Applied Econometrics

Applied Econometrics

A Modern Approach using
EViews and Microfit
Revised Edition

Dimitrios Asteriou
and
Stephen G. Hall

palgrave
macmillan

First edition 2006
Revised edition 2007
Published by
PALGRAVE MACMILLAN
Houndmills, Basingstoke, Hampshire RG21 6XS and
175 Fifth Avenue, New York, N.Y. 10010
Companies and representatives throughout the world.

PALGRAVE MACMILLAN is the global academic imprint of the Palgrave Macmillan division of St. Martin's Press, LLC and of Palgrave Macmillan Ltd. Macmillan® is a registered trademark in the United States, United Kingdom and other countries. Palgrave is a registered trademark in the European Union and other countries.

ISBN-13: 978–0–230–50640–4
ISBN-10: 0–230–50640–2

This book is printed on paper suitable for recycling and made from fully managed and sustained forest sources. Logging, pulping and manufacturing processes are expected to conform to the environmental regulations of the country of origin.

A catalogue record for this book is available from the British Library.

A catalog record for this book is available from the Library of Congress.

Library of Congress Catalogue Card Number - 220651708

10 9 8 7 6 5 4 3
16 15 14 13 12 11 10 09 08

Printed and bound in China

To Athina, for all her love and encouragement – D.A.
To Jacquie, for all her help and understanding – S.G.H.

Contents

List of Figures

List of Tables

Preface

The purpose of this book is to provide the reader with a thorough grounding in the central ideas and techniques of econometric theory, as well as to give all the tools needed to carry out an empirical project.

For the first task, regarding the econometric theory, the book adopts a very analytical and simplified approach in explaining the theories presented in the text. The use of mathematics in econometrics is practically unavoidable, but the book tries to satisfy both those readers who do not have a solid mathematical background as well as those who prefer the use of mathematics for a more thorough understanding. To achieve this task, the book adopts an approach that provides, when it is required, both a general and a mathematical treatment of the subject in two separate sections. Thus, the reader who doesn't want to get involved with proofs and mathematical manipulations may concentrate on the 'general (verbal) approach' skipping the 'more mathematical' approach, without any loss of continuity. Similarly, readers who want to go through the mathematics involved in every topic are able to do so by studying the relevant sections in each chapter. Having this choice, in cases thought of as important, the text also uses matrix algebra to prove mathematically some of the points; while the main points of that analysis are also presented in a simplified manner to make the text accessible even to those who have not taken a course in matrix algebra.

Another important feature regarding the use of mathematics in the text is that it presents all calculations required to get the reader from one equation to another, as well as providing explanations of mathematical tricks used in order to obtain these equations when necessary. Thus readers with a limited background in mathematics will also find some of the mathematical proofs quite accessible, and should therefore not be disheartened in progressing through them.

From the practical or applied econometrics point of view, the book is innovative in two ways: (a) it presents very analytically (step by step) all the statistical tests, and (b) after each test presentation it explains how these tests can be carried out using appropriate econometric softwares such as EViews and Microfit. We think that this is one of the strongest features of the book, and we hope that the reader will find it very useful in applying those techniques using real data. This approach was chosen because from our teaching experience we have realized that students find econometrics quite a hard course of study, simply because they cannot see the 'beauty' of it, which emerges only when they are able to obtain results from actual data and know how to interpret those results to draw conclusions. Applied econometric analysis is the essence of econometrics, and we hope that the use of EViews and/or Microfit will make the practice of econometrics more satisfying and enjoyable, and its study fascinating too. For readers who need a basic introduction regarding the use of EViews and Microfit, they can start the book from the last chapter (Chapter 21) which discusses practical issues in using those two econometrics packages.

While the text is introductory (and is thus mostly suitable for undergraduates), it can also be useful to those who undertake postgraduate courses that require applied work (perhaps through an MSc project). All of the empirical results from the examples reported in the book are reproducible. A website has been established including all the files that are required for plotting the figures, reestimating the regressions and all other relevant tests presented in the book. The files are given in three different formats, namely xls (for excel), wf1 (for EViews) and fit (for Microfit). If any errors or typos are detected please let Dimitrios know by e-mailing him at D.Asteriou@city.ac.uk.

DIMITRIOS ASTERIOU

&

STEPHEN G. HALL

Acknowledgements

I would like to thank my friend and colleague Keith Pilbeam from City University, for his constant encouragement. I am also gratefully indebted to Simon Blackett from Palgrave Macmillan for sharing my enthusiasm for the project from the beginning. I would also like to thank Dionysios Glycopantis, John Thomson, Alistair McGuire, Costas Siriopoulos, George Agiomirgianakis, Kerry Patterson and Vassilis Monastiriotis.

DA

Any remaining mistakes or omissions are of course our responsibility.

DA and SGH

1 Introduction

What is econometrics?

The study of econometrics has become an essential part of every undergraduate course in Economics and it is not an exaggeration to say that it is also a very essential part of every economist's training. This is because the importance of applied economics is constantly increasing while the quantification and evaluation of economic theories and hypotheses constitutes now, more than ever, a bare necessity. Theoretical economics may suggest that there is a relationship among two, or more, variables but applied economics demands both evidence that this relationship is a real one, observed in everyday life, and quantification of the relationship between the two variables as well. The study of the methods that enable us to quantify economic relationships using actual data is known as econometrics.

Literally, econometrics means 'measurement (which is the meaning of the Greek word metrics) in economics'. However, in essence, econometrics include all those statistical and mathematical techniques that are utilized in the analysis of economic data. The main target of using these statistical and mathematical tools in economic data is to attempt to prove or disprove certain economic propositions and models.

The stages of applied econometric work

Applied econometric work in practice always has (or should at least, have) as a starting point a model or an economic theory. From this theory, the first task of the applied econometrician is to formulate an econometric model that can be used in an empirically testable form. Then, the next task is to collect data that can be used to perform the test, and after that to proceed with the estimation of the model.

After the estimation of the model is done, the applied econometrician has to perform specification tests to make sure that the model she/he used was the appropriate one, as well as some diagnostic checking in order to check the performance and the accuracy of the estimation procedure. If those tests suggest that the model is adequate, then the next test is to apply hypothesis testing in order to test the validity of the theoretical predictions, and then she/he will be able to use the model for making predictions and policy recommendations. If it is found that the specification tests and the diagnostics suggest that the model used was not an appropriate one, then the econometrician will have to go back to the econometric model formulation stage and revise the model, repeating the whole procedure from the beginning (for a graphical depiction of these stages see Figure 1.1). The aim of this book is to deal with these issues and provide readers with all the basic mathematical and analytical tools that will enable them to carry out applied econometric work of this kind.

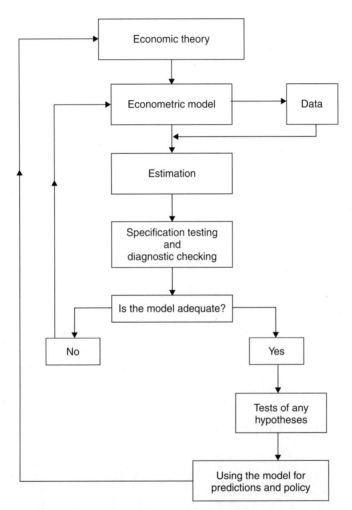

Figure 1.1 The stages of applied econometric analysis

Source: Based on Maddala (2001).

Part

I

Statistical Background and Basic Data Handling

2 The Structure of Economic Data

Economic data sets come in various forms. While some econometric methods can be applied straightforwardly to different types of data sets, it is essential to examine the special features of some sets. In the next sections we describe the most important data structures encountered in applied econometric work.

Cross-sectional data

A cross-sectional data set consists of a sample of individuals, households, firms, countries, regions, cities or any other type of units at a specific point in time. In some cases, the data across all units do not correspond to exactly the same time period. Consider a survey that collects data from questionnaires applied to different families that were surveyed during different days within a month. In this case, we can ignore the minor time differences in collecting the data and the data collected will still be viewed as a cross-sectional data set.

In econometrics, cross-sectional variables are usually denoted by the subscript i, with i taking values from $1, 2, 3, \ldots, N$; for N number of cross-sections. So, if for example Y denotes the income data we have collected for N number of individuals, this variable, in a cross-sectional framework, will be denoted by:

$$Y_i \quad \text{for } i = 1, 2, 3, \ldots, N \tag{2.1}$$

Cross-sectional data are widely used in economics and other social sciences. In economics, the analysis of cross-sectional data is mainly associated with applied microeconomics. Labour economics, state and local public finance, business economics, demographic economics and health economics are some of the most common fields included within microeconomics. Data on individuals, households, firms, cities and regions at a given point in time are utilized in these cases in order to test microeconomic hypotheses and evaluate economic policies.

Time series data

A time series data set consists of observations on one or several variables over time. So, time series data are arranged in chronological order and can have different time frequencies, such as biannual, annual, quarterly, monthly, weekly, daily and hourly. Examples of time series data can include stock prices, gross domestic product (GDP), money supply, ice-cream sale figures, among many others.

Time series data are denoted with the subscript t. So, for example, if Y denotes the GDP of a country from 1990 to 2002 then we denote that as:

$$Y_t \quad \text{for } t = 1, 2, 3, \ldots, T \tag{2.2}$$

where $t = 1$ for 1990 and $t = T = 13$ for 2002.

Because past events can influence future events and lags in behaviour are prevalent in social sciences, time is a very important dimension in time series data sets. A variable which is lagged one period will be denoted as Y_{t-1} and obviously when it is lagged s periods will denoted as Y_{t-s}. Similarly if it is leading k period will be denoted as Y_{t+k}.

A key feature of time series data, that makes it more difficult to analyse than cross-sectional data, is the fact that economic observations are commonly dependent across time. By this we mean that most economic time series are closely related to their recent histories. So, while most econometric procedures can be applied with both cross-sectional and time series data sets, in the case of time series there is a need for more things to be done in specifying the appropriate econometric model. Additionally, the fact that economic time series display clear trends over time has led to new econometric techniques that try to address these features.

Another important feature is that time-series data that follow certain frequencies might exhibit a strong seasonal pattern. This feature is encountered mainly with weekly, monthly and quarterly time series. Finally, it's important to say that time series data are mainly associated with macroeconomic applications.

Panel data

A panel data set consists of a time series for each cross-sectional member in the data set; as an example we could consider the sales and the number of employees for 50 firms over a five-year period. Panel data can also be collected on a geographical basis; for example we might have GDP and money supply data for a set of 20 countries and for 20-year periods.

Panel data are denoted by the use of both i and t subscripts that we have used before for cross-sectional and time series data respectively. This is simply because panel data have both cross-sectional and time series dimensions. So, we will denote GDP for a set of countries and for a specific time period as:

$$Y_{it} \quad \text{for } t = 1, 2, 3, \ldots, T \text{ and } i = 1, 2, 3, \ldots, N \tag{2.3}$$

To better understand the structure of panel data consider a cross-sectional and a time series variable as $N \times 1$ and $T \times 1$ matrices respectively:

$$Y_t^{ARGENTINA} = \begin{pmatrix} Y_{1990} \\ Y_{1991} \\ Y_{1992} \\ \vdots \\ \vdots \\ Y_{2002} \end{pmatrix}; \quad Y_i^{1990} = \begin{pmatrix} Y_{ARGENTINA} \\ Y_{BRAZIL} \\ Y_{PARAGUAY} \\ \vdots \\ \vdots \\ Y_{VENEZUELA} \end{pmatrix} \tag{2.4}$$

Here $Y_t^{ARGENTINA}$ is GDP for Argentina from 1990 to 2002 and Y_i^{1990} is GDP for 1990 for 20 different Latin American countries.

The panel data Y_{it} variable will then be an $N \times T$ matrix of the following form:

$$Y_{it} = \begin{pmatrix} Y_{ARG,1990} & Y_{BRA,1990} & Y_{VEN,1990} \\ Y_{ARG,1991} & Y_{BRA,1991} & Y_{VEN,1991} \\ \vdots & \vdots & \vdots \\ Y_{ARG,2002} & Y_{BRA,2002} & Y_{VEN,2002} \end{pmatrix}_{T \times N} \tag{2.5}$$

where the t dimension is depicted vertically and the i dimension horizontally.

Most undergraduate econometrics books do not contain discussion of the econometrics of panel data. However, the advantages of panel data, combined with the fact that many issues in economics are difficult, if not impossible, to analyse satisfactorily without the use of panel data makes their use more than necessary. The final part of this textbook, is, for this reason, devoted to the analysis of panel data techniques and methods of estimation.

3 Working with Data: Basic Data Handling

Before going straight into the statistical and econometric tools, a preliminary analysis is extremely important in order to get a basic 'feel' for the data. This chapter briefly describes ways of viewing and analysing data by examining various types of graphs and summary statistics. This process provides the necessary background for the sound application of regression analysis and interpretation of results. In addition, we shall see how to apply several types of transformation to the raw data, so as to isolate or remove one or more components of a time series, and/or to obtain the format most suitable for the ultimate regression analysis. While the focus is on time series data, some of the points and procedures apply to cross-sectional data as well.

Looking at raw data

The point of departure is simply to look at the numbers in a spreadsheet, taking note of the number of series, start and end dates, range of values, and so on. If we look more closely at the figures, we may notice outliers or certain discontinuities/structural breaks (e.g. a large jump in the values at a point in time). These are very important as they can have a substantial impact on regression results, and must therefore be kept in mind when formulating the model and interpreting the output.

Graphical analysis

Looking at the raw data (i.e. the actual numbers) may tell us certain things, but various graphs facilitate the inspection process considerably. Graphs are essential tools for seeing the 'big picture', and they reveal a large amount of information about the series in one view. They also make checking for outliers or structural breaks much easier than poring through a spreadsheet! The main graphical tools are:

1 Histograms: give an indication of the distribution of a variable;
2 Scatter plots: give combinations of values from two series for the purpose of determining their relationship (if any);
3 Line graphs: facilitate comparisons of series;
4 Bar graphs; and
5 Pie charts.

Graphs in MFit

Creating graphs

To create a line graph of a variable against time, we need to type in the Microfit Command Editor window:

```
plot x
```

The above command produces a plot of variable x against time over the entire sample period. If we need a certain sample period then we need to type:

```
sample t₀ t₁; plot x
```

where t_0 and t_1 stand for the start and the end of our subsample period respectively. For example,

```
sample 1990q1 1994q4; plot x
```

Furthermore, we can plot up to a maximum of 50 variables against another variable. When issuing this command, namely xplot, we must specify at least two variable names. For example:

```
xplot x y
```

or

```
sample 1990q1 1994q4; xplot x y z
```

The above commands produce a plot of the variables x and z against the variable y regarding the subsample period 1990q1 1994q4 (note that all graphs are produced in the Process Menu). The default graph display may be edited using the graph control facility. Click the **graph** button to access it. Graph control contains many options for adjusting the various features of the graph; each option has its own property page. Click the appropriate page tab to view it. To apply a change we have made without closing graph control, click the **apply now** button. To exit graph control without implementing the changes click **cancel**. The most commonly used page tabs are: **2D Gallery**, **Titles**, **Trends** and **Background**.

Saving graphs

When we plot a graph, the Graph Editor window opens. A displayed graph can be saved as a bitmap (BMP) (click on the 2nd button) or as a Windows metafile (WMF) (click on the 3rd button). If we are using MS Word then we can copy and paste the graph by clicking on the 4th button first, and then open MS Word and paste the graph. The 1st button sends the graph to the nearest printer.

Graphs in EViews

In EViews we can plot/graph the data in a wide variety of ways. One way is to double-click on the variable of interest (the one we want to obtain a graph from) and a new window will appear that will actually look like a spreadsheet with the values of the variable we double-clicked. Then in order to obtain graphs we need to go to **View/Line Graph** in order to obtain a plot of the series against time (if it is a time series) or against observations (for **undated or irregular** – cross sectional data). Another option is to click on **View/Bar Graph** which gives the same figure as with the line option but with bars for every observation instead of a line plot. Obviously the line graph option is preferable in describing time series, and the bar graph for cross-sectional data.

In case we need to plot together more than one series, we may first open/create a **group** of series in EViews. In order to open a group we either select the series we want to be in the group by clicking on them with the mouse one by one, having the control button pressed, or by typing on the EViews command line the word:

```
group
```

and then pressing enter. This will lead to a new EViews window in which to specify the series to include in the group. So, in this window, we need to type the name of the series we want to plot together, and then click **OK**. Again, a spreadsheet appears with the values for the variables selected to appear in the group. By clicking on **View** there are two graphs options: **Graph** will create graphs of all series together in the group, whilst **Multiple Graphs** will create graphs for each individual series in the group. In both **Graph** and **Multiple Graphs** options there are different types of graphs that can be obtained. One which can be very useful in econometric analysis is the scatter plot. In order to obtain a scatter plot of two series in EViews we may open a group (following the procedure described above) with the two series we want to plot and then go to **View/Graph/Scatter**. There follow four different options of scatter plots, (a) simple scatter, (b) scatter with a fitted regression line, (c) scatter with a line that fits as close as possible to the data and (d) a scatter with a kernel density function.

Another simple and convenient way of obtaining a scatter plot in EViews is by use of the command:

```
scat X Y
```

where X and Y should be replaced by the names of the series to be plotted on the X and Y axes respectively. Similarly, a very easy way of obtaining a time plot of a time series, can be done by the command

```
plot X
```

where again X is the name of the series we want to plot. The plot command can be used in order to obtain time plots of more than one series in the same graph by specifying more than one variable separated by spaces such as:

```
plot X Y Z
```

A final option to obtain graphs in EViews is to click on **Quick/Graph** and then specify the names of the series that we need to plot (either one or more). A new window opens that offers different options of graph types and different options of scales. After making the choice, press **OK** to obtain the relevant graph.

After a graph is obtained, we can easily copy and paste graphs from EViews into a document in a word processor. To do this we first need to make sure that the active object is the window that contains the graph (the title bar of the window should have a bright colour, if it does not click anywhere on the graph and it will be activated – the title bar will become bright). We then either press **ctrl+c**, or alternatively click on **Edit/Copy**. The **Copy Graph as Metafile** window appears with various options: to either copy the file to the clipboard in order to paste it into the programme required (the word processor for example), or alternatively to copy the file to a disk file. Also, we can choose whether the graph will be in colour or use bold lines. If we copy the graph to the clipboard we can paste it in a different programme very easily by either pressing **ctrl+v** or by clicking on **Edit/Paste**. Conventional Windows programmes allow the graph to be edited, changing its size or position in the programme.

Summary statistics

To gain a more precise idea of the distribution of a variable x_t we can estimate various simple measures such as the mean (or average), often defined as $\bar{x}$, the variance often defined as σ_x^2 and its square root, the standard deviation again stated as σ_x. Thus

$$\bar{x} = \frac{1}{T}\sum_{i=1}^{T} x_i \tag{3.1}$$

$$\sigma_x^2 = \frac{1}{T-1}\sum_{i=1}^{T}(x_i - \bar{x})^2 \tag{3.2}$$

$$\sigma_x = \sqrt{\sigma_x^2} \tag{3.3}$$

To analyse two or more variables we might also consider their covariance and correlations defined later. However, we would stress that these summary statistics contain far less information than a graph and the starting point for any good piece of empirical analysis should be a graphical check of all the data.

Summary statistics in MFit

In order to obtain summary statistics in Microfit we need to type the command:

```
cor X
```

where X is the name of the variable needed to obtain summary statistics from. Apart from summary statistics (minimum, maximum, mean, standard deviation, skewness, kurtosis and coefficient of variation) Microfit will also give the autocorrelation function of this variable. In order to obtain the histogram of a variable the respective command is:

```
hist X
```

The histogram may be printed, copied and saved like every other graph from Microfit.

Summary statistics in EViews

In order to obtain summary descriptive statistics in EViews we need again either to double-click and open the series window, or to create a group with more than one series as described in the graphs section above. After that click on **View/Descriptive Statistics/Histogram and Stats** for the one variable window case. This will provide summary statistics like the mean, median, minimum, maximum, standard deviation, skewness, kurtosis and the Jarque-Berra Statistic for testing for normality of the series together with its respective probability limit. If opening a group, clicking **View/Descriptive Statistics** provides two different choices: one using a common sample for all series, and another using the most possible observation by not caring about different sample sizes among different variables.

Components of a time series

An economic or financial time series consists of up to four components:

1 trend (smooth, long-term/consistent upward or downward movement);

2 cycle (rise and fall over periods longer than a year, e.g. due to a business cycle);

3 seasonal (within-year pattern seen in weekly, monthly or quarterly data); or

4 irregular (random component; can be subdivided into episodic [unpredictable but identifiable] and residual [unpredictable and unidentifiable]).

Note that not all time series have all four components, although the irregular component is present in every series. As we shall see later, various techniques are available for removing one or more components from a time series.

Indices and base dates

An index is a number that expresses the relative change in value (e.g. price or quantity) from one period to another. The changes are measured relative to the value in a base date (which may be revised from time to time). Common examples of indices are the consumer price index (CPI) and the JSE all-share price index. In many cases, such as the preceding examples, indices are used as a convenient way of summarizing many prices in one series (the all-share index is comprised of many individual companies' share prices). Note that two indices may only be compared directly if they have the same base date, which may lead to the need to change the base date of a certain index.

Splicing two indices and changing the base date of an index

Suppose we have the following data:

Year	Price index (1985 base year)	Price index (1990 base year)	Standardized price index (1990 base)
1985	100		45.9
1986	132		60.6
1987	196		89.9
1988	213		97.7
1989	258		118.3
1990	218	100	100
1991		85	85
1992		62	62

In this (hypothetical) example, the price index for the years 1985 to 1990 (column 2) uses 1985 as its base year (i.e. the index takes on a value of 100 in 1985), while from 1991 onwards (column 3) the base year is 1990. To make the two periods compatible, we need to convert the data in one of the columns so that a single base year is used. This procedure is known as splicing two indices.

- If we want 1990 as our base year, then we need to divide all the previous values (i.e. in column 2) by a factor of 2.18 (so that the first series now takes on a value of 100 in 1990). The standardized series is shown in the last column in the table.

- Similarly, to obtain a single series in 1985 prices, we would need to multiply the values for the years 1991 to 1993 by a factor of 2.18.

Even if we have a complete series with a single base date, we may for some reason want to change that base date. The procedure is similar: simply multiply or divide – depending on whether the new base date is earlier or later than the old one – the entire series by the appropriate factor to get a value of 100 for the chosen base year.

Data transformations

Changing the frequency of time series data

EViews allows us to convert the frequency of a time series (e.g. reducing the frequency from monthly to quarterly figures). The choice of method for calculating the reduced frequency depends partly on whether we have a stock variable or a flow variable. In general, for stock variables (and indices such as the CPI) we would choose specific dates (e.g. beginning, middle or end of period) or averaging, while for flow variables we would use the total sum of the values (e.g. annual gross domestic product, GDP, in 1998 is the sum of quarterly GDP in each of the four quarters of 1998). Increasing the frequency of a time series (e.g. from quarterly to monthly) involves extrapolation and should be used with great caution. The resultant series will appear quite smooth and is a 'manufactured' series which would normally be used for ease of comparison with a series of similar frequency.

Nominal versus real data

A rather tricky question in econometrics is the choice between nominal and real terms for our data. The problem with nominal series is that they incorporate a price component that can obscure the fundamental features that we are interested in. This is particularly problematic when two nominal variables are being compared, since the dominant price component in each will produce close matches between the series, resulting in a spuriously high correlation coefficient. To circumvent this problem, one can convert nominal series to real terms by using an appropriate price deflator (e.g. the CPI for consumption expenditure or the PPI for manufacturing production). However, sometimes an appropriate deflator is not available, which renders the conversion process somewhat arbitrary.

The bottom line is: think carefully about the variables you are using and the relationships you are investigating, and choose the most appropriate format for the data – and be consistent.

Logs

Logarithmic transformations are very popular in econometrics, for several reasons. First, many economic time series exhibit a strong trend (i.e., a consistent upward or downward movement in the values). When this is caused by some underlying growth process, a plot of the series will reveal an exponential curve. In such cases, the exponential/growth component dominates other features of the series (e.g. cyclical and irregular components of time series) and may thus obscure the more interesting relationship between this variable and another growing variable. Taking the natural logarithm of such a series effectively linearizes the exponential trend (since the log function is the inverse of an exponential function). For example, one may want to work with the (natural) log of GDP, which will appear on a graph roughly as a straight line, rather than the exponential curve exhibited by the raw GDP series.

Second, logs may also be used to linearize a model which is non-linear in the parameters. An example is the Cobb–Douglas production function:

$$Y = AL^a K^\beta e^u \tag{3.4}$$

(where u is a disturbance term and e is the base of the natural log).

Taking logs of both sides we obtain:

$$\ln(Y) = \ln(A) + a\ln(K) + b\ln(L) + u \tag{3.5}$$

Each variable (and the constant term) can be redefined as follows: $y = \ln(Y)$; $k = \ln(K)$; $l = \ln(L)$; $a = \ln(A)$; so that the transformed model becomes:

$$y = a + ak + bl + u \tag{3.6}$$

which is linear in the parameters and hence can easily be estimated using ordinary least squares (OLS) regression.

A third advantage of using logarithmic transformations is that it allows the regression coefficients to be interpreted as elasticities, since for small changes in any variable x, (change in $\log x$) $\simeq$ (relative change in x itself). (This follows from elementary differentiation: $d(\ln x)/dx = 1/x$ and thus $d(\ln x) = dx/x$.)

In the log-linear production function above, a measures the change in $\ln(Y)$ associated with a small change in $\ln(K)$, i.e. it represents the elasticity of output with respect to capital.

Differencing

In the previous section it was noted that a log transformation linearizes an exponential trend. If one wants to remove the trend component from a (time) series entirely – i.e. to render it stationary – one needs to apply differencing, i.e. compute absolute changes from one period to the next. Symbolically,

$$\Delta Y_t = Y_t - Y_{t-1} \tag{3.7}$$

which is known as first-order differencing. If a differenced series still exhibits a trend, it needs to be differenced again (one or more times) to render it stationary. Thus we have second-order differencing:

$$\Delta^2 Y_t = \Delta(Y_t - Y_{t-1}) = \Delta Y_t - \Delta Y_{t-1}$$
$$= (Y_t - Y_{t-1}) - (Y_{t-1} - Y_{t-2}) \tag{3.8}$$

and so on.

Growth rates

In many instances, it makes economic sense to analyse data and model relationships in growth-rate terms. A prime example is GDP, which is far more commonly discussed in growth-rate terms rather than levels. Using growth rates allows one to investigate the way that changes (over time) in one variable are related to changes (over the same time period) in another variable. Because of the differencing involved, the calculation of growth rates in effect removes the trend component from a series.

There are two types of growth rates: discretely compounded and continuously compounded. Discretely compounded growth rates are computed as follows:

$$\text{growth rate of } Y_t = (Y_t - Y_{t-1})/Y_{t-1}$$

where t refers to the time period.

It is more usual in econometrics to calculate continuously compounded growth rates, which essentially combine the logarithmic and differencing transformations. Dealing with annual data is simple: the continuously compounded growth rate is the natural log of the ratio of the value of the variable in one period to the value in the previous period (or, alternatively, the difference between the logged value in one year and the logged value in the previous year):

$$\text{growth rate of } Y_t = \ln(Y_t/Y_{t-1}) = \ln(Y_t) - \ln(Y_{t-1})$$

For monthly data, there is a choice between calculating the (annualized) month-on-previous-month growth rate and the year-on-year growth rate. The advantage of the former is that it provides the most up-to-date rate and is therefore less biased than a year-on-year rate. Month-on-month growth rates are usually annualized, i.e. multiplied by a factor of 12 to give the amount the series would grow in a whole year if that monthly rate applied throughout the year. The relevant formulae are as follows:

$$\text{annualized month-on-month growth rate}$$
$$= 12 * \ln(Y_t/Y_{t-1}) \quad \text{(continuous)}$$
$$\text{OR } [(Y_t/Y_{t-1})^{12} - 1] \quad \text{(discrete)}$$

annualized quarter-on-quarter growth rate
$$= 4 * \ln(Y_t/Y_{t-1}) \quad \text{(continuous)}$$
$$\text{OR } [(Y_t/Y_{t-1})^4 - 1] \quad \text{(discrete)}$$

(Multiply these growth rates by 100 to obtain percentage growth rates.)

However, month-on-previous-month growth rates (whether annualized or not) are often highly volatile, in large part because time series are frequently subject to seasonal factors (the Christmas boom being the best-known). It is in order to avoid this seasonal effect that growth rates usually compare a period with the corresponding period a year earlier (e.g. January 2000 with January 1999). This is how the headline inflation rate is calculated, for instance. Similar arguments apply to quarterly and other data. (Another advantage of using these rates in regression analysis is that it allows one year for the impact of one variable to take effect on another variable.) This type of growth rate computation involves seasonal differencing:

$$\Delta^s Y_t = Y_t - Y_{t-s}$$

The formula for calculating the year-on-year growth rate using monthly data is:

$$growth\ rate\ of\ Y_t = \ln(Y_t/Y_{t-12}) = \ln(Y_t) - \ln(Y_{t-12})$$

In sum, calculating year-on-year growth rates simultaneously removes trend and seasonal components from time series, and thus facilitates the examination (say, in correlation or regression analysis) of other characteristics of the data (such as cycles or irregular components).

Part

II

The Classical Linear Regression Model

4 Simple Regression

Introduction to regression: the classical linear regression model (CLRM)

Why do we do regressions?

Econometric methods such as a regression can help to overcome the problem of complete uncertainty and provide guidelines on planning and decision-making. Of course, building up a model is not an easy task. Models should meet certain criteria (for example the model should not suffer from serial correlation) in order to be valid and a lot of work is usually needed before we end up with a good model. Furthermore, much decision-making is required on which variables to include or not include in the model. Too many may cause problems (unneeded variables misspecification), while too few may cause other problems (omitted variables misspecification or incorrect functional form).

The classical linear regression model

The classical linear regression model is a way of examining the nature and form of the relationship among two or more variables. In this chapter we consider the case of only two variables. One important issue in the regression analysis is the direction of causation between the two variables; in other words, we want to know which variable is causing/affecting the other. Alternatively, this can be stated as which variable depends on the other. Therefore, we refer to the two variables as the dependent variable (usually denoted by Y) and the independent or explanatory variable (usually denoted by X). We want to explain/predict the value of Y for different values of the explanatory variable X. Let us assume that X and Y are linked by a simple linear relationship:

$$E(Y_t) = a + \beta X_t \tag{4.1}$$

where $E(Y_t)$ denotes the average value of Y_t for given X_t and unknown population parameters a and β (the subscript t indicates that we have time series data). Equation (4.1) is called the population regression equation. The actual value of Y_t will not always equal its expected value $E(Y_t)$. There are various factors that can 'disturb' its actual behaviour and therefore we can write actual Y_t as

$$Y_t = E(Y_t) + u_t$$

or

$$Y_t = a + \beta X_t + u_t \tag{4.2}$$

where u_t is a disturbance. There are several reasons why a disturbance exists:

1 Omission of explanatory variables. There might be other factors (other than X_t) affecting Y_t that have been left out of equation (4.2). This may be possible either because we do not know these factors, or even knowing them there might be

a possibility that we are unable to measure them in order to use them in a regression analysis.

2 Aggregation of variables. In some cases it is desirable to avoid having too many variables and therefore we attempt to summarize in aggregate a number of relationships in only one variable. Therefore, we end up with only a good approximation of Y_t, having discrepancies which are captured by the disturbance term.

3 Model specification. We might have a misspecified model in terms of its structure. For example, it might be that Y_t is not affected by X_t, but that it is affected by the value of X in the previous period (i.e. X_{t-1}). In this case, if X_t and X_{t-1} are closely related, estimation of (4.2) will lead to discrepancies which again are captured by the error term.

4 Functional misspecification. The relationship between X and Y might be a non-linear relationship. We will deal with non-linearities in other chapters of this text.

5 Measurement errors. If the measurement of one or more variables is not correct then errors appear in the relationship and this contributes to the disturbance term.

Now the question is whether it is possible or not to estimate the population regression function based on sample information. The answer is that we may not be able to estimate it 'accurately' because of sampling fluctuations. However, although the population regression equation is unknown – and will remain unknown – to any investigator, it is possible to estimate it after gathering data from a sample. A first step for the researcher is to do a scatter plot of the sample data and try to fix (one way or another) a straight line to the scatter of points as shown in Figure 4.1.

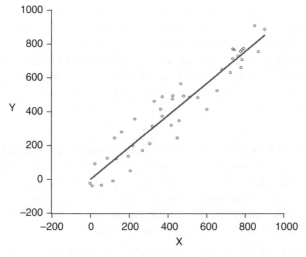

Figure 4.1 Scatter plot of *Y* on *X*

There are many ways of fixing a line including:

1 By eye.

2 Connecting the first with the last observation.

3 Taking the average of the first two observations and the average of the last two observations and connecting those two points.

4 Applying the method of ordinary least squares (OLS).

The first three methods are naïve ones, while the last is the most appropriate method for this type of situation. The OLS method is the topic of the next section.

The ordinary least squares (OLS) method of estimation

Consider again the population regression equation

$$Y_t = a + \beta X_t + u_t \tag{4.3}$$

This equation is not directly observable. However, we can gather data and obtain estimates of a and β from a sample of the population. This gives us the following relationship which is a fitted straight line with intercept $\hat{a}$ and slope $\hat{\beta}$:

$$\hat{Y}_t = \hat{a} + \hat{\beta} X_t \tag{4.4}$$

Equation (4.4) can be referred to as the sample regression equation. Here, $\hat{a}$ and $\hat{\beta}$ are sample estimates of the population parameters a and β, and $\hat{Y}_t$ denotes the predicted value of Y. (Once we have the estimated sample regression equation we can easily predict Y for various values of X.)

When we fit a sample regression line to a scatter of points, it is obviously desirable to select a line in such a manner that it is as close as possible to the actual Y, or, in other words that provides residuals that are the smallest possible. In order to do this we adopt the following criterion: choose the sample regression function in such a way that the sum of the squared residuals is as small as possible (i.e. is minimized). This method of estimation has some desirable properties that make it the most popular technique in uncomplicated applications of regression analysis. Namely:

1 By using the squared residuals we eliminate the effect of the sign of the residuals so it is not possible for a positive and negative residual to offset each other. For example if we were to minimize the sum of the residuals this could be achieved by setting the forecast for $Y(\hat{Y})$ equal to the mean of $Y(\bar{Y})$. But this would not be a very well fitting line at all. So clearly we want a transformation which makes all the residuals the same sign before making them as small as possible.

2 By squaring the residuals, we give more weight to the larger residuals and so we, in effect, work harder to reduce the very large errors.

3 The OLS method chooses $\hat{a}$ and $\hat{\beta}$ estimators that follow some numerical and statistical properties (such as unbiasedness and efficiency) that we will discuss later.

We can now see how to derive the OLS estimators. Denoting by *RSS* the sum of the squared residuals, we have:

$$RSS = \hat{u}_1^2 + \hat{u}_2^2 + \cdots + \hat{u}_n^2 = \sum_{t=1}^{n} \hat{u}_t^2 \qquad (4.5)$$

However, we know that:

$$\hat{u}_t = (Y_t - \hat{Y}_t) = (Y_t - \hat{a} - \hat{\beta}X_t) \qquad (4.6)$$

and therefore:

$$RSS = \sum_{t=1}^{n} \hat{u}_t^2 = \sum_{t=1}^{n}(Y_t - \hat{Y}_t)^2 = \sum_{t=1}^{n}(Y_t - \hat{a} - \hat{\beta}X_t)^2 \qquad (4.7)$$

To minimize equation (4.7), the first-order condition is to take the partial derivatives of *RSS* with respect to $\hat{a}$ and $\hat{\beta}$ and set them to zero. Thus, we have:

$$\frac{\partial RSS}{\partial \hat{a}} = -2\sum_{t=1}^{n}(Y_t - \hat{a} - \hat{\beta}X_t) = 0 \qquad (4.8)$$

and

$$\frac{\partial RSS}{\partial \hat{\beta}} = -2\sum_{t=1}^{n}X_t(Y_t - \hat{a} - \hat{\beta}X_t) = 0 \qquad (4.9)$$

The second-order partial derivatives are:

$$\frac{\partial^2 RSS}{\partial \hat{a}^2} = 2n \qquad (4.10)$$

$$\frac{\partial^2 RSS}{\partial \hat{\beta}^2} = 2\sum_{t=1}^{n}X_t^2 \qquad (4.11),$$

$$\frac{\partial^2 RSS}{\partial \hat{a}\partial \hat{\beta}} = 2\sum_{t=1}^{n}X_t \qquad (4.12)$$

Therefore, it is easy to verify that the second-order conditions for a minimum are met.

Since $\sum \hat{a} = n\hat{a}$ (for simplicity of notation we omit the upper and lower limits of the summation symbol), we can (by using that and rearranging), rewrite equations (4.8) and (4.9) as follows:

$$\sum Y_t = n\hat{a} - \hat{\beta}\sum X_t \qquad (4.13)$$

and

$$\sum X_t Y_t = \hat{a} \sum X_t + \hat{\beta} \sum X_t^2 \tag{4.14}$$

The only unknowns in the above two equations are $\hat{a}$ and $\hat{\beta}$. Therefore, we can solve the above system of two equations with two unknowns in order to obtain $\hat{a}$ and $\hat{\beta}$. First, we divide both sides of (4.13) by n to have:

$$\frac{\sum Y_t}{n} = \frac{n\hat{a}}{n} - \frac{\hat{\beta} \sum X_t}{n} \tag{4.15}$$

Denoting by $\bar{Y} = \sum Y_t/n$ and $\bar{X} = \sum X_t/n$, and rearranging, we obtain:

$$\hat{a} = \bar{Y} - \hat{\beta}\bar{X} \tag{4.16}$$

Substituting (4.16) in (4.14) we get:

$$\sum X_t Y_t = \bar{Y} \sum X_t - \hat{\beta}\bar{X} \sum X_t + \hat{\beta} \sum X_t^2 \tag{4.17}$$

or

$$\sum X_t Y_t = \frac{1}{n} \sum Y_t \sum X_t - \hat{\beta}\frac{1}{n} \sum X_t \sum X_t + \hat{\beta} \sum X_t^2 \tag{4.18}$$

and finally, factorizing the $\hat{\beta}$ terms:

$$\sum X_t Y_t = \frac{\sum Y_t \sum X_t}{n} + \hat{\beta}\left[\sum X_t^2 - \frac{(\sum X_t)^2}{n}\right] \tag{4.19}$$

Thus, we can obtain $\hat{\beta}$ as:

$$\hat{\beta} = \frac{\sum X_t Y_t - 1/n \sum Y_t \sum X_t}{\sum X_t^2 - 1/n (\sum X_t)^2} \tag{4.20}$$

And given $\hat{\beta}$ we can use (4.16) to obtain $\hat{a}$.

Alternative expressions for $\hat{\beta}$

We can express the numerator and denominator of (4.20) as follows:

$$\sum (X_t - \bar{X})(Y_t - \bar{Y}) = \sum X_t Y_t - \frac{1}{n} \sum Y_t \sum X_t \tag{4.21}$$

$$\sum (X_t - \bar{X})^2 = \sum X_t^2 - \frac{1}{n}\left(\sum X_t\right)^2 \tag{4.22}$$

and then have that:

$$\hat{\beta} = \frac{\sum(X_t - \bar{X})(Y_t - \bar{Y})}{\sum(X_t - \bar{X})^2} \tag{4.23}$$

or even:

$$\hat{\beta} = \frac{\sum x_t y_t}{\sum x_t^2} \tag{4.24}$$

where obviously $x_t = (X_t - \bar{X})$, and $y_t = (Y_t - \bar{Y})$, which are deviations from their respective means.

Alternatively, we can use the definitions of $Cov(X, Y)$ and $Var(X)$ in order to obtain an alternative expression for $\hat{\beta}$ as illustrated below:

$$\hat{\beta} = \frac{\sum X_t Y_t - 1/n \sum Y_t \sum X_t}{\sum X_t^2 - 1/n (\sum X_t)^2} = \frac{\sum X_t Y_t - \bar{Y}\bar{X}}{\sum X_t^2 - (\bar{X})^2} \tag{4.25}$$

or

$$\hat{\beta} = \frac{\sum(X_t - \bar{X})(Y_t - \bar{Y})}{\sum(X_t - \bar{X})^2} \tag{4.26}$$

If we further divide both nominator and denominator by $1/n$ we have

$$\hat{\beta} = \frac{1/n \sum(X_t - \bar{X})(Y_t - \bar{Y})}{1/n \sum(X_t - \bar{X})^2} \tag{4.27}$$

and finally express $\hat{\beta}$ as:

$$\hat{\beta} = \frac{Cov(X_t, Y_t)}{Var(X_t)} \tag{4.28}$$

where $Cov(X_t, Y_t)$ and $Var(X_t)$ are sample variances and covariances.

The assumptions of the CLRM

General

In the previous section we described the desirable properties of estimators. However, we need to make clear that there is no guarantee that the OLS estimators will possess any of these properties. Unless a number of assumptions – which this section presents – hold.

In general, when we calculate estimators of population parameters from sample data we are bound to make some initial assumptions about the population distribution. Usually, they amount to a set of statements about the distribution of the variables that we are investigating, without which our model and estimates cannot be justified. Therefore, it is very important not only to present the assumptions but also to move beyond them, to the extent that we will at least study what happens when they go wrong, and how we may test whether they have gone wrong. This will be examined in the third part of this book.

The assumptions

The CLRM consists of eight basic assumptions about the ways in which the observations are generated:

1 *Linearity*. The first assumption is that the dependent variable can be calculated as a linear function of a specific set of independent variables, plus a disturbance term. This can be expressed mathematically as follows: the regression model is linear in the unknown coefficients α and β so that, $Y_t = \alpha + \beta X_t + u_t$, for $t = 1, 2, 3, \ldots, n$.

2 X_t *has some variation*. By this assumption we mean that not all observations of X_t are the same, at least one has to be different so that the sample $Var(X)$ is not 0. It is important to distinguish between the sample variance which simply shows how much X varies over the particular sample and the stochastic nature of X. In many places in this book we will make the assumption that X is non stochastic (see point 3 below). This means that the variance of X at any point of time is zero so $Var(X_t) = 0$ and if we could somehow repeat the world over again X would always take exactly the same values. But of course over any sample there will (indeed must) be some variation in X.

3 X_t *is non-stochastic and fixed in repeated samples*. By this assumption we first mean that X_t is a variable whose values are not determined by some chance mechanism, they are determined by an experimenter or investigator, and second that it is possible to repeat the sample with the same independent variable values. This implies that $Cov(X_s, u_t) = 0$ for all s, and $t = 1, 2, \ldots, n$, that is that X_t and u_t are uncorrelated.

4 *The expected value of the disturbance term is zero*. This means that the disturbance is a genuine disturbance, so that if we took a large number of samples the mean disturbance would be zero. This can be shown as $E(u_t) = 0$. We need this assumption in order to be able to interpret the deterministic part of a regression model, $\alpha + \beta X_t$, as a 'statistical average' relation.

5 *Homoskedasticity*. This requires that all disturbance terms have the same variance, so that $Var(u_t) = \sigma^2 = $ constant for all t.

6 *Serial independence*. This requires that all disturbance terms are independently distributed, or more easily are not correlated with one another, so that $Cov(u_t, u_s) = E(u_t - Eu_t)(u_s - Eu_s) = E(u_t u_s) = 0$ for all $t \neq s$. This assumption has a special significance in economics; to grasp what it means in practice, recall that we nearly always obtain our data from time series in which each t is one year, or one-quarter, or one week, ahead of the last. The condition means, therefore, that the disturbance in one period should not be related to the disturbance in the next or previous periods. This condition is frequently violated since, if there is a disturbing effect at one time, it is likely to persist. In this discussion we will be studying violations of this assumption quite carefully.

7 *Normality of residuals*. The disturbance $u_1, u_2, \ldots, u_n$ are assumed to be independently and identically normally distributed with mean zero and common variance σ^2.

8 $n > 2$ *and multicollinearity*. This says that the number of observations must be at least greater than two, or in general it must be greater than the number of independent variables and that there are no exact linear relationships among the variables.

Violations of the assumptions

The first three assumptions basically state that X_t is a 'well-behaved' variable that was not chosen by chance, and that we can in some sense 'control' for it by choosing it again and again. These are needed because X_t is used to explain what is happening (the explanatory variable).

Violation of assumption one creates problems which are in general called misspecification errors, such as wrong regressors, nonlinearities and changing parameters. We discuss those problems analytically in Chapter 9. Violation of assumptions two and three results in errors in variables and problems which are discussed in Chapter 11. Violation of the fourth assumption leads to a biased intercept, while violations of assumptions 5 and 6 lead to problems of heteroskedasticity and serial correlation respectively. These problems are discussed in Chapters 7 and 8 respectively. Finally, assumption seven has important implications in hypothesis testing, and violation of assumption 8 leads to problems of perfect multicollinearity which are discussed in Chapter 6 (see Table 4.1).

Properties of the OLS estimators

We now return to the properties that we would like our estimators to have. Based on the assumptions of the CLRM we can prove that the OLS estimators are Best Linear Unbiased

Table 4.1   The assumptions of the CLRM

Assumption	Mathematical expression	Violation may imply	Chapter
(1) Linearity of the model	$Y_t = \alpha + \beta X_t + u_t$	Wrong regressors Nonlinearity Changing parameters	9 9 9
(2) X is variable	$Var(X)$ is not 0	Errors in variables	9
(3) X is non-stochastic and fixed in repeated samples	$Cov(X_s, u_t) = 0$ for all s and $t = 1, 2, \ldots, n$	Autoregression	11
(4) Expected value of disturbance is zero	$E(u_t) = 0$	Biased intercept	—
(5) Homoskedasticity	$Var(u_t) = \sigma^2 = $ constant	Heteroskedasticity	7
(6) Serial independence	$Cov(u_t, u_s) = 0$ for all $t \neq s$	Autocorrelation	8
(7) Normality of disturbance	$u_t \sim N(\mu, \sigma^2)$	Outliers	9
(8) No linear relationships	$\sum_{t=1}^{T}(\delta_i X_{it} + \delta_j X_{jt}) \neq 0 \quad i \neq j$	Multicollinearity	6

Estimators (BLUE). In order to do that, we first have to decompose the regression coefficients estimated under OLS into their random and non-random components.

As a starting point note that Y_t has a non-random component $(a + \beta X_t)$, as well as a random component which is captured by the residuals u_t. Therefore, the $Cov(X, Y)$ – which depends on values of Y_t – will have a random and non-random component:

$$Cov(X, Y) = Cov(X_t, [a + \beta X + u]) \tag{4.29}$$

$$= Cov(X, a) + Cov(X, \beta X) + Cov(X, u)$$

However, because α and β are constants we have that $Cov(X, a) = 0$ and that $Cov(X, \beta X) = \beta Cov(X, X) = \beta Var(X)$. Thus:

$$Cov(X, Y) = \beta Var(X) + Cov(X, u) \tag{4.30}$$

and substituting that in equation (4.28) yields:

$$\hat{\beta} = \frac{Cov(X, Y)}{Var(X)} = \beta + \frac{Cov(X, u)}{Var(X)} \tag{4.31}$$

which says that the OLS coefficient $\hat{\beta}$ estimated from any sample has a non-random component, β, and a random component which depends on the $Cov(X_t, u_t)$.

Linearity

Based on assumption 3, we have that X is non-stochastic and fixed in repeated samples. Therefore, the X values can be treated as constants so that what we need is merely to concentrate on the Y values. If the OLS estimators are linear functions of the Y values then they are linear estimators. From (4.24) we have that:

$$\hat{\beta} = \frac{\sum x_t y_t}{\sum x_t^2} \tag{4.32}$$

Since the X_t are regarded as constants, then x_t are regarded as constants as well. We have that:

$$\hat{\beta} = \frac{\sum x_t y_t}{\sum x_t^2} = \frac{\sum x_t (Y_t - \bar{Y})}{\sum x_t^2} = \frac{\sum x_t Y_t - \bar{Y} \sum x_t}{\sum x_t^2} \tag{4.33}$$

but because $\bar{Y} \sum x_t = 0$, we can have that

$$\hat{\beta} = \frac{\sum x_t Y_t}{\sum x_t^2} = \sum z_t Y_t \tag{4.34}$$

where $z_t = x_t / \sum x_t^2$ can also be regarded as constant and, therefore, $\hat{\beta}$ is indeed a linear estimator of the Y_t.

Unbiasedness

Unbiasedness of $\hat{\beta}$

To prove that $\hat{\beta}$ is an unbiased estimator of β we need to show that $E(\hat{\beta}) = \beta$. We have:

$$E(\hat{\beta}) = E\left[\beta + \frac{Cov(X,u)}{Var(X)}\right] \tag{4.35}$$

However, β is a constant, and using assumption 3 – that X_t is non-random – we can take $Var(X)$ as a fixed constant to take them out of the expectation expression and have:

$$E(\hat{\beta}) = E(\beta) + \frac{1}{Var(X)}E[Cov(X,u)] \tag{4.36}$$

Therefore, it is enough to show that $E[Cov(X,u)] = 0$. We know that:

$$E[Cov(X,u)] = E\left[\frac{1}{n}\sum_{t=1}^{n}(X_t - \bar{X})(u_t - \bar{u})\right] \tag{4.37}$$

where $1/n$ is constant, so we can take it out of the expectation, while we can also break the sum into the sum of its expectations to give:

$$E[Cov(X_t, u_t)] = \frac{1}{n}\left[E(X_1 - \bar{X})(u_1 - \bar{u}) + \cdots + E(X_n - \bar{X})(u_n - \bar{u})\right]$$

$$= \frac{1}{n}\sum_{t=1}^{n}E\left[(X_t - \bar{X})(u_t - \bar{u})\right] \tag{4.38}$$

Furthermore, because X_t is non-random (again from assumption 3) we can take it out of the expectation term to give

$$E[Cov(X,u)] = \frac{1}{n}\sum_{t=1}^{n}(X_t - \bar{X})E(u_t - \bar{u}) \tag{4.39}$$

Finally, using assumption 4, we have that $E(u_t) = 0$ and therefore $E(\bar{u}) = 0$. So, $E[Cov(X,u)] = 0$ and this proves that

$$E(\hat{\beta}) = \beta$$

or, to put it in words, that $\hat{\beta}$ is an unbiased estimator of the true population parameter β.

Unbiasedness of $\hat{a}$

We know that $\hat{a} = \bar{Y} - \hat{\beta}\bar{X}$, so

$$E(\hat{a}) = E(\bar{Y}) - E(\hat{\beta})\bar{X} \tag{4.40}$$

But we also have that

$$E(Y_t) = a + \beta X_t + E(u_t) = a + \beta X_t \tag{4.41}$$

where we eliminated the $E(u_t)$ term because, according to assumption 4, $E(u_t) = 0$. So:

$$E(\bar{Y}) = a + \beta \bar{X} \tag{4.42}$$

Substituting (4.42) into (4.40) gives:

$$E(\hat{a}) = a + \beta \bar{X} - E(\hat{\beta})\bar{X} \tag{4.43}$$

But we have proved before that $E(\hat{\beta}) = \beta$, therefore:

$$E(\hat{a}) = a + \beta \bar{X} - \beta \bar{X} = a \tag{4.44}$$

which proves that $\hat{a}$ is an unbiased estimator of a.

Efficiency and BLUEness

Under assumptions 5 and 6, we can prove that the OLS estimators are the most efficient among all unbiased linear estimators. Thus, we can conclude that the OLS procedure yields BLU estimators.

The proof that the OLS estimators are BLU is relatively complicated. It entails a procedure which goes the opposite way to that followed so far. First we start the estimation from the beginning trying to derive a BLU estimator of β, based on the properties of linearity, unbiasedness and minimum variance one by one, and then we check whether the BLU estimator, derived by this procedure, is the same as the OLS estimator.

So, we want to derive the BLU estimator of β, say $\check{\beta}$, concentrating first on the property of linearity. For $\check{\beta}$ to be linear we need to have:

$$\check{\beta} = \delta_1 Y_1 + \delta_2 Y_2 + \cdots + \delta_n Y_n = \sum \delta_t Y_t \tag{4.45}$$

where the δ_t terms are constants the values of which are to be determined.

Proceeding with the property of unbiasedness, for $\check{\beta}$ to be unbiased we must have $E(\check{\beta}) = \beta$. We know that:

$$E(\check{\beta}) = E\left(\sum \delta_t Y_t\right) = \sum \delta_t E(Y_t) \tag{4.46}$$

Substituting $E(Y_t) = a + \beta X_t$ (because $Y_t = a + \beta X_t + u_t$, and also because X_t is non-stochastic and $E(u_t) = 0$; given by the basic assumptions of the model), we get:

$$\cdot E(\check{\beta}) = \sum \delta_t (a + \beta X_t) = a \sum \delta_t + \beta \sum \delta_t X_t \tag{4.47}$$

and therefore, in order to have unbiased $\breve{\beta}$ we need:

$$\sum \delta_t = 0 \quad \text{and} \quad \sum \delta_t X_t = 1 \tag{4.48}$$

Next, we proceed by deriving an expression for the variance (that we need to minimize) of the $\breve{\beta}$.

$$\begin{aligned} Var(\breve{\beta}) &= E\left[\breve{\beta} - E(\breve{\beta})\right]^2 \\ &= E\left[\sum \delta_t Y_t - E\left(\sum \delta_t Y_t\right)\right]^2 \\ &= E\left[\sum \delta_t Y_t - \sum \delta_t E(Y_t)\right]^2 \\ &= E\left[\sum \delta_t (Y_t - E(Y_t))\right]^2 \end{aligned} \tag{4.49}$$

In this expression we can use $Y_t = a + \beta X_t + u_t$ and $E(Y_t) = a + \beta X_t$ to give:

$$\begin{aligned} Var(\breve{\beta}) &= E\left[\sum \delta_t (a + \beta X_t + u_t - (a + \beta X_t))\right]^2 \\ &= E\left(\sum \delta_t u_t\right)^2 \\ &= E(\delta_1^2 u_1^2 + \delta_2^2 u_2^2 + \delta_3^2 u_3^2 + \cdots + \delta_n^2 u_n^2 \\ &\quad + 2\delta_1 \delta_2 u_1 u_2 + 2\delta_1 \delta_3 u_1 u_3 + \cdots) \\ &= \delta_1^2 E(u_1^2) + \delta_2^2 E(u_2^2) + \delta_3^2 E(u_3^2) + \cdots + \delta_n^2 E(u_n^2) \\ &\quad + 2\delta_1 \delta_2 E(u_1 u_2) + 2\delta_1 \delta_3 E(u_1 u_3) + \cdots) \end{aligned} \tag{4.50}$$

Using assumptions 5 ($Var(u_t) = \sigma^2$) and 6 ($Cov(u_t, u_s) = E(u_t u_s) = 0$ for all $t \neq s$) we obtain that:

$$Var(\breve{\beta}) = \sum \delta_t^2 \sigma^2 \tag{4.51}$$

We now need to choose δ_t in the linear estimator (4.46) to be such as to minimize the variance (4.51) subject to the constraints (4.49), which ensure unbiasedness (with this then having a linear, unbiased minimum variance estimator). We formulate the Langrangean function:

$$L = \sigma^2 \sum \delta_t^2 - \lambda_1 \left(\sum \delta_t\right) - \lambda_2 \left(\sum \delta_t X_t - 1\right) \tag{4.52}$$

where λ_1 and λ_2 are Langrangean multipliers.

Following the regular procedure, which is to take the first-order conditions (i.e. the partial derivatives of L with respect to δ_t, λ_1 and λ_2) and set them equal to zero; and after rearrangement and mathematical manipulations (we omit the mathematical details of the derivation because it is very lengthy and tedious, and because it does not use any of the assumptions of the model anyway) we obtain the optimal δ_t as:

$$\delta_t = \frac{x_t}{\sum x_t^2} \tag{4.53}$$

Therefore, we have that $\delta_t = z_t$ of the OLS expression given by (4.34). So, substituting this into our linear estimator $\breve{\beta}$ we have:

$$\begin{aligned}
\breve{\beta} &= \sum \delta_t Y_t = \sum z_t Y_t \\
&= \sum z_t (Y_t - \bar{Y} + \bar{Y})^* \\
&= \sum z_t (Y_t - \bar{Y}) + \bar{Y} \sum z_t \\
&= \sum z_t y_t = \frac{\sum x_t y_t}{\sum x_t^2} \\
&= \hat{\beta}
\end{aligned} \tag{4.54}$$

Thus, the $\hat{\beta}$ of the OLS is the BLUE.

The advantage of the BLUEness condition is that it provides us with an expression for the variance by substituting the optimal δ_t given in (4.53) into (4.51) to give:

$$\begin{aligned}
Var(\breve{\beta}) = Var(\hat{\beta}) &= \sum \left(\frac{x_t}{\sum x_t^2}\right)^2 \sigma^2 \\
&= \frac{\sum x_t^2 \sigma^2}{\left(\sum x_t^2\right)^2} = \sigma^2 \frac{1}{\sum x_t^2}
\end{aligned} \tag{4.55}$$

Consistency

Consistency is the idea that as the sample becomes infinitely large the parameter estimate given by a procedure such as OLS converges on the true parameter value. This is obviously true when the estimator is unbiased, as shown above, as consistency is really just a weaker form of unbiasedness. However the proof above rests on our assumption 3 that the X variables are fixed. If we relax this assumption then it is no longer possible to prove the unbiasedness of OLS but we can still establish that it is a consistent estimator. So when we relax assumption 3 OLS is no longer a BLU estimator but it is still consistent.

We showed in equation (4.31) that $\hat{\beta} = \beta + Cov(X, u)/Var(X)$, dividing the top and the bottom of the last term by n gives

$$\hat{\beta} = \beta + \frac{Cov(X, u)/n}{Var(X)/n} \tag{4.56}$$

---

* We add and subtract $\bar{Y}$.

Using the law of large numbers, we know that $Cov(X, u)/n$ converges to its expectation which is $Cov(X_t, u_t)$. Similarly, $Var(X)/n$ converges to $Var(X_t)$. So, as $n \to \infty$; $\hat{\beta} \to \beta + Cov(X_t, u_t)/Var(X_t)$, which is equal to the true population parameter β if $Cov(X_t, u_t) = 0$ (i.e. if X_t and u_t are uncorrelated). Thus $\hat{\beta}$ is a consistent estimator of the true population parameter β.

The overall goodness of fit

We showed before that the regression equation obtained from the OLS method fits a scatter diagram quite closely. However, we need to know how close it is to the scattered observed values to be able to judge whether a particular line describes the relationship among Y_t and X_t better than an alternative line. In other words, it is desirable to know a measure which describes the closeness of fit. This measure will also inform us about how well the obtained equation accounts for the behaviour of the dependent variable.

In order to obtain such a measure, we first have to decompose the actual value of Y_t into a predicted value, which comes from the regression equation $\hat{Y}_t$ plus the equation's residuals:

$$Y_t = \hat{Y}_t + \hat{u}_t \qquad (4.57)$$

subtracting $\bar{Y}$ from both sides we have:

$$Y_t - \bar{Y} = \hat{Y}_t - \bar{Y} + \hat{u}_t \qquad (4.58)$$

We need to obtain a measure of the total variation in Y_t from its mean $\bar{Y}$. Therefore, we take the sum of equation (4.58):

$$\sum (Y_t - \bar{Y}) = \sum (\hat{Y}_t - \bar{Y} + \hat{u}_t) \qquad (4.59)$$

Then square both terms to get:

$$\sum (Y_t - \bar{Y})^2 = \sum (\hat{Y}_t - \bar{Y} + \hat{u}_t)^2 \qquad (4.60)$$

Note, that if we divide the measure that we have on the left-hand side of the above equation by n, we would simply get the sample variance of Y_t. So $\sum (Y_t - \bar{Y})^2$ is an appropriate measure of the total variation in Y_t, often called the total sum of squares (TSS). Continuing:

$$\sum (Y_t - \bar{Y})^2 = \sum (\hat{Y}_t - \bar{Y})^2 + \sum \hat{u}_t^2 + 2 \sum (\hat{Y}_t - \bar{Y})\hat{u}_t \qquad (4.61)$$

where $\sum (\hat{Y}_t - \bar{Y})^2$ is the explained sum of squares from the OLS – usually called ESS – and $\sum \hat{u}_t^2$ is the unexplained part of the total variation in Y_t, or alternatively the remaining or residual sum of squares (RSS). It is easy to show that the cross-product term drops out of the equation using the properties of the OLS residuals (from the first order conditions we had that $-2\sum(Y_t - \hat{a} - \hat{\beta}X_t) = 0$ and $-2\sum X_t(Y_t - \hat{a} - \hat{\beta}X_t) = 0$ which says that $-2\sum \hat{u}_t = 0$ and $-2\sum X_t\hat{u}_t = 0$):

$$\sum(Y_t - \bar{Y})\hat{u}_t = \sum(\hat{a} + \hat{\beta}X_t - \bar{Y})\hat{u}_t$$
$$= \hat{a}\sum \hat{u}_t + \hat{\beta}\sum X_t\hat{u}_t - \bar{Y}\sum \hat{u}_t = 0 \qquad (4.62)$$

Thus equation (4.61) reduces to:

$$TSS = ESS + RSS \qquad (4.63)$$

where both TSS and ESS are expressed in units of Y squared. By relating ESS to TSS we can derive a pure number called the coefficient of determination (and denoted by R^2):

$$R^2 = \frac{ESS}{TSS} \qquad (4.64)$$

which measures the proportion of the total variation in Y_t (TSS) that is explained by the sample regression equation (ESS). By dividing each of the terms in (4.63) by TSS we can obtain an alternative equation which gives us the range of the values of R^2:

$$1 = R^2 + \frac{RSS}{TSS} \qquad (4.65)$$

When the sample regression function fails to account for any of the variation in Y_t then ESS = 0 and all the variation in Y_t is left unexplained: RSS = TSS. In this case $R^2 = 0$ and this is its lower bound. At the opposite extreme, when the sample regression equation predicts perfectly every value of Y_t no equation error occurs, thus RSS = 0 and ESS = TSS which gives us an R^2 equal to its upper bound value of 1.

Therefore, the values of R^2 lie in between 0 and 1, and show how closely the equation fits the data. An R^2 of 0.4 is better than a value of 0.2, but not twice as good. The value of 0.4 indicates that 40% of the variation in Y_t is explained by the sample regression equation (or by the regressors).

Problems associated with R^2

There are a number of serious problems associated with the use of R^2 in judging the performance of a single equation, or as a basis of comparison of different equations:

1 *Spurious regression problem (this problem will be fully discussed in chapters 16 and 17).* In the case where two or more variables are actually unrelated, but exhibit strong trend like behaviour, the R^2 can take on very high values (sometimes even greater than 0.9). This may mislead the researcher into believing that there is actually a strong relationship between the variables.

2 *High correlation of X_t with another variable Z_t.* It might be that there is a variable Z_t that determines the behaviour of Y_t and is highly correlated with X_t. Then, even

though a large value of R^2 shows the importance of X_t in determining Y_t, the omitted variable Z_t may be responsible for this.

3 *Correlation does not necessarily implies causality.* No matter how high the value of R^2, this cannot suggest causality among Y_t and X_t, because R^2 is a measure of correlation between the observed value Y_t and the predicted value $\hat{Y}_t$. To whatever extent possible, refer to economic theory, previous empirical work and intuition to determine a causally related variable to include in a sample regression.

4 *Time series equation vs cross section equations.* Time series equations almost always generate higher R^2 values than cross-section equations. This arises because cross-sectional data contain a great deal of random variation (usually called 'noise') which makes ESS small relative to TSS. On the other hand, even badly specified time series equations can give R^2s of 0.999 for the spurious regression reasons presented in point 1 above. Therefore, comparisons of time series and cross-sectional equations using R^2 are not possible.

5 *Low R^2 does not mean wrong choice of X_t.* Low values of R^2 are not necessarily the result of using a wrong explanatory variable. The functional form that is used might be an inappropriate one (i.e. linear instead of quadratic) or – in the case of time series – the choice of time period might be incorrect and lagged terms might need to be included instead.

6 *R^2s from equations with different forms of Y_t are not comparable.* Assume we estimate the following population regression equations:

$$Y_t = a_0 + b_0 X_t + e_t \tag{4.66}$$

$$\ln Y_t = a_1 + b_1 \ln X_t + u_t \tag{4.67}$$

comparing their R^2 is not correct. This is due to the definition of R^2. The R^2 in the first equation shows the proportion of variation in Y_t explained by X_t, while in the second equation shows the proportion of the variation in the natural logarithm of Y_t explained by the natural logarithm of X_t. In general, whenever the dependent variable is changed in anyway, the R^2 should not be used to compare the models.

Hypothesis testing and confidence intervals

Under the assumptions of the CLRM, we know that the estimators $\hat{a}$ and $\hat{\beta}$ obtained by OLS follow a normal distribution with means a and β and variances $\sigma_{\hat{a}}^2$ and $\sigma_{\hat{\beta}}^2$ respectively. It follows that the variables:

$$\frac{\hat{a} - a}{\sigma_{\hat{a}}} \quad \text{and} \quad \frac{\hat{\beta} - \beta}{\sigma_{\hat{\beta}}} \tag{4.68}$$

have a standard normal distribution (i.e. a normal distribution with 0 mean and variance 1). If we replace the unknown $\sigma_{\hat{a}}$ and $\sigma_{\hat{\beta}}$ by their estimates $s_{\hat{a}}$ and $s_{\hat{\beta}}$ this is no longer true. However, it is relatively easy (the proof of this, however, is beyond the scope of this book) to show that the following random variables (after the replacement):

$$\frac{\hat{a} - a}{s_{\hat{a}}} \quad \text{and} \quad \frac{\hat{\beta} - \beta}{s_{\hat{\beta}}} \tag{4.69}$$

follow the student's t-distribution with $n - 2$ degrees of freedom. The student's t-distribution is close to the standard normal distribution except that it has fatter tails, particularly when the number of degrees of freedom is small.

Testing the significance of the OLS coefficients

Knowing the distribution of our estimated coefficients we are able to conduct hypothesis testing in order to assess their statistical significance. In general the following steps should be involved:

Step 1   Set the null and alternative hypothesis. It can be either H_0: $\beta = 0$; H_a: $\beta \neq 0$ (two-tailed test), or if there is prior knowledge about the sign of the estimated coefficient (let's assume positive), H_0: $\beta = 0$; H_a: $\beta > 0$ (one-tail test).

Step 2   Calculate the t-statistic by $t = (\hat{\beta} - \beta)/s_{\hat{\beta}}$, where here because β under null is equal to zero it becomes $\hat{\beta}/s_{\hat{\beta}}$ (note that this is the t-statistic that is automatically provided by EViews and Microfit in their standard regression outputs).

Step 3   Find from the t-tables the t-critical for $n - 2$ degrees of freedom.

Step 4   If $|t_{stat}| > |t_{crit}|$ reject the null hypothesis.

Note that if we want to test a different hypothesis (i.e. that $\beta = 1$), then we need to change our null and alternative hypothesis in step 1 and calculate manually the t-statistic by the $t = (\hat{\beta} - \beta)/s_{\hat{\beta}}$ formula. In this case it is not appropriate to use the t-statistic which is provided by EViews and Microfit.

A rule of thumb of significance tests

The procedure for hypothesis testing outlined above presupposes that the researcher selects a significance level and then compares the value of the t-statistic with the critical value for this level. Several rules of thumb based on this approach have been developed, and these are useful in the sense that we do not need to consult statistical tables in cases of large samples (degrees of freedom >30).

Note that the critical value for a 5% level of significance and for a very large sample ($n \rightarrow \infty$) reaches the value of ± 1.96. For the same level and for 30 degrees of freedom it is ± 2.045, while for 60 degrees of freedom it is exactly ± 2.00. Therefore, for large samples it is quite safe to use as a rule of thumb a critical value of $|t| > 2$. For a one-tail test the rule of thumb changes with the t-value being $|t| > 1.65$. The rules stated above are nothing more that convenient approximations to these values. For 'small' samples we must use the specific values given in the t-table, as the above rules are not safe to apply.

The p-value approach

EViews and Microfit apart from reporting t statistics for the estimated coefficients also report p values which can be used as an alternative approach in assessing the significance of regression coefficients. The p value shows what is the smallest level at which we would be able to accept the null hypothesis of a test. It is very useful because the significance levels chosen for a test are always arbitrary. Why, for example, 5% and not 1% or 10%. The p value approach is also more informative than the 'choice of significance levels and find critical values' approach, because one can obtain exactly the level of significance of the estimated coefficient. For example, a p-value of 0.339 says that if the true $\beta = 0$ there is a probability of 0.339 of observing an estimated value of $\hat{\beta}$ which is greater than or equal to the OLS estimate purely by chance. So the estimated value could have arisen by chance with a fairly high probability even if the true value is zero. Similarly if the p-value was 0.01, this says that there is a very small probability of a value for $\hat{\beta}$ equal or greater than the OLS estimate arising purely by chance when the true value of β is zero. Furthermore, if we have in mind a conventional significance level (lets say 5% or 0.05) we conclude that the coefficient is significantly different from zero at the 5% level if the p-value is less than or equal to 0.05. If it is greater than 0.05 then we cannot reject the null hypothesis that the coefficient is actually zero at our 5% significance level.

Confidence intervals

For the null hypothesis that $H_0:\beta = \beta_1$ and for an $r\%$ significance level we can accept the null when our 't' test lies in the following region:

$$-t_{r,n-2} \leq \frac{\hat{\beta} - \beta_1}{s_{\hat{\beta}}} \leq t_{r,n-2} \tag{4.70}$$

where $t_{r,n-2}$ is the critical value from the student 't' tables for an $r\%$ significance level and $n - 2$ degrees of freedom (as we assume there are only two parameters being estimated). So we can construct a confidence interval for the range of values of β_1 for which we would accept the null hypothesis.

$$\hat{\beta} - t_{r,n-2}s_{\hat{\beta}} \leq \beta_1 \leq \hat{\beta} + t_{r,n-2}s_{\hat{\beta}} \tag{4.71}$$

or alternatively

$$\hat{\beta} \pm t_{r,n-2}s_{\hat{\beta}} \tag{4.72}$$

of course the same holds for α being $\hat{\alpha} \pm t_{r,n-2}s_{\hat{\alpha}}$.

How to estimate a simple regression in Microfit and EViews

Simple regression in Microfit

Step 1: Open Microfit.

Step 2: Click on **File/New** in order to create a new file.

Step 3: Choose the required frequency for time series or 'undated' for cross-sectional data and specify the number of variables as well as the start and end for time series data or the number of observations for cross-sectional data.

Step 4: When asked to provide names and descriptions for variables give the names Y and X, and the descriptions that you want and think will enable you to remember the definitions of your variables (giving descriptions is optional but is recommended as it is sometimes really helpful). Press <GO>.

Step 5: Either type the data into Microfit or copy/paste the data from Excel®. Be very careful pasting the data, to provide appropriate information required by Microfit. Press <GO> at the end.

Step 6: Once you have put the data in Microfit, you then have to create a constant. Either go to the **process** editor (by pressing the **process** button) and type C = 1 (and then press <GO>), or click on **Edit/Constant (intercept) term** and provide a name for your intercept by typing it in the corresponding window (let us assume that you name your constant term C).

Step 7: Go to the single editor (by clicking the **'single'** button) and type into the single editor:

```
Y C X
```

and then click <START>. The regression output is presented in a new window which provides estimates for alpha (the coefficient of the constant term), beta (the coefficient of X) and some additional statistics that will be discussed in later chapters of this book.

Simple regression in EViews

Step 1: Open EViews.

Step 2: Click on **File/New/Workfile** in order to create a new file.

Step 3: Choose the frequency of the data in the case of time series data, or [**Undated or Irregular**] in the case of cross-sectional data and specify the start and end of your data set. You will have a new window, which automatically contains a constant (**c**) and a residual (**resid**) series.

Step 4: In the command line type:

```
genr x=0 (press 'enter')
genr y=0 (press 'enter')
```

which creates two new series named x and y that contain zeros for every observation. Open x and y as a group by selecting them and double clicking with your mouse.

Step 5: Then either type the data into EViews or copy/paste the data from Excel. In order to be able to type (edit) the data of your series or to paste anything into the EViews cells, the '**edit** $+/-$' button must be pressed. After finishing with editing the series press the '**edit** $+/-$' button again to lock or secure the data.

Step 6: Once the data have been entered into EViews, the regression line (to obtain alpha and beta) may be estimated either by typing:

```
ls y c x (press 'enter')
```

on the command line, or by clicking on **Quick/Estimate equation** and then writing your equation (i.e. y c x) in the new window. Note that the option for OLS (LS – Least Squares (NLS and ARMA)) is automatically chosen by EViews and the sample is automatically chosen to be the maximum possible.

Either way, the regression result output is obtained in a new window which provides estimates for alpha (the coefficient of the constant term), beta (the coefficient of X) and some additional statistics that will be discussed in later chapters of this book.

Reading the EViews simple regression results output

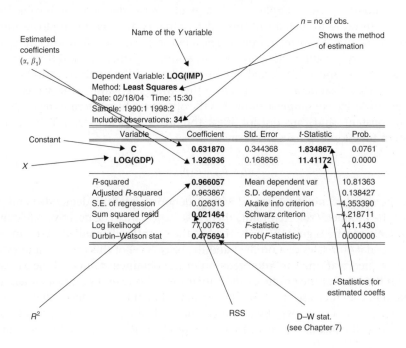

Presentation of regression results

The results of a regression analysis can be presented in various different ways. However, the most common way is to write the estimated equation with standard errors of coefficients written in brackets below the estimated coefficients and include some more statistics below the equation. For the consumption function that will be presented in Computer Example 2, the results are summarized as shown below:

$$\hat{C}_t = 15.116 + 0.160 Y_t^d$$

$$(6.565) \quad (0.038) \tag{4.73}$$

$$R^2 = 0.932 \quad n = 20 \quad \hat{\sigma} = 6.879 \tag{4.74}$$

From this summary we can (a) read estimated effects of changes in the explanatory variables on the dependent variable, (b) predict values of the dependent variable for given values of the explanatory variable, (c) perform hypothesis testing for the estimated coefficients, and (d) construct confidence intervals for the estimated coefficients.

Applications

Application 1: the demand function

From economic theory we know that the demand for a commodity depends basically on the price of that commodity (the law of demand). Other possible determinants can include prices of other competing goods (close substitutes) or those that complement that commodity (close complements), and of course the level of income of the consumer. In order to include all those determinants we need to employ a multiple regression analysis. However, for pedagogical purposes we have to restrict ourselves to one explanatory variable. Therefore, we can assume a partial demand function where the quantity demanded is affected only by the price of the product. (Another way of doing this is to assume a *ceteris paribus* (other things remaining the same) demand function, in which we simply assume that the other variables entering the relationship remain constant, and thus do not affect the quantity demanded.) The population regression function will have the form:

$$q_t = a_0 + a_1 p_t + u_t \tag{4.75}$$

where the standard notation is used with q_t denoting quantity demanded and p_t the price of the product. From economic theory we expect a_1 to be negative reflecting the law of demand (the higher the price the less the quantity demanded). We can collect time series data for sales of a product and the price level of this product and estimate the above specification. The interpretation of the obtained results will be as follows. For a_1: if the price of the product will be increased by one unit of measurement (i.e. if measured in £ an increase of £1.00), the consumption of this product will be decreased (because a_1 will be negative) by $\hat{a}_1$ units. For a_0: if the price of the product is zero consumers will consume $\hat{a}_0$ quantity of this product. R^2 is expected to be somehow low (lets say 0.6) suggesting that there are additional variables that affect the quantity demanded, that we did not include in our equation, while it is also possible to obtain the price elasticity of this product for a given year (lets say 1999) from the equation:

$$\frac{p_{99}}{\hat{q}_{99}}\frac{\Delta q}{\Delta p} = \frac{p_{99}}{\hat{q}_{99}}\hat{a}_1 \tag{4.76}$$

Application 2: a production function

One of the most basic relationships in economic theory is the production function, that, usually, relates output (denoted by Y) to the possible factor inputs affecting production, such as labour (L) and capital (K). The general form of this relationship can be expressed by:

$$Y_t = f(K_t, L_t) \tag{4.77}$$

A frequently utilized form of this function – due to its properties that we will see later – is the well-known Cobb–Douglas production function:

$$Y_t = AK_t^a L_t^\beta \tag{4.78}$$

where a and β are constant terms that express the responsiveness of output to capital and labour respectively. A can be regarded as an exogenous efficiency/technology parameter. Obviously the greater is A, the higher is maximum output keeping labour and capital constant. In the short run we can assume that the stock of capital is fixed (short-run can be viewed here as a period that once the decision about capital has been made it cannot be changed by the producer until the next period). Then, in the short run, maximum output depends only on the labour input, and the production function becomes:

$$Y_t = g(L_t) \tag{4.79}$$

Using the Cobb–Douglas form of function (and for K_t constant and equal to K_0) we will have:

$$Y_t = (AK_0^a)L_t^\beta = A^*L_t^\beta \tag{4.80}$$

where $A^* = (AK_0^a)$. This short-run production function is now a bivariate model, and after applying a logarithmic transformation can be estimated with the OLS method. Taking the natural logarithm of both sides and adding an error term we have:

$$\ln Y_t = \ln(A^*) + \beta \ln(L_t) + u_t$$
$$= c + \beta \ln(L_t) + u_t \tag{4.81}$$

where $c = \ln(A^*)$, and β is the elasticity of output with respect to labour (one of the properties of the Cobb–Douglas production function). This elasticity denotes the percentage change in output that results from a 1 per cent change in the labour input.

We may use time series data on production and employment for the manufacturing sector of a country (or aggregate GDP and employment data) to obtain estimates of c and β for the above model.

Application 3: Okun's law

Okun (1962) developed an empirical relationship, using quarterly data from 1947:2 to 1960:4, between changes in the state of the economy (captured by changes in GNP) and changes in the unemployment rate, known as Okun's law. His results provide an important insight into the sensitivity of the unemployment rate to economic growth. The basic relationship is that of connecting the growth rate of unemployment (UNEMP) (which constitutes the dependent variable) to a constant and the growth rate of GNP (the independent variable) as follows:

$$\Delta UNEMP_t = a + b\Delta GNP_t + u_t \tag{4.82}$$

Applying OLS the sample regression equation that Okun obtained was:

$$\Delta \widehat{UNEMP}_t = 0.3 - 0.3\Delta GNP_t$$

$$R^2 = 0.63 \tag{4.83}$$

The constant in this equation shows the mean change in the unemployment rate when the growth rate of the economy is equal to zero, so from the obtained results we conclude that when the economy does not grow the unemployment rate rises by 0.3 per cent. The negative b coefficient suggests that when the state of the economy improves, the unemployment rate falls. The relationship, though, is less than one to one. A 1 per cent increase in GNP is connected with only a 0.3 per cent decrease in the unemployment rate. This result is called Okun's law. It is easy to collect data on GNP and unemployment, calculate their respective growth rates and check whether Okun's law is valid for different countries and different time periods.

Application 4: the Keynesian consumption function

Another basic relationship in economic theory is the Keynesian consumption function that simply states that consumption (C_t) is a positive linear function of disposable (after tax) income (Y_t^d). The relationship is as follows:

$$C_t = a + \delta Y_t^d \tag{4.84}$$

where a is the autonomous consumption (consumption even when disposable income is zero) and δ is the marginal propensity to consume. In this function we expect $a > 0$ and $0 > \delta > 1$. A $\hat{\delta} = 0.7$ means that the marginal propensity to consume is 0.7. A Keynesian consumption function is estimated below as a worked-out computer exercise example.

Computer example: the Keynesian consumption function

Table 4.2 provides data for consumption and disposable income for 20 randomly selected people.

(a) Put the data in Excel and calculate α and β assuming a linear relationship among X and Y using both expressions for β as given by (4.20) and (4.28).

(b) Calculate α and β using the 'Data Analysis' menu provided in Excel® and check whether the results are the same as the ones obtained in (a).

(c) Create a scatter plot of X and Y.

(d) Use Microfit and EViews to calculate α and β and scatter plots of X and Y.

Solution

(a) First, we have to obtain the products $X * Y$ and X^2 as well as the summations of X, Y, $X * Y$ and X^2. These are given in Table 4.3.

The command for cell C2 is '=B2*A2'; C3 is '=B3*A3' and so on; D2 is '=B2*B2' or '=B2^2'. For the summations in A22 the command is '=SUM(A2:A21)' and similarly for B22 is '=SUM(B2:B21)' and so on.

We can then calculate α and β using (4.20) as follows: For β we need to type in a cell the following '=(C22-(A22*B22)/20)/(D22-((B22^2)/20))'. For α we need to type in a different cell the following '=AVERAGE(A2:A21)-G2*AVERAGE(B2:B21)'.

If we do this correctly we should find that $\beta = 0.610888903$ and $\alpha = 15.11640873$.

Table 4.2 Data for simple regression example

Consumption Y	Disposable income X
72.30	100
91.65	120
135.20	200
94.60	130
163.50	240
100.00	114
86.50	126
142.36	213
120.00	156
112.56	167
132.30	189
149.80	214
115.30	188
132.20	197
149.50	206
100.25	142
79.60	112
90.20	134
116.50	169
126.00	170

Table 4.3 Excel calculations

	A	B	C	D
1	Y	X	X*Y	X-squared
2	72.30	100.00	7230.00	10000.00
3	91.65	120.00	10998.00	14400.00
4	135.20	200.00	27040.00	40000.00
5	94.60	130.00	12298.00	16900.00
6	163.50	240.00	39240.00	57600.00
7	100.00	114.00	11400.00	12996.00
8	86.50	126.00	10899.00	15876.00
9	142.36	213.00	30322.68	45369.00
10	120.00	156.00	18720.00	24336.00
11	112.56	167.00	18797.52	27889.00
12	132.30	189.00	25004.70	35721.00
13	149.80	214.00	32057.20	45796.00
14	115.30	188.00	21676.40	35344.00
15	132.20	197.00	26043.40	38809.00
16	149.50	206.00	30797.00	42436.00
17	100.25	142.00	14235.50	20164.00
18	79.60	112.00	8915.20	12544.00
19	90.20	134.00	12086.80	17956.00
20	116.50	169.00	19688.50	28561.00
21	126.00	170.00	21420.00	28900.00
22	2310.32	3287.00	398869.90	571597.00

Table 4.4 Excel calculations (continued)

	A	...	F	G	H
1	Y	...			
2	72.30	...	beta	0.610888903	
3	91.65	...	alpha	15.11640873	
4	135.20	...			
5	94.60	...		Y	X
6	163.50	...	Y	628.096654	
7	100.00	...	X	958.4404	1568.9275

Alternatively, using equation (4.28), we may go to the menu **Tools/Data Analysis** and from the data analysis menu choose the command **covariance**. We are then asked to specify the **Input Range**, the columns that contain the data for Y and X (i.e. enter '$A$1:$B$21' or simply select this area using the mouse). Note that if we include the labels (Y, X) in our selection we have to tick the **Labels in the First Row** box. We are asked to specify our **Output Range** as well, which can be either a different sheet (not recommended) or any empty cell in the current sheet (i.e. we might specify cell F5). By clicking <OK> we obtain the display shown in Table 4.4.

In order to obtain beta we have to write in cell G2 '=G7/H7'. The command for alpha remains the same as in the previous case.

(b) Go to **Tools/Data Analysis** and from the data analysis menu choose the command **Regression**. We are then asked to specify our **Input Y Range** which is the column that contains the data for the dependent (Y) variable (i.e. write '$A$1:$A$21') and **Input X Range** which is the column that contains the data for the independent (X) variable (i.e. write '$B$1:$B$21'). Again we can select those two areas using the mouse, and if

Table 4.5 Regression output from Excel

Regression Statistics					
Multiple *R*	0.9654959				
R Square	0.93218233				
Adjusted *R* square	0.92841469				
Standard error	6.87960343				
Observations	20				
ANOVA					
	df	*SS*	*MS*	*F*	*Significance F*
Regression	1	11710.0121	11710.0121	247.41757	5.80822E-12
Residual	18	851.9209813	47.3289434		
Total	19	12561.93308			
	Coefficients	*Standard error*	*t Stat*	*P-value*	*Lower 95%*
Intercept	15.1164087	6.565638115	2.302351799	0.0334684	1.322504225
X	0.6108889	0.038837116	15.72951266	5.808E-12	0.529295088

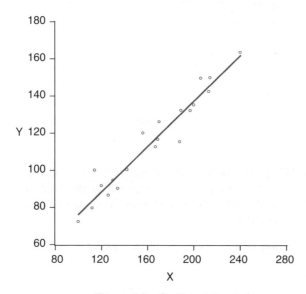

Figure 4.2 Scatter plot

we include the labels (Y, X) in our selection we have to tick the **Labels in the First Row** box. We will also be asked to specify **Output Range** similarly as above. By clicking <OK> the display shown in Table 4.5 is obtained.

Apart from estimates for α (which is the coefficient of the Intercept) and β (which is the coefficient of X), Table 4.5 shows more statistics that will be discussed in the Chapters.

(c) To obtain a scatter plot of Y and X, click on the **chart wizard** button and then specify **XY scatter** and click **next** – go to **series** and enter the values for X and Y using the mouse, click **next** again – enter titles for the diagram and the X and Y variables and then click **finish** to obtain the graph. By clicking on the dots of the scatter plot and using the right button of the mouse, **add Trendline** can be chosen for the graph. The graph will look like that shown in Figure 4.2.

(d) To obtain the regression results in Microfit we need to apply the following steps:

1 Open Microfit.

2 Choose **File/New** in order to create a new file.

3 Choose **Undated** and specify the number of variables (in this case 2) as well as the number of observations (in this case 20).

4 When asked to provide names and descriptions for the variables, give the names Y and X, and the descriptions 'Consumption' and 'Disposable Income' respectively (giving descriptions is optional but it is recommended to give descriptions of your variables because sometimes it is really helpful). Press <**GO**>.

5 Either type the data into Microfit or copy/paste the data from Excel®. Press <**GO**> at the end.

6 Having entered the data in Microfit, we need to create a constant. Either go to the **process** editor (by pressing the **process** button) and write:

$C = 1$ (and then press <**GO**>)

or go to **Edit/Constant (intercept) term** and provide a name for the intercept by typing it in the corresponding window (let's assume that we name the constant term as C).

7 Go to the single editor (by clicking the **single** button) and write:

        Y C X

and click <**START**>. The output shown in Table 4.6 is shown in a new window and provides estimates for alpha (the coefficient of the constant term), beta (the coefficient of X) and some additional statistics that will be discussed enter in the next sections of the chapter.

(e) To obtain regression results in EViews, the following steps are required:

1 Open EViews.

2 Choose **File/New/Workfile** in order to create a new file.

3 Choose **Undated or Irregular** and specify the number of observations (in this case 20). A new window appears which automatically contains a constant (**c**) and a residual (**resid**) series.

4 In the command line type:

        genr x=0 (press enter)
        genr y=0 (press enter)

which creates two new series named **x** and **y** that contain zeros for every observation. Open **x** and **y** as a group by selecting them and double clicking with the mouse.

5 Either type the data in EViews or copy/paste the data from Excel®. To edit the series press the **edit +/−** button. After finishing with editing the series press the **edit +/−** button again to lock or secure the data.

Table 4.6 Microfit Results from a Simple Regression Model

Dependent variable is Y
20 observations used for estimation from 1 to 20

Regressor	Coefficient	Standard Error	T-Ratio[Prob]
C	15.1164	6.5656	2.3024 [.033]
X	0.61089	0.038837	15.7295 [.000]

R-Squared	0.93218	R-bar-squared	0.92841
S.E. of regression	6.8796	F-stat. F(1, 18)	247.4176 [.000]
Mean of dependent variable	115.5160	S.D. of dependent variable	25.7129
Residual sum of squares	851.9210	Equation log-likelihood	−65.8964
Akaike info. criterion	−67.8964	Schwarz bayesian criterion	−68.8921
DW-statistic	2.2838		

Diagnostic Tests			
Test Statistics	LM Version		F Version
A: Serial Correlation	CHSQ(1) = 0.72444 [0.395]		$F(1, 17) = 0.63891$ [.435]
B: Functional Form	CHSQ(1) = 0.19091 [0.662]		$F(1, 17) = 0.16384$ [.691]
C: Normality	CHSQ(2) = 0.35743 [0.836]		Not applicable
D: Heteroscedasticity	CHSQ(1) = 0.40046 [0.527]		$F(1, 18) = 0.36778$ [.552]

A   Lagrange multiplier test of residual serial correlation.
B   Ramsey's RESET test using the square of the fitted values.
C   Based on a test of skewness and kurtosis of residuals.
D   Based on the regression of squared residuals on squared fitted values.

Table 4.7   EViews results from a simple regression model

Dependent Variable: Y
Method: Least Squares
Date: 01/09/04 Time: 16:13
Sample: 1–20
Included observations: 20

Variable	Coefficient	Std. Error	t-Statistic	Prob.
C	15.11641	6.565638	2.302352	0.0335
X	0.610889	0.038837	15.72951	0.0000

R-squared	0.932182	Mean dependent var	115.5160
Adjusted R-squared	0.928415	S.D. dependent var	25.71292
S.E. of regression	6.879603	Akaike info criterion	6.789639
Sum squared resid	851.9210	Schwarz criterion	6.889212
Log likelihood	−65.89639	F-statistic	247.4176
Durbin–Watson stat	2.283770	Prob(F-statistic)	0.000000

6 After entering the data into EViews, the regression line (to obtain alpha and beta) can be estimated either by writing:

```
ls y c x (press enter)
```

on the EViews command line, or by clicking on **Quick/Estimate equation** and then writing the equation (i.e. y c x) in the new window. Note that the option for **OLS (LS – Least Squares (NLS and ARMA))** is automatically chosen by EViews and the sample is automatically chosen to be from 1 to 20.

Either way the output shown in Table 4.7 is shown in a new window which provides estimates for alpha (the coefficient of the constant term) and beta (the coefficient of X).

Questions and exercises

Questions

1 An outlier is an observation that is very far from the sample regression function. Suppose the equation is initially estimated using all observations and then reestimated omitting outliers. How will the estimated slope coefficient change? How will R^2 change? Explain.

2 Regression equations are sometimes estimated using an explanatory variable that is a deviation from some value of interest. An example is a capacity utilization rate–unemployment rate equation, such as:

$$u_t = a_0 + a_1(CAP_t - CAP_t^f) + e_t$$

where CAP_t^f is a single value representing the capacity utilization rate corresponding to full employment (the value of 87.5% is sometimes used for this value).

(a) Will the estimated intercept from this equation differ from that in the equation with only CAP_t as an explanatory variable? Explain.

(b) Will the estimated slope coefficient from this equation differ from that in the equation with only CAP_t as an explanatory variable? Explain.

3 Prove that the OLS coefficient for the slope parameter in the simple linear regression model is unbiased.

4 Prove that the OLS coefficient for the slope parameter in the simple linear regression model is BLUE.

5 State the assumptions of the simple linear regression model and explain why they are necessary.

Exercise 4.1

The following data refer to the quantity sold for a good Y (measured in kg), and the price of that good X (measured in pence per kg), for 10 different market locations:

Y:	198	181	170	179	163	145	167	203	251	147
X:	23	24.5	24	27.2	27	24.4	24.7	22.1	21	25

(a) Assuming a linear relationship among the two variables, obtain the OLS estimators of a and β.

(b) On a scatter diagram of the data, draw in your OLS sample regression line.

(c) Estimate the elasticity of demand for this good at the point of sample means (i.e. when $Y = \bar{Y}$ and $X = \bar{X}$).

Exercise 4.2

The table below shows the average growth rates of GDP and employment for 25 OECD countries for the period 1988–97.

Countries	Empl.	GDP	Countries	Empl.	GDP
Australia	1.68	3.04	Korea	2.57	7.73
Austria	0.65	2.55	Luxembourg	3.02	5.64
Belgium	0.34	2.16	Netherlands	1.88	2.86
Canada	1.17	2.03	New Zealand	0.91	2.01
Denmark	0.02	2.02	Norway	0.36	2.98
Finland	−1.06	1.78	Portugal	0.33	2.79
France	0.28	2.08	Spain	0.89	2.60
Germany	0.08	2.71	Sweden	−0.94	1.17
Greece	0.87	2.08	Switzerland	0.79	1.15
Iceland	−0.13	1.54	Turkey	2.02	4.18
Ireland	2.16	6.40	United Kingdom	0.66	1.97
Italy	−0.30	1.68	United States	1.53	2.46
Japan	1.06	2.81			

(a) Assuming a linear relationship obtain the OLS estimators.

(b) Provide an interpretation of the coefficients.

Exercise 4.3

In the Keynesian consumption function:

$$C_t = a + \delta Y_t^d$$

the estimated marginal propensity to consume is simply $\hat{\delta}$ while the average propensity to consume is $C/Y^d = \hat{a}/Y^d + \hat{\delta}$. Using data from 200 UK households on annual income and consumption (both of which were measured in UK£) we found the following regression equation:

$$C_t = 138.52 + 0.725 Y_t^d \quad R^2 = 0.862$$

(a) Provide an interpretation of the constant in this equation and comment about its sign and magnitude.

(b) Calculate the predicted consumption of a hypothetical household with annual income £40,000.

(c) With Y_t^d on the x-axis draw a graph of the estimated MPC and APC.

Exercise 4.4

Obtain annual data for the inflation rate and the unemployment rate of a country.

(a) Estimate the following regression which is known as the Phillips curve:

$$\pi_t = a_0 + a_1 UNEMP_t + u_t$$

where π_t is inflation and $UNEMP_t$ is unemployment. Present the results in the usual way.

(b) Estimate the alternative model:

$$\pi_t - \pi_{t-1} = a_0 + a_1 UNEMP_{t-1} + u_t$$

and calculate the NAIRU (i.e. when $\pi_t - \pi_{t-1} = 0$).

(c) Reestimate the above equations splitting your sample into different decades. What factors account for differences in the results? Which period has the 'best-fitting' equation? State the criteria you have used.

Exercise 4.5

The following equation has been estimated by OLS:

$$\hat{R}_t = 0.567 + 1.045 R_{mt} \quad n = 250$$

$$(0.33) \quad (0.066)$$

where R_t and R_{mt} denote the excess return of a stock and the excess return of the market index for the London Stock Exchange.

(a) Derive a 95% confidence interval for each coefficient.

(b) Are these coefficients statistically significant? Explain what is the meaning of your findings regarding the CAPM theory.

(c) Test the hypothesis H_0: $\beta = 1$ and H_a: $\beta < 1$ at the 1% level of significance. If you reject H_0 what does this indicate about this stock?

Exercise 4.6

Obtain time series data on real business fixed investment (I) and an appropriate rate of interest (r). Consider the following population regression function:

$$I_t = \alpha_0 + \alpha_1 r_t + e_t$$

(a) What are the expected signs of the coefficients in this equation?

(b) Explain the rationale for each of these signs.

(c) How can you use this equation to estimate the interest elasticity of investment?

(d) Estimate the population regression function.

(e) Which coefficients are statistically significant? Are the signs those expected?

(f) Construct a 99% confidence interval for the coefficient of r_t.

(g) Estimate the log-linear version of the population regression function:

$$\ln I_t = a_0 + a_1 \ln r_t + u_t$$

(h) Is the estimated interest rate elasticity of investment significant?

(i) Do you expect this elasticity to be elastic or inelastic and why?

(j) Perform a hypothesis test of whether investment is interest-elastic.

Exercise 4.7

The file salaries_01.wf1 contains data for senior officers from a large number of UK firms. The variable *salary* is the salary that each one of them gets, measured in thousand pounds. The variable *years_senior* measures the number of years for which they are senior officers, while the variable *years_comp* measures the number of years for which they have worked in the company at the time of the research.

(a) Find summary statistics for the three above-mentioned variables and discuss them.

(b) Estimate a simple regression that explains whether and how salary level is affected by the years for which they are senior officers. Estimate another regression that now explains whether and how salary level is affected by the years for which they have worked in the same company. Report your results and comment on them. Which relationship seems to be more robust and why?

5 Multiple Regression

So far, we have restricted ourselves to the single case of a two-variable relationship in a regression equation. However, in economics it is quite rare to have such relationships. Usually the dependent variable, Y, depends on a big set of explanatory variables or regressors, and so we have to extend our analysis to more than one regressor. The multiple regression model generally has the following form:

$$Y_t = \beta_1 X_{1t} + \beta_2 X_{2t} + \beta_3 X_{3t} + \cdots + \beta_k X_{kt} + u_t \qquad (5.1)$$

where X_{1t} is a vector equal to unity (to allow for the constant term) and can be omitted from (5.1), and X_{jt} ($j = 2, 3, \ldots, k$) is the set of explanatory variables or regressors. From this it follows that (5.1) contains k parameters to be estimated, which gives the degrees of freedom as well.

Derivation of the multiple regression coefficients

The three-variable model

The three-variable model relates Y to a constant and two explanatory variables X_2 and X_3. Thus, we have:

$$Y_t = \beta_1 + \beta_2 X_{2t} + \beta_3 X_{3t} + u_t \qquad (5.2)$$

As before we need to minimize the sum of the squared residuals (RSS):

$$RSS = \sum_{t=1}^{n} \hat{u}_t^2 \qquad (5.3)$$

where $\hat{u}_t$ is the difference between the actual Y_t and the fitted $\hat{Y}_t$, predicted by the regression equation. Therefore:

$$\hat{u}_t = Y_t - \hat{Y}_t = Y_t - \hat{\beta}_1 - \hat{\beta}_2 X_{2t} - \hat{\beta}_3 X_{3t} \qquad (5.4)$$

substituting (5.4) into (5.3) we get:

$$RSS = \sum_{t=1}^{n} \hat{u}_t^2 = \sum_{t=1}^{n} \left(Y_t - \hat{\beta}_1 - \hat{\beta}_2 X_{2t} - \hat{\beta}_3 X_{3t} \right)^2 \qquad (5.5)$$

The next step is to take the First Order Conditions (F.O.C.s) for a minimum:

$$\frac{\partial RSS}{\partial \hat{\beta}_1} = -2 \sum_{t=1}^{n} \left(Y_t - \hat{\beta}_1 - \hat{\beta}_2 X_{2t} - \hat{\beta}_3 X_{3t} \right) = 0 \qquad (5.6)$$

$$\frac{\partial RSS}{\partial \hat{\beta}_2} = -2 \sum_{t=1}^{n} X_{2t} \left(Y_t - \hat{\beta}_1 - \hat{\beta}_2 X_{2t} - \hat{\beta}_3 X_{3t} \right) = 0 \qquad (5.7)$$

$$\frac{\partial RSS}{\partial \hat{\beta}_3} = -2 \sum_{t=1}^{n} X_{3t} \left(Y_t - \hat{\beta}_1 - \hat{\beta}_2 X_{2t} - \hat{\beta}_3 X_{3t} \right) = 0 \qquad (5.8)$$

And again we end up with a system of three equations with three unknowns $\hat{\beta}_1$, $\hat{\beta}_2$ and $\hat{\beta}_3$, which can be easily solved to give estimates of the unknowns. Equation (5.6) can be transformed, for example, easily to give:

$$\sum_{t=1}^{n} Y_t = \sum_{t=1}^{n} \hat{\beta}_1 + \sum_{t=1}^{n} \hat{\beta}_2 X_{2t} + \sum_{t=1}^{n} \hat{\beta}_3 X_{3t} \qquad (5.9)$$

$$\sum_{t=1}^{n} Y_t = n\hat{\beta}_1 + \hat{\beta}_2 \sum_{t=1}^{n} X_{2t} + \hat{\beta}_3 \sum_{t=1}^{n} X_{3t} \qquad (5.10)$$

dividing throughout by n and defining $\bar{X}_i = \sum_{t=1}^{n} X_i / n$:

$$\bar{Y}_t = \hat{\beta}_1 + \hat{\beta}_2 \bar{X}_2 + \hat{\beta}_3 \bar{X}_3 \qquad (5.11)$$

and we obtain a solution for $\hat{\beta}_1$:

$$\hat{\beta}_1 = \bar{Y} - \hat{\beta}_2 \bar{X} - \hat{\beta}_3 \bar{X} \qquad (5.12)$$

Using equation (5.12) and the second and third of the F.O.C.s, and after manipulations, we obtain a solution for $\hat{\beta}_2$:

$$\hat{\beta}_2 = \frac{Cov(X_2, Y)Var(X_3) - Cov(X_3, Y)Cov(X_2, X_3)}{Var(X_2)Var(X_3) - [Cov(X_2, X_3)]^2} \qquad (5.13)$$

and $\hat{\beta}_3$ will be similar to (5.13) by rearranging X_{2t} and X_{3t}:

$$\hat{\beta}_3 = \frac{Cov(X_3, Y)Var(X_2) - Cov(X_2, Y)Cov(X_3, X_2)}{Var(X_3)Var(X_2) - [Cov(X_3, X_2)]^2} \qquad (5.14)$$

The *k*-variables case

With k explanatory variables the model is as presented initially in equation (5.1), so we have:

$$Y_t = \beta_1 X_{1t} + \beta_2 X_{2t} + \beta_3 X_{3t} + \cdots + \beta_k X_{kt} + u_t \qquad (5.15)$$

while again we obtain fitted values as:

$$\hat{Y}_t = \hat{\beta}_1 X_{1t} + \hat{\beta}_2 X_{2t} + \hat{\beta}_3 X_{3t} + \cdots + \hat{\beta}_k X_{kt} \qquad (5.16)$$

and

$$\hat{u}_t = Y_t - \hat{Y}_t = Y_t - \hat{\beta}_1 X_{1t} - \hat{\beta}_2 X_{2t} - \hat{\beta}_3 X_{3t} - \cdots - \hat{\beta}_k X_{kt} \tag{5.17}$$

Furthermore we again want to minimize RSS, so:

$$RSS = \sum_{t=1}^{n} \hat{u}_t^2 = \sum_{t=1}^{n} \left(Y_t - \hat{\beta}_1 X_{1t} - \hat{\beta}_2 X_{2t} - \hat{\beta}_3 X_{3t} - \cdots - \hat{\beta}_k X_{kt} \right)^2 \tag{5.18}$$

Taking the F.O.C.s for a minimum this time we obtain k equations for k unknown regression coefficients, as:

$$\sum_{t=1}^{n} Y_t = n\hat{\beta}_1 + \hat{\beta}_2 \sum_{t=1}^{n} X_{2t} + \cdots + \hat{\beta}_k \sum_{t=1}^{n} X_{kt} \tag{5.19}$$

$$\sum_{t=1}^{n} Y_t X_{2t} = \hat{\beta}_1 \sum_{t=1}^{n} X_{2t} + \hat{\beta}_2 \sum_{t=1}^{n} X_{2t}^2 + \cdots + \hat{\beta}_k \sum_{t=1}^{n} X_{kt} X_{2t} \tag{5.20}$$

$$\cdots \tag{5.21}$$

$$\sum_{t=1}^{n} Y_t X_{k-1,t} = \hat{\beta}_1 \sum_{t=1}^{n} X_{k-1t} + \hat{\beta}_2 \sum_{t=1}^{n} X_{2t} X_{k-1t} + \cdots + \hat{\beta}_k \sum_{t=1}^{n} X_{kt} X_{k-1,t} \tag{5.22}$$

$$\sum_{t=1}^{n} Y_t X_{k,t} = \hat{\beta}_1 \sum_{t=1}^{n} X_{kt} + \hat{\beta}_2 \sum_{t=1}^{n} X_{2t} X_{k,t} + \cdots + \hat{\beta}_k \sum_{t=1}^{n} X_{kt}^2 \tag{5.23}$$

The above k equations can be solved uniquely for the βs, and it is easy to show that:

$$\hat{\beta}_1 = \bar{Y} - \hat{\beta}_2 \bar{X}_2 - \cdots - \hat{\beta}_k \bar{X}_k \tag{5.24}$$

However, the expressions for $\hat{\beta}_2, \hat{\beta}_3, \ldots, \hat{\beta}_k$ are very complicated and the mathematics will not be presented here. The analysis should be done with the use of matrix algebra which is the context of the next section. Standard computer programmes do all the calculations and provide estimates immediately.

Derivation of the coefficients with matrix algebra

Equation (5.1) can be easily written in matrix notation as:

$$\mathbf{Y} = \mathbf{X}\boldsymbol{\beta} + \mathbf{u} \tag{5.25}$$

where

$$\mathbf{Y} = \begin{pmatrix} Y_1 \\ Y_2 \\ \vdots \\ Y_T \end{pmatrix}, \quad \mathbf{X} = \begin{pmatrix} 1 & X_{21} & X_{31} & \cdots & X_{k1} \\ 1 & X_{22} & X_{32} & \cdots & X_{k3} \\ \vdots & \vdots & \vdots & & \vdots \\ 1 & X_{2T} & X_{3T} & \cdots & X_{kT} \end{pmatrix},$$

$$\boldsymbol{\beta} = \begin{pmatrix} \beta_1 \\ \beta_2 \\ \vdots \\ \beta_k \end{pmatrix}, \quad \mathbf{u} = \begin{pmatrix} u_1 \\ u_2 \\ \vdots \\ u_n \end{pmatrix}$$

Thus, $\mathbf{Y}$ is a $T \times 1$ vector, $\mathbf{X}$ is an $T \times k$ matrix, $\boldsymbol{\beta}$ is a $k \times 1$ vector and $\mathbf{u}$ is an $T \times 1$ vector. Our aim is to minimize *RSS*. Note that in matrix notation $RSS = \hat{\mathbf{u}}'\hat{\mathbf{u}}$. Thus, we have:

$$\hat{\mathbf{u}}'\hat{\mathbf{u}} = (\mathbf{Y} - \mathbf{X}\hat{\boldsymbol{\beta}})'(\mathbf{Y} - \mathbf{X}\hat{\boldsymbol{\beta}}) \tag{5.26}$$

$$= (\mathbf{Y}' - \hat{\boldsymbol{\beta}}'\mathbf{X}')(\mathbf{Y} - \mathbf{X}\hat{\boldsymbol{\beta}}) \tag{5.27}$$

$$= \mathbf{Y}'\mathbf{Y} - \mathbf{Y}'\mathbf{X}\hat{\boldsymbol{\beta}} - \hat{\boldsymbol{\beta}}'\mathbf{X}'\mathbf{Y} + \hat{\boldsymbol{\beta}}'\mathbf{X}'\mathbf{X}\hat{\boldsymbol{\beta}} \tag{5.28}$$

$$= \mathbf{Y}'\mathbf{Y} - 2\mathbf{Y}\mathbf{X}'\hat{\boldsymbol{\beta}}' + \hat{\boldsymbol{\beta}}'\mathbf{X}'\mathbf{X}\hat{\boldsymbol{\beta}} \tag{5.29}$$

We now need to differentiate the above expression with respect to $\hat{\boldsymbol{\beta}}$ and set this result equal to zero:

$$\frac{\partial RSS}{\partial \hat{\boldsymbol{\beta}}} = -2\mathbf{X}'\mathbf{Y} + 2\mathbf{X}'\mathbf{X}\hat{\boldsymbol{\beta}} = 0 \tag{5.30}$$

which is a set of *k* equations and *k* unknowns. Re-writing (5.30) we have:

$$\mathbf{X}'\mathbf{X}\hat{\boldsymbol{\beta}} = \mathbf{X}'\mathbf{Y} \tag{5.31}$$

and multiplying both sides by the inverse matrix $(\mathbf{X}'\mathbf{X})^{-1}$ we finally get:

$$\hat{\boldsymbol{\beta}} = (\mathbf{X}'\mathbf{X})^{-1}\mathbf{X}'\mathbf{Y} \tag{5.32}$$

which is the solution for the OLS estimators in the case of multiple regression analysis.

The structure of the X'X and X'Y matrices

For a better understanding of the above solution, it is quite useful to examine the structure of the $(\mathbf{X}'\mathbf{X})$ and $(\mathbf{X}'\mathbf{Y})$ matrices that give us the solution for $\hat{\boldsymbol{\beta}}$. Recall that $\tilde{x}_t = (X_t - \bar{X})$ denote deviations of variables from their means, so, we have that:

$$(\bar{\mathbf{x}}'\bar{\mathbf{x}}) = \begin{pmatrix} \sum \tilde{x}_{2t}^2 & \sum \tilde{x}_{2t}\tilde{x}_{3t} & \sum \tilde{x}_{2t}\tilde{x}_{4t} & \cdots & \sum \tilde{x}_{2t}\tilde{x}_{kt} \\ \sum \tilde{x}_{3t}\tilde{x}_{2t} & \sum \tilde{x}_{3t}^2 & \sum \tilde{x}_{3t}\tilde{x}_{4t} & \cdots & \sum \tilde{x}_{3t}\tilde{x}_{kt} \\ \sum \tilde{x}_{4t}\tilde{x}_{2t} & \sum \tilde{x}_{4t}\tilde{x}_{3t} & \sum \tilde{x}_{4t}^2 & \cdots & \sum \tilde{x}_{4t}\tilde{x}_{kt} \\ \cdots & \cdots & \cdots & & \cdots \\ \sum \tilde{x}_{kt}\tilde{x}_{2t} & \sum \tilde{x}_{kt}\tilde{x}_{3t} & \sum \tilde{x}_{kt}\tilde{x}_{4t} & \cdots & \sum \tilde{x}_{kt}^2 \end{pmatrix} \tag{5.33}$$

and:

$$(\bar{x}'y) = \begin{pmatrix} \sum \tilde{x}_{2t}\tilde{y}_t \\ \sum \tilde{x}_{3t}\tilde{y}_t \\ \sum \tilde{x}_{4t}\tilde{y}_t \\ \dots \\ \sum \tilde{x}_{kt}\tilde{y}_t \end{pmatrix} \quad (5.34)$$

It is simple to see that the matrix $(x'x)$ in the case of a four explanatory variables regression model ($k = 4$) will reduce to its 3×3 equivalent; for $k = 3$ to its 2×2 and so on. When we have the simple linear regression model with two explanatory variables ($k = 2$, the constant and the slope coefficient), we will have $(x'x) = \sum \tilde{x}_{2t}^2$ and $(x'y) = \sum \tilde{x}_{2t}\tilde{y}_t$. Therefore the OLS formula will be:

$$\hat{\beta}_2 = (x'x)^{-1}(x'y)$$

$$= \left(\sum \tilde{x}_2^2 \right)^{-1} \left(\sum \tilde{x}_2\tilde{y} \right) \quad (5.35)$$

$$= \frac{\sum \tilde{x}_2\tilde{y}}{\sum \tilde{x}_2^2} = \hat{\beta}^* \quad (5.36)$$

which is the same with expression (4.24) that we derived analytically without matrix algebra in Chapter 4.

The assumptions of the multiple regression model

Very briefly we can state again the assumptions of the model which are not much different from the simple two-variable case:

1 The dependent variable is a linear function of the explanatory variables.

2 All explanatory variables are non-random.

3 All explanatory variables have values that are fixed in repeated samples, and as $n \to \infty$ the variance of their sample values $1/n \sum (X_{jt} - \bar{X}_j)^2 \to Q_j$ ($j = 2, 3, \dots, k$) where the Q_j are fixed constants.

4 $E(u_t) = 0$ for all t.

5 $Var(u_t) = E(u_t^2) = \sigma^2 = $ constant for all t.

6 $Cov(u_t, u_j) = E(u_t, u_j) = 0$ for all $j \neq t$.

7 Each u_t is normally distributed.

8 There are no exact linear relationships among the sample values of any two or more of the explanatory variables.

The variance–covariance matrix of the errors

Recall from the matrix representation of the model that we have an $n \times 1$ vector $\mathbf{u}$ of error terms. If we form an $n \times n$ matrix $\mathbf{u}'\mathbf{u}$ and take the expected value of this matrix we get:

$$E(\mathbf{uu}') = \begin{pmatrix} E(u_1^2) & E(u_1 u_2) & E(u_1 u_3) & \cdots & E(u_1 u_n) \\ E(u_2 u_1) & E(u_2^2) & E(u_2 u_3) & \cdots & E(u_2 u_n) \\ E(u_3 u_1) & E(u_3 u_2) & E(u_3^2) & \cdots & E(u_3 u_n) \\ \cdots & \cdots & \cdots & & \cdots \\ E(u_n u_1) & E(u_n u_2) & E(u_n u_3) & \cdots & E(u_n^2) \end{pmatrix} \qquad (5.37)$$

Now, since each error term, u_t, has a zero mean, the diagonal elements of this matrix will represent the variance of the disturbances, and the non-diagonal terms will be the covariances among the different disturbances. Hence, this matrix is called the variance–covariance matrix of the errors, and using assumptions 5 ($Var(u_t) = E(u_t^2) = \sigma^2$) and 6 ($Cov(u_t, u_j) = E(u_t, u_j) = 0$) will be like:

$$E(\mathbf{uu}') = \begin{pmatrix} \sigma^2 & 0 & 0 & \cdots & 0 \\ 0 & \sigma^2 & 0 & 0 & 0 \\ 0 & 0 & \sigma^2 & \cdots & 0 \\ \cdots & \cdots & \cdots & & \cdots \\ 0 & 0 & 0 & \cdots & \sigma^2 \end{pmatrix} = \sigma^2 \mathbf{I_n} \qquad (5.38)$$

where $\mathbf{I_n}$ is an $n \times n$ identity matrix.

Properties of the multiple regression model OLS estimators

As in the simple two-variable regression model, based on the assumptions of the CLRM, we can prove that the OLS estimators are Best Linear Unbiased Estimators (BLUE). We concentrate on the slope coefficients ($\beta_2, \beta_3, \beta_4, \ldots, \beta_k$) rather than the constant (β_1) because these are the parameters of greatest interest.

Linearity

For OLS estimators to be linear, assumptions 2 and 3 are needed. Since the values of the explanatory variables are fixed constants, it can easily be shown that the OLS estimators are linear functions of the Y values. Recall the solution for $\hat{\beta}$:

$$\hat{\beta} = (\mathbf{X}'\mathbf{X})^{-1}\mathbf{X}'\mathbf{Y} \qquad (5.39)$$

where since $\mathbf{X}$ is a matrix of fixed constants then $\mathbf{W} = (\mathbf{X}'\mathbf{X})^{-1}\mathbf{X}'$ is also a $n \times k$ matrix of fixed constants. Since $\mathbf{W}$ is a matrix of fixed constants, $\hat{\beta}$ is a linear function of Y, so by definition it is a linear estimator.

Unbiasedness

We know that:

$$\hat{\beta} = (X'X)^{-1}X'Y \tag{5.40}$$

and we also have that:

$$Y = X\beta + \mathbf{u} \tag{5.41}$$

Substituting this into equation (5.40) above we obtain:

$$\begin{aligned}
\hat{\beta} &= (X'X)^{-1}X'(X\beta + \mathbf{u}) \\
&= (X'X)^{-1}X'X\beta + (X'X)^{-1}X'\mathbf{u} \\
&= \beta + (X'X)^{-1}X'\mathbf{u} \quad [\text{since } (X'X)^{-1}X'X = I]
\end{aligned} \tag{5.42}$$

Taking expectations of (5.42) yields:

$$E(\hat{\beta}) = E(\beta) + (X'X)^{-1}X'E(\mathbf{u}) \tag{5.43}$$

$$= \beta \quad [\text{since } E(\beta) = \beta \text{ and } E(\mathbf{u}) = 0] \tag{5.44}$$

Therefore $\hat{\beta}$ is an unbiased estimator of β.

Consistency

Unbiasedness simply means that whatever the sample size we expect that on average the estimated $\hat{\beta}$ will equal the true β, however the above proof of this rests on the assumption that X is fixed and this is a strong and often unrealistic assumption. If we relax this assumption however we can still establish that $\hat{\beta}$ is consistent, this simply means that as the estimation sample size goes to infinity $\hat{\beta}$ will converge in probability on its true value. Thus $p\lim(\hat{\beta}) = \beta$. The proof of consistency will not be presented here as it is tedious and beyond the scope of this book. However the key assumption to this proof is that the X variable while not being fixed must be uncorrelated with the error term.

BLUEness

Before we proceed with the proof that the OLS estimators for the multiple regression model are BLUEs, it is good to first find expressions for the variances and convariances of the OLS estimators.

Consider the symmetric $k \times k$ matrix of the form:

$$E(\hat{\beta} - \beta)(\hat{\beta} - \beta)'$$

$$= \begin{pmatrix} E(\hat{\beta}_1 - \beta_1)^2 & E(\hat{\beta}_1 - \beta_1)(\hat{\beta}_2 - \beta_2) & \cdots & E(\hat{\beta}_1 - \beta_1)(\hat{\beta}_k - \beta_k) \\ E(\hat{\beta}_2 - \beta_2)(\hat{\beta}_1 - \beta_1) & E(\hat{\beta}_2 - \beta_2)^2 & \cdots & E(\hat{\beta}_2 - \beta_2)(\hat{\beta}_k - \beta_k) \\ \cdots & \cdots & & \cdots \\ E(\hat{\beta}_k - \beta_k)(\hat{\beta}_1 - \beta_1) & E(\hat{\beta}_k - \beta_k)(\hat{\beta}_2 - \beta_2) & \cdots & E(\hat{\beta}_k - \beta_k)^2 \end{pmatrix} \quad (5.45)$$

Because of unbiasedness of $\hat{\beta}$ we have that $E(\hat{\beta}) = \beta$. So:

$$E(\hat{\beta} - \beta)(\hat{\beta} - \beta)' = \begin{pmatrix} Var(\hat{\beta}_1)^2 & Cov(\hat{\beta}_1, \hat{\beta}_2) & \cdots & Cov(\hat{\beta}_1, \hat{\beta}_k) \\ Cov(\hat{\beta}_2, \hat{\beta}_1) & Var(\hat{\beta}_2) & \cdots & Cov(\hat{\beta}_2, \hat{\beta}_k) \\ \cdots & \cdots & & \cdots \\ Cov(\hat{\beta}_k, \hat{\beta}_1) & Cov(\hat{\beta}_k, \hat{\beta}_2) & \cdots & Var(\hat{\beta}_k) \end{pmatrix} \quad (5.46)$$

which is called the variance–covariance matrix of $\hat{\beta}$. We need to find an expression for this. Consider that from (5.32) we have:

$$\hat{\beta} = (X'X)^{-1}X'Y \quad (5.47)$$

substituting $Y = X\beta + u$, we get:

$$\hat{\beta} = (X'X)^{-1}X'(X\beta + u)$$
$$= (X'X)^{-1}X'X\beta + (X'X)^{-1}X'u$$
$$= \beta + (X'X)^{-1}X'u \quad (5.48)$$

or

$$\hat{\beta} - \beta = (X'X)^{-1}X'u \quad (5.49)$$

By the definition of variance–covariance we have that:

$$Var(\hat{\beta}) = \mathbf{E}[(\hat{\beta} - \beta)(\hat{\beta} - \beta)']$$
$$= E\{[(X'X)^{-1}X'u][(X'X)^{-1}X'u]'\}$$
$$= E\{(X'X)^{-1}X'uu'X(X'X)^{-1}\}^*$$
$$= (X'X)^{-1}X'E(uu')X(X'X)^{-1\dagger}$$
$$= (X'X)^{-1}X'\sigma^2 IX(X'X)^{-1}$$
$$= \sigma^2(X'X)^{-1} \quad (5.50)$$

---

* This is because $(BA)' = A'B'$.
† This is because, by assumption 2, the Xs are non-random.

Now for the BLUEness of the $\hat{\beta}$, let us assume that there is $\hat{\beta}^*$ which is any other linear estimator of β, which can be expressed as:

$$\hat{\beta}^* = [(X'X)^{-1}X' + Z](Y) \tag{5.51}$$

where Z is a matrix of constants. Substituting for $Y = X\beta + u$, we get:

$$\hat{\beta}^* = [(X'X)^{-1}X' + Z](X\beta + u)$$
$$= \beta + ZX\beta + (X'X)^{-1}X'u + Zu \tag{5.52}$$

and for $\hat{\beta}^*$ to be unbiased we require that:

$$ZX = 0 \tag{5.53}$$

Using (5.53), we can rewrite (5.52) as:

$$\hat{\beta}^* - \beta = (X'X)^{-1}X'u + Zu \tag{5.54}$$

Going back to the definition of the variance–covariance:

$$E[(\hat{\beta} - \beta)(\hat{\beta} - \beta)'] = \{(X'X)^{-1}X'u + Zu\}\{(X'X)^{-1}X'u + Zu\}' \tag{5.55}$$
$$= \sigma^2(X'X)^{-1} + \sigma^2 ZZ' \tag{5.56}$$

which says that the variance–covariance matrix of the alternative estimator $\hat{\beta}^*$ is equal to the variance–covariance matrix of the OLS estimator $\hat{\beta}$ plus σ^2 times ZZ', and therefore greater than the variance–covariance of $\hat{\beta}$. Hence $\hat{\beta}$ is BLUE.

R^2 and adjusted R^2

The regular coefficient of determination, R^2 is again a measure of the closeness of fit in the multiple regression model as in the simple two-variable model. However, R^2 cannot be used as a means of comparing two different equations containing different numbers of explanatory variables. This is because when additional explanatory variables are included, the proportion of variation in Y explained by the Xs, R^2, will always be increased. Therefore, we will always obtain a higher R^2 regardless of the importance or not of the additional regressor. For this reason we need a different measure that will take into account the number of explanatory variables included in each model. This measure is called the adjusted R^2 (and is denoted by $\bar{R}^2$) because it is adjusted for the number of regressors (or adjusted for the degrees of freedom).

Recall that $R^2 = ESS/TSS = 1 - RSS/TSS$, so that the adjusted R^2 is just:

$$\bar{R}^2 = 1 - \frac{RSS/(n-k)}{TSS/(n-1)} = 1 - \frac{RSS(n-1)}{TSS(n-k)} \tag{5.57}$$

Thus, an increase in the number of Xs included in the regression function, increases k and this will reduce RSS (which if we do not adjust will increase R^2). Dividing now, RSS by $n - k$, the increase in k tends to offset the fall in RSS and this is why $\bar{R}^2$ is a 'fairer' measure in comparing different equations. The criterion of selecting a model is to include an extra variable only if it increases $\bar{R}^2$. Note that because $(n - 1)/(n - k)$ is never less than 1, $\bar{R}^2$ will never be higher than R^2. However, while R^2 has values between 0 and 1 only, and can never be negative, $\bar{R}^2$ can have a negative value in some cases. A negative $\bar{R}^2$ indicates that the model does not adequately describe the data-generating process.

General criteria for model selection

We said before that increasing the number of explanatory variables in a multiple regression model will decrease the RSS, and R^2 will therefore increase. However, the cost of that is a loss in terms of degrees of freedom. A different method – apart from $\bar{R}^2$ – of allowing for the number of Xs to change when assessing goodness of fit is to use different criteria for model comparison, such as the Akaike Information Criterion (AIC) developed by Akaike (1974) and given by:

$$AIC = \left(\frac{RSS}{n} \right) e^{2k/n} \tag{5.58}$$

the Finite Prediction Error (FPE) developed again by Akaike (1970):

$$FPE = \left(\frac{RSS}{n} \right) \frac{n + k}{n - k} \tag{5.59}$$

the Schwarz Bayesian Criterion (SBC) developed by Schwarz (1978):

$$SBC = \left(\frac{RSS}{n} \right) e^{k/n} \tag{5.60}$$

or the Hannan and Quin (1979) Criterion (HQC):

$$HQC = \left(\frac{RSS}{n} \right) (\ln n)^{2k/n} \tag{5.61}$$

among many others. (Other criteria include those by Shibata, 1981, Rice, 1984, and a Generalized Gross Validation, GCV, method developed by Craven and Wahba, 1979.) Note that some programmes including Eviews reports the logarithm of the AIC (5.58) and (5.61).

Ideally, we select the model that minimizes all those statistics, as compared to an alternative one. In general, however, it is quite common to have contradictory results coming from different criteria. For example, the SBC penalizes model complexity more heavily than any other measure, and might therefore give a different conclusion. A model that outperforms another in several of these criteria might generally be preferred. However, in general the AIC is one of the most commonly used in time series analysis. Both AIC and SBC are provided by EViews in the standard regression results output, while Microfit provides only SBC.

Multiple regression estimation in Microfit and EViews

Multiple regression in Microfit

Step 1 Open Microfit.

Step 2 Click on **File/New** in order to create a new file or **File/Open** to open an existing file.

Step 3 If it is a new file follow the steps 3–6 described in the simple regression case.

Step 4 Go to the single editor (by clicking the '**single**' button) and type into the single editor:

```
Y C X2 X3 X4 ... XK
```

where X2, ..., XK are the names of the variables to add into the explanatory variables list. Of course Y is the dependent variable and C is the constant created in Microfit. After determining the equation, click <**START**>. The regression result outputs in a new window which provides estimates for β_1 (the coefficient of the constant term C), and $\beta_2, ..., \beta_k$ (the coefficients of Xs) and some additional statistics that will be discussed in later chapters of this book.

Multiple regression in EViews

Step 1 Open EViews.

Step 2 Click **File/New/Workfile** in order to create a new file or **File/Open** to open an existing file.

Step 3 If a new file, follow steps 3–5 described in the simple regression case.

Step 4 Once the data have been entered in EViews, then the regression line can be estimated (to obtain β_1 (the coefficient of the constant term C) and $\beta_2, ..., \beta_k$ (the coefficients of Xs)) through two different ways. One is by typing in the EViews command line:

```
ls y c x2 x3 ... xk (press 'enter')
```

where y is to be substituted with the name of the dependent variable as it appears in the EViews file, and, similarly, x2, ... xk will be the names of the explanatory variables.

The second way is to click on **Quick/Estimate equation** and then write the equation (i.e. y c x2 ... xk) in the new window. Note that the option for OLS (LS – Least Squares (NLS and ARMA)) is automatically chosen by EViews and the sample is automatically chosen to be the maximum possible.

Below we show an example of a regression result output from EViews (the case of Microfit is similar).

Reading the EViews multiple regression results output

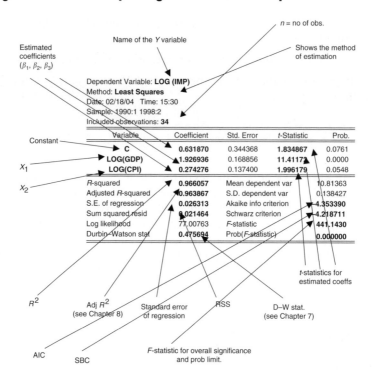

Hypothesis testing

Testing individual coefficients

As in simple regression analysis, in multiple regression a single test of hypothesis on a regression coefficient is carried out as a normal t test. We can again have one-tail tests (if there is some prior belief/theory for the sign of the coefficient) or two-tail tests, carried out in the usual way ($(\hat{\beta} - \beta)/s_{\hat{\beta}}$ follows t_{n-k}), and we can immediately make a decision about the significance or not of the $\hat{\beta}$s using the criterion $|t\text{-}stat| > |t\text{-}crit|$ having the t-statistic provided immediately by either Microfit or EViews (note that especially for large samples we can use the 'rule of thumb' $|t\text{-}stat| > 2$).

Testing linear restrictions

Sometimes in economics we need to test whether there are particular relationships between the estimated coefficients. Take for example a production function of the standard Cobb–Douglas type:

$$Q = AL^a K^\beta \tag{5.62}$$

where Q is output, L denotes labour units, K is capita and A is an exogenous technology parameter. If we take logarithms and add an error term we have:

$$\ln Q = c + a \ln L + \beta \ln K + u \tag{5.63}$$

where $c = \ln A$, a constant and a and β coefficients are simply the elasticities of labour and capital respectively. In this example it might be desirable to test whether $a + \beta = 1$, which implies constant returns to scale (i.e. if we double inputs the output will be doubled as well).

Therefore, we have estimates $\hat{a}$ and $\hat{\beta}$ that we want them to obey a linear restriction. If we impose this restriction to the Cobb–Douglas production function we will have:

$$\ln Q = c + (1 - \beta) \ln L + \beta \ln K + u$$
$$\ln Q - \ln L = c + \beta(\ln K - \ln L) + u \tag{5.64}$$
$$Q^* = c + \beta K^* + u$$

where $Q^* = \ln Q - \ln L$ and $K^* = \ln K - \ln L$. Thus, we can estimate (5.64) to get $\hat{\beta}$ and then obtain $\hat{a} = 1 - \hat{\beta}$. The estimates obtained this way are known as restricted least squares estimates and equation (5.64) is referred to as the restricted equation while obviously (5.63) is the unrestricted equation.

Sometimes, it is even possible to impose more than just one restriction at a time. For example suppose we have the unrestricted equation:

$$Y_t = \beta_1 + \beta_2 X_{2t} + \beta_3 X_{3t} + \beta_4 X_{4t} + \beta_5 X_{5t} + e_t \tag{5.65}$$

and we need to impose the following restrictions:

$$\beta_3 + \beta_4 = 1 \quad \text{and} \quad \beta_2 = \beta_5$$

Substituting the restrictions to the unrestricted equation we have:

$$
\begin{aligned}
Y_t &= \beta_1 + \beta_5 X_{2t} + (1 - \beta_4) X_{3t} + \beta_4 X_{4t} + \beta_5 X_{5t} + e_t \\
Y_t &= \beta_1 + \beta_5 X_{2t} + X_{3t} - \beta_4 X_{3t} + \beta_4 X_{4t} + \beta_5 X_{5t} + e_t \\
Y_t - X_{3t} &= \beta_1 + \beta_5(X_{2t} + X_{5t}) + \beta_4(X_{4t} - X_{3t}) + e_t \\
Y_t^* &= \beta_1 + \beta_5(X_{1t}^*) + \beta_4(X_{2t}^*) + e_t
\end{aligned} \tag{5.66}
$$

where $Y_t^* = Y_t - X_{3t}$, $X_{1t}^* = X_{2t} + X_{5t}$ and $X_{2t}^* = X_{4t} - X_{3t}$.

Therefore, in this case we can estimate the restricted equation (5.66) and get $\hat{\beta}_1, \hat{\beta}_5$ and $\hat{\beta}_4$ and then calculate $\hat{\beta}_3$ and $\hat{\beta}_2$ from the restrictions imposed above.

So far, things are simple. However, the problem is that usually we are not able to just accept the restrictions as given without testing for their validity. There are three basic ways of constructing a test; the Likelihood Ratio procedure, the Wald procedure and the Lagrange Multiplier (or LM) procedure. The exact derivation of these procedures is beyond the scope of this book but we will attempt to give an intuitive account of these three. The idea of most tests is to asses the difference between an unrestricted model and a restricted version of the same model. If the restriction does not affect the fit of the model very much then we would want to accept the restriction as being valid. If on the other hand the model fits much worse then we would reject the model. Of course this means we have to have some firm measure of how much worse the fit can get and still be insignificant. In general this measure comes from a measure of how good a model is which is called the likelihood function, at an intuitive level this shows us how likely the model is to be correct. The exact way we use this to form a test is based on the fact that if we take twice the difference between the likelihood function of the unrestricted and restricted model this value will have a χ^2 distribution with the number of degrees of freedom equal to the number of restrictions imposed on the model. This gives rise to the basic Likelihood Ratio test which simply involves estimating the model both with the restriction and without it and constructing a test based on these two estimates. The χ^2 distribution is an asymptotic one, which means that it is really only the correct one for an infinitely large sample, however in some cases we can calculate a version of the Likelihood Ratio test which is correct in small samples and then it may have an F distribution for example. Any test which involves estimating the model BOTH with and without the restriction is a form of Likelihood Ratio test. There are however two approximations to the Likelihood Ratio test which only require us to estimate one model. If we only estimate the unrestricted model and then use a formulae to approximate the full likelihood ratio test this is called a Wald test. The 't' test associated with OLS coefficients for example are a particular form of Wald test. We estimate the unrestricted model and then we can test the hypothesis that the true coefficient is zero, but we do not actually estimate the complete model subject to this restriction. The final method (the LM procedure) only estimates a restricted model and then tests for a relaxation of these restrictions by again applying a formulae but not actually re-estimating the model. This final procedure has proved very useful in recent years as it allows us to test a model for many possible forms of misspecification without having to estimate many different models. All three forms may have asymptotic χ^2 distributions or they may have distributions which correct for the small sample such as an F or 't' distribution.

The F-form of the likelihood ratio test

The most common method is to estimate both the unrestricted equation and the restricted equation and to take the *RSS* of both models denoted as RSS_U and RSS_R respectively (the subscript U stands for unrestricted, R for restricted).

It should be obvious that $RSS_R > RSS_U$. However, if the restrictions are valid, then this difference should be minimal. It is beyond the scope of this text to prove that there is a statistic given by the following expression:

$$\frac{(RSS_R - RSS_U)/(k_U - k_R)}{SSR_U/(n - k_U)} \tag{5.67}$$

that follows an F-type distribution with $(k_U - k_R, n - k_U)$ degrees of freedom, and that is the appropriate statistic to help us determine whether the restrictions are valid or not. So, summarizing, the F-test (which is a special form of the likelihood ratio procedure) for testing linear restrictions can be conducted as follows:

Step 1   The null hypothesis is that the restrictions are valid.

Step 2   Estimate both the restricted and unrestricted models and obtain RSS_R and RSS_U.

Step 3   Calculate F-statistical by expression (5.67) above where k_U and k_R are the number of regressors in each model.

Step 4   Find F-critical for $(k_U - k_R, n - k_U)$ degrees of freedom from the F-tables.

Step 5   If F-statistical $>$ F-critical reject the null hypothesis.

Testing the joint significance of the Xs

This is simply the F-type test for the overall goodness of fit, but it can be understood more easily as a special case of a LR-type test. Consider the following two (unrestricted and super-restricted) models:

$$Y_t = \beta_1 + \beta_2 X_{2t} + \beta_3 X_{3t} + \beta_4 X_{4t} + \beta_5 X_{5t} + e_t \tag{5.68}$$

$$Y_t = \beta_1 + \epsilon_t \tag{5.69}$$

The second model is called super-restricted because we imposed a number of restrictions equal to the number of explanatory variables excluding the constant (i.e. $k - 1$ restrictions).

The null hypothesis in this case is $\beta_2 = \beta_3 = \beta_4 = \beta_5 = 0$, or to put it in words 'none of the coefficients in the model apart from the intercept is statistically significant'. If we fail to reject this hypothesis, this means that we have a very poor model and we must reformulate it.

In this special case we can show that we do not need to estimate both models in order to calculate the F statistic. First, we can get RSS_U by estimating the full model. Then we can get RSS_{SR} by minimizing $\sum \epsilon_t^2 = \sum (Y_t - \beta_1)^2$ with respect to β_1. However, we know that $\beta_1 = \bar{Y}_t$ and therefore $RSS_{SR} = \sum (Y_t - \bar{Y}_t)^2$ which is the same as TSS_U.

Therefore, the F statistic is now:

$$\frac{(TSS_U - RSS_U)/(k-1)}{RSS_U/(n-k)} = \frac{ESS_U/(k-1)}{RSS_U/(n-k)} = \frac{R^2/(k-1)}{(1 - R^2)/(n-k)} \tag{5.70}$$

which can easily be calculated by the R^2 of the unrestricted model.

F-test for overall significance in Microfit and EViews

Both Microfit and EViews provide the F statistic for the overall significance of the Xs as a part of the summary statistics for a regression model. What we need is just to make sure that F-statistical $> F$-critical $(k - 1, n - k)$ in order to reject the null hypothesis. If we cannot reject the null, then we have to reformulate our model.

Adding or deleting explanatory variables

Frequently we might face problems of deciding whether to add or delete one or more explanatory variables from an estimated model. When only one variable is involved, a safe criterion is to check its t-ratio, but when a set of variables is involved then we might need to assess their combined influence in the model. Consider the following model:

$$Y_t = \beta_1 + \beta_2 X_{2t} + \cdots + \beta_k X_{kt} + e_t \tag{5.71}$$

$$Y_t = \beta_1\beta_1 + \beta_2 X_{2t} + \cdots + \beta_k X_{kt} + \beta_{k+1}X_{k+1t} + \cdots + \beta_m X_{mt} + \epsilon_t \tag{5.72}$$

In this case we again have a restricted and unrestricted model with $n - k$ more variables which we are interested in to assess their combined effect. The null hypothesis here is $\beta_{k+1} = \beta_{k+2} = \cdots = \beta_m = 0$ which says that the joint significance of these omitted variables is zero. Alternatively, we can have model (5.72) as the initial model and might want to test that variables $X_{k+1} = X_{k+2} = \cdots = X_{mt}$ are redundant to this model. This can be tested by either a regular F-test or by a likelihood ratio (LR) test. The F-type test as we explained before is based on the difference of the RSS of the restricted and unrestricted regressions.

The *LR* statistic is computed as:

$$LR = -2(l_R - l_U)$$

where l_R and l_U are the maximized values of the log-likelihood function of the unrestricted and restricted equations respectively. The *LR* statistic follows a χ^2 distribution with degrees of freedom equal to the number of restrictions (i.e. the number of omitted or added variables).

Omitted and redundant variables test in EViews

Suppose that we have estimated the unrestricted model:

$$ls \; Y \; C \; X1 \; X2 \; X3$$

and want to test whether $X4$ and $X5$ are omitted from the model. From the regression window select **View/Coefficient tests/Omitted Variables-Likelihood Ratio**. A new window with a dialog box opens, where we specify the names of the variables we want to test (i.e. write $X4 \; X5$) and click <**OK**>. EViews reports the two statistics concerning the hypothesis testing (i.e. the F and *LR* statistics with their probability limits). If F-stat $> F$-critical or if LR-stat $> \chi^2$-critical then we reject the null that the two series do not belong to the equation. Similar steps have to be carried out for a variable deletion test, where we choose **View/Coefficient tests/Redundant Variables-Likelihood Ratio** and specify the names of the variables that were included in the initial model and whose significance we want to test.

Omitted and redundant variables test in Microfit

Similarly, in Microfit, after estimating a regression and closing the results window a new window pops out with 10 different choices numbered consecutively from 0 to 9. Choice 2 is about hypothesis testing, which is exactly what we discussed in the second part of this chapter. Choosing 2: **Move to hypothesis testing menu** and clicking <OK> a new window again opens with 10 different choices. From those choices, choice 5 concerns the variable deletion test and choice 6 the variable addition test. In each case we need to specify the names/labels of variables to add or delete. Microfit reports results of *LR*, *F* and Lagrange multiplier (LM) test statistics. In each case, if the statistical value is bigger than the critical value we reject the null hypothesis about the validity of the restrictions.

How to perform the Wald test in EViews and Microfit

As noted above a particular set of restrictions or hypothesis may be tests in 3 different ways, the Likelihood Ratio procedure gives rise to the *F*-test above which involves estimating the model twice and this may be cumbersome to do. The Wald procedure however allows us to test any restriction on a model once we have estimated it without estimating any further models. It is therefore often quite convenient to use a series of Wald tests after we have estimated our model.

The Wald test in EViews

We can test various linear restrictions in EViews and Microfit using the Wald test. For EViews we first estimate the unrestricted equation, then from the regression output window we choose **View/Coefficient Tests/Wald-Coefficient Restrictions** .... We then need to enter the restrictions in the new dialog box (in the case of more than one restriction we have to separate them by commas). The restrictions should be entered as equations involving the estimated coefficients and constants. The coefficients should be referred to as **C(1)** for the constant, **C(2)** for the coefficient of the first explanatory variable and so on. After entering the restrictions click <**OK**>. EViews reports the F statistic of the Wald test and a Chi-square statistic. If the statistical value is bigger than the critical then we reject the null hypothesis.

The Wald test in Microfit

Similarly, in Microfit, after estimating a regression and closing the results window a new window pops out with 10 different choices numbered consecutively from 0 to 9. Choosing 2: **Move to hypothesis testing menu** and clicking <OK> a new window opens, again with 10 different choices. From those choices, choice 7 concerns the Wald test for linear restrictions. We need to specify the restrictions as equations, where this time the coefficients should be referred to as **A1** for the constant, **A2** for the coefficient of the first explanatory variable, and so on. Microfit reports the Wald statistics as a Chi-square distributed statistic. If the statistical value is bigger than the critical value, then we reject the null hypothesis.

The *t* test (A special case of the Wald procedure)

A third method is to test the restriction without actually estimating the restricted equation, but simply using a *t* test on the actual restriction. Think of the Cobb–Douglas production function:

$$\ln Q = c + a \ln L + \beta \ln K + u \tag{5.73}$$

and the restriction $a + \beta = 1$. What we can do is to obtain by OLS $\hat{a}$ and $\hat{\beta}$ and test whether $\hat{a} + \hat{\beta} = 1$. We know that $\hat{a}$ and $\hat{\beta}$ are normally distributed:

$$\hat{a} \sim N\left(a, \sigma_{\hat{a}}^2\right) \quad \text{and} \quad \hat{\beta} \sim N\left(\beta, \sigma_{\hat{\beta}}^2\right)$$

where σ^2 refers to the respective variances. Furthermore, we know that any linear combination of two normal variables will also be normal. So, we have:

$$\hat{a} + \hat{\beta} \sim N(a + \beta, Var(\hat{a} + \hat{\beta}))$$

where

$$Var(\hat{a} + \hat{\beta}) = Var(\hat{a}) + Var(\hat{\beta}) + 2Cov(\hat{a}, \hat{\beta})$$

Converting the above into standard normal distribution

$$\frac{\hat{a} + \hat{\beta} - (a + \beta)}{Var(\hat{a}) + Var(\hat{\beta}) + 2Cov(\hat{a}, \hat{\beta})} \sim N(0, 1)$$

or

$$\frac{\hat{a} + \hat{\beta} - 1}{Var(\hat{a}) + Var(\hat{\beta}) + 2Cov(\hat{a}, \hat{\beta})} \sim N(0, 1)$$

because under the null hypothesis $a + \beta = 1$. Also, we do not know the variances and covariances exactly, but these can be estimated. If we substitute
an estimated value for the denominator in the above equation (let's say u) which can be taken from the residuals variance/covariance matrix, then its statistical distribution changes to the student's *t* distribution with $n - k$ degrees of freedom. Thus, we can apply a *t* test calculating the following:

$$t_{stat} = \frac{\hat{a} + \hat{\beta} - 1}{Var(\hat{a}) + Var(\hat{\beta}) + 2Cov(\hat{a}, \hat{\beta})} \tag{5.74}$$

and as always if $|t_{stat}| > |t\text{-}crit|$ then we reject the null. Because this test requires several auxiliary calculations, one of the previously presented methods is generally recommended.

The LM test

The final way to test a set of restrictions on a model rests on only estimating the restricted model, this is the Lagrange Multiplier (LM) test, it is particularly useful, as we will see later, as it allows us to test for more general models which might often be much more difficult to estimate. Let's assume that we have again the unrestricted model:

$$Y_t = \beta_1 + \beta_2 X_{2t} + \beta_3 X_{3t} + \beta_4 X_{4t} + \beta_5 X_{5t} + u_t \qquad (5.75)$$

and after imposing

$$\beta_3 + \beta_4 = 1 \quad \text{and} \quad \beta_2 = \beta_5$$

we have:

$$Y_t^* = \beta_1 + \beta_5(X_{1t}^*) + \beta_4(X_{2t}^*) + u_t \qquad (5.76)$$

as was shown above.

The LM test involves the following steps:

Step 1 The null hypothesis is that the restrictions are valid.

Step 2 Estimate the restricted model in (5.76) and save the residuals $\hat{u}_R$.

Step 3 Regress $\hat{u}_R$ on the four explanatory variables of the unrestricted model in (5.75):

$$\hat{u}_R = \hat{\delta}_1 + \hat{\delta}_2 X_{2t} + \hat{\delta}_3 X_{3t} + \hat{\delta}_4 X_{4t} + \hat{\delta}_5 X_{5t} + \varepsilon_t$$

Step 4 Calculate the χ^2-statistic $= nR^2$ which is distributed with h degrees of freedom, where h is the number of restrictions (in this case 2).

Step 5 Find χ^2-critical for h degrees of freedom.

Step 6 If χ^2-statistical $> \chi^2$-critical reject the null hypothesis.

The LM test in Microfit and EViews

There is no routine to use to calculate the LM procedure to test simple linear restrictions in Microfit and EViews as it is almost always more convenient to use a Wald or Likelihood Ratio test, so to calculate the LM test for the above restrictions we would have to manually follow the steps above. However when we come to test more complex departures from our model such as serial correlation or ARCH effects the LM procedure becomes very useful and both programmes have a number of routines which make use of this procedure as we will see later.

Computer example: Wald, omitted and redundant variables tests

The file wage.xls contains data regarding wage rates (*wage*), years of education (*educ*), years of working experience (*exper*) and years spent with the same company (*tenure*) for 900 UK financial analysts. We want to estimate an equation which includes as determinants of the logarithm of the wage rate the variables, *educ*, *exper* and *tenure*.

First we need to construct/generate the dependent variable. In order to do that we have to type the following command in the EViews command line:

```
genr lnwage = log(wage)
```

Then, in order to estimate the multiple regression model, we have to select from the EViews toolbar **Quick/Estimate Equation** and type into the **Equation Specification** box the required model as:

```
lnwage c educ exper tenure
```

The results from this equation are shown in Table 5.1.

We can also save the equation (named **unrestrict01**) and save the regression results (by clicking on the '**freeze**' button) at an output table (named **Table01** in the file). As may be seen from the equation, all three variables have positive coefficients. These are all above the 'rule of thumb' critical *t*-value of 2, hence all are significant. So, it may be said that wages will increase as education, experience and tenure increases. Despite the significance of these three variables, the adjusted R^2 is quite low (0.145) as there are probably other variables that affect wages.

A Wald test of coefficient restrictions

Let's now assume that we want to test whether the effect of the *tenure* variable is the same with that of experience (*exper* variable). Referring to the estimation equation, we can see that the coefficient of *exper* is $C(3)$ and the coefficient of *tenure* is $C(4)$.

In order to test the hypothesis that the two effects are equal we need to conduct a Wald test in EViews. This can be done by clicking on **View/Coefficient Tests/Wald-Coefficient Restrictions**, in the regression results output and then by typing the restriction as:

$$C(3) = C(4) \tag{5.77}$$

Table 5.1   Results from the wage equation

Dependent Variable: LNWAGE
Method: Least Squares
Date: 02/02/04 Time: 11:10
Sample: 1 900
Included observations: 900

Variable	Coefficient	Std. Error	t-Statistic	Prob.
C	5.528329	0.112795	49.01237	0.0000
EDUC	0.073117	0.006636	11.01871	0.0000
EXPER	0.015358	0.003425	4.483631	0.0000
TENURE	0.012964	0.002631	4.927939	0.0000
R-squared	0.148647	Mean dependent var		6.786164
Adjusted R-squared	0.145797	S.D. dependent var		0.420312
S.E. of regression	0.388465	Akaike info criterion		0.951208
Sum squared resid	135.2110	Schwarz criterion		0.972552
Log likelihood	−424.0434	F-statistic		52.14758
Durbin–Watson stat	1.750376	Prob(F-statistic)		0.000000

in the **Wald Test** window (and then click <**OK**>). EViews then generates the *F* statistic (we saved this output as **Table02WALD**). The results of the Wald test are reported in Table 5.2.

The *F* statistic is equal to 0.248, which is lower than the *F* critical value of 3.84. As *F*-statistical is less than *F*-critical, we cannot reject the null hypothesis. The null hypothesis is that the two coefficients are the same, and hence we accept this conclusion.

A redundant variable test

Suppose we want to conduct a redundant variable test for the explanatory variable *tenure*, i.e. years with current employer, to determine whether this variable is significant in determining the logarithm of the wage rate. In order to do that we need to click on **View/Coefficient Tests/Redundant variables-Likelihood ratio**, and type the name of the variable (*tenure*) that we want to check. The results of this test are shown in Table 5.3.

We can now save this output as **Table03REDUNDANT**. The results give us an *F*-statistic of 24.285, for comparison to the value of *F*-critical of 3.84. As *F*-statistical is

Table 5.2   Wald test results

Equation: Untitled			
Null Hypothesis: C(3) = C(4)			
F-statistic	0.248656	Probability	0.618145
Chi-square	0.248656	Probability	0.618023

Table 5.3   Redundant variable test results

Redundant Variables: TENURE			
F-statistic	24.28459	Probability	0.000001
Log likelihood ratio	24.06829	Probability	0.000001

Test Equation:
Dependent Variable: LNWAGE
Method: Least Squares
Date: 01/30/04 Time: 16:47
Sample: 1 900
Included observations: 900

Variable	Coefficient	Std. Error	t-Statistic	Prob.
C	5.537798	0.114233	48.47827	0.0000
EDUC	0.075865	0.006697	11.32741	0.0000
EXPER	0.019470	0.003365	5.786278	0.0000
R-squared	0.125573	Mean dependent var		6.786164
Adjusted R-squared	0.123623	S.D. dependent var		0.420312
S.E. of regression	0.393475	Akaike info criterion		0.975728
Sum squared resid	138.8757	Schwarz criterion		0.991736
Log likelihood	−436.0776	F-statistic		64.40718
Durbin–Watson stat	1.770020	Prob(F-statistic)		0.000000

greater than *F*-critical, we can reject the null hypothesis. Therefore, we can conclude that the coefficient of the variable *tenure* is not zero, and therefore *tenure* is not redundant i.e. it has a significant effect in determining the wage rate.

An omitted variable test

Suppose now, that we want to conduct an omitted variable test for the explanatory variable *educ*. To do that, we first need to estimate a model that does not include

Table 5.4   Wage equation test results

Dependent Variable: LNWAGE
Method: Least Squares
Date: 02/02/04 Time: 11:57
Sample: 1 900
Included observations: 900

Variable	Coefficient	Std. Error	t-Statistic	Prob.
C	6.697589	0.040722	164.4699	0.0000
EXPER	−0.002011	0.003239	−0.621069	0.5347
TENURE	0.015400	0.002792	5.516228	0.0000
R-squared	0.033285	Mean dependent var		6.786164
Adjusted R-squared	0.031130	S.D. dependent var		0.420312
S.E. of regression	0.413718	Akaike info criterion		1.076062
Sum squared resid	153.5327	Schwarz criterion		1.092070
Log likelihood	−481.2280	F-statistic		15.44241
Durbin–Watson stat	1.662338	Prob(F-statistic)		0.000000

Table 5.5   Omitted variable test results

Omitted Variables: EDUC

F-Statistic	121.4120	Probability	0.000000
Log likelihood ratio	114.3693	Probability	0.000000

Test Equation:
Dependent Variable: LNWAGE
Method: Least Squares
Date: 02/02/04 Time: 12:02
Sample: 1 900
Included observations: 900

Variable	Coefficient	Std. Error	t-Statistic	Prob.
C	5.528329	0.112795	49.01237	0.0000
EXPER	0.015358	0.003425	4.483631	0.0000
TENURE	0.012964	0.002631	4.927939	0.0000
EDUC	0.073117	0.006636	11.01871	0.0000
R-squared	0.148647	Mean dependent var		6.786164
Adjusted R-squared	0.145797	S.D. dependent var		0.420312
S.E. of regression	0.388465	Akaike info criterion		0.951208
Sum squared resid	135.2110	Schwarz criterion		0.972552
Log likelihood	−424.0434	F-statistic		52.14758
Durbin–Watson stat	1.750376	Prob(F-statistic)		0.000000

educ as an explanatory variable and then check whether the omission of *educ* was of importance in the model or not. So we estimate the following equation by typing on the EViews command line:

```
ls lnwage c exper tenure
```

and the results of this regression model are shown in the Table 5.4.

In order to conduct the omitted variable test we now need to click on **View/Coefficient Tests/Omitted variables-Likelihood ratio**, and type the name of the variable (*educ*) that we want to check. The results of this test are shown in Table 5.5.

We see from these results that the *F* statistic is equal to 121.41 which is much bigger than the critical value (see also the very small value of the probability limit), suggesting that the variable *educ* was really an omitted variable that plays a very important role in the determination of the log of wage rate.

Questions and exercises

Questions

1 Derive the OLS solutions for $\hat{\beta}$ for the k explanatory variables case using matrix algebra.

2 Prove that the OLS estimates for the k explanatory variables case are BLUE.

3 Show how one can test for constant returns to scale for the following Cobb–Douglas type production function:

$$Q = AL^a K^\beta$$

where Q is output, L denotes labour units, K is capita and A is an exogenous technology parameter.

4 Describe the steps involved for performing the Wald test for linear restrictions.

5 Write down a regression equation and show how you can test whether one of the explanatory variables in redundant.

Exercise 5.1

The file health.xls contains data for the following variables: *birth_weight* = the weight of infants after birth, when low can put an infant in risk of illnesses; *cig* = number of cigarettes that the mother was smoking during pregnancy; and *fam_inc* = the income of the family, the higher the family income the better the access to parental care from the family in general. Therefore, we would expect that both variables should affect *birth_weight*.

(a) Run a regression that includes both variables and explain the signs of the coefficients.

(b) Estimate a regression that includes only *fam_inc*, and comment on your results.

(c) Estimate a regression that includes only *cig* and comment on your results.

(d) Present all three regressions summarized in a table and comment on your results, especially by comparing the changes in the estimated effects and the R^2 of the three different models. What does the F statistic suggest about the joint significance of the explanatory variables in the multiple regression case?

(e) Test the hypothesis that the effect of *cig* is two times bigger than the respective effect of *fam_inc* using the Wald test.

Exercise 5.2

Use the data from the file wage.wf1 and estimate an equation which includes as determinants of the logarithm of the wage rate the variables, *educ, exper* and *tenure*.

(a) Comment on your results.

(b) Conduct a test of whether another year of general workforce experience (captured by *exper*) has the same effect on log(wage) as another year of education (captured by *educ*). State clearly your null and alternative hypotheses and your restricted and unrestricted models. Use the Wald test to check for that hypothesis.

(c) Conduct a redundant variable test for the explanatory variable *exper*. Comment on your results.

(d) Estimate a model with *exper* and *educ* only and then conduct an omitted variable test for *tenure* in the model. Comment on your results.

Exercise 5.3

Use the data in the file money_uk.wf1 to estimate the parameters α, β and γ, in the equation below:

$$\ln(M/P)_t = a + \beta \ln Y_t + \gamma \ln R_t + u_t$$

(a) Briefly outline the theory behind the aggregate demand for money. Relate your discussion to the specification of the equation given above. In particular explain, first the meaning of the dependent variable and then the interpretation of β and γ.

(b) Perform appropriate tests of significance on the estimated parameters in order to investigate each of the following propositions: (i) that the demand for money increases with the level of real income, (ii) the demand for money is income-elastic, and (iii) the demand for money is inversely related to the rate of interest.

Exercise 5.4

The file living.xls contains data for a variety of economic and social measures for a sample of 20 different countries, where:

Y = GNP per capita, 1984 $US;
X2 = average % annual inflation rate (1973–84);

X3 = % of labour force in agriculture;
X4 = life expectancy at birth, 1984 (years);
X5 = number enrolled in secondary education as % of age group.

(a) Insert the data in EViews or Microfit.

(b) Estimate the regression coefficients in each of the following equations:

$$Y_t = \beta_1 + \beta_2 X_{2t} + u_t$$

$$Y_t = \beta_1 + \beta_2 X_{2t} + \beta_3 X_{3t} + u_t$$

$$Y_t = \beta_1 + \beta_2 X_{2t} + \beta_3 X_{3t} + \beta_4 X_{4t} + u_t$$

$$Y_t = \beta_1 + \beta_2 X_{2t} + \beta_3 X_{3t} + \beta_4 X_{4t} + \beta_5 X_{5t} + u_t$$

(c) How robust are the estimated coefficients? By this we mean, to what extent do the estimated values of each β_i change as further explanatory variables are added to the right-hand side of the equation?

(d) Assuming Y to be an index of economic development, carry out tests of significance on all slope coefficients in the final regression equation model. State clearly the null and alternative hypotheses for each case and give reasons for setting them like that.

Exercise 5.5

The file Cobb_Douglas_us.wf1 contains data for output (Y), labour (L) and stock of capital (K) for the United States. Estimate a Cobb–Douglas type regression equation and check for constant returns to scale using the Wald test.

Part

III Violating the Assumptions of the CLRM

6 Multicollinearity

Assumption number 8 of the CLRM requires that there are no exact linear relationships among the sample values of the explanatory variables. This requirement can also be stated as the absence of perfect multicollinearity. In this chapter we will show how the existence of perfect multicollinearity leads to the fact that the method of OLS cannot provide estimates for the population parameters, while we will also examine the more common and realistic case of imperfect multicollinearity and its effects on OLS estimators. Finally, we will examine possible ways of detecting problematic multicollinearity and ways of resolving these problems.

Perfect multicollinearity

To understand multicollinearity consider the following model:

$$Y = \beta_1 + \beta_2 X_2 + \beta_3 X_3 + u \qquad (6.1)$$

where hypothetical sample values for X_2 and X_3 are given below:

$$
\begin{array}{llllll}
X_2': & 1 & 2 & 3 & 4 & 5 & 6 \\
X_3': & 2 & 4 & 6 & 8 & 10 & 12
\end{array}
$$

From this we can easily observe that $X_3 = 2X_2$. Therefore, while equation (6.1) seems to contain two explanatory variables X_2 and X_3 which are distinct, in fact the information provided by X_3 is not distinct from that of X_2. This is because, as we have seen, X_3 is an exact linear function of X_2. When this situation occurs, X_2 and X_3 are said to be linearly dependent, which implies that X_2 and X_3 are perfectly collinear. More formally, two variables X_2 and X_3 are linearly dependent if one variable can be expressed as a linear function of the other variable. When this occurs then the equation:

$$\delta_1 X_2 + \delta_2 X_3 = 0 \qquad (6.2)$$

can be satisfied for non-zero values of both δ_1 and δ_2. In our example we have: $X_3 = 2X_2$, therefore $(-2)X_2 + (1)X_3 = 0$, so $\delta_1 = -2$ and $\delta_2 = 1$. Obviously if the only solution in (6.2) is $\delta_1 = \delta_2 = 0$ (usually called the trivial solution) the X_2 and X_3 are linearly independent. The absence of perfect multicollinearity requires that 6.2 does not hold exactly.

In the case of more than two explanatory variables (lets take five), the case for linear dependence is that one variable can be expressed as an exact linear function of one or more or even all of the other variables. So this time the expression

$$\delta_1 X_1 + \delta_2 X_2 + \delta_3 X_3 + \delta_4 X_4 + \delta_5 X_5 = 0 \qquad (6.3)$$

can be satisfied with at least two non-zero coefficients.

An application to better understand this situation can be given by the dummy variable trap. Take for example X_1 to be the intercept (so as $X_1 = 1$) and X_2, X_3, X_4 and X_5 to be seasonal dummies for quarterly time series data (i.e. X_2 takes the value of 1 for the first quarter, zero otherwise; X_3 takes the value of 1 for the second quarter, zero otherwise and so on). Therefore, in this case we have that $X_2 + X_3 + X_4 + X_5 = 1$;

and because $X_1 = 1$ then $X_1 = X_2 + X_3 + X_4 + X_5$. So, the solution is $\delta_1 = 1$, $\delta_2 = -1$, $\delta_3 = -1$, $\delta_4 = -1$, and $\delta_5 = -1$, and this set of variables is linearly dependent.

Consequences of perfect multicollinearity

It is fairly easy to show that under conditions of perfect multicollinearity, the OLS estimators are not unique. Consider, for example, the model:

$$Y = \beta_1 + \beta_2 X_2 + \beta_3 X_3 + u_t \qquad (6.4)$$

where we have that $X_3 = \delta_1 + \delta_2 X_2$; and δ_1 and δ_2 are known constants. Substituting this into (6.4) gives:

$$
\begin{aligned}
Y &= \beta_1 + \beta_2 X_2 + \beta_3(\delta_1 + \delta_2 X_2) + u \\
&= (\beta_1 + \beta_3 \delta_1) + (\beta_2 + \beta_3 \delta_2) X_2 + u \\
&= \vartheta_1 + \vartheta_2 X_2 + \varepsilon \qquad (6.5)
\end{aligned}
$$

where of course $\vartheta_1 = (\beta_1 + \beta_3 \delta_1)$ and $\vartheta_2 = (\beta_2 + \beta_3 \delta_2)$.

So what we can estimate from our sample data is the coefficients ϑ_1 and ϑ_2. However, no matter how good the estimates of ϑ_1 and ϑ_2 will be, we will never be able to obtain unique estimates of β_1, β_2 and β_3. In order to obtain those we have to solve the following equations:

$$\hat{\vartheta}_1 = \hat{\beta}_1 + \hat{\beta}_3 \delta_1$$

$$\hat{\vartheta}_2 = \hat{\beta}_2 + \hat{\beta}_3 \delta_2$$

However, this is a system of two equations and three unknowns $\hat{\beta}_1$, $\hat{\beta}_2$ and $\hat{\beta}_3$. Unfortunately, as in any system that has more variables than equations, this will have an infinite number of solutions. For example, select an arbitrary value for $\hat{\beta}_3$, lets say k. Then for $\hat{\beta}_3 = k$ we can find $\hat{\beta}_1$ and $\hat{\beta}_2$ as

$$\hat{\beta}_1 = \hat{\vartheta}_1 - \delta_1 k$$

$$\hat{\beta}_2 = \hat{\vartheta}_2 - \delta_2 k$$

Since there are infinite values that can be used for k we can have an infinite number of solutions for $\hat{\beta}_1$, $\hat{\beta}_2$ and $\hat{\beta}_3$. So under perfect multicollinearity no estimation method can provide us with unique estimates for the population parameters. In terms of matrix notation, and for a more general case if one of the columns of matrix X is an exact linear function of one or more of the other column then the matrix X'X will be singular, which implies that its determinant will be zero ($|X'X| = 0$). Since the OLS estimators are given by:

$$\hat{\beta} = (X'X)^{-1} X'Y$$

we need the inverse matrix of $\mathbf{X'X}$ which is calculated by the expression

$$(\mathbf{X'X})^{-1} = \frac{1}{|\mathbf{X'X}|}[\mathbf{adj}(\mathbf{X'X})]$$

and because $|\mathbf{X'X}| = 0$ then it cannot be inverted.

Another way of showing this is by trying to evaluate the expression for the least squares estimator, for from (5.13):

$$\hat{\beta}_2 = \frac{Cov(X_2, Y)Var(X_3) - Cov(X_3, Y)Cov(X_2, X_3)}{Var(X_2)Var(X_3) - [Cov(X_2, X_3)]^2}$$

substituting $X_3 = \delta_1 + \delta_2 X_2$

$$\hat{\beta}_2 = \frac{Cov(X_2, Y)Var(\delta_1 + \delta_2 X_2) - Cov(\delta_1 + \delta_2 X_2, Y)Cov(X_2, \delta_1 + \delta_2 X_2)}{Var(X_2)Var(\delta_1 + \delta_2 X_2) - [Cov(X_2, \delta_1 + \delta_2 X_2)]^2}$$

dropping the additive δ_1 term:

$$\hat{\beta}_2 = \frac{Cov(X_2, Y)Var(\delta_2 X_2) - Cov(\delta_2 X_2, Y)Cov(X_2, \delta_2 X_2)}{Var(X_2)Var(\delta_2 X_2) - [Cov(X_2, \delta_2 X_2)]^2}$$

taking out of the *Var* and *Cov* the term δ_2

$$\hat{\beta}_2 = \frac{Cov(X_2, Y)\delta_2^2 Var(X_2) - \delta_2 Cov(X_2, Y)\delta_2 Cov(X_2, X_2)}{Var(X_2)\delta_2^2 Var(X_2) - [\delta_2 Cov(X_2, X_2)]^2}$$

and using the fact that $Cov(X_2, X_2) = Var(X_2)$

$$\hat{\beta}_2 = \frac{\delta_2^2 Cov(X_2, Y)Var(X_2) - \delta_2^2 Cov(X_2, Y)Var(X_2)}{\delta_2^2 Var(X_2)^2 - \delta_2^2 Var(X_2)^2} = \frac{0}{0}$$

which means that the regression coefficient is indeterminate. So, we have seen that the consequences of perfect multicollinearity are extremely serious. However, perfect multicollinearity seldom arises with actual data. The occurrence of perfect multicollinearity often results from correctable mistakes, such as the dummy variable trap presented before, or including variables as $\ln X$ and $\ln X^2$ in the same equation. So, the more relevant question and the real problem is how to deal with the more realistic case of imperfect multicollinearity, which will be examined in the next section.

Imperfect multicollinearity

Imperfect multicollinearity exists when the explanatory variables in an equation are correlated, but this correlation is less than perfect. Imperfect multicollinearity can be expressed as follows: when the relationship among the two explanatory variables in (6.4) for example is $X_3 = X_2 + v$ where v is a random variable that can be viewed as the 'error' in the exact linear relationship among the two variables; if v has non-zero values then we can obtain OLS estimates. As a practical note, in reality every multiple regression equation will contain some degree of correlation among its explanatory variables. For example, time series data frequently contain a common upward time trend causing variables of this kind to be highly correlated. So, the problem is to identify whether the degree of multicollinearity observed in one relationship is sufficiently high as to create problems. Before proceeding to that point we need to examine the effects of imperfect multicollinearity in the OLS estimators.

Consequences of imperfect multicollinearity

In general, when imperfect multicollinearity exists among two or more explanatory variables, not only are we able to obtain OLS estimates but these estimators will also be the best (BLUE). However, the BLUEness of these estimators should be examined in a more detailed way. Implicit in the BLUE property is the efficiency of the OLS coefficients. As we will show later, although OLS estimators are those with the smallest possible variance of all linear unbiased estimators, imperfect multicollinearity affects the attainable values of these variances and therefore estimation precision. Using the matrix solution again, imperfect multicollinearity implies that one column of the X matrix is now an approximate linear function of one or more of the others. Therefore, now matrix $|\mathbf{X}'\mathbf{X}|$ will be close to singularity which implies again that its determinant will be close to zero. As we have said before, when forming the inverse $(\mathbf{X}'\mathbf{X})^{-1}$ we have to divide by the reciprocal of $|\mathbf{X}'\mathbf{X}|$, which means that the elements (and particularly the diagonal elements) of $(\mathbf{X}'\mathbf{X})^{-1}$ will be large. Hence, because the variance of $\hat{\beta}$ is given by:

$$var(\hat{\beta}) = \sigma^2 (\mathbf{X}'\mathbf{X})^{-1} \tag{6.6}$$

we see that the variances and consequently the standard errors of the OLS estimators will tend to be large when there is a relatively high degree of multicollinearity. In other words, while OLS provides linear unbiased estimators with the minimum variance property, these variances are often substantially larger than those obtained in the absence of multicollinearity.

To explain this in more detail consider the expression that gives the variance of the partial slope of variable X_j which is given by (for the case of two explanatory variables):

$$var(\hat{\beta}_2) = \frac{\sigma^2}{\sum (X_2 - \bar{X}_2)^2 (1 - r^2)} \tag{6.7}$$

$$var(\hat{\beta}_3) = \frac{\sigma^2}{\sum (X_3 - \bar{X}_3)^2 (1 - r^2)} \tag{6.8}$$

where r^2 is the square of the sample correlation coefficient between X_2 and X_3. It can be seen that (keeping other things equal) a rise in r (which means higher degree of multicollinearity) will lead to an increase in the variances and therefore to an increase in the standard errors of the OLS estimators.

Extending this to more than two explanatory variables, the variance of β_j will be given by:

$$var(\hat{\beta}_j) = \frac{\sigma^2}{\sum (X_j - \bar{X}_j)^2 (1 - R_j^2)} \tag{6.9}$$

where R_j^2 is the coefficient of determination from the auxiliary regression of X_j on all other explanatory variables in the original equation. The expression can be re-written as:

$$var(\hat{\beta}_j) = \frac{\sigma^2}{\sum(X_j - \bar{X}_j)^2} \frac{1}{(1 - R_j^2)} \qquad (6.10)$$

The second term in this expression is called the variance inflation factor (*VIF*) for X_j:

$$VIF_j = \frac{1}{(1 - R_j^2)}$$

This name is given because it is easy to show that cases of high degrees of intercorrelation among the Xs will result in a high value of R_j^2 which inflates the variance of $\hat{\beta}_j$. If $R_j^2 = 0$ then $VIF = 1$ (which is its lowest value). As R_j^2 rises, VIF_j rises at an increasing rate, approaching infinity in the case of perfect multicollinearity ($R_j^2 = 1$). The table below presents various values for R_j^2 and the corresponding VIF_j.

R_j^2	VIF_j
0	1
0.5	2
0.8	5
0.9	10
0.95	20
0.975	40
0.99	100
0.995	200
0.999	1000

VIF values that exceed 10 are generally viewed as evidence of the existence of problematic multicollinearity as we will discuss below. From the table we can see that this occurs when $R^2 > 0.9$. Concluding, imperfect multicollinearity can substantially diminish the precision with which the OLS estimators are obtained. This has obviously more negative effects on the estimated coefficients. One important consequence is that large standard errors will lead to confidence intervals for the $\hat{\beta}_j$ parameters that are calculated by:

$$\hat{\beta}_j \pm t_{a,n-k} \, s_{\hat{\beta}_j}$$

to be very wide, increasing uncertainty about the true parameter values.

Another consequence has to do with the statistical inference regarding the OLS estimates. Recall that the *t*-ratio is given by $t = \hat{\beta}_j / s_{\hat{\beta}_j}$. The inflated variance associated with multicollinearity, raises the denominator of this statistic causing its value to fall. Therefore, we might have *t*-statistics which suggest the insignificance of the coefficients while this is only due to multicollinearity. Note here that the existence of multicollinearity does not necessarily mean small *t*-stats. This can be because the variance is also affected by the variance of X_j (presented by writing $\sum(X_j - \bar{X}_j)^2$) and the residual's variance (σ^2). Multicollinearity affects not only the variances of the OLS estimators, but the covariances as well. By this fact, the possibility of sign reversal arises. Also, when severe multicollinearity is present, the addition or deletion of just a few sample observations can substantially change the estimated coefficient causing 'unstable' OLS estimators. Concluding, the consequences of imperfect multicollinearity can be summarized as follows:

1 Estimates of the OLS coefficients may be imprecise in the sense that large standard errors lead to wider confidence intervals.

2 Affected coefficients may fail to attain statistical significance due to low t-statistics, which may lead us to wrongly drop an influential variable from our regression model.

3 The signs of the estimated coefficients can be the opposite of those expected.

4 The addition or deletion of a few observations may result in substantial changes in the estimated coefficients.

Detecting problematic multicollinearity

Simple correlation coefficient

Multicollinearity is caused by intercorrelations among the explanatory variables. Therefore, the most logical way in order to detect multicollinearity problems would appear to be through the correlation coefficient for those two variables. When an equation contains only two explanatory variables, the simple correlation coefficient is an adequate measure for detecting multicollinearity. If the value of the correlation coefficient is large, then problems from multicollinearity might emerge. The problem here is to define what value can be considered as large, and most researchers appear to consider the value of 0.9 as the threshold beyond which problems are likely to occur. This can be understood from the *VIF* for a value of $r = 0.9$ as well.

R^2 from auxiliary regressions

In the case where we have more than two variables, the use of the simple correlation coefficient to detect bivariate correlations and therefore problematic multicollinearity is highly unreliable. This is because an exact linear dependency can occur among three or more variables simultaneously. Therefore, in these cases we use auxiliary regressions. Candidates for dependent variables in auxiliary regressions are those displaying the symptoms of problematic multicollinearity discussed in the previous section. If a near-linear dependency exists, the auxiliary regression will display a small equation standard error, a large R^2 and a statistically significant t-value for the overall significance of the regressors.

Computer examples

Example 1: induced multicollinearity

The file multicol.wf1 contains data for three different variables, namely Y, $X2$ and $X3$, where $X2$ and $X3$ are constructed to be highly collinear. The correlation matrix of the three variables can be obtained from EViews by opening all three variables together in a group, by clicking on **Quick/Group Statistics/Correlations**. EViews requires us to define the series list that we want to include in the group and we type:

```
Y X2 X3
```

and then click <**OK**>. The results will be as shown in Table 6.1.

The results are of course symmetrical, while the diagonal elements are equal to 1 because they are correlation coefficients of the same series. We can see that Y is highly positively correlated with both $X2$ and $X3$, and also that $X2$ and $X3$ are nearly the same variables (the correlation coefficient is equal to 0.999995, i.e. very close to 1). From this we obviously suspect that there will be a very high possibility of the negative effects of multicollinearity.

Estimating a regression with both explanatory variables by typing in the EViews command line:

```
ls y c x2 x3
```

Table 6.1   Correlation matrix

	Y	$X2$	$X3$
Y	1	0.8573686	0.857437
$X2$	0.8573686	1	0.999995
$X3$	0.8574376	0.999995	1

Table 6.2   Regression results (full model)

Dependent Variable: Y
Method: Least Squares
Date: 02/17/04 Time: 01:53
Sample: 1 25
Included observations: 25

Variable	Coefficient	Std. Error	t-Statistic	Prob.
C	35.86766	19.38717	1.850073	0.0778
X2	−6.326498	33.75096	−0.187446	0.8530
X3	1.789761	8.438325	0.212099	0.8340

R-squared	0.735622	Mean dependent var	169.3680
Adjusted R-squared	0.711587	S.D. dependent var	79.05857
S.E. of regression	42.45768	Akaike info criterion	10.44706
Sum squared resid	39658.40	Schwarz criterion	10.59332
Log likelihood	−127.5882	F-statistic	30.60702
Durbin–Watson stat	2.875574	Prob(F-statistic)	0.000000

we get the results shown in Table 6.2. Here we see that the effect of $X2$ on Y is negative and the effect of $X3$ is positive, while both variables appear to be insignificant. This latter result is very strange considering the fact that both variables are highly correlated with Y as we have seen above. However, estimating the model including only $X2$, either by typing on the EViews command line:

```
ls y c x2
```

or by clicking on the **Estimate** button of the **Equation Results** window and respecifying the equation by excluding/deleting the $X3$ variable, we get the results shown in Table 6.3. This time we see that $X2$ is positive and statistically significant (with a t statistic of 7.98).

Reestimating the model, this time including only $X3$, we get the results shown in Table 6.4. This time we see that $X3$ is highly significant and positive.

Table 6.3   Regression results (omitting $X3$)

Dependent Variable: Y
Method: Least Squares
Date: 02/17/04 Time: 01:56
Sample: 1 25
Included observations: 25

Variable	Coefficient	Std. Error	t-Statistic	Prob.
C	36.71861	18.56953	1.977358	0.0601
X2	0.832012	0.104149	7.988678	0.0000
R-squared	0.735081	Mean dependent var		169.3680
Adjusted R-squared	0.723563	S.D. dependent var		79.05857
S.E. of regression	41.56686	Akaike info criterion		10.36910
Sum squared resid	39739.49	Schwarz criterion		10.46661
Log likelihood	−127.6138	F-statistic		63.81897
Durbin–Watson stat	2.921548	Prob(F-statistic)		0.000000

Table 6.4   Regression results (omitting $X2$)

Dependent Variable: Y
Method: Least Squares
Date: 02/17/04 Time: 01:58
Sample: 1 25
Included observations: 25

Variable	Coefficient	Std. Error	t-Statistic	Prob.
C	36.60968	18.57637	1.970766	0.0609
X3	0.208034	0.026033	7.991106	0.0000
R-squared	0.735199	Mean dependent var		169.3680
Adjusted R-squared	0.723686	S.D. dependent var		79.05857
S.E. of regression	41.55758	Akaike info criterion		10.36866
Sum squared resid	39721.74	Schwarz criterion		10.46617
Log likelihood	−127.6082	F-statistic		63.85778
Durbin–Watson stat	2.916396	Prob(F-statistic)		0.000000

Table 6.5   Auxiliary regression results (regressing $X2$ to $X3$)

Dependent Variable: $X2$
Method: Least Squares
Date: 02/17/04 Time: 02:03
Sample: 1 25
Included observations: 25

Variable	Coefficient	Std. Error	t-Statistic	Prob.
C	−0.117288	0.117251	−1.000310	0.3276
X3	0.250016	0.000164	**1521.542**	0.0000

R-squared	**0.999990**	Mean dependent var	159.4320
Adjusted R-squared	0.999990	S.D. dependent var	81.46795
S.E. of regression	0.262305	Akaike info criterion	0.237999
Sum squared resid	1.582488	Schwarz criterion	0.335509
Log likelihood	− 0.974992	F-statistic	2315090.
Durbin–Watson stat	2.082420	Prob(F-statistic)	0.000000

Finally, running an auxiliary regression of $X2$ on a constant and $X3$ yields the results shown in Table 6.5. Here note that the value of the t statistic is extremely high (1521.542!) while R^2 is nearly 1.

The conclusions from this analysis can be summarized as follows:

1 The correlation among the explanatory variables was very high, which might suggest that multicollinearity is present and that it might be serious. However, we mentioned in the theory that looking just at the correlation coefficients of the explanatory variables is not enough to detect multicollinearity.

2 Standard errors or t-ratios of the estimated coefficients changed from estimation to estimation, suggesting that the problem of multicollinearity in this case was really serious.

3 The stability of the estimated coefficients was also very problematic, with negative and positive coefficients being estimated for the same variable in two alternative specifications.

4 R^2 from auxiliary regressions are substantially high suggesting that multicollinearity really exists and that it unavoidably affects our estimations.

Example 2: with the use of real economic data

Let us now examine the problem of multicollinearity once more, this time using real economic data. The file imports_uk.wf1 contains quarterly data for four different variables, namely, imports (*IMP*), gross domestic product (*GDP*), the consumer price index (*CPI*) and the producer price index (*PPI*) for the UK economy.

The correlation matrix of the three variables can be obtained from EViews by opening all the variables together in a group, by clicking on **Quick/Group Statistics/Correlations**. EViews asks us to define the series list that we want to include in the group and we type in:

```
imp gdp cpi ppi
```

Table 6.6   Correlation matrix

	IMP	GDP	CPI	PPI
IMP	1.000000	0.979713	0.916331	0.883530
GDP	0.979713	1.000000	0.910961	0.899851
CPI	0.916331	0.910961	1.000000	**0.981983**
PPI	0.883530	0.899851	0.981983	1.000000

Table 6.7   First model regression results (including only *CPI*)

Dependent Variable: LOG(IMP)
Method: Least Squares
Date: 02/17/04 Time: 02:16
Sample: 1990:1 1998:2
Included observations: 34

Variable	Coefficient	Std. Error	t-Statistic	Prob.
C	0.631870	0.344368	1.834867	0.0761
LOG(GDP)	1.926936	0.168856	11.41172	0.0000
LOG(CPI)	0.274276	0.137400	1.996179	0.0548

R-squared	0.966057	Mean dependent var	10.81363
Adjusted R-squared	0.963867	S.D. dependent var	0.138427
S.E. of regression	0.026313	Akaike info criterion	−4.353390
Sum squared resid	0.021464	Schwarz criterion	−4.218711
Log likelihood	77.00763	F-statistic	441.1430
Durbin–Watson stat	0.475694	Prob(F-statistic)	0.000000

and then click <OK>. The results are shown in Table 6.6. From the correlation matrix we can see that in general the correlations among the variables are very high, but the highest correlation is among *CPI* and *PPI* (0.98) as expected.

Estimating a regression with the logarithm of imports as the dependent variable and the logarithms of *GDP* and *CPI* only as explanatory variables by typing in the EViews command line:

```
ls log(imp) c log(gdp) log(cpi)
```

we get the results shown in Table 6.7. The R^2 of this regression is very high, and both variables appear to be positive with the log(*GDP*) being very highly significant as well. The log(*CPI*) is also significant but only marginally.

Estimating, however, the model including the logarithm of *PPI* as well, either by typing on the EViews command line:

```
ls log(imp) c log(gdp) log(cpi) log(ppi)
```

or by clicking on the **Estimate** button of the **Equation Results** window and respecifying the equation by adding the log(*PPI*) variable in the list of variables, we get the results shown in Table 6.8. Now log(*CPI*) is highly significant, while log(*PPI*) (which is highly correlated with log(*CPI*) and therefore should have more or less the same effect on log(*IMP*)) is negative and highly significant. This of course is due to the inclusion of both price indices in the same equation specification, due to the problem of multicollinearity.

Table 6.8   Second model regression results (including both *CPI* and *PPI*)

Dependent Variable: LOG(IMP)
Method: Least Squares
Date: 02/17/04 Time: 02:19
Sample: 1990:1 1998:2
Included observations: 34

Variable	Coefficient	Std. Error	t-Statistic	Prob.
C	0.213906	0.358425	0.596795	0.5551
LOG(GDP)	1.969713	0.156800	12.56198	0.0000
LOG(CPI)	1.025473	0.323427	3.170645	0.0035
LOG(PPI)	−0.770644	0.305218	−2.524894	0.0171

R-squared	0.972006	Mean dependent var		10.81363
Adjusted R-squared	0.969206	S.D. dependent var		0.138427
S.E. of regression	0.024291	Akaike info criterion		−4.487253
Sum squared resid	0.017702	Schwarz criterion		−4.307682
Log likelihood	80.28331	F-statistic		347.2135
Durbin – Watson stat	0.608648	Prob(F-statistic)		0.000000

Table 6.9   Third model regression results (including only *PPI*)

Dependent Variable: LOG(IMP)
Method: Least Squares
Date: 02/17/04 Time: 02:22
Sample: 1990:1 1998:2
Included observations: 34

Variable	Coefficient	Std. Error	t-Statistic	Prob.
C	0.685704	0.370644	1.850031	0.0739
LOG(GDP)	2.093849	0.172585	12.13228	0.0000
LOG(PPI)	0.119566	0.136062	0.878764	0.3863

R-squared	0.962625	Mean dependent var		10.81363
Adjusted R-squared	0.960213	S.D. dependent var		0.138427
S.E. of regression	0.027612	Akaike info criterion		−4.257071
Sum squared resid	0.023634	Schwarz criterion		−4.122392
Log likelihood	75.37021	F-statistic		399.2113
Durbin–Watson stat	0.448237	Prob(F-statistic)		0.000000

Estimating the equation this time without log(*CPI*) but with log(*PPI*) we get the results shown in Table 6.9, which shows that log(*PPI*) is positive and insignificant! So, it is clear that the significance of log(*PPI*) in the specification above was due to the linear relationship that connects the two price variables.

So, the conclusions from this analysis are similar to the case of the collinear data set in Example 1 above, and can be summarized as follows:

1 The correlation among the explanatory variables was very high.

2 Standard errors or *t*-ratios of the estimated coefficients changed from estimation to estimation.

3 The stability of the estimated coefficients was also quite problematic, with negative and positive coefficients being estimated for the same variable in two alternative specifications.

In this case it is clear that multicollinearity is present, and that it is also serious, because we included two price variables which are quite strongly correlated. We leave it as an exercise for the reader to check the presence and the seriousness of multicollinearity only with the inclusion of log(*GDP*) and log(*CPI*) as explanatory variables (Exercise 6.1 below).

Questions and exercises

Questions

1 Define multicollinearity and explain its consequences in simple OLS estimates.
2 In the following model:

$$Y = \beta_1 + \beta_2 X_2 + \beta_3 X_3 + \beta_4 X_4 + u_t$$

assume that X_4 is a perfect linear combination of X_2. Show that in this case it is impossible to obtain OLS estimates.

3 From Chapter 5 we know that $\hat{\beta} = (X'X)^{-1}(X'Y)$. What happens to $\hat{\beta}$ when there is perfect collinearity among the Xs? How would you know if perfect collinearity exists.

4 Explain what the VIF is and what is its use.

5 Show how we can proceed in order to detect possible multicollinearity in a regression model.

Exercise 6.1

The file imports_uk.wf1 contains quarterly data for imports (*imp*), gross domestic product (*gdp*) and the consumer price index (*cpi*) for the USA. Use these data to estimate the following model:

$$\ln imp_t = \beta_1 + \beta_2 \ln gdp_t + \beta_3 \ln cpi_t + u_t$$

Check whether there is multicollinearity in the data. Calculate the correlation matrix of the variables and comment regarding the possibility of multicollinearity. Also, run the following additional regressions:

$$\ln imp_t = \beta_1 + \beta_2 \ln gdp_t + u_t$$
$$\ln imp_t = \beta_1 + \beta_2 \ln cpi_t + u_t$$
$$\ln gdp_t = \beta_1 + \beta_2 \ln cpi_t + u_t$$

What can you conclude about the nature of multicollinearity from these results?

Exercise 6.2

The file imports_uk_y.wf1 contains yearly observations of the variables mentioned in Exercise 6.1. Repeat Exercise 6.1 using the yearly data. Do your results change?

Exercise 6.3

The file imports_us.wf1 contains data for imports (I), gross national product (Y) and the consumer price index (P) for the USA. Use these data to estimate the following model:

$$\ln I_t = \beta_1 + \beta_2 \ln Y_t + \beta_3 \ln P_t + u_t$$

Check whether there is multicollinearity in the data. Calculate the correlation matrix of the variables and comment regarding the possibility of multicollinearity. Also, run the following additional regressions:

$$\ln I_t = \beta_1 + \beta_2 \ln Y_t + u_t$$
$$\ln I_t = \beta_1 + \beta_2 \ln P_t + u_t$$
$$\ln Y_t = \beta_1 + \beta_2 \ln P_t + u_t$$

What can you conclude about the nature of multicollinearity from these results?

Exercise 6.4

The file cars.wf1 contains data on new cars sold in the United States as a function of various variables. Develop a suitable model for estimating a demand function for cars in the United States. If you include all variables as regressors, do you expect to find multicollinearity and why? Provide alternative estimated models and check their respective coefficients. Do they change significantly? Explain how you could attempt to resolve this problem.

Exercise 6.5

Use the data in the file money_uk02.wf1 to estimate the parameters α, β and γ, in the equation below:

$$\ln(M/P)_t = a + \beta \ln Y_t + \gamma \ln R_{1t} + u_t$$

where R_{1t} is the 3-months treasury bill rate. For the rest of the variables the usual notation applies.

(a) Use as an additional variable in the above equation R_{2t} which is the dollar interest rate.

(b) Do you expect to find multicollinearity and why?

(c) Calculate the correlation matrix of all the variables. Which correlation coefficient is the largest?

(d) Calculate auxiliary regressions and conclude whether the degree of multicollinearity in (a) is serious or not.

7

Heteroskedasticity

Introduction: what is heteroskedasticity?

A good start might be made by first defining the words homoskedasticity and heteroskedasticity. Some authors spell the former homoscedasticity, but McCulloch (1985) appears to have settled this controversy in favour of homoskedasticity, based on the fact that the word has a Greek origin. From our teaching experience we have realized that students are somehow 'afraid' of the term heteroskedasticity, and that they use the term quite a lot when they want to demonstrate the difficulty of econometrics. We think, therefore, that it is essential to make clear both the meaning and origin of the word. On the positive side, Studenmund (2001) very nicely states that, although difficult to spell, it provides a really impressive comeback when parents ask 'what'd you learn for all that money?'

Both words can be split into two parts, having as a first part the Greek words homo (which means same or equal) or hetero (which means different or unequal), and as a second part the Greek word skedastic (which means spread or scatter). So, homoskedasticity means equal spread, and heteroskedasticity, on the other hand, means unequal spread. In econometrics the measure we usually use for spread is the variance, and therefore heteroskedasticity deals with unequal variances.

Recalling the assumptions of the classical linear regression model presented in Chapters 4 and 5, assumption 5 was that the disturbances should have a constant (equal) variance independent of i, given in mathematical form by the following equation:*

$$var(u_i) = \sigma^2 \tag{7.1}$$

Therefore, having an equal variance means that the disturbances are homoskedastic.

However, it is quite common in regression analysis to have cases where this assumption is violated. (In general heteroskedasticity is more likely to take place in a cross-sectional framework. However, this does not mean that heteroskedasticity in time series models is impossible.) In such cases we say that the homoskedasticity assumption is violated, and that the variance of the error terms depends on exactly which observation is discussed, i.e.:

$$var(u_i) = \sigma_i^2 \tag{7.2}$$

Note that the only difference between (7.1) and (7.2) is the subscript i attached to the σ^2, which means that the variance can change for every different observation in the sample $i = 1, 2, 3, \ldots, n$.

In order to make this clearer, it is useful to go back to the simple two-variable regression model of the form:

$$Y_i = a + \beta X_i + u_i \tag{7.3}$$

Consider, first, a scatter plot with a population regression line of the form given in Figure 7.1 and compare it with that of Figure 7.2. Points X_1, X_2 and X_3 in Figure 7.1, although referring to different values of $X(X_1 < X_2 < X_3)$, have an effect on Y that

---

*Because heteroskedasticity is often analysed in a pure cross section setting in most of this chapter we will index our variables by i rather than t.

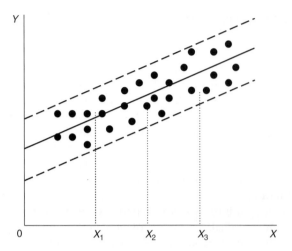

Figure 7.1   Data with a constant variance

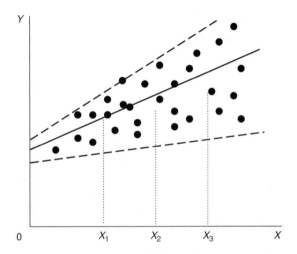

Figure 7.2   An example of heteroskedasticity with increasing variance

they are concentrated closely around the regression line with an equal spread above and below the regression line (i.e. equal spread=homoskedastic).

On the other hand, points X_1, X_2 and X_3 in Figure 7.2 again refer to different values of X but, this time, it is clear that the higher the value of X the higher is the 'speed' around the line. In this case the spread is different or unequal for each X_i (given from the dashed lines above and below the regression line), and therefore we have heteroskedasticity. It is now clear that in Figure 7.3 we have the opposite case (for lower X_i the variance is higher).

An example for the first case of heteroskedasticity (depicted in Figure 7.2) can be given in terms of income and consumption patterns. People with low levels of income do not have much flexibility in spending their money. A large proportion of their income will be spent on buying food, clothing and transportation; so, at low levels

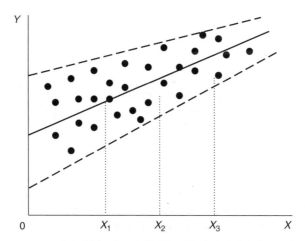

Figure 7.3 An example of heteroskedasticity with falling variance

of income, consumption patterns will not differ much and the spread will be more or less low. On the other hand, rich people have a much wider choice and flexibility in spending. Some might consume a lot, some might be large savers or investors in the stockmarket, implying that the average consumption (given by the regression line) can be quite different from the actual consumption. So the spread for high incomes will be definitely higher than that for lower incomes.

An example of the opposite case (such as the one depicted in Figure 7.3) can be attributed either to improvements in data-collection techniques (think here of large banks that have sophisticated data-processing facilities and therefore are able to calculate with fewer errors customer estimates compared to smaller banks with no such facilities), or to error-learning models where experience decreases the chances of making large errors (think for example of the Y variable being score performance on a test and the X variable being the times that individuals have taken the test in the past, or hours of preparation for the test; the larger the X, the smaller the variability in terms of Y will be).

The aim of this chapter is, after examining the consequences of heteroskedasticity on OLS estimators, to present tests for detecting heteroskedasticity in econometric models, as well as to show ways of resolving heteroskedasticity.

Consequences of heteroskedasticity on OLS estimators

A general approach

Consider the classical linear regression model:

$$Y_i = \beta_1 + \beta_2 X_{2i} + \beta_3 X_{3i} + \cdots + \beta_k X_{ki} + u_i \tag{7.4}$$

If the error term u_i in this equation is known to be heteroskedastic, then the consequences on the OLS estimators $\hat{\beta}s$ (or $\hat{\beta}$), can be summarized as follows:

1 The OLS estimators for the $\hat{\beta}s$ are still unbiased and consistent. This is because none of the explanatory variables is correlated with the error term. So, a correctly specified equation that suffers only from the presence of heteroskedasticity will give us values of $\hat{\beta}s$ which are relatively good.

2 Heteroskedasticity affects the distribution of the $\hat{\beta}s$ increasing the variances of the distributions and therefore making the estimators of the OLS method inefficient (because it violates the minimum variance property). To understand this consider Figure 7.4 which shows the distribution of an estimator $\hat{\beta}$ with and without heteroskedasticity. It is obvious that heteroskedasticity does not cause bias because $\hat{\beta}$ is centred around β (so $E(\hat{\beta}) = \beta$) but widening the distribution makes it no longer efficient. So OLS is no longer the most efficient estimator.

3 Heteroskedasticity also affects the variances (and therefore the standard errors as well) of the estimated $\hat{\beta}s$. In fact the presence of heteroskedasticity causes the OLS method to underestimate the variances (and standard errors) hence leading to higher than expected values of t statistics and F statistics. Therefore, heteroskedasticity has a wide impact on hypothesis testing: neither the t statistics or the F statistics are reliable any more for hypothesis testing because they will lead us to reject the null hypothesis too often.

A mathematical approach

We want to see how the presence of heteroskedasticity affects the OLS estimators. In order to do that, first we will show what happens in the simple regression model, then we will present the effect of heteroskedasticity in the form of the variance–covariance

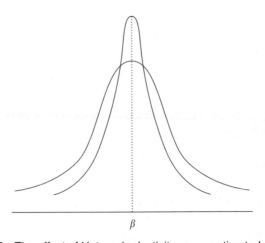

Figure 7.4   The effect of Heteroskedasticity on an estimated parameter

matrix of the error terms of the multiple regression model, and after that we will be able to show with the use of matrix algebra the effect of heteroskedasticity in a multiple regression framework.

Effect on the OLS estimators of the simple regression model

So, for the simple linear regression model – with only one explanatory variable and a constant regressed on Y, as the one we analysed in Chapter 4 – it is easy to show that the variance of the slope estimator will be affected by the presence of heteroskedasticity. Recall from equation (4.56) for the variance of the OLS coefficient $\hat{\beta}$, we had that:

$$
\begin{aligned}
Var(\hat{\beta}) &= \sum \left(\frac{x_i}{\sum x_i^2} \right)^2 \sigma^2 \\
&= \frac{\sum x_i^2 \sigma^2}{\left(\sum x_i^2 \right)^2} = \sigma^2 \frac{1}{\sum x_i^2}
\end{aligned}
\tag{7.5}
$$

this is only in the case when the error terms are homoskedastic so that the variance of the residuals is constant σ^2. The only difference between (4.56) and the equation presented here is that we use the subscript i instead of t, because in this chapter we mainly have models of cross-sectional data. This is because heteroskedasticity is more likely to appear in cases of cross-sectional data, as we have mentioned above. In the case of heteroskedasticity, the variance changes with every individual observation i, and therefore the variance of $\hat{\beta}$ will now be given by:

$$
Var(\hat{\beta}) = \sum \left(\frac{x_i}{\sum x_i^2} \right)^2 \sigma_i^2 = \frac{\sum x_i^2 \sigma_i^2}{\left(\sum x_i^2 \right)^2}
\tag{7.6}
$$

which is clearly different from (7.5). Now we are able to explain the bias that occurs in the presence of heteroskedasticity. If heteroskedasticity is present and we calculate the variance of $\hat{\beta}$ given by the standard OLS formula (7.5) instead of the correct (7.6), then we will be bound to underestimate the true variance and standard error of $\hat{\beta}$. Therefore, we will have t-ratios that will be falsely high, incorrectly leading us to the conclusion that an explanatory variable X is statistically significant, while its impact on Y is in fact zero. Also, the confidence intervals for β will be narrower than their correct values, leading us again to think that we have a higher precision in our estimates than the true, statistically justifiable case.

Effect on the variance–covariance matrix of the error terms

Second, it is useful to see how the presence of heteroskedasticity will affect the form of the variance–covariance matrix of the error terms of the classical linear multiple regression model.

Recall from Chapter 5 (p. 66ff.) that the variance–covariance matrix of the errors, because of assumptions 5 and 6, looks like:

$$E(\mathbf{uu'}) = \begin{pmatrix} \sigma^2 & 0 & 0 & \cdots & 0 \\ 0 & \sigma^2 & 0 & 0 & 0 \\ 0 & 0 & \sigma^2 & \cdots & 0 \\ \cdots & \cdots & \cdots & & \cdots \\ 0 & 0 & 0 & \cdots & \sigma^2 \end{pmatrix} = \sigma^2 \mathbf{I_n} \qquad (7.7)$$

where $\mathbf{I_n}$ is an $n \times n$ identity matrix.

The presence of heteroskedasticity, states clearly that assumption 5 is no longer valid. Therefore, the variance–covariance matrix of the residuals will no longer look like the classical case, but will be as follows:

$$E(\mathbf{uu'}) = \begin{pmatrix} \sigma_1^2 & 0 & 0 & \cdots & 0 \\ 0 & \sigma_2^2 & 0 & 0 & 0 \\ 0 & 0 & \sigma_3^2 & \cdots & 0 \\ \cdots & \cdots & \cdots & & \cdots \\ 0 & 0 & 0 & \cdots & \sigma_n^2 \end{pmatrix} = \Omega \qquad (7.8)$$

Effect on the OLS estimators of the multiple regression model

Recall that the variance–covariance matrix of the OLS estimators $\hat{\beta}$ is given by:

$$\begin{aligned} Cov(\hat{\boldsymbol{\beta}}) &= \mathbf{E}[(\hat{\beta} - \beta)(\hat{\beta} - \beta)'] \\ &= E\{[(\mathbf{X'X})^{-1}\mathbf{X'u}][(\mathbf{X'X})^{-1}\mathbf{X'u}]'\} \\ &= E\{(\mathbf{X'X})^{-1}\mathbf{X'uu'X}(\mathbf{X'X})^{-1}\}^* \\ &= (\mathbf{X'X})^{-1}\mathbf{X'}E(\mathbf{uu'})\mathbf{X}(\mathbf{X'X})^{-1\dagger} \\ &= (\mathbf{X'X})^{-1}\mathbf{X'}\Omega\mathbf{X}(\mathbf{X'X})^{-1} \end{aligned} \qquad (7.9)$$

which is totally different from the classical expression $\sigma^2(\mathbf{X'X})^{-1}$. This is because assumption 5 no longer holds, and of course Ω denotes the new variance-covariance matrix presented above, whatever form it may happen to take. Therefore, using the classical expression to calculate the variances, standard errors and t-statistics of the estimated $\hat{\beta}$s will lead us to the wrong conclusions. Formulae 7.9 forms the basis for what is often called 'Robust' inference, i.e. the derivation of standard errors and 't' statistics which are correct even when some of the OLS assumptions are violated. Basically what happens is that we assume a particular form for the Ω matrix and then use (7.9) to calculate a corrected covariance matrix.

---

* This is because $(AB)' = B'A'$.

† This is because, according to assumption 2, the Xs are non-random.

Detecting heteroskedasticity

In general there are two ways of detecting the presence of heteroskedasticity. The first is by inspection of different graphs, and this is called the informal way, while the second way is by applying appropriate tests that can detect heteroskedasticity. The informal way is the topic of the next section. The formal methods include various tests for the presence of heteroskedasticity, some of which will be presented in later sections.

The informal way

In the informal way, and in the two variable case that we have seen before, it is obvious that we can easily detect heteroskedasticity by simple inspection of the scatter plot. However, this cannot be done in the multiple regression case. In this case useful information regarding the possible presence of heteroskedasticity can be given by plotting the squared residuals against the dependent variable and/or the explanatory variables.

Gujarati (1978) presents cases in which from the pattern of graphs of this kind, we can deduct useful information regarding heteroskedasticity. The possible patterns are presented in Figures 7.5–7.9 respectively. In Figure 7.5 we see that there is no systematic pattern among the two variables, which suggests that we have a 'healthy' model, or at least one that does not suffer from heteroskedasticity. In the next figures, though we have evidence of heteroskedasticity, in Figure 7.6 we see a clear pattern that suggests heteroskedasticity, in Figure 7.7 there is a clear linear relationship between Y_i (or X_i) and u_i^2, while Figures 7.8 and 7.9 exhibit a quadratic relationship. Knowing the relationship between the two variables can be very useful because it enables us to transform the data in such a manner as to eliminate the heteroskedasticity.

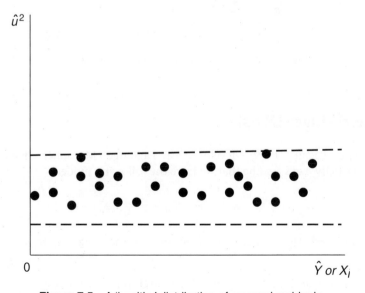

Figure 7.5 A 'healthy' distribution of squared residuals

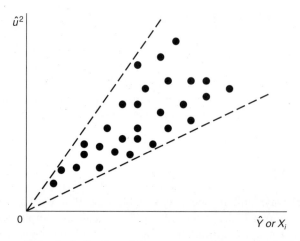

Figure 7.6   An indication of the presence of heteroskedasticity

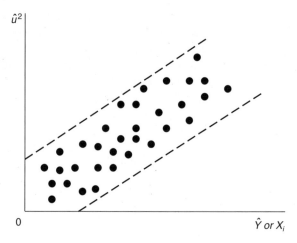

Figure 7.7   Another indication of Heteroskedasticity

The Breusch–Pagan LM test

Breusch and Pagan (1979) developed a Lagrange Multiplier (LM) test for heteroskedasticity. Let's assume that we have the following model:

$$Y_i = \beta_1 + \beta_2 X_{2i} + \beta_3 X_{3i} + \cdots + \beta_k X_{ki} + u_i \tag{7.10}$$

where $var(u_i) = \sigma_i^2$. The Breusch–Pagan test involves the following steps:

Step 1   Run a regression of model (7.10) and obtain the residuals $\hat{u}_i$ of this regression equation.

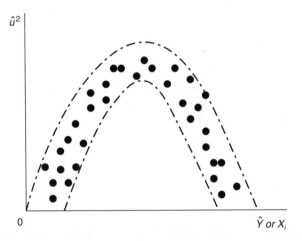

Figure 7.8 A non linear relationship leading to heteroskedasticity

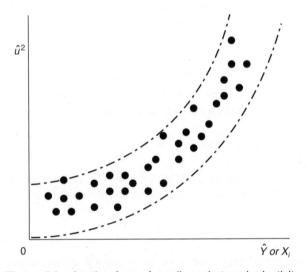

Figure 7.9 Another form of non linear heteroskedasticity

Step 2 Run the following auxiliary regression:

$$\hat{u}_i^2 = a_1 + a_2 Z_{2i} + a_3 Z_{3i} + \cdots + a_p Z_{pi} + v_i \tag{7.11}$$

where Z_{ki} is a set of variables that we think determine the variance of the error term. (Usually for Z_{ki} we use the explanatory variables of the original regression equation, i.e. the Xs.)

Step 3 Formulate the null and the alternative hypotheses. The null hypothesis of homoskedasticity is that:

$$H_0: \quad a_1 = a_2 = \cdots = a_p = 0 \tag{7.12}$$

while the alternative is that at least one of the as is different from zero and that at least one of the Zs affects the variance of the residuals which will be different for different t.

Step 4   Compute the $LM = nR^2$ statistic, where n is the number of observations used in order to estimate the auxiliary regression in step 2, and R^2 is the coefficient of determination of this regression. The LM statistic follows the χ^2 distribution with $p - 1$ degrees of freedom.

Step 5   Reject the null and conclude that there is significant evidence of heteroskedasticity when LM-statistical is bigger than the critical value (LM-$stat >$ $\chi^2_{p-1,\alpha}$). Alternatively, compute the p value and reject the null if the p value is less than the level of significance α (usually $\alpha = 0.05$).

In this – as also in all other LM tests that we will examine later – the auxiliary equation is implicitly making an assumption about the form of heteroskedasticity we expect to find in the data. There are three more LM tests which introduce different forms of auxiliary regressions, suggesting different functional forms about the relationship of the squared residuals ($\hat{u}_i^2$, which is a proxy for σ^2 since it is not known) and the explanatory variables.

The Breusch–Pagan test in EViews

The Breusch–Pagan test can be performed in EViews as follows. First we need to estimate the regression equation model with OLS; so we need to use the command

```
ls y c x1 x2 x3 ... xk
```

where y is our dependent variable and x1 to xk are our explanatory variables. Then to obtain the residuals we use the generate (genr) command as follows:

```
genr ut=resid
```

Note that it is important to type and execute this command immediately after obtaining the equation results so that the resid vector has the residual of the equation estimated previously. Here ut is just a name we provide for the error terms of this model.
   We then need to calculate the squared residuals as follows:

```
genr utsq=ut^2
```

and after that obtain the estimate of the auxiliary regression from the command:

```
ls utsq c z1 z2 z3 ... zp
```

To compute the LM statistic we need to do the calculation $LM = n * R^2$, where n is the number of observations and R^2 is the coefficient of determination of the auxiliary regression.
   After that we need to compare LM-critical with LM-statistical and conclude.

The Glesjer LM test

Glesjer's (1969) test involves the following steps (Note that the steps are the same as the Breusch–Pagan test above with the only exception of step 2 that involves a different auxiliary regression equation.):

Step 1 Run a regression of model (7.10) and obtain the residuals $\hat{u}_i$ of this regression equation.

Step 2 Run the following auxiliary regression:

$$|\hat{u}_i| = a_1 + a_2 Z_{2i} + a_3 Z_{3i} + \cdots + a_p Z_{pi} + v_i \tag{7.13}$$

Step 3 Formulate the null and the alternative hypotheses. The null hypothesis of homoskedasticity is that:

$$H_0: \quad a_1 = a_2 = \cdots = a_p = 0 \tag{7.14}$$

while the alternative is that at least one of the as is different from zero.

Step 4 Compute the $LM = nR^2$ statistic, where n is the number of observations used in order to estimate the auxiliary regression in step 2, and R^2 is the coefficient of determination of this regression. The LM statistic follows the χ^2 distribution with $p - 1$ degrees of freedom.

Step 5 Reject the null and conclude that there is significant evidence of heteroskedasticity when LM-statistical is bigger than the critical value ($LM\text{-}stat > \chi^2_{p-1,\alpha}$). Alternatively, compute the p-value and reject the null if the p-value is less than the level of significance α (usually $\alpha = 0.05$).

The Glesjer test in EViews

The Glesjer test can be performed in EViews as follows. First we need to estimate the regression equation model with OLS, so, we need to use the command:

```
ls y c x1 x2 x3 ... xk
```

where y is our dependent variable and x1 to xk are our explanatory variables. Then to obtain the residuals we use the generate (genr) command as follows:

```
genr ut=resid
```

Note that it is important to type and execute this command immediately after obtaining the equation results so that the resid vector has the residual of the equation estimated previously. Here ut is just a name we provide for the error terms of this model. We then need to calculate the squared residuals as follows:

```
genr absut=abs(ut)
```

and after that obtain the estimate of the auxiliary regression from the command:

```
ls absut c z1 z2 z3 ... zp
```

To compute the *LM* statistic we need to do the calculation $LM = n * R^2$, where n is the number of observations and R^2 is the coefficient of determination of the auxiliary regression.

After that we need to compare *LM*-critical with *LM*-statistical and conclude.

The Harvey–Godfrey LM test

Harvey (1976) and Godfrey (1978) developed the following test:

Step 1 Run a regression of model (7.10) and obtain the residuals $\hat{u}_i$ of this regression equation.

Step 2 Run the following auxiliary regression:

$$\ln(\hat{u}_i^2) = a_1 + a_2 Z_{2i} + a_3 Z_{3i} + \cdots + a_p Z_{pi} + v_i \qquad (7.15)$$

Step 3 Formulate the null and the alternative hypotheses. The null hypothesis of homoskedasticity is that:

$$H_0: \quad a_1 = a_2 = \cdots = a_p = 0 \qquad (7.16)$$

while the alternative is that at least one of the *as* is different from zero.

Step 4 Compute the $LM = nR^2$ statistic, where n is the number of observations used in order to estimate the auxiliary regression in step 2, and R^2 is the coefficient of determination of this regression. The *LM* statistic follows the χ^2 distribution with $p - 1$ degrees of freedom.

Step 5 Reject the null and conclude that there is significant evidence of hetero-skedasticity when *LM*-statistical is bigger than the critical value (*LM-stat* $>$ $\chi^2_{p-1,\alpha}$). Alternatively, compute the *p*-value and reject the null if the *p*-value is less than the level of significance α (usually $\alpha = 0.05$).

The Harvey–Godfrey test in EViews

The Harvey–Godfrey test can be performed in EViews as follows. First we need to estimate the regression equation model with OLS, so we use the command:

```
ls y c x1 x2 x3 ... xk
```

where y is our dependent variable and x1 to xk are our explanatory variables. Then to obtain the residuals we use the generate (genr) command as follows:

```
genr ut=resid
```

Note that it is important to type and execute this command immediately after obtaining the equation results so that the resid vector has the residual of the equation estimated previously. Here ut is just a name we provide for the error terms of this model.

We then need to calculate the squared residuals as follows:

```
genr utsq=ut^2
```

and after that obtain the estimate of the auxiliary regression from the command:

```
ls log(utsq) c z1 z2 z3 ... zp
```

To compute the *LM* statistic we need to do the calculation $LM = n * R^2$, where n is the number of observations and R^2 is the coefficient of determination of the auxiliary regression.

After that we need to compare *LM*-critical with *LM*-statistical and conclude.

The Park LM test

Park (1966) developed an alternative LM test, involving the following steps:

Step 1 Run a regression of model (7.10) and obtain the residuals $\hat{u}_i$ of this regression equation.

Step 2 Run the following auxiliary regression:

$$\ln(\hat{u}_i^2) = a_1 + a_2 \ln Z_{2i} + a_3 \ln Z_{3i} + \cdots + a_p \ln Z_{pi} + v_i \qquad (7.17)$$

Step 3 Formulate the null and the alternative hypotheses. The null hypothesis of homoskedasticity is that:

$$H_0: \quad a_1 = a_2 = \cdots = a_p = 0 \qquad (7.18)$$

while the alternative is that at least one of the *a*s is different from zero and then at least one of the *Z*s affects the variance of the residuals which will be different for different *t*.

Step 4 Compute the $LM = nR^2$ statistic, where n is the number of observations used in order to estimate the auxiliary regression in step 2, and R^2 is the coefficient of determination of this regression. The *LM* statistic follows the χ^2 distribution with $p-1$ degrees of freedom.

Step 5 Reject the null and conclude that there is significant evidence of heteroskedasticity when *LM*-statistical is bigger than the critical value (*LM-stat* $> \chi^2_{p-1,\alpha}$). Alternatively, compute the *p*-value and reject the null if the *p*-value is less than the level of significance α (usually $\alpha = 0.05$).

The Park test in EViews

The Park test can be performed in EViews as follows. First we need to estimate the regression equation model with OLS, so we need to use the command:

```
ls y c x1 x2 x3 ... xk
```

where y is our dependent variable and x1 to xk are our explanatory variables. Then to obtain the residuals we need to use the generate (genr) command as follows:

```
genr ut=resid
```

Note that it is important to type and execute this command immediately after obtaining the equation results so that the resid vector has the residual of the equation estimated previously. Here ut is just a name we provide for the error terms of this model. We then need to calculate the squared residuals as follows:

```
.genr utsq=ut^2
```

and after that to obtain the estimation of the auxiliary regression from this command:

```
ls log(utsq) c log(z1) log(z2) log(z3) ... log(zp)
```

To compute the *LM* statistic we need to do the calculation $LM = n * R^2$, where n is the number of observations and R^2 is the coefficient of determination of the auxiliary regression.

After that we need to compare *LM*-critical with *LM*-statistical and conclude.

An obvious criticism for all the above LM tests is that they require a prior knowledge about what might be causing the heteroskedasticity captured in the form of the auxiliary equation. Alternative models have been proposed and they are presented below.

The Goldfeld–Quandt test

Goldfeld and Quandt (1965) proposed an alternative test based on the idea that if the variances of the residuals are the same across all observations (i.e. homoskedastic), then the variance for one part of the sample should be the same as the variance for another part of the sample. What is necessary for the test to be applicable is to identify a variable to which the variance of the residuals is mostly related (this can be done with plots of the residuals against the explanatory variables). The steps of the Goldfeld–Quandt test are as follows:

Step 1 Identify one variable that is closely related to the variance of the disturbance term, and order (or rank) the observations of this variable in descending order (starting with the highest and going to the lowest value).

Step 2 Split the ordered sample into two equally sized sub-samples by omitting c central observations, so that the two sub-samples will contain $\frac{1}{2}(n - c)$

observations. The first will contain the largest values and the second will contain the lowest ones.

Step 3 Run an OLS regression of Y on the X variable that you have used in step 1 for each sub-sample and obtain the RSS for each equation.

Step 4 Calculate the F-statistic as follows:

$$F = \frac{RSS_1}{RSS_2} \tag{7.19}$$

where in the nominator (RSS_1) you put the *RSS* with the largest value. The F statistic is distributed with $F_{(1/2(n-c)-k,1/2(n-c)-k)}$ degrees of freedom.

Step 5 Reject the null hypothesis of homoskedasticity if F-statistical > F-critical.

The idea behind the formula is that if the error terms are homoskedastic, then the variance of the residuals will be the same for each sample so that the ratio is unity. If the ratio is significantly larger then the null of equal variances will be rejected. One question here is what the appropriate value of c would be. This is arbitrarily chosen and it should usually be between 1/6 and 1/3 of the observations.

The problem with the Goldfeld–Quandt test is that it does not take into account cases where heteroskedasticity is caused by more than one variable and it is not always suitable for time series data. However, it is a very popular model for the simple regression case (with only one explanatory variable).

The Goldfeld–Quandt test in EViews

To perform the Goldfeld–Quandt test in EViews we first need to sort the data in descending order according to the variable that we identified and that we think causes the heteroskedasticity X. To do this click on **Procs/Sort Series**, enter the name of the variable (in this case X) in the sort key dialog box and check descending for the sort order. We then need to break the sample into two different sub-samples and run OLS of Y on X for both sub-samples in order to obtain the RSSs. For this we need to use the following commands:

```
smpl start end
ls y c x
scalar rss1=@ssr
for the first sample
and
smpl start end
ls y c x
scalar rss2=@ssr
```

where in both cases the start and the end points should be defined appropriately depending on the frequency of our data set and of the number of middle point observations that should be excluded.

We then need to calculate the F stat which is given by RRS1/RSS2 or by the following command:

```
genr F_GQ=RSS1/RSS2
```

and compare this with the *F*-critical value given by:

```
genr f-crit=@qfdist(.95,n1-k,n2-k)
```

or alternatively to obtain the *p*-value and conclude from it by:

```
genr p-value=1-@fdist(.05,n1-k,n2-k)
```

White's test

White (1980) developed a more general test for heteroskedasticity that eliminates the problems that appeared in the previous tests. White's test is also an LM test, but it has the advantages that (a) it does not assume any prior knowledge of heteroskedasticity, (b) it does not depend on the normality assumption as the Breusch–Pagan test and (c) it proposes a particular choice for the Zs in the auxiliary regression.

The steps involved in White's test assuming a model with two explanatory variables like the one presented here:

$$Y_i = \beta_1 + \beta_2 X_{2i} + \beta_3 X_{3i} + u_i \qquad (7.20)$$

are the following:

Step 1 Run a regression of model (7.20) and obtain the residuals $\hat{u}_i$ of this regression equation.

Step 2 Run the following auxiliary regression:

$$\hat{u}_i^2 = a_1 + a_2 X_{2i} + a_3 X_{3i} + a_4 X_{2i}^2 + a_5 X_{3i}^2 + a_6 X_{2i} X_{3i} + v_i \qquad (7.21)$$

i.e. regress the squared residuals on a constant, all the explanatory variables, the squared explanatory variables, and their respective cross products.

Step 3 Formulate the null and the alternative hypotheses. The null hypothesis of homoskedasticity is that:

$$H_0: \quad a_1 = a_2 = \cdots = a_p = 0 \qquad (7.22)$$

while the alternative is that at least one of the *a*s is different from zero.

Step 4 Compute the $LM = nR^2$ statistic, where *n* is the number of observations used in order to estimate the auxiliary regression in step 2, and R^2 is the coefficient of determination of this regression. The *LM* statistic follows the χ^2 distribution with $6 - 1$ degrees of freedom.

Step 5 Reject the null and conclude that there is significant evidence of heteroskedasticity when *LM*-statistical is bigger than the critical value (*LM-stat* > $\chi^2_{6-1,\alpha}$). Alternatively, compute the *p*-value and reject the null if the *p*-value is less than the level of significance α (usually $\alpha = 0.05$).

Because White's test is more general, and because of its advantages, presented above, it is recommended over all the previous tests, although one practical problem is that due to the cross product terms the number of regressors in (7.21) can become large.

White's test in EViews

EViews already has a routine after obtaining results by OLS for executing White's test for heteroskedasticity. After obtaining the OLS results, we click on **View/Residual Tests/White Heteroskedasticity (no cross terms)** if we don't want to include the cross-product terms of our explanatory variables in the auxiliary regression; or, alternatively, click on **View/Residual Tests/White Heteroskedasticity (cross terms)** if we want to include the cross-product terms of our explanatory variables in the auxiliary regression. EViews in both cases provides us with the results of the auxiliary regression equation that is estimated in each case, as well as with the LM test and its respective p-value.

Computer example: heteroskedasticity tests

The file houseprice.wf1 contains data regarding the house prices of a sample of 88 London houses together with some characteristics regarding those houses. Analytically, we have the following variables:

> *Price* = the price of the houses measured in pounds.
>
> *Rooms* = the number of bedrooms in each house.
>
> *Sqfeet* = the size of the house measured in square feet.

We would like to see whether the number of bedrooms and the size of the house play an important role in determining the price of each house.

By a simple scatter plot inspection of the two explanatory variables against the dependent variable we can see (Figures 7.10 and 7.11) that there is clear evidence of heteroskedasticity in the relationship regarding the *Rooms* variable, but also some evidence of the same problem for the size proxy (*Sqfeet*) variable with larger variations in prices for larger houses.

The Breusch–Pagan test

Testing for heteroskedasticity in a more formal way, we can first apply the Breusch–Pagan test:

Step 1 We estimate the regression equation:

$$price = b_1 + b_2 rooms + b_3 sqfeet + u$$

the results of which are presented in Table 7.1.

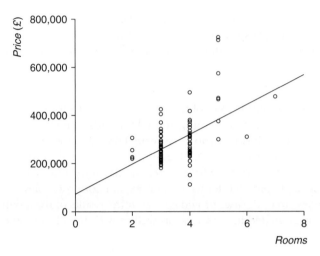

Figure 7.10   Clear evidence of heteroskedasticity

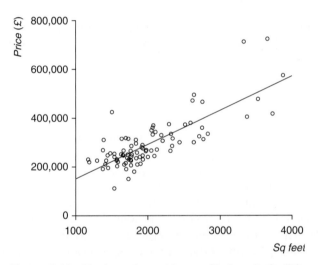

Figure 7.11   Much weaker evidence of heteroskedasticity

Step 2   We then obtain the residuals of this regression model (we name them as ut) by typing the following command in the command line:

```
genr ut=resid
```

and the squared residuals by typing the command:

```
genr utsq=ut^sq
```

Table 7.1 Basic regression model results

Dependent Variable: PRICE
Method: Least Squares
Date: 02/03/04 Time: 01:52
Sample: 1 88
Included observations: 88

Variable	Coefficient	Std. Error	t-Statistic	Prob.
C	−19315.00	31046.62	−0.622129	0.5355
Rooms	15198.19	9483.517	1.602590	0.1127
Sqfeet	128.4362	13.82446	9.290506	0.0000

R-squared	0.631918	Mean dependent var	293546.0
Adjusted R-squared	0.623258	S.D. dependent var	102713.4
S.E. of regression	63044.84	Akaike info criterion	24.97458
Sum squared resid	3.38E+11	Schwarz criterion	25.05903
Log likelihood	−1095.881	F-statistic	72.96353
Durbin–Watson stat	1.858074	Prob(F-statistic)	0.000000

Table 7.2 The Breusch–Pagan test auxiliary regression

Dependent Variable: UTSQ
Method: Least Squares
Date: 02/03/04 Time: 02:09
Sample: 1 88
Included observations: 88

Variable	Coefficient	Std. Error	t-Statistic	Prob.
C	−8.22E+09	3.91E+09	−2.103344	0.0384
Rooms	1.19E+09	1.19E+09	0.995771	0.3222
Sqfeet	3881720.	1739736.	2.231213	0.0283

R-squared	0.120185	Mean dependent var	3.84E+09
Adjusted R-squared	0.099484	S.D. dependent var	8.36E+09
S.E. of regression	7.93E+09	Akaike info criterion	48.46019
Sum squared resid	5.35E+21	Schwarz criterion	48.54464
Log likelihood	−2129.248	F-statistic	5.805633
Durbin–Watson stat	2.091083	Prob(F-statistic)	0.004331

Then we estimate the auxiliary regression using as Zs the explanatory variables that we have in our original equation model:

$$utsq = a_1 + a_2 rooms + a_3 sqfeet + v$$

The results of this equation are presented in Table 7.2.

The *LM* statistic is distributed under a chi-square distribution with degrees of freedom equal to the number of slope coefficients included in the auxiliary regression (or k − 1) which in our case is 2. The chi-square critical can be given by:

```
genr chi=@qchisq(.95,2)
```

and is equal to 5.991465.

Step 3 Because the *LM*-stat > chi-square critical value we conclude that the null can be rejected, and therefore there is evidence of heteroskedasticity.

The Glesjer test

For the Glesjer test the steps are similar to the above but the dependent variable in the auxiliary regression is now the absolute value of the error terms. So, we need to construct this variable as follows:

```
genr absut=abs(ut)
```

and then estimate the auxiliary equation of the form:

$$absut = a_1 + a_2 rooms + a_3 sqfeet + v$$

The results of this model are given in Table 7.3. Again we need to calculate the *LM* statistic:

$$LM = \text{obs} * R^2 = 88 * 0.149244 = 13.133472$$

which is again bigger than the chi-square critical value, and therefore we again conclude that there is sufficient evidence of heteroskedasticity.

The Harvey–Godfrey test

For the Harvey–Godfrey test the auxiliary regression has the form:

$$log(utsq) = a_1 + a_2 rooms + a_3 sqfeet + v$$

Table 7.3 The Glesjer test auxiliary regression

Dependent Variable: ABSUT
Method: Least Squares
Date: 02/03/04 Time: 02:42
Sample: 1 88
Included observations: 88

Variable	Coefficient	Std. Error	t-Statistic	Prob.
C	−23493.96	19197.00	−1.223835	0.2244
Rooms	8718.698	5863.926	1.486836	0.1408
Sqfeet	19.04985	8.548052	2.228560	0.0285
R-squared	0.149244	Mean dependent var		45976.49
Adjusted R-squared	0.129226	S.D. dependent var		41774.94
S.E. of regression	38982.40	Akaike info criterion		24.01310
Sum squared resid	1.29E+11	Schwarz criterion		24.09756
Log likelihood	−1053.577	F-statistic		7.455547
Durbin–Watson stat	2.351422	Prob(F-statistic)		0.001039

Table 7.4 The Harvey–Godfrey test auxiliary regression

Dependent Variable: LOG(UTSQ)
Method: Least Squares
Date: 02/03/04 Time: 02:46
Sample: 1 88
Included observations: 88

Variable	Coefficient	Std. Error	t-Statistic	Prob.
C	17.77296	0.980629	18.12405	0.0000
Rooms	0.453464	0.299543	1.513852	0.1338
Sqfeet	0.000625	0.000437	1.432339	0.1557
R-squared	0.098290	Mean dependent var		20.65045
Adjusted R-squared	0.077073	S.D. dependent var		2.072794
S.E. of regression	1.991314	Akaike info criterion		4.248963
Sum squared resid	337.0532	Schwarz criterion		4.333418
Log likelihood	−183.9544	F-statistic		4.632651
Durbin–Watson stat	2.375378	Prob(F-statistic)		0.012313

and the results of this auxiliary regression model are given in Table 7.4. In this case the *LM* statistic is:

$$LM = \text{obs} * R^2 = 88 * 0.098290 = 8.64952$$

which is again bigger than the chi-square critical value, and therefore we again conclude that there is sufficient evidence of heteroskedasticity.

The Park test

Finally, for the Park test the auxiliary regression has the form:

$$log(utsq) = a_1 + a_2 log(rooms) + a_3 log(sqfeet) + v \qquad (7.23)$$

the results of which are given in Table 7.5. In this case the *LM* statistic is:

$$LM = \text{obs} * R^2 = 88 * 0.084176 = 7.407488$$

which is again bigger than the chi-square critical value, and therefore we again conclude that there is sufficient evidence of heteroskedasticity.

The Goldfeld–Quandt test

The Goldfeld–Quandt test requires that we first order the observations according to the variable that we think mostly causes the heteroskedasticity. Taking this to be the *rooms*

Table 7.5   The Park test auxiliary regression

Dependent Variable: LOG(UTSQ)
Method: Least Squares
Date: 02/03/04 Time: 02:50
Sample: 1 88
Included observations: 88

Variable	Coefficient	Std. Error	t-Statistic	Prob.
C	9.257004	6.741695	1.373097	0.1733
Log(Rooms)	1.631570	1.102917	1.479322	0.1428
Log(Sqfeet)	1.236057	0.969302	1.275204	0.2057
R-squared	0.084176	Mean dependent var		20.65045
Adjusted R-squared	0.062627	S.D. dependent var		2.072794
S.E. of regression	2.006838	Akaike info criterion		4.264494
Sum squared resid	342.3290	Schwarz criterion		4.348949
Log likelihood	−184.6377	F-statistic		3.906274
Durbin–Watson stat	2.381246	Prob(F-statistic)		0.023824

variable, we perform this test following the steps described below:

Step 1   First we click on **Procs/Sort Series** and enter the name of the variable (in this case *rooms*) in the sort key dialog box and click on the box to check **descending** for the sort order.

Step 2   We then need to break the sample into two different sub-samples, subtracting c number of intermediate observations. Choosing c close to 1/6 of the total observations we have that $c = 14$. Therefore each sub-sample will contain $(88 - 14)/2 = 37$ observations. The first sample will have observations 1 to 37 and the second will have observations 51 to 88.

Step 3   Now we need to run an OLS of *price* on rooms for both sub-samples in order to obtain the RSSs. For this we need to use the following commands:

```
smpl   1 37          [sets the sample to
                      sub-sample 1]
ls price c rooms     [estimates the regression
                      equation]
scalar rss1=@ssr     [creates a scalar which will
                      be the value of the RSS
                      of the regression equation
                      estimated by the previous
                      command]
```

Similarly for the second sub-sample we type the following commands:

```
smpl 51 88
ls price c rooms
scalar rss2=@ssr
```

and the results for both sub-samples are presented in Tables 7.6 and 7.7. Since *RSS1* is bigger than *RSS2*, the *F* statistic can be calculated as follows:

```
genr F_GQ=RSS1/RSS2
```

Table 7.6   The Goldfeld–Quandt test (first sub-sample results)

Dependent Variable: PRICE
Method: Least Squares
Date: 02/03/04 Time: 03:05
Sample: 1 37
Included observations: 37

Variable	Coefficient	Std. Error	t-Statistic	Prob.
C	−150240.0	124584.0	−1.205933	0.2359
Rooms	110020.7	28480.42	3.863028	0.0005

R-squared	0.298920	Mean dependent var		325525.0
Adjusted R-squared	0.278889	S.D. dependent var		134607.0
S.E. of regression	114305.9	Akaike info criterion		26.18368
Sum squared resid	**4.57E+11**	Schwarz criterion		26.27076
Log likelihood	−482.3981	F-statistic		14.92298
Durbin–Watson stat	1.718938	Prob(F-statistic)		0.000463

Table 7.7   The Goldfeld–Quandt test (second sub-sample results)

Dependent Variable: PRICE
Method: Least Squares
Date: 02/03/04 Time: 03:05
Sample: 51 88
Included observations: 38

Variable	Coefficient	Std. Error	t-Statistic	Prob.
C	227419.1	85213.84	2.668805	0.0113
Rooms	11915.44	29273.46	0.407039	0.6864

R-squared	0.004581	Mean dependent var		261911.2
Adjusted R-squared	−0.023069	S.D. dependent var		54751.89
S.E. of regression	55379.83	Akaike info criterion		24.73301
Sum squared resid	**1.10E+11**	Schwarz criterion		24.81920
Log likelihood	−467.9273	F-statistic		0.165681
Durbin–Watson stat	1.983220	Prob(F-statistic)		0.686389

and F-critical will be given by:

```
genr F_crit=@qfdist(.95,37,37)
```

The F-statistic $= 4.1419$ is bigger than F-critical $= 1.7295$, and therefore we conclude that there is evidence of heteroskedasticity.

The White test

For the White Test, we simply need to estimate the equation model (presented in the first table with results of this example) and then click on **View/Residual Tests/White (no cross products)** to get the results shown in Table 7.8. Note that the auxiliary regression does not include the cross products of the explanatory variables in this case. The *LM-stat* $= 16.20386$ is bigger than the critical value and the p-value also next to the *LM*-test provided by EViews is 0.02757, both suggesting evidence of heteroskedasticity.

Table 7.8   The White test (no cross products)

White Heteroskedasticity Test:

F-statistic	4.683121	Probability	0.001857
Obs*R-squared	**16.20386**	**Probability**	**0.002757**

Test Equation:
Dependent Variable: RESID^2
Method: Least Squares
Date: 02/03/04 Time: 03:15
Sample: 1 88
Included observations: 88

Variable	Coefficient	Std. Error	t-Statistic	Prob.
C	7.16E + 09	1.27E + 10	0.562940	0.5750
Rooms	7.21E + 09	5.67E + 09	1.272138	0.2069
Rooms^2	−7.67E + 08	6.96E + 08	−1.102270	0.2735
Sqfeet	−20305674	9675923.	−2.098577	0.0389
Sqfeet^2	5049.013	1987.370	2.540550	0.0129

R-squared	0.184135	Mean dependent var	3.84E + 09
Adjusted R-squared	0.144816	S.D. dependent var	8.36E + 09
S.E. of regression	7.73E + 09	Akaike info criterion	48.43018
Sum squared resid	4.96E + 21	Schwarz criterion	48.57094
Log likelihood	−2125.928	F-statistic	4.683121
Durbin–Watson stat	1.640895	Prob(F-statistic)	0.001857

If we choose the version of the White test with the cross products (by clicking on **View/Residual Tests/White (cross products)** we get the results shown in Table 7.9. In this case as well, as in all cases above, we have that the *LM*-stat (17.22519) is bigger than the critical and therefore there is evidence of heteroskedasticity.

Engle's ARCH test[*]

So far we have examined for the presence of autocorrelation in the error terms of a regression model. Engle (1982) introduced a new concept allowing for autocorrelation to occur in the variance of the error terms, rather than in the error terms themselves. To capture this autocorrelation Engle developed the Autoregressive Conditional Heteroskedasticity (ARCH) model, the key idea behind which is that the variance of u_t depends on the size of the squared error term lagged one period (that is u_{t-1}^2).
More analytically, consider the regression model:

$$Y_t = \beta_1 + \beta_2 X_{2t} + \beta_3 X_{3t} + \cdots + \beta_k X_{kt} + u_t \tag{7.24}$$

and assume that the variance of the error term follows an ARCH(1) process:

$$Var(u_t) = \sigma_t^2 = \gamma_0 + \gamma_1 u_{t-1}^2 \tag{7.25}$$

If there is no autocorrelation in $Var(u_t)$, then γ_1 should be zero and therefore $\sigma_t^2 = \gamma_0$. So, we have a constant (homoskedastic) variance.

---

[*] This test only applies to a time series context and so in this section we revert to indexing our variables by t.

Table 7.9 The White test (cross products)

White Heteroskedasticity Test:

F-statistic	3.991436	Probability	0.002728
Obs*R-squared	**17.22519**	**Probability**	**0.004092**

Test Equation:
Dependent Variable: RESID^2
Method: Least Squares
Date: 02/03/04 Time: 03:18
Sample: 1 88
Included observations: 88

Variable	Coefficient	Std. Error	t-Statistic	Prob.
C	1.08E + 10	1.31E + 10	0.822323	0.4133
Rooms	7.00E + 09	5.67E + 09	1.234867	0.2204
Rooms^2	−1.28E + 09	8.39E + 08	−1.523220	0.1316
Rooms*Sqfeet	1979155.	1819402.	1.087805	0.2799
Sqfeet	−23404693	10076371	−2.322730	0.0227
Sqfeet^2	4020.876	2198.691	1.828759	0.0711

R-squared	0.195741	Mean dependent var	3.84E + 09
Adjusted R-squared	0.146701	S.D. dependent var	8.36E + 09
S.E. of regression	7.72E + 09	Akaike info criterion	48.43858
Sum squared resid	4.89E + 21	Schwarz criterion	48.60749
Log likelihood	−2125.297	F-statistic	3.991436
Durbin–Watson stat	1.681398	Prob(F-statistic)	0.002728

The model can easily be extended for higher-order ARCH(p) effects having that:

$$Var(u_t) = \sigma_t^2 = \gamma_0 + \gamma_1 u_{t-1}^2 + \gamma_2 u_{t-2}^2 + \cdots + \gamma_p u_{t-p}^2 \qquad (7.26)$$

and here the null hypothesis is that:

$$H_0: \quad \gamma_1 = \gamma_2 = \cdots = \gamma_p = 0 \qquad (7.27)$$

that is, no ARCH effects present. The steps involved in the ARCH test are:

Step 1 Estimate equation (7.24) by OLS and obtain the residuals, $\hat{u}_t$.

Step 2 Regress the squared residuals (u_t^2) against a constant, u_{t-1}^2, u_{t-2}^2, ..., u_{t-p}^2 (the value of p will be determined by the order of ARCH(p) for which you want to test).

Step 3 Compute the *LM* statistic $= (n - p)R^2$, from the regression in step 2. If $LM > \chi_p^2$ for a given level of significance reject the null of no ARCH effects and conclude that ARCH effects are indeed present.

The ARCH-LM test in EViews and Microfit

After estimating a regression equation in EViews, in order to perform the ARCH LM test we go from the estimation results window to **View/Residual Tests/ARCH LM test**... EViews asks for the number of lags to be included in the test, and after specifying that and clicking on <**OK**> we obtain the results of the test. The interpretation is as usual.

In Microfit after estimating the regression model, close the results window by clicking on <**close**> to obtain the **Post Regression** menu. From that menu choose option 2, and move to the **Hypothesis Testing** menu and click <**OK**>. From the hypothesis testing menu choose option 2, **Autoregressive Conditional Heteroskedasticity tests (OLS & NLS)**, and again click <**OK**>. We are then asked to determine the number of lags in the **Input an integer** window and after clicking <**OK**> we obtain the results of the test. An example with the use of EViews is given below.

Computer example of the ARCH-LM test

To apply the ARCH-LM test we first need to estimate the equation and then click on **View/Residual Tests/ARCH LM Test** and specify the lag order. Applying the ARCH-LM test to the initial model (for ARCH(1) effects, i.e. in lag order we typed 1):

$$C_t = b_1 + b_2 D_t + b_3 P_t + u_t \tag{7.28}$$

we obtain the results shown in Table 7.10, where it is obvious from both the LM statistic (and the probability limit) as well as from the t statistic of the lagged squared residual term that it is highly significant that this equation has ARCH(1) effects.

Resolving heteroskedasticity

If we find that heteroskedasticity is present, there are two ways of proceeding: (a) we can re-estimate the model in a way which fully recognizes the presence of the problem, this would involve applying the generalized (or weighted) least squares method. This would then produce a new set of parameter estimates which would be more efficient than the

Table 7.10   The ARCH-LM test results

ARCH Test:

F-statistic	12.47713	Probability	0.001178
Obs*R-squared	**9.723707**	Probability	**0.001819**

Test Equation:
Dependent Variable: RESID^2
Method: Least Squares
Date: 02/12/04 Time: 23:21
Sample(adjusted): 1985:2 1994:2
Included observations: 37 after adjusting endpoints

Variable	Coefficient	Std. Error	t-Statistic	Prob.
C	0.000911	0.000448	2.030735	0.0499
RESID^2(−1)	0.512658	0.145135	**3.532298**	0.0012

R-squared	0.262803	Mean dependent var.	0.001869
Adjusted R-squared	0.241740	S.D. dependent var.	0.002495
S.E. of regression	0.002173	Akaike info. criterion	−9.373304
Sum squared resid	0.000165	Schwarz criterion	−9.286227
Log likelihood	175.4061	F-statistic	12.47713
Durbin–Watson stat	1.454936	Prob(F-statistic)	0.001178

OLS ones and a correct set of covariances and 't' statistics. Or (b) we can recognize that while OLS is no longer best it is still consistent and the real problem is the covariances and 't' statistics which are simply wrong. We can then correct the covariances and 't' statistics by basing them on a formulae such as (7.9). Of course this will not change the actual parameter estimates which will remain less than fully efficient.

Generalized (or weighted) least squares

Generalized least squares

Consider the following model:

$$Y_i = \beta_1 + \beta_2 X_{2i} + \beta_3 X_{3i} + \cdots + \beta_k X_{ki} + u_i \tag{7.29}$$

where the variance of the error term instead of being constant is heteroskedastic, i.e. is $Var(u_i) = \sigma_i^2$.

If we divide each term in (7.29) by the standard deviation of the error term, σ_i, then we obtain the modified model:

$$\frac{Y_i}{\sigma_i} = \beta_1 \frac{1}{\sigma_i} + \beta_2 \frac{X_{2i}}{\sigma_i} + \beta_3 \frac{X_{3i}}{\sigma_i} + \cdots + \beta_k \frac{X_{ki}}{\sigma_i} + \frac{u_i}{\sigma_i} \tag{7.30}$$

or

$$Y_i^* = \beta_1 X_{1i}^* + \beta_2 X_{2i}^* + \beta_3 X_{3i}^* + \cdots + \beta_k X_{ki}^* + u_i^* \tag{7.31}$$

For the modified model, we have that:

$$Var(u_i^*) = Var\left(\frac{u_i}{\sigma_i}\right) = \frac{Var(u_i)}{\sigma_i^2} = 1 \tag{7.32}$$

Therefore, estimates obtained by OLS of regressing Y_i^* to $X_{1i}^*, X_{2i}^*, X_{3i}^*, \ldots, X_{ki}^*$ are now BLUE. This procedure is called generalized least squares (GLS).

Weighted least squares

The GLS procedure is also the same as the weighted least squares (WLS), where we have weights, ω_i, adjusting our variables. To see the similarity define $\omega_i = \frac{1}{\sigma_i}$, and rewrite the original model as:

$$\omega_i Y_i = \beta_1 \omega_i + \beta_2 (X_{2i}\omega_i) + \beta_3 (X_{3i}\omega_i) + \cdots + \beta_k (X_{ki}\omega_i) + (u_i\omega_i) \tag{7.33}$$

which if we define as $\omega_i Y_i = Y_i^*$, and $(X_{ki}\omega_i) = X_{ki}^*$, we have the same equation as (7.31):

$$Y_i^* = \beta_1 X_{1i}^* + \beta_2 X_{2i}^* + \beta_3 X_{3i}^* + \cdots + \beta_k X_{ki}^* + u_i^* \tag{7.34}$$

Assumptions regarding the structure of σ^2

Although GLS and WLS are simple to grasp and appear to be straightforward, one major practical problem is that σ_i^2 is unknown and therefore estimation of (7.31) and/or (7.33) is not possible without making explicit assumptions regarding the structure of σ_i^2.

However, if we have a prior belief about the structure of σ_i^2, then GLS and WLS work in practice. In order to see this, consider the case where in (7.29) we know that:

$$Var(u_i) = \sigma_i^2 = \sigma^2 Z_i^2 \tag{7.35}$$

where Z_i is a variable of which the values are known for all i. Dividing every term in (7.35) by Z_i we get:

$$\frac{Y_i}{Z_i} = \beta_1 \frac{1}{Z_i} + \beta_2 \frac{X_{2i}}{Z_i} + \beta_3 \frac{X_{3i}}{Z_i} + \cdots + \beta_k \frac{X_{ki}}{Z_i} + \frac{u_i}{Z_i} \tag{7.36}$$

or

$$Y_i^* = \beta_1 X_{1i}^* + \beta_2 X_{2i}^* + \beta_3 X_{3i}^* + \ldots + \beta_k X_{ki}^* + u_i^* \tag{7.37}$$

where starred terms denote variables divided by Z_i. In this case we have that:

$$Var(u_i^*) = Var\left(\frac{u_i}{Z_i}\right) = \sigma^2 \tag{7.38}$$

So, the heteroskedasticity problem has been resolved from the original model. Note, however, that this equation has no constant term; the constant in the original regression (β_1 in 7.24) becomes the coefficient on X_i^* in 7.37. Care should be taken in interpreting the coefficients especially when Z_i is an explanatory variable in the original model (7.29). Assume, for example, that $Z_i = X_{3i}$, then we have that:

$$\frac{Y_i}{Z_i} = \beta_1 \frac{1}{Z_i} + \beta_2 \frac{X_{2i}}{Z_i} + \beta_3 \frac{X_{3i}}{Z_i} + \cdots + \beta_k \frac{X_{ki}}{Z_i} + \frac{u_i}{Z_i} \tag{7.39}$$

or

$$\frac{Y_i}{Z_i} = \beta_1 \frac{1}{Z_i} + \beta_2 \frac{X_{2i}}{Z_i} + \beta_3 + \cdots + \beta_k \frac{X_{ki}}{Z_i} + \frac{u_i}{Z_i} \tag{7.40}$$

If this form of WLS is used, then the coefficients obtained should be interpreted very carefully. Note that β_3 is now the constant term of (7.37) while it was a slope coefficient in (7.29); and on the other hand, β_1 is now a slope coefficient in (7.37), while it was the intercept in the original model (7.29). Therefore a researcher interested in the effect of X_{3i} in (7.29) should examine the intercept in (7.37), and similarly for the other case.

Heteroskedasticity-consistent estimation methods

White (1980) proposed a method of obtaining consistent estimators of the variances and covariances of the OLS estimators. We will not present the mathematical details of this method here as they are quite tedious and beyond the scope of this text. However, several computer packages (EViews is one of them) are now able to compute White's heteroskedasticity-corrected variances and standard errors. An example of using White's method of estimation in EViews is given in the computer example below.

Computer example: resolving heteroskedasticity

Recall the example above concerning heteroskedasticity tests. Since with all tests we found evidence of heteroskedasticity, alternative methods of estimation than OLS need to be used. If we estimate the equation by OLS we get the results shown in Table 7.11.

However, we know that because of heteroskedasticity, the standard errors of the OLS coefficients estimates are incorrect. In order to obtain White's corrected standard error estimates we need to click on **Quick/Estimate Equation** and click on the **Options** button which is located at the lower right of the **Equation Specification** window. After that the **Estimation Options** window opens where we need to click on the **Heteroskedasticity Consistent Covariance** box, and then similarly to click on the box next to **White** and then on <**OK**>. When we return to the Equation Specification window, we must enter the required regression equation by typing:

```
price c rooms sqfeet
```

and then click <**OK**>. The results obtained will be as shown in Table 7.11 where now the White's standard errors are not the same as those from the simple OLS case although the coefficients are, of course, identical.

Calculating the confidence interval for the coefficient of *sqfeet* for the simple OLS case (the incorrect case) we have (the t-stat for 0.05 and 86 degrees of freedom is 1.662765):

$$128.4362 - 1.662765 * 13.82446 < b_3 < 128.4362 + 1.662765 * 13.82446$$

$$105.44 < b_3 < 151.42$$

Table 7.11   Regression results with heteroskedasticity

Dependent Variable: PRICE
Method: Least Squares
Date: 02/03/04   Time: 01:52
Sample: 1 88
Included observations: 88

Variable	Coefficient	Std. Error	t-Statistic	Prob.
C	−19315.00	31046.62	−0.622129	0.5355
Rooms	15198.19	9483.517	1.602590	0.1127
Sqfeet	128.4362	13.82446	9.290506	0.0000

R-squared	0.631918	Mean dependent var	293546.0
Adjusted R-squared	0.623258	S.D. dependent var	102713.4
S.E. of regression	63044.84	Akaike info criterion	24.97458
Sum squared resid	3.38E+11	Schwarz criterion	25.05903
Log likelihood	−1095.881	F-statistic	72.96353
Durbin–Watson stat	1.858074	Prob(F-statistic)	0.000000

while for the White corrected case it will be:

$$128.4362 - 1.662765 * 19.59089 < b_3 < 128.4362 + 1.662765 * 19.59089$$

$$112.44 < b_3 < 144.38$$

Therefore, the White's corrected standard errors provide us with a better (more accurate) estimation.

Table 7.12 Heteroskedasticity-corrected regression results (White's method)

Dependent Variable: PRICE
Method: Least Squares
Date: 02/05/04 Time: 20:30
Sample: 1 88
Included observations: 88
White Heteroskedasticity-Consistent Standard Errors & Covariance

Variable	Coefficient	Std. Error	t-Statistic	Prob.
C	−19315.00	**41520.50**	−0.465192	0.6430
Rooms	15198.19	**8943.735**	1.699311	0.0929
Sqfeet	128.4362	**19.59089**	6.555914	0.0000

R-squared	0.631918	Mean dependent var	293546.0
Adjusted R-squared	0.623258	S.D. dependent var	102713.4
S.E. of regression	63044.84	Akaike info criterion	24.97458
Sum squared resid	3.38E + 11	Schwarz criterion	25.05903
Log likelihood	−1095.881	F-statistic	72.96353
Durbin–Watson stat	1.757956	Prob(F-statistic)	0.000000

Table 7.13 Heteroskedasticity-corrected regression results (weighted LS method)

Date: 02/05/04 Time: 20:54
Sample: 1 88
Included observations: 88
Weighting series: SQFEET^(−.5)
White Heteroskedasticity-Consistent Standard Errors & Covariance

Variable	Coefficient	Std. Error	t-Statistic	Prob.
C	8008.412	36830.04	0.217442	0.8284
Rooms	11578.30	9036.235	1.281319	0.2036
Sqfeet	121.2817	18.36504	6.603944	0.0000

Weighted Statistics

R-squared	0.243745	Mean dependent var	284445.3
Adjusted R-squared	0.225950	S.D. dependent var	67372.90
S.E. of regression	59274.73	Akaike info criterion	24.85125
Sum squared resid	2.99E+11	Schwarz criterion	24.93570
Log likelihood	−1090.455	F-statistic	53.20881
Durbin–Watson stat	1.791178	Prob(F-statistic)	0.000000

Unweighted Statistics

R-squared	0.628156	Mean dependent var	293546.0
Adjusted R-squared	0.619406	S.D. dependent var	102713.4
S.E. of regression	63366.27	Sum squared resid	3.41E+11
Durbin–Watson stat	1.719838		

Alternatively, EViews allows us to use the weighted or generalized least squares method as well. If we assume that the variable which is causing the heteroskedasticity is the *sq feet* variable, or in mathematical notation we assume that:

$$Var(u_i) = \sigma_i^2 = \sigma^2 sqfeet \tag{7.41}$$

then the weight variable will be $1/\sqrt{sqfeet}$. To do this we need to click on **Quick/Estimate Equation** and then on **Options**, this time checking next to the **Weighted LS/TSLS** box and enter the weighting variable $1/\sqrt{sqfeet}$ in the box by typing:

```
sqfeet^(-.5)
```

The results from this method are given in Table 7.13 below and are clearly different from the simple OLS estimation. We will leave it as an exercise for the reader to calculate and compare standard errors and confidence intervals for this case.

Questions and exercises

Questions

1 State briefly what are the consequences of heteroskedasticity in simple OLS.

2 Describe the Goldfeld–Quandt test for detection of heteroskedasticity.

3 Show how one can apply the method of weighted least squares in order to resolve heteroskedasticity.

4 Discuss and show mathematically what is the problem in terms of interpretation of the estimated coefficients, when applying WLS and the weight is an explanatory variable of the original model.

5 Consider the following model:

$$Y_i = \beta_1 + \beta_2 X_{2i} + \beta_3 X_{3i} + u_i$$

where $Var(u_i) = \sigma^2 X_{2i}$. Find the generalized least squares estimates.

6 Define heteroskedasticity and provide examples of econometric models where heteroskedasticity is likely to exist.

Exercise 7.1

Use the data in the file houseprice.wf1 to estimate a model of:

$$price_i = \beta_1 + \beta_2 sqfeet_i + u_i$$

Check for heteroskedasticity using the White and the Goldfeld–Quandt tests. Obtain the generalized least squares estimates for the following assumptions: (a) $Var(u_i) = \sigma^2 sqfeet_i$ and (b) $Var(u_i) = \sigma^2 sqfeet_i^2$. Comment on the sensitivity of the estimates and their standard errors to the heteroskedastic specification. For each of the two cases, use both the White and the Goldfeld–Quandt tests to see whether heteroskedasticity has been eliminated.

Exercise 7.2

Use the data in Greek_SME.wf1 to estimate the effect of size (proxied by number of employees) to the profit/sales ratio. Check whether the residuals in this equation are heteroskedastic by applying all the tests we have described (both formal and informal) for detection of heteroskedacity. If there is heteroskedasticity, obtain the White's corrected standard error estimates and construct confidence intervals to see the differences of the simple OLS and the White's estimates.

Exercise 7.3

Use the data in police.wf1 to estimate the equation that relates the actual value of the current budget (Y) with the expected value of the budget (X). Check for heteroskedasticity in this regression equation with all the known tests described in this chapter.

Exercise 7.4

The file sleep.xls contains data for 706 individuals concerning sleeping habits and possible determinants of sleeping time. Estimate the following regression equation:

$$sleep = b_0 + b_1 totwrk + b_2 educ + b_3 age + b_4 yngkid + b_5 male + u \qquad (7.42)$$

(a) Check whether there is evidence of heteroskedasticity.

(b) Is the estimated variance of u higher for men than women?

(c) Reestimate the model correcting for heteroskedasticity. Compare the results obtained in (c) with those in part from the simple OLS estimation.

Exercise 7.5

Use the data in the file houseprice.xls to estimate the following equation:

$$price = b_0 + b_1 lotsize + b_2 sqrft + b_3 bdrms + u \qquad (7.43)$$

(a) Check whether there is evidence of heteroskedasticity.

(b) Reestimate the equation but this time instead of *price* use log(*price*) as the dependent variable. Check for heteroskedasticity again. Is there any change in your conclusion in (a)?

(c) What does this example suggest about heteroskedasticity and the transformation used for the dependent variable?

8 Autocorrelation

Introduction: what is autocorrelation?

We know that the use of OLS to estimate a regression model leads us to BLUE Estimates of the parameters only when all the assumptions of the CLRM are satisfied. In the previous chapter we examined the case where assumption 5 does not hold. This chapter examines the effects on the OLS estimators when assumption 6 of the CLRM is violated.

Assumption 6 of the CLRM states that the covariances and correlations between different disturbances are all zero:

$$Cov(u_t, u_s) = 0 \quad \text{for all } t \neq s \tag{8.1}$$

This assumption states that the error terms u_t and u_s are independently distributed, which is called serial independence. If this assumption is no longer true, then the disturbances are not pairwise independent, but are pairwise autocorrelated (or serially correlated). In this situation:

$$Cov(u_t, u_s) \neq 0 \quad \text{for some } t \neq s \tag{8.2}$$

which means that an error occurring at period t may be correlated with one at period s.

Autocorrelation is most likely to occur in a time-series framework. When data are ordered in chronological order, the error in one period may affect the error in the next (or other) time period(s). (It is highly likely that there will be intercorrelations among successive observations especially when the interval is short, such as daily, weekly or monthly frequencies compared to a cross-sectional data set.) For example an unexpected increase in consumer confidence can cause a consumption function equation to underestimate consumption for two or more periods. In cross-sectional data, the problem of autocorrelation is less likely to exist because we can easily change the arrangement of the data without meaningfully altering the results. (However, this is not true in the case of spatial autocorrelation, but this is beyond the scope of this text.)

What causes autocorrelation?

One factor that can cause autocorrelation is *omitted variables*. Suppose that Y_t is related to X_{2t} and X_{3t} but we, wrongfully, do not include X_{3t} in our model. The effect of X_{3t} will be captured by the disturbances u_t. If X_{3t}, as many economic time series depends on $X_{3,t-1}, X_{3,t-2}$ and so on. This will lead to unavoidable correlation among u_t and u_{t-1}, u_{t-2} and so on. Thus, omitted variables can be a cause for autocorrelation.

Autocorrelation can also occur due to *misspecification* of the model. Suppose that Y_t is connected to X_{2t} with a quadratic relationship $Y_t = \beta_1 + \beta_2 X_{2t}^2 + u_t$, but we, wrongfully, assume and estimate a straight line $Y_t = \beta_1 + \beta_2 X_{2t} + u_t$. Then, the error term obtained from the straight line specification will depend on X_{2t}^2. If X_{2t} is increasing or decreasing over time, u_t will also be increasing or decreasing over time, indicating autocorrelation.

A third factor is *systematic errors in measurement*. Suppose a company updates its inventory at a given period in time; if a systematic error occurred in its measurement, then the cumulative inventory stock will exhibit accumulated measurement errors. These errors will show up as an autocorrelated procedure.

First and higher order autocorrelation

The simplest and most commonly observed case of autocorrelation is first-order serial correlation. (The terms serial correlation and autocorrelation are identical and will be used in this text interchangeably.) Consider the multiple regression model:

$$Y_t = \beta_1 + \beta_2 X_{2t} + \beta_3 X_{3t} + \cdots + \beta_k X_{kt} + u_t \tag{8.3}$$

in which the current observation of the error term (u_t) is a function of the previous (lagged) observation of the error term (u_{t-1}) i.e.:

$$u_t = \rho u_{t-1} + \varepsilon_t \tag{8.4}$$

where ρ is the parameter depicting the functional relationship among observations of the error term (u_t) and ε_t is a new error term which is iid (identically independently distributed). The coefficient ρ is called the first-order autocorrelation coefficient and takes values from -1 to 1 (or $|\rho| < 1$) in order to avoid explosive behaviour (we will explain this analytically in Chapter 13, where we describe the ARIMA models).

It is obvious that the size of ρ will determine the strength of serial correlation, and we can differentiate three cases:

(a) If ρ is zero, then we have no serial correlation, because $u_t = \varepsilon_t$ and therefore an iid error term.

(b) If ρ approaches unity, the value of the previous observation of the error (u_{t-1}) becomes more important in determining the value of the current error term (u_t) and therefore greater positive serial correlation exists. In this case the current observation of the error term tends to have the same sign as the previous observation of the error term (i.e. negative will lead to negative, and positive will lead to positive). This is called positive serial correlation. Figure 8.1 shows how the residuals of a case of positive serial correlation appear.

(c) If ρ approaches -1, again obviously the strength of serial correlation will be very high. This time, however, we now have negative serial correlation. Negative serial correlation implies that there is some saw tooth like behaviour in the time plot of

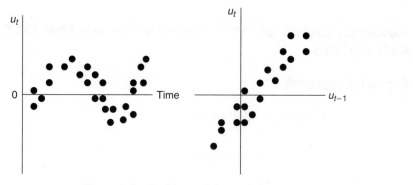

Figure 8.1 Positive serial correlation

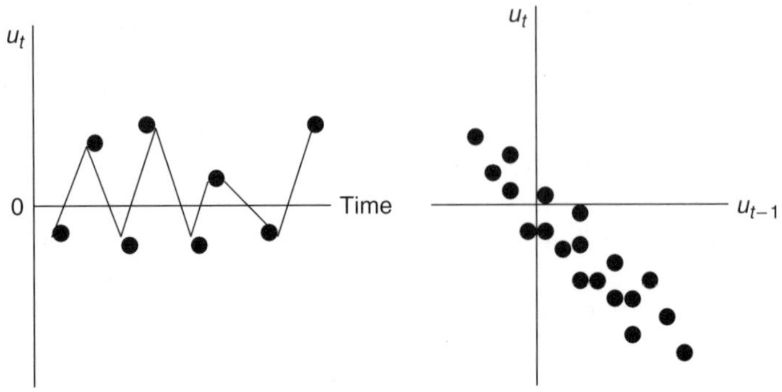

Figure 8.2 Negative serial correlation

the error terms. The signs of the error terms have a tendency to switch signs from negative to positive and vice versa in consecutive observations. Figure 8.2 depicts the case of negative serial correlation.

In general, in economics, negative serial correlation is much less likely to happen that positive serial correlation.

Serial correlation can take many forms and we can have disturbances that follow higher orders of serial correlation. Consider the following model:

$$Y_t = \beta_1 + \beta_2 X_{2t} + \beta_3 X_{3t} + \cdots + \beta_k X_{kt} + u_t \tag{8.5}$$

where

$$u_t = \rho_1 u_{t-1} + \rho_2 u_{t-2} + \cdots + \rho_p u_{t-p} + \varepsilon_t \tag{8.6}$$

In this case, we say that we have pth-order serial correlation. If we have quarterly data and we omit seasonal effects, for example, we might expect to find that a 4th-order serial correlation is present; while, similarly, monthly data might exhibit 12th-order serial correlation. In general, however, cases of higher-order serial correlation are not as likely to happen as the first-order type that we analytically examined before.

Consequences of autocorrelation on the OLS estimators

A general approach

Consider the classical linear regression model:

$$Y_t = \beta_1 + \beta_2 X_{2t} + \beta_3 X_{3t} + \cdots + \beta_k X_{kt} + u_t \tag{8.7}$$

If the error term (u_t) in this equation is known to exhibit serial correlation, then the consequences on the OLS estimates can be summarized as follows:

1 The OLS estimators of the $\hat{\beta}$s are still unbiased and consistent. This is because both unbiasedness and consistency do not depend on assumption 6 (see the proofs of unbiasedness and consistency in Chapters 4 and 5) which is in this case violated.

2 The OLS estimators will be inefficient and therefore no longer BLUE.

3 The estimated variances of the regression coefficients will be biased and inconsistent, and therefore hypothesis testing is no longer valid. In most of the cases, R^2 will be overestimated (indicating a better fit than the one that truly exists) and the t-statistics will tend to be higher (indicating higher significance of our estimates than the correct one).

A more mathematical approach

First we will examine how serial correlation affects the form of the variance–covariance matrix of the residuals, and then we will use this to show why the variance of the $\hat{\beta}$s in a multiple regression model will no longer be correct.

Effect on the variance–covariance matrix of the error terms

Recall from Chapter 5 (p. 66ff.) that the variance–covariance matrix of the residuals, because of assumptions 5 and 6, looks like:

$$E(\mathbf{uu'}) = \begin{pmatrix} \sigma^2 & 0 & 0 & \cdots & 0 \\ 0 & \sigma^2 & 0 & 0 & 0 \\ 0 & 0 & \sigma^2 & \cdots & 0 \\ \cdots & \cdots & \cdots & & \cdots \\ 0 & 0 & 0 & \cdots & \sigma^2 \end{pmatrix} = \sigma^2 \mathbf{I_n} \tag{8.8}$$

where $\mathbf{I_n}$ is an $n \times n$ identity matrix.

The presence of serial correlation shows clearly that assumption 6 is violated. Therefore, the non-diagonal terms of the variance–covariance matrix of the residuals will no longer be zero. Let's assume that the error terms are serially correlated of order one. We therefore have that:

$$u_t = \rho u_{t-1} + \varepsilon_t \tag{8.9}$$

Using the lag operator, $LX_t = X_{t-1}$, equation (8.9) can be rewritten as:

$$(1 - \rho L)u_t = \varepsilon_t \tag{8.10}$$

or

$$u_t = \frac{1}{(1 - \rho L)}\varepsilon_t$$

$$= (1 + \rho L + \rho^2 L^2 + \cdots)\varepsilon_t$$

$$= \varepsilon_t + \rho\varepsilon_{t-1} + \rho^2\varepsilon_{t-2} + \rho^3\varepsilon_{t-3} + \cdots \tag{8.11}$$

Squaring both sides of (8.11) and taking expectations, yields:

$$E(u_t^2) = Var(u_t) = \frac{\sigma_\varepsilon^2}{1 - \rho^2} \tag{8.12}$$

Note that the solution for $Var(u_t)$ does not involve t, therefore the u_t series has a constant variance given by:

$$\sigma_u^2 = \frac{\sigma_\varepsilon^2}{1 - \rho^2} \tag{8.13}$$

Using (8.11) it is simple to show that the covariances $E(u_t, u_{t-1})$ will be given by:

$$E(u_t, u_{t-1}) = \rho \sigma_u^2 \tag{8.14}$$

$$E(u_t, u_{t-2}) = \rho^2 \sigma_u^2 \tag{8.15}$$

$$\cdots \tag{8.16}$$

$$E(u_t, u_{t-s}) = \rho^s \sigma_u^2 \tag{8.17}$$

Thus the variance–covariance matrix of the disturbances (for the first-order serial correlation case) will be given by:

$$E(\mathbf{uu}') = \sigma^2 \begin{pmatrix} 1 & \rho & \rho^2 & \cdots & \rho^{n-1} \\ \rho & 1 & \rho & \cdots & \rho^{n-2} \\ \cdots & \cdots & \cdots & & \cdots \\ \rho^{n-1} & \rho^{n-2} & \rho^{n-3} & \cdots & 1 \end{pmatrix} = \Omega_2\,{}^* \tag{8.18}$$

Effect on the OLS estimators of the multiple regression model

Recall that the variance–covariance matrix of the OLS estimators $\hat{\beta}$ is given by:

$$\begin{aligned} Cov(\hat{\beta}) &= \mathbf{E}[(\hat{\beta} - \beta)(\hat{\beta} - \beta)'] \\ &= E\{[(X'X)^{-1}X'\mathbf{u}][(X'X)^{-1}X'\mathbf{u}]'\} \\ &= E\{(X'X)^{-1}X'\mathbf{uu}'X(X'X)^{-1}\}^\dagger \\ &= (X'X)^{-1}X'E(\mathbf{uu}')X(X'X)^{-1}{}^\ddagger \\ &= (X'X)^{-1}X'\Omega_2 X(X'X)^{-1} \end{aligned} \tag{8.19}$$

which is totally different from the classical expression $\sigma^2(X'X)^{-1}$. This is because assumption 6 is no longer valid, and of course Ω_2 denotes the new variance–covariance matrix presented above, whatever form it may happen to take. Therefore, using the classical expression to calculate the variances, standard errors and t-statistics of

---

* We denote this matrix of Ω_2 in order to differentiate from the Ω matrix in the heteroskedasticity case in Chapter 10.

† This is because $(AB)' = B'A'$.

‡ This is because, according to assumption 2, the Xs are non-random.

the estimated $\hat{\beta}$s will lead us to incorrect conclusions. Formulae 8.19 (which is also similar to 7.9) forms the basis for what is often called 'Robust' inference, i.e. the derivation of standard errors and 't' statistics which are correct even when some of the OLS assumptions are violated. Basically what happens is that we assume a particular form for the Ω matrix and then use (8.19) to calculate a corrected covariance matrix.

Detecting autocorrelation

The graphical method

One simple way to detect autocorrelation is by examining whether the residual plots against time and the scatter plot of $\hat{u}_t$ against $\hat{u}_{t-1}$ exhibit patterns similar to those presented in Figures 8.1 and 8.2 above. In such cases we say that we have evidence of positive serial correlation when the pattern is similar to that of Figure 8.1, and negative serial correlation if similar to that of Figure 8.2. An example with real data is given below.

Example: detecting autocorrelation using the graphical method

The file ser_corr.wf1 contains the following quarterly data from 1985q1 to 1994q2:
  lcons = the consumer's expenditure on food in £millions at constant 1992 prices.
  ldisp = disposable income in £millions at constant 1992 prices.
  lprice = the relative price index of food (1992 = 100).
Denoting *lcons*, *ldisp* and *lprice* by C_t, D_t and P_t respectively, we estimate in EViews the following regression equation:

$$C_t = b_1 + b_2 D_t + b_3 P_t + u_t$$

by typing in the EViews command line:

```
ls lcons c ldisp lprice
```

Results from this regression are shown in Table 8.1.
  After estimating the regression, we store the residuals of the regression in a vector by typing the command:

```
genr res01=resid
```

A plot of the residuals obtained by the command:

```
plot res01
```

is presented in Figure 8.3, while a scatter plot of the residuals against the residuals at $t-1$ obtained by using the command:

```
scat res01 (-1) res01
```

is given in Figure 8.4.

Table 8.1   Regression results from the computer example

Dependent Variable: LCONS
Method: Least Squares
Date: 02/12/04 Time: 14:25
Sample: 1985:1 1994:2
Included observations: 38

Variable	Coefficient	Std. Error	t-Statistic	Prob.
C	2.485434	0.788349	3.152708	0.0033
LDISP	0.529285	0.292327	1.810589	0.0788
LPRICE	−0.064029	0.146506	−0.437040	0.6648

R-squared	0.234408	Mean dependent var	4.609274
Adjusted R-squared	0.190660	S.D. dependent var	0.051415
S.E. of regression	0.046255	Akaike info criterion	−3.233656
Sum squared resid	0.074882	Schwarz criterion	−3.104373
Log likelihood	64.43946	F-statistic	5.358118
Durbin–Watson stat	0.370186	Prob(F-statistic)	0.009332

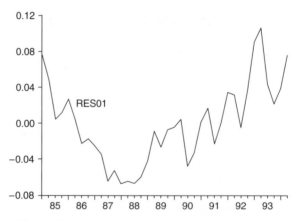

Figure 8.3   Residuals plot from computer example

From both these figures it is clear that the residuals are serially correlated and particularly positively serially correlated.

The Durbin–Watson test

The most frequently used statistical test for the presence of serial correlation is the Durbin–Watson (DW) test (see Durbin and Watson, 1950), which is valid when the following assumptions are met:

(a) the regression model includes a constant;

(b) serial correlation is assumed to be of first-order only; and

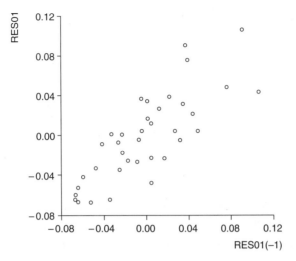

Figure 8.4 Residuals scatter plot from computer example

(c) the equation does not include a lagged dependent variable as an explanatory variable.

Consider the model:

$$Y_t = \beta_1 + \beta_2 X_{2t} + \beta_3 X_{3t} + \cdots + \beta_k X_{kt} + u_t \tag{8.20}$$

where:

$$u_t = \rho u_{t-1} + \varepsilon_t \quad |\rho| < 1 \tag{8.21}$$

Then under the null hypothesis H_0: $\rho = 0$ the DW test involves the following steps:

Step 1 Estimate the model by using OLS and obtain the residuals $\hat{u}_t$.

Step 2 Calculate the DW test statistic given by:

$$d = \frac{\sum_{t=2}^{n}(\hat{u}_t - \hat{u}_{t-1})^2}{\sum_{t=1}^{n}\hat{u}_t^2} \tag{8.22}$$

Step 3 Construct Table 8.2, substituting with your calculated d_U, d_L, $4-d_U$ and $4-d_L$ that you will obtain from the DW critical values table that is given in the Appendix. Note that table of critical values is according to k' which is the number of explanatory variables excluding the constant.

Step 4a To test for positive serial correlation the hypotheses are:

$$H_0: \quad \rho = 0 \text{ no autocorrelation.}$$

$$H_a: \quad \rho > 0 \text{ positive autocorrelation.}$$

Table 8.2 The DW test

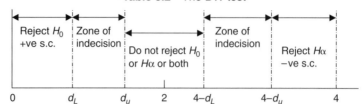

1 If $d \leq d_L$ we reject H_0 and conclude in favour of positive serial correlation.

2 If $d \geq d_U$ we cannot reject H_0 and therefore there is no positive serial correlation.

3 In the special case where $d_L < d < d_U$ the test is inconclusive.

Step 4b To test for negative serial correlation the hypotheses are:

$$H_0: \quad \rho = 0 \text{ no autocorrelation.}$$

$$H_a: \quad \rho < 0 \text{ negative autocorrelation.}$$

1 If $d \geq 4 - d_L$ we reject H_0 and conclude in favour of negative serial correlation.

2 If $d \leq 4 - d_U$ we cannot reject H_0 and therefore there is no negative serial correlation.

3 In the special case where $4 - d_U < d < 4 - d_L$ the test is inconclusive.

The inconclusiveness of the DW test comes from the fact that the small sample distribution for the DW statistic depends on the X variables and is difficult to determine in general a prefered testing procedure is the LM test to be described later.

A rule of thumb for the DW test

From the estimated residuals we can get an estimate of ρ as:

$$\hat{\rho} = \frac{\sum_{t=2}^{n} \hat{u}_t \hat{u}_{t-1}}{\sum_{t=1}^{n} \hat{u}_t^2} \tag{8.23}$$

It is shown in the Appendix that the DW statistic is approximately equal to $d = 2(1 - \hat{\rho})$. Because ρ by definition ranges from -1 to 1, the range for d will be from 0 to 4. Therefore, we can have three different cases:

(a) $\rho = 0$; $d = 2$: therefore, a value of d near to 2 indicates that there is no evidence of serial correlation.

(b) $\rho \simeq 1$; $d \simeq 0$: a strong positive autocorrelation means that ρ will be close to $+1$, and thus d will get very low values (close to zero) for positive autocorrelation.

(c) $\rho \simeq -1$; $d \simeq 4$: similarly, when ρ is close to -1 then d will be close to 4 indicating strong negative serial correlation.

From this analysis we can see that, as a rule of thumb, when the DW test statistic is very close to 2 then we do not have serial correlation.

The DW test in EViews and Microfit

Both EViews and Microfit report the DW test statistic directly in the diagnostics of every regression output; the DW statistic is reported in the final line of the left-hand corner. The only work that remains for the researcher is to construct the table with the critical values and check whether serial correlation exists or not, and of what kind. An example is given below.

Computer example of the DW test

From the regression results output of the previous example (graphical detection of autocorrelation) we observe that the DW statistic is equal to 0.37. Finding the critical values d_L and d_U for $n = 38$ and $k' = 2$ and putting those in the DW table we have the results shown in Table 8.3. It is obvious that $d = 0.37$ is less than $d_L = 1.11$, and therefore there is strong evidence of positive serial correlation.

The Breusch–Godfrey LM test for serial correlation

The DW test has several drawbacks that make its use inappropriate in various cases. For instance (a) it may give inconclusive results, (b) it is not applicable when a lagged dependent variable is used, and (c) it can't take into account higher orders of serial correlation.

For these reasons Breusch (1978) and Godfrey (1978) developed an *LM* test which can accommodate all the above cases. Consider the model:

$$Y_t = \beta_1 + \beta_2 X_{2t} + \beta_3 X_{3t} + \cdots + \beta_k X_{kt} + u_t \tag{8.24}$$

Table 8.3 An example of the DW test

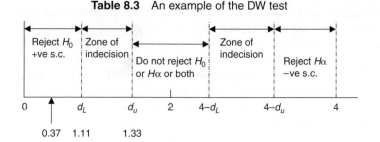

where

$$u_t = \rho_1 u_{t-1} + \rho_2 u_{t-2} + \cdots + \rho_p u_{t-p} + \varepsilon_t \tag{8.25}$$

The Breusch–Godfrey *LM* test combines these two equations:

$$Y_t = \beta_1 + \beta_2 X_{2t} + \beta_3 X_{3t} + \cdots + \beta_k X_{kt} + \rho_1 u_{t-1} + \rho_2 u_{t-2} + \cdots$$
$$+ \rho_p u_{t-p} + \varepsilon_t \tag{8.26}$$

and therefore the null and the alternative hypotheses are:

H_0: $\rho_1 = \rho_2 = \cdots = \rho_p = 0$ no autocorrelation.

H_a: at least one of the ρs is not zero, thus, serial correlation.

The steps for carrying out the test are the following:

Step 1   Estimate (8.24) by OLS and obtain $\hat{u}_t$.

Step 2   Run the following regression model with the number of lags used (p) being determined according to the order of serial correlation you are willing to test.

$$\hat{u}_t = \alpha_0 + \alpha_1 X_{2t} \ldots \alpha_R X_{Rt} + \alpha_{R+1} \hat{u}_{t-1} \ldots \alpha_{R+P} \hat{u}_{t-p}$$

Step 3   Compute the *LM* statistic $= (n - p)R^2$ from the regression run in step 2. If this *LM* statistic is bigger than the χ_p^2 critical value for a given level of significance, then we reject the null of serial correlation and conclude that serial correlation is present. Note that the choice of p is arbitrary. However, the periodicity of the data (quarterly, monthly, weekly etc.) will often give us a suggestion for the size of p.

The Breusch–Godfrey test in EViews and Microfit

After estimating a regression equation in EViews, in order to perform the Breusch–Godfrey LM test we move from the estimation results window to **View/Residual Tests/Serial Correlation LM test**... EViews asks for the number of lags to be included in the test, and after specifying that and clicking on <**OK**> the results of the test are obtained. The interpretation is as usual.

Microfit reports the LM test for first-order serial correlation directly in the diagnostic tests section of the regression results output. The Breusch – Godfrey *LM* test is for Microfit test A. If we need to test for higher-order serial correlation we close the results window by clicking on <**close**> to obtain the **Post Regression** menu. From that menu choose option 2. Move to the **Hypothesis Testing** menu and click <**OK**>. From the hypothesis testing menu choose option 1, **LM tests for Serial Correlation (OLS, IV, NLS and IV-NLS)**, and click <**OK**>. You will then be asked to determine the number of lags in the **Input an integer** window and after clicking <**OK**> the results of the test will be obtained. An example with the use of EViews is given below.

Computer example of the Breusch–Godfrey test

Continuing with the consumption, disposable income and price relationship, we proceed by testing for fourth-order serial correlation due to the fact that we have quarterly data. In order to test for serial correlation of fourth order we use the Breusch–Godfrey LM test. From the estimated regression results window we go to **View/Residual Tests/Serial Correlation LM Test** and specify as the number of lags the number 4. The results of this test are shown in Table 8.4.

We can see from the first columns that the values of both the *LM* statistic and the *F* statistic are quite high, suggesting the rejection of the null of no serial correlation. It is also evident that this is so due to the fact that the *p*-values are very small (smaller than 0.05 for a 95% confidence interval). So, serial correlation is definitely present. However, if we observe the regression results, we see that only the first lagged residual term is statistically significant, indicating, most probably, that the serial correlation is of first order. Rerunning the test for a first-order serial correlation the results are as shown in Table 8.5.

This time the *LM* statistic is much higher, as well as the *t* statistic of the lagged residual term. So, the autocorrelation is definitely of first order.

Durbin's *h* test in the presence of lagged dependent variables

We mentioned before in the assumptions of the DW test, that the DW test is not applicable when our regression model includes lagged dependent variables as

Table 8.4 Results of the Breusch–Godfrey test (4th order s.c.)

Breusch-Godfrey Serial Correlation LM Test:

F-statistic	17.25931	Probability	0.000000
Obs*R-squared	**26.22439**	Probability	**0.000029**

Test Equation:
Dependent Variable: RESID
Method: Least Squares
Date: 02/12/04 Time: 22:51

Variable	Coefficient	Std. Error	t-Statistic	Prob.
C	−0.483704	0.489336	−0.988491	0.3306
LDISP	0.178048	0.185788	0.958341	0.3453
LPRICE	−0.071428	0.093945	−0.760322	0.4528
RESID(−1)	0.840743	0.176658	**4.759155**	0.0000
RESID(−2)	−0.340727	0.233486	−1.459306	0.1545
RESID(−3)	0.256762	0.231219	1.110471	0.2753
RESID(−4)	0.196959	0.186608	1.055465	0.2994

R-squared	0.690115	Mean dependent var	1.28E−15
Adjusted R-squared	0.630138	S.D. dependent var	0.044987
S.E. of regression	0.027359	Akaike info criterion	−4.194685
Sum squared resid	0.023205	Schwarz criterion	−3.893024
Log likelihood	86.69901	F-statistic	11.50621
Durbin–Watson stat	1.554119	Prob(F-statistic)	0.000001

Table 8.5   Results of the Breusch–Godfrey test (1st order s.c.)

Breusch–Godfrey Serial Correlation LM Test:

F-statistic	53.47468	Probability	0.000000
Obs*R-squared	**23.23001**	Probability	**0.000001**

Test Equation:
Dependent Variable: RESID
Method: Least Squares
Date: 02/12/04 Time: 22:55

Variable	Coefficient	Std. Error	t-Statistic	Prob.
C	−0.585980	0.505065	−1.160208	0.2540
LDISP	0.245740	0.187940	1.307546	0.1998
LPRICE	−0.116819	0.094039	−1.242247	0.2226
RESID(−1)	0.828094	0.113241	**7.312638**	0.0000

R-squared	0.611316	Mean dependent var	1.28E − 15
Adjusted R-squared	0.577020	S.D. dependent var	0.044987
S.E. of regression	0.029258	Akaike info criterion	−4.126013
Sum squared resid	0.029105	Schwarz criterion	−3.953636
Log likelihood	82.39425	F-statistic	17.82489
Durbin–Watson stat	1.549850	Prob(F-statistic)	0.000000

explanatory variables. Therefore, if the model under examination has the form:

$$Y_t = \beta_1 + \beta_2 X_{2t} + \beta_3 X_{3t} + \cdots + \beta_k X_{kt} + \gamma Y_{t-1} + u_t \qquad (8.27)$$

the DW test is no longer valid.

Durbin (1970) devised a test statistic that can be used for such models, and this h statistic has the form:

$$h = \left(1 - \frac{d}{2}\right) \sqrt{\frac{n}{1 - n\sigma_{\hat{\gamma}}^2}} \qquad (8.28)$$

where n is the number of observations, d is the regular DW statistic defined in (8.22) and $\sigma_{\hat{\gamma}}^2$ is the estimated variance of the coefficient of the lagged dependent variable. For large samples this statistic follows a normal distribution. So, the steps involved in the h test are the following:

Step 1   Estimate (8.27) by OLS to obtain the residuals and calculate the DW statistic given by (8.22). (As we noted before, in practical terms this step using EViews involves only the estimation of the equation by OLS. EViews provides the DW statistic in its reported regression diagnostics. Using Microfit this step alone will also give the h statistic so step 2 is not needed.)

Step 2   Calculate the h statistic given by (8.28).

Step 3   The hypotheses are:

$$H_0: \quad \rho = 0 \text{ no autocorrelation.}$$

$$H_a: \quad \rho < 0 \text{ autocorrelation is present.}$$

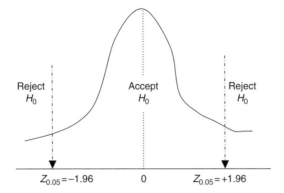

Figure 8.5 Durbin's *h* test, graphically

Step 4 Compare the *h* statistic with the critical value (for large samples and for $\alpha = 0.05$, $z = \pm 1.96$). If the *h* statistic exceeds the critical value, then H_0 is rejected and we conclude that there is serial correlation (see also Figure 8.5).

The *h* test in EViews and Microfit

EViews reports only the DW test, independently of whether a lagged dependent variable is used as a regressor or not. Therefore step 2 is needed in order to calculate the *h* statistic. In Microfit, though, inclusion of a lagged dependent variable gives by default the *h* statistic in the diagnostics of the regression results output window. This is located next to the DW statistic and is the last line of the right-hand corner. Microfit also reports the probability limit for this statistic, so if it is bigger than 0.05 the reader can understand very quickly that serial correlation is not present in this case. An example of the *h* test using EViews is given below.

Computer example of Durbin's *h* test

If we want to estimate the following regression model:

$$C_t = b_1 + b_2 D_t + b_3 P_t + b_4 C_{t-1} + u_t$$

which includes a lagged dependent variable, we know that the DW test is no longer valid. Thus, in this case we need to use either Durbin's *h* test or the LM test. Running the regression model by typing:

```
ls lcons c ldisp lprice lcons(-1)
```

we get the results shown in Table 8.6.

Table 8.6   Regression results with a lagged dependent variable

Dependent Variable: LCONS
Method: Least Squares
Date: 02/12/04 Time: 22:59
Sample(adjusted): 1985:2 1994:2
Included observations: 37 after adjusting endpoints

Variable	Coefficient	Std. Error	t-Statistic	Prob.
C	−0.488356	0.575327	−0.848831	0.4021
LDISP	0.411340	0.169728	2.423524	0.0210
LPRICE	−0.120416	0.086416	−1.393442	0.1728
LCONS(−1)	0.818289	**0.103707**	7.890392	0.0000

R-squared	0.758453	Mean dependent var		4.608665
Adjusted R-squared	0.736494	S.D. dependent var		0.051985
S.E. of regression	0.026685	Akaike info criterion		−4.307599
Sum squared resid	0.023500	Schwarz criterion		−4.133446
Log likelihood	83.69058	F-statistic		34.53976
Durbin–Watson stat	**1.727455**	Prob(F-statistic)		0.000000

The DW statistic is equal to 1.727455, and from this we can get the h statistic from the formula:

$$h = \left(1 - \frac{d}{2}\right) \sqrt{\frac{n}{1 - n\sigma_{\hat{\gamma}}^2}}$$

where $\sigma_{\hat{\gamma}}^2$ is the variance of the coefficient of LCONS$(-1) = (0.103707)^2 = 0.0107551$. Typing in EViews the following command we get the value of the h statistic:

```
scalar h= (1-1.727455/2)(37/(1-37*0.103707))^(.5)
```

and by double clicking on the scalar h we can see the value at the low left-hand corner as:

```
scalar h=1.0682889
```

and therefore because $h < z -$ critical $= 1.96$ we fail to reject the H_0 hypothesis and conclude that this model does not suffer from serial correlation.

Applying the LM test for this regression equation by clicking on **View/Residual Tests/Serial Correlation LM Test** and specifying the lag order to be equal to 1 (by typing 1 in the relevant box) we get the results shown in Table 8.7. From these results it is again clear that there is no serial correlation in this model.

Resolving autocorrelation

Since the presence of autocorrelation provides us with inefficient OLS estimators, it is important to have ways of correcting our estimates, and two different cases are presented in the next two sections.

Table 8.7   The Breusch–Godfrey LM test (again)

Breusch–Godfrey Serial Correlation LM Test:

F-statistic	0.680879	Probability	0.415393
Obs*R-squared	**0.770865**	Probability	**0.379950**

Test Equation:
Dependent Variable: RESID
Method: Least Squares
Date: 02/12/04 Time: 23:10

Variable	Coefficient	Std. Error	t-Statistic	Prob.
C	0.153347	0.607265	0.252521	0.8023
LDISP	0.018085	0.171957	0.105171	0.9169
LPRICE	0.003521	0.086942	0.040502	0.9679
LCONS(−1)	−0.054709	0.123515	−0.442932	0.6608
RESID(−1)	0.174392	0.211345	0.825154	0.4154

R-squared	0.020834	Mean dependent var	9.98E-16
Adjusted R-squared	−0.101562	S.D. dependent var	0.025549
S.E. of regression	0.026815	Akaike info criterion	−4.274599
Sum squared resid	0.023010	Schwarz criterion	−4.056908
Log likelihood	84.08009	F-statistic	0.170220
Durbin–Watson stat	1.855257	Prob(F-statistic)	0.952013

When ρ is known

Consider the model:

$$Y_t = \beta_1 + \beta_2 X_{2t} + \beta_3 X_{3t} + \cdots + \beta_k X_{kt} + u_t \tag{8.29}$$

where we know that u_t is autocorrelated and we speculate that it follows a first-order serial correlation, so that:

$$u_t = \rho u_{t-1} + \varepsilon_t \tag{8.30}$$

If (8.29) holds for period t, it will hold for period $t-1$ as well, so:

$$Y_{t-1} = \beta_1 + \beta_2 X_{2t-1} + \beta_3 X_{3t-1} + \cdots + \beta_k X_{kt-1} + u_{t-1} \tag{8.31}$$

Multiplying both sides of (8.31) by ρ, yields:

$$\rho Y_{t-1} = \beta_1 \rho + \beta_2 \rho X_{2t-1} + \beta_3 \rho X_{3t-1} + \cdots + \beta_k \rho X_{kt-1} + \rho u_{t-1} \tag{8.32}$$

and subtracting (8.32) from (8.29) we obtain:

$$Y_t - \rho Y_{t-1} = \beta_1(1-\rho) + \beta_2(X_{2t} - \rho X_{2t-1}) + \beta_3(X_{3t} - \rho X_{3t-1}) + \cdots$$
$$+ \beta_k(X_{kt} - \rho X_{kt-1}) + (u_t - \rho u_{t-1}) \tag{8.33}$$

or

$$Y_t^* = \beta_1^* + \beta_2 X_{2t}^* + \beta_3 X_{3t}^* + \cdots + \beta_k X_{kt}^* + \varepsilon_t \tag{8.34}$$

Table 8.8 Regression results for determining the value of ρ

Dependent Variable: RES01
Method: Least Squares
Date: 02/12/04 Time: 23:26
Sample(adjusted): 1985:2 1994:2
Included observations: 37 after adjusting endpoints

Variable	Coefficient	Std. Error	t-Statistic	Prob.
RES01(−1)	**0.799544**	0.100105	7.987073	0.0000

R-squared	0.638443	Mean dependent var	−0.002048
Adjusted R-squared	0.638443	S.D. dependent var	0.043775
S.E. of regression	0.026322	Akaike info criterion	−4.410184
Sum squared resid	0.024942	Schwarz criterion	−4.366646
Log likelihood	82.58841	Durbin–Watson stat	1.629360

Table 8.9 The generalized differencing regression results

Dependent Variable: LCONS_STAR
Method: Least Squares
Date: 02/12/04 Time: 23:49
Sample: 1985:1 1994:2
Included observations: 38

Variable	Coefficient	Std. Error	t-Statistic	Prob
BETA1_STAR	4.089403	1.055839	3.873131	0.0004
LDISP_STAR	0.349452	0.231708	1.508155	0.1405
LPRICE_STAR	−0.235900	0.074854	−3.151460	0.0033

R-squared	0.993284	Mean dependent var	0.974724
Adjusted R-squared	0.992900	S.D. dependent var	0.302420
S.E. of regression	0.025482	Akaike info criterion	−4.426070
Sum squared resid	0.022726	Schwarz criterion	−4.296787
Log likelihood	87.09532	Durbin–Watson stat	1.686825

where $Y_t^* = Y_t - \rho Y_{t-1}$, $\beta_1^* = \beta_1(1-\rho)$, and $X_{it}^* = (X_{it} - \rho X_{it-1})$.

Note that with this differencing procedure we lose one observation. In order to avoid this loss of one observation it is suggested that Y_1 and X_{i1} should be transformed for the first observation as follows:

$$Y_1^* = Y_1\sqrt{1-\rho^2} \quad \text{and} \quad X_{i1}^* = X_{i1}\sqrt{1-\rho^2} \tag{8.35}$$

The transformation that generated Y_t^*, β_1^* and X_{it}^* is known as quasi-differencing or generalized differencing. Note that the error term in (8.34) satisfies all the CLRM assumptions. So, if ρ is known we can apply OLS to (8.34) and obtain estimates that are BLUE. An example of the use of generalized differencing is provided below.

Computer example of the generalized differencing approach

In order to apply the generalized differencing estimators we first need to find an estimate of the ρ coefficient. Remember that from the first computer example we obtained the residual terms and we named them *res*01. Running a regression of *res*01 to *res*01(-1) we get the results shown in Table 8.9, from which we have that the ρ coefficient is equal to 0.799.

In order then to transform the variables for the first observation we need to enter the following commands in the EViews command window:

```
scalar rho=c(1)  [saves the estimate of the  r coefficient]
smpl 1985:1 1985:1 [sets the sample to be only the first observation]
genr lcons_star=((1-rho^2)^(0.5))*lcons
genr ldisp_star=((1-rho^2)^(0.5))*ldisp
genr lprice_star=((1-rho^2)^(0.5))*lprice
genr beta1_star=((1-rho^2)^(0.5))
```

where the three commands generate the starred variables and the final command creates the new constant.

To transform the variables for observations 2 to 38 we need to type the following commands in the EViews command window:

```
smpl 1985:2 1994:2
genr lcons_star=lcons-rho*lcons(-1)
genr ldisp_star=ldisp-rho*disp(-1)
genr lprice_star=lprice-rho*lprice(-1)
genr beta1_star=1-rho
```

And in order then to estimate the generalized differenced equation we need first to change the sample to all observations by typing:

```
smpl 1985:1 1994:2
```

and then to execute the following command:

```
ls lcons_star beta1_star ldisp_star lprice_star
```

the results of which are shown in Table 8.9.

When ρ is unknown

Although the method of generalized differencing seems to be very easy to apply, in practice the value of ρ is not known. Therefore, alternative procedures need to be developed in order to provide us with estimates of ρ and then of the regression model (8.34). Several procedures have been developed, with two being the most popular and important: (a) the Cochrane–Orcutt iterative procedure, and (b) the Hildreth–Lu search procedure. These two procedures are presented below.

The Cochrane–Orcutt iterative procedure

Cochrane and Orcutt (1949) developed an iterative procedure that can be presented through the following steps:

Step 1 Estimate the regression model (8.29) and obtain the residuals $\hat{u}_t$.

Step 2 Estimate the first-order serial correlation coefficient ρ by OLS from $\hat{u}_t = \rho \hat{u}_{t-1} + \varepsilon_t$.

Step 3 Transform the original variables as $Y_t^* = Y_t - \hat{\rho} Y_{t-1}, \beta_1^* = \beta_1(1 - \hat{\rho})$, and $X_{it}^* = (X_{it} - \hat{\rho} X_{it-1})$ for $t = 2, \ldots, n$ and as $Y_1^* = Y_1\sqrt{1 - \hat{\rho}^2}$ and $X_{i1}^* = X_{i1}\sqrt{1 - \hat{\rho}^2}$ for $t = 1$.

Step 4 Run the regression using the transformed variables and find the residuals of this regression. Since we do not know that the $\hat{\rho}$ obtained from step 2 is the 'best' estimate of ρ, go back to step 2 and repeat step 2 to step 4 for several rounds until the following stopping rule holds.

Stopping rule The iterative procedure can be stopped when the estimates of ρ from two successive iterations differ by no more than some preselected (very small) value, such as 0.001. The final $\hat{\rho}$ is used to get the estimates of (8.34). In general, the iterative procedure converges quickly and does not require more than 3 to 6 iterations.

EViews utilizes an iterative non-linear method for estimating generalized differencing results with AR(1) errors (autoregressive errors of order 1) in the presence of serial correlation. Since the procedure is iterative, it requires a number of repetitions in order to achieve convergence which is reported in the EViews results below the **included observations** information. The estimates from this iterative method can be obtained by simply adding the AR(1) error terms to the end of the equation specification list. So, if we have a model with variables Y and X, the simple linear regression command is:

```
ls y c x
```

If we know that the estimates suffer from serial correlation of order 1, then results can be obtained through the iterative process by using the command:

```
ls y c x ar(1)
```

EViews provides results in the regular way about the constant and the coefficient of the X variable, together with an estimate for ρ which will be the coefficient of the AR(1) term. An example is provided at the end of this section.

The Hildreth–Lu search procedure

Hildreth and Lu (1960) developed an alternative method to the Cochrane–Orcutt iterative procedure, their method consisting of the following steps:

Step 1 Choose a value for ρ (say ρ_1), and for this value transform the model as in (8.34) and estimate it by OLS.

Step 2 From the estimation in step 1 obtain the residuals $\hat{\varepsilon}_t$ and the residual sum of squares (RSS(ρ_1)). Next choose a different value of ρ (say ρ_2) and repeat steps 1 and 2.

Step 3 By varying ρ from -1 to $+1$ in some predetermined systematic way (lets say at steps of length 0.05), we can get a series of values of RSS(ρ_i). We choose that ρ for which RSS is minimized and the equation (8.34) that was estimated using that optimal ρ as the optimal solution.

This procedure is very hectic and involves lots of calculations. EViews provides results very quickly with the Cochrane–Orcutt iterative method (as we have shown above), and is usually preferred in cases of autocorrelation.

Computer example of the iterative procedure

To obtain results with the EViews iterative method and assuming a serial correlation of order one, we type the following command in EViews:

```
ls lcons c ldisp lprice ar(1)
```

the results from which are shown in Table 8.10.

We observe that it required 13 iterations in order to obtain convergent results. Also, the AR(1) coefficient (which is in fact the ρ) is equal to 0.974 which is much bigger than obtained in the previous computer example. However, this is not always the case; other examples lead to smaller discrepancies. The case here might be affected by the quarterly frequency of the data. If we use an AR(4) term in addition by the

Table 8.10   Results with the iterative procedure

Dependent Variable: LCONS
Method: Least Squares
Date: 02/12/04 Time: 23:51
Sample(adjusted): 1985:2 1994:2
Included observations: 37 after adjusting endpoints
Convergence achieved after 13 iterations

Variable	Coefficient	Std. Error	t-Statistic	Prob.
C	9.762759	1.067582	9.144742	0.0000
LDISP	-0.180461	0.222169	-0.812269	0.4225
LPRICE	-0.850378	0.057714	-14.73431	0.0000
AR(1)	**0.974505**	0.013289	**73.33297**	0.0000

R-squared	0.962878	Mean dependent var.		4.608665
Adjusted R-squared	0.959503	S.D. dependent var.		0.051985
S.E. of regression	0.010461	Akaike info. criterion		-6.180445
Sum squared resid	0.003612	Schwarz criterion		-6.006291
Log likelihood	118.3382	F-statistic		285.3174
Durbin–Watson stat	2.254662	Prob(F-statistic)		0.000000

Inverted AR Roots	0.97	

Table 8.11   Results with the iterative procedure and AR(4) term

Dependent Variable: LCONS
Method: Least Squares
Date: 02/12/04 Time: 23:57
Sample(adjusted): 1986:1 1994:2
Included observations: 34 after adjusting endpoints
Convergence achieved after 11 iterations

Variable	Coefficient	Std. Error	t-Statistic	Prob.
C	10.21009	0.984930	10.36632	0.0000
LDISP	−0.308133	0.200046	−1.540312	0.1343
LPRICE	−0.820114	0.065876	−12.44932	0.0000
AR(1)	**0.797678**	0.123851	**6.440611**	0.0000
AR(4)	0.160974	0.115526	1.393404	0.1741

R-squared	0.967582	Mean dependent var		4.610894
Adjusted R-squared	0.963111	S.D. dependent var		0.053370
S.E. of regression	0.010251	Akaike info criterion		−6.187920
Sum squared resid	0.003047	Schwarz criterion		−5.963455
Log likelihood	110.1946	F-statistic		216.3924
Durbin–Watson stat	2.045794	Prob(F-statistic)		0.000000

Inverted AR Roots	0.97	0.16+0.55i	0.16−0.55i	−0.50

command:

```
ls lcons c ldisp lprice ar(1) ar(4)
```

we get a ρ coefficient (see Table 8.11) which is very close to the one from the previous example.

Questions and exercises

Questions

1 What is autocorrelation? Which assumption of the CLRM is violated and why?

2 Explain what are the consequences of autocorrelation and how can it be resolved when ρ is known.

3 Explain how autocorrelation can be resolved when ρ is unknown.

4 Describe the steps of the DW test for autocorrelation. What are its disadvantages and which alternative tests can you suggest?

Exercise 8.1

The file investment.wf1 contains data for the following variables, I = investment, Y = income and R = interest rate. Estimate a regression equation that has as dependent variable the investment, and as explanatory variables income and the interest rate. Check for autocorrelation using both the informal and all the formal ways (tests) that we have covered in Chapter 8. If autocorrelation exists, use the Cochrane–Orcutt iterative procedure to resolve autocorrelation.

Exercise 8.2

The file product.wf1 contains data for the following variables, q = quantity of a good produced during various years, p = price of the good, f = amount of fertilizer used in the production of this good and r = amount of rainfall during each production year. Estimate a regression equation that explains the quantity produced of this product. Check for autocorrelation using both the informal and all the formal ways (tests) that we have covered in Chapter 8. If autocorrelation exists, use the Cochrane–Orcutt iterative procedure to resolve autocorrelation.

Appendix

The DW test statistic given in (8.22) can be expanded to give:

$$d = \frac{\sum_{t=2}^{n} \hat{u}_t^2 + \sum_{t=2}^{n} \hat{u}_{t-1}^2 - 2\sum_{t=2}^{n} \hat{u}_t \hat{u}_{t-1}}{\sum_{t=1}^{n} \hat{u}_t^2} \tag{8.36}$$

Because $\hat{u}_t$ are generally small, the summations from 2 to n or from 2 to $n-1$ will both be approximately equal to the summation from 1 to n. Thus:

$$\sum_{t=2}^{n} \hat{u}_t^2 \simeq \sum_{t=2}^{n} \hat{u}_{t-1}^2 \simeq \sum_{t=1}^{n} \hat{u}_t^2 \tag{8.37}$$

So, we have that (8.36) is now:

$$d \simeq 1 + 1 - \frac{2\sum_{t=2}^{n} \hat{u}_t \hat{u}_{t-1}}{\sum_{t=1}^{n} \hat{u}_t^2} \tag{8.38}$$

but from equation (8.23) we have that $\hat{\rho} = 2\sum_{t=2}^{n} \hat{u}_t \hat{u}_{t-1} / \sum_{t=1}^{n} \hat{u}_t^2$, and therefore:

$$d \simeq 2 - 2\rho \simeq 2(1 - \rho) \tag{8.39}$$

Finally, because ρ takes values from $+1$ to -1, then d will take values from 0 to 4.

9 Misspecification: Wrong Regressors, Measurement Errors and Wrong Functional Forms

One of the most important problems in econometrics is that in reality we are never certain about the form or specification of the equation we want to estimate. For example one of the most common specification errors is to estimate an equation which omits one or more influential explanatory variables or an equation that contains explanatory variables that do not belong to the 'true' specification. We will first see how these problems affect the OLS estimates, and then provide ways of resolving these problems.

Other misspecification problems due to the functional form can result from the assumption which states that the relation among the Y and Xs is linear being no longer true. Therefore, here we present a variety of models that allow us to formulate and estimate various non-linear relationships.

Furthermore, we examine the problems emerging from measurement errors regarding our variables, as well as formal tests for misspecification. Finally, alternative approaches to selecting the best model are presented in the final section.

Omitting influential or including non-influential explanatory variables

Consequences of omitting influential variables

Omitting explanatory variables that play an important role in the determination of the dependent variable causes these variables to become a part of the error term in the population function. Therefore, one or more of the CLRM assumptions will be violated. To explain this in detail, consider the population regression function:

$$Y = \beta_1 + \beta_2 X_2 + \beta_3 X_3 + u \tag{9.1}$$

where $\beta_2 \neq 0$ and $\beta_3 \neq 0$, and let's assume that this is the 'correct' form of this relationship.

However, let us also suppose that we make an error in our specification and we estimate:

$$Y = \beta_1 + \beta_2 X_2 + u^* \tag{9.2}$$

where X_3 is wrongly omitted. In this equation we are forcing u to include the omitted variable X_3 as well as any other purely random factors. In fact in equation (9.2) the error term is:

$$u^* = \beta_3 X_3 + u \tag{9.3}$$

Based on the assumptions of the CLRM, now the assumption that the mean error is zero is violated:

$$E(u^*) = E(\beta_3 X_3 + u) = E(\beta_3 X_3) + E(u) = E(\beta_3 X_3) \neq 0 \tag{9.4}$$

and, furthermore, if the excluded variable X_3 happens to be correlated with X_2 then the error term in equation (9.2) is no longer independent of X_2. The result of both these complications lead to estimators of β_1 and β_2 that are biased and inconsistent. This is often called omitted variable bias. It is easy to show that the case is the same when we omit more than one variable from the 'true' population equation.

Including a non-influential variable

We have seen that omitting influential explanatory variables causes special complications for the OLS estimators. However, if an estimated equation includes variables that are not influential the problem is not so serious. In this case let's assume that the correct equation is:

$$Y = \beta_1 + \beta_2 X_2 + u \qquad (9.5)$$

and this time estimate:

$$Y = \beta_1 + \beta_2 X_2 + \beta_3 X_3 + u \qquad (9.6)$$

where X_3 is wrongly included in the model specification.

In this case since X_3 does not belong to equation (9.6), its population coefficient should be equal to zero ($\beta_3 = 0$). If $\beta_3 = 0$ then none of the CLRM assumptions are violated when we estimate equation (9.6) and therefore OLS estimators will yield both unbiased and consistent estimators. However, although the inclusion of an irrelevant variable does not lead to bias, the OLS estimators of β_1 and β_2 are unlikely to be fully efficient. In the case that X_3 is correlated with X_2, then an unnecessary element of multicollinearity will be introduced to the estimation, which will unavoidably lead to a higher standard error in the coefficient of X_2. This might lead to the wrong conclusion of having non-significant t values for explanatory variables that are influential.

Therefore, because of the inclusion of irrelevant variables, it does not necessarily follow that a coefficient with an insignificant t statistic is non-relevant. So, dropping insignificant variables from a regression model has to be dealt with very cautiously. In general, in non-influential conditions we should expect that:

1 The value of $\bar{R}^2$ will fall, since degrees of freedom increase, while the *RSS* should remain more or less unchanged.

2 Sign reversal will not occur for the coefficients of the remaining regressors, nor should their magnitudes change appreciably.

3 t statistics of the remaining variables are not affected appreciably.

However, selection of a non-influential variable that is highly correlated with one or more of the remaining variables can alter their t statistics. Thus, those guidelines are valid only under ideal circumstances, as we have mentioned before. Intuition, economic theory and previous empirical findings should be used to determine whether or not to delete variables from an equation.

Omission and inclusion of relevant and irrelevant variables at the same time

In this case suppose that the correct equation is:

$$Y = \beta_1 + \beta_2 X_2 + \beta_3 X_3 + u \tag{9.7}$$

and we estimate:

$$Y = \beta_1 + \beta_2 X_2 + \beta_4 X_4 + u^* \tag{9.8}$$

Therefore, here we not only omit the relevant variable X_3, but we also include the non-influential variable X_4 at the same time. As we analysed above, the consequences of the first case are to have biased and inconsistent estimates, and the second gives inefficient estimates. In general, the consequences of omitting an influential variable are very serious and we therefore need to have a way of detecting such problems. One way of doing this is by observing a lot of the residuals of the estimated equation. We saw in the discussion in Chapter 8 that visual observation of the residuals can give us an indication of problems of autocorrelation, where we will also describe formal tests to detect autocorrelation and to resolve it also.

The plug-in solution in the omitted variable bias

Sometimes, it is possible to face omitted variable bias because a key variable that affects Y is not available. For example, consider a model where the monthly salary of an individual is associated with whether or not he/she is male or female (*sex*), and the years each individual has spent in education (*education*). Both of these factors can be easily quantified and included in the model. However, if we also assume that the salary level can be affected by the socio-economic environment in which each person was brought up, then it is hard to find a variable that captures that to be included in what should be the appropriate equation:

$$(salary\_level) = \beta_1 + \beta_2(sex) + \beta_3(education) + \beta_4(background) \tag{9.9}$$

Not including the *background* variable in this model may lead to biased and inconsistent estimates of β_2 and β_3. Our major interest, however, is to get appropriate estimates for those two slope coefficients. We do not care that much for β_1, and we can never hope for a consistent estimator of β_3 since *background* is unobserved. Therefore a way to resolve this problem and effectively get appropriate slope coefficients is to include a proxy variable for the omitted variable, such as, in this example, the family-income (*fm_inc*) of each individual. In this case, of course, *fm_inc* does not have to be the same as *background*, but we need *fm_inc* to be correlated with the unobserved variable *background*.

In order to illustrate this more properly, consider the following model:

$$Y = \beta_1 + \beta_2 X_2 + \beta_3 X_3 + \beta_4 X_4^* + u \tag{9.10}$$

where X_2 and X_3 are variables that are observed (such as *sex* and *education*), while X_4^* is unobserved (such as *background*), but we have a variable X_4 which is a 'good' proxy variable for X_4^* (such as *fm_inc*).

For X_4 we require at least some relationship to X_4^*, for example a simple linear form such as:

$$X_4^* = \gamma_1 + \gamma_2 X_4 + e \qquad (9.11)$$

where an error e should be included because X_4^* and X_4 are not exactly related. Obviously, if then the variable X_4^* is not an appropriate proxy for X_4, while in general we include proxies that have a positive correlation, so, $\gamma_2 > 0$. The coefficient γ_1 is included in order to allow X_4^* and X_4 to be measured on different scales, and obviously they can be either positive or negatively related.

Therefore, in order to resolve the omitted variable bias, we can assume that X_4 and X_4^* are the same and therefore run the regression:

$$
\begin{aligned}
Y &= \beta_1 + \beta_2 X_2 + \beta_3 X_3 + \beta_4(\gamma_1 + \gamma_2 X_4 + e) + u \\
  &= (\beta_1 + \beta_4 \gamma_1) + \beta_2 X_2 + \beta_3 X_3 + \beta_4 \gamma_2 X_4 + (u + \beta_4 e) \\
  &= a_1 + \beta_2 X_2 + \beta_3 X_3 + a_4 X_4 + \varkappa \qquad (9.12)
\end{aligned}
$$

where $\varkappa = u + \beta_4 e$, is a composite error which depends on the model of interest (9.10) and the error from the proxy variable equation (9.11). Obviously, $a_1 = (\beta_1 + \beta_4 \gamma_1)$ is the new intercept and $a_4 = \beta_4 \gamma_2$ is the slope parameter of the proxy variable. As we mentioned earlier, by estimating (9.12) we do not get unbiased estimators of β_1 and β_4, but we do get unbiased estimators of a_1, β_2, β_3 and a_4. The important thing is we get 'appropriate' estimates for the parameters β_2 and β_3 which are of most interest in our analysis.

On the other hand, it is easy to show that using a proxy variable can still lead to bias. Suppose that the unobserved variable X_4^* is related to all (or some) of the observed variables. Then equation (9.11) becomes:

$$X_4^* = \gamma_1 + \gamma_2 X_2 + \gamma_3 X_3 + \gamma_4 X_4 + w \qquad (9.13)$$

Equation (9.11) simply assumes that $\gamma_2 = \gamma_3 = 0$, and by substituting equation (9.13) into equation (9.10) we get:

$$
\begin{aligned}
Y &= (\beta_1 + \beta_4 \gamma_1) + (\beta_2 + \beta_4 \gamma_2) X_2 + (\beta_3 + \beta_4 \gamma_3) X_3 \\
  &\quad + \beta_4 \gamma_4 X_4 + (u + \beta_4 w) \qquad (9.14)
\end{aligned}
$$

from which we get that $plim(\hat{\beta}_2) = \beta_2 + \beta_4 \gamma_2$ and $plim(\hat{\beta}_3) = \beta_3 + \beta_4 \gamma_3$. Therefore, connecting this to the previous example, if *education* has a positive partial correlation with *fm_inc*, we will have a positive bias (inconsistency) in the estimate of the *education* coefficient. However, we can reasonably hope that the bias we face in this case will be smaller than in the case of ignoring the problem of omitted variable entirely.

Various functional forms

Introduction

A different situation where we may face specification errors is that of using an incorrect functional form. The most obvious case has to do with the basic assumption of having an equation that can be represented by a linear relationship. If this is not true, then we might adopt a linear estimating equation while the real population relationship is non-linear.

For example, if the true regression equation is:

$$Y = AX_2^{\beta} X_3^{\gamma} e^{u} \qquad (9.15)$$

and we estimate the linear form given by:

$$Y = a + \beta X_2 + \gamma X_3 + u \qquad (9.16)$$

then the parameters β and γ in the non-linear model represent elasticities, while β (and γ) in the linear model show an estimate of the change in Y after a one-unit change in β (and γ). Therefore, β and γ are clearly incorrect estimators of the true population parameters.

One way to detect wrong functional forms is to visually observe the pattern of the residuals. If we observe a systematic pattern in the residuals then we can suspect the possibility of misspecification. However, apart from that it is also useful to know the various possible non-linear functional forms that we might have to estimate together with the properties regarding marginal effects and elasticities. Table 9.1 presents a summary of the forms and features of the various alternative models.

Linear-log functional form

In a linear-log model, the dependent variable remains the same but the independent variable appears in logs. Thus the model is:

$$Y = \beta_1 + \beta_2 \ln X + u \qquad (9.17)$$

Table 9.1 Forms and features of different functional forms

Name	Functional form	Marginal effect (dY/dX)	Elasticity $(X/Y)(dY/dX)$
Linear	$Y = \beta_1 + \beta_2 X$	β_2	$\beta_2 X / Y$
Linear-log	$Y = \beta_1 + \beta_2 \ln X$	β_2 / X	β_2 / Y
Reciprocal	$Y = \beta_1 + \beta_2 (1/X)$	$-\beta_2 / X^2$	$-\beta_2 / (XY)$
Quadratic	$Y = \beta_1 + \beta_2 X + \beta_3 X^2$	$\beta_2 + 2\beta_3 X$	$(\beta_2 + 2\beta_3 X)X/Y$
Interaction	$Y = \beta_1 + \beta_2 X + \beta_3 XZ$	$\beta_2 + \beta_3 Z$	$(\beta_2 + \beta_3 Z)X/Y$
Log-linear	$\ln Y = \beta_1 + \beta_2 X$	$\beta_2 Y$	$\beta_2 X$
Log-reciprocal	$\ln Y = \beta_1 + \beta_2 (1/X)$	$-\beta_2 Y / X^2$	$-\beta_2 X$
Log-quadratic	$\ln Y = \beta_1 + \beta_2 X + \beta_3 X^2$	$Y(\beta_2 + 2\beta_3 X)$	$X(\beta_2 + 2\beta_3 X)$
Double-log	$\ln Y = \beta_1 + \beta_2 \ln X$	$\beta_2 Y / X$	β_2
Logistic	$\ln[Y/(1-Y)] = \beta_1 + \beta_2 X$	$\beta_2 Y(1-Y)$	$\beta_2 (1-Y)X$

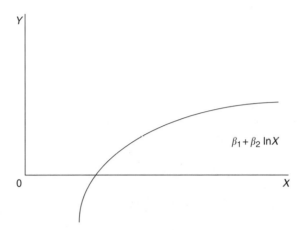

Figure 9.1   A linear-log functional form

This relation gives a marginal effect (dY/dX) equal to $dY/dX = \beta_2/X$. Solving this for dY:

$$dY = \beta_2 \frac{dX}{X} = \frac{\beta_2}{100}\left[100\frac{dX}{X}\right] = \frac{\beta_2}{100} \quad (\% \text{ change in } X) \tag{9.18}$$

So, a 1% change in X will lead to $\beta_2/100$ units change on Y (note that this is not a percentage but a unit change).

A plot of this function for positive β_1 and β_2 is given in Figure 9.1, while an example from economic theory can be the production of total output of an agricultural product (Y) with respect to hectares of land used for its cultivation (X).

Reciprocal functional form

A different example is that of:

$$Y = \beta_1 + \beta_2(1/X) + u \tag{9.19}$$

a plot of which is shown in Figure 9.2.

This form is frequently used with demand curve applications. Note that because demand curves are typically downward-sloping we expect that β_2 is positive and also, while X becomes sufficiently large, Y asymptotically approaches β_1.

Polynomial functional form

This model will include terms of the explanatory variable X increased in different powers according to the degree of the polynomial (k). We have:

$$Y = \beta_1 + \beta_2 X + \beta_3 X^2 + \cdots + \beta_k X^k + u \tag{9.20}$$

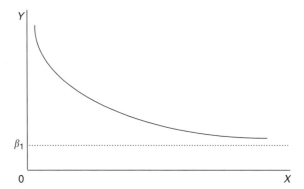

Figure 9.2 A reciprocal functional form

To estimate this model we simply generate new variables X^2, X^3 and so on and then regress these variables to Y. Obviously if $k = 3$ then the polynomial is cubic, while for $k = 2$ it is quadratic. Quadratic formulations are frequently used in order to fit U-shaped curves (like for example cost functions). In general, polynomials of order higher than 2 should be avoided, first because of reduction of the degrees of freedom, and second because there is a possibility of high correlation between X and X^2 and the estimated coefficients are unreliable.

Functional form including interaction terms

Sometimes it is possible that the marginal effect of a variable depends on another variable. For example Klein and Morgan (1951) suggested that the marginal propensity to consume is affected by asset holdings of individuals, meaning that a wealthier person is likely to have a higher marginal propensity to consume out of his income. Thus in the Keynesian consumption function:

$$C = a + \beta Y + u \tag{9.21}$$

where C denotes consumption and y income, β is the marginal propensity to consume; we have that $\beta = \beta_1 + \beta_2 A$, where A denotes assets. Substituting this into (9.21) we get:

$$C = a + (\beta_1 + \beta_2 A)Y + u$$
$$= a + \beta_1 Y + \beta_2 AY + u \tag{9.22}$$

The term AY is known as the interaction term. Note that in this case the marginal effect will be given by $dC/dY = \beta_2 + \beta_2 A$, so we need to know the value of A in order to calculate it.

Log-linear functional form

So far we have examined models where non-linearity emerges only from the explanatory variables. Now we examine a model in which the dependent variable appears transformed. Consider the model:

$$\ln Y = \beta_1 + \beta_2 X + u \tag{9.23}$$

β_2, now, is the marginal effect of C on $\ln Y$ and not on Y. This is known as the instantaneous rate of growth. Differentiating both sides with respect to X we obtain:

$$\beta_2 = \frac{d \ln Y}{dX} = \frac{1}{Y}\frac{dY}{dX} = \frac{dY}{Y}\frac{1}{dX} \tag{9.24}$$

The term dY/Y is the change in Y divided by Y. Therefore, when multiplied by 100, β_2 gives the change in Y per unit change in X.

The log-linear model is widely applied in economics (and lately especially in the human capital literature). This theory suggests, for example, that the more educated a person is, the higher should be his/her salary. Therefore, let us say that there is a return to an extra year of education, labelled as θ. Then for the first period, the monthly salary will be equal to $s_1 = (1+\theta)s_0$, for a two year return it will be $s_2 = (1+\theta)^2 s_0$, and so on. Then for k years it will be $s_k = (1+\theta)^k s_0$. Taking logarithms of both sides we have that:

$$\ln s_k = k \ln(1+\theta) + \ln(s_0) = \beta_1 + \beta_2 k \tag{9.25}$$

where of course k is years in education for each individual. Thus, we have obtained a log-linear relationship between salary and years of education, where the OLS coefficient β_2 is that one more year of education will give $100\beta_2$ per cent more in monthly salary earnings.

The double-log functional form

The double-log model is very popular in cases where we expect variables to have constant ratios. A common specification is the Cobb–Douglas type of production function of the form:

$$Y_t = A K_t^a L_t^\beta \tag{9.26}$$

where the standard notation is used. Taking logarithms of both sides and adding an error term we get:

$$\ln Y_t = \gamma + a \ln K_t + \beta \ln L_t + u_t \tag{9.27}$$

and it is easy to show, here, that a and β are the elasticities of K_t and L_t respectively. To demonstrate that, consider changes in K while keeping L constant; then we have:

$$a = \frac{d \ln Y}{d \ln K} = \frac{(1/Y)dY}{(1/K)dK} = \frac{K}{Y}\frac{dY}{dK} \tag{9.28}$$

Also, another way to show this is by taking the derivative of Y with respect to K; from the initial function (9.26):

$$\frac{dY}{dK} = aAK_t^{a-1}L_t^{\beta} = a\frac{AK_t^aL_t^{\beta}}{K} = a\frac{Y}{K} \tag{9.29}$$

and therefore:

$$a = \frac{dY}{dK}\frac{K}{Y} \tag{9.30}$$

It is easy to show that the same holds for β. We leave this as an exercise for the reader. Table 9.2 provides interpretations of the marginal effects in the various logarithmic models.

The Box–Cox transformation

As we demonstrated above, the choice of the functional form plays a very important role in the interpretation of the estimated coefficients, and therefore we need to have a formal test which will be able to direct us to choose which functional form to use in cases where we are uncertain about the population relationship.

For example, think of a model with two explanatory variables (X_2 and X_3). We must be able to determine whether to use the linear, log-linear, linear-log or double-log specification. When the choice is between the linear and linear-log model, or among the log-linear and double-log specification, things are easy because we have the same dependent variable in each of the two models. So, we can estimate both models and choose the functional form that yields the higher R^2. However, in cases where the dependent variable is not the same, as for example in the linear form:

$$Y = \beta_1 + \beta_2 X \tag{9.31}$$

Table 9.2 Interpretation of marginal effects in logarithmic models

Name	Functional form	Marginal effect	Interpretation
Linear	$Y = \beta_1 + \beta_2 X$	$\Delta Y = \beta_2 \Delta X$	1 *unit* change in X will induce a β_2 *unit* change in Y
Linear-log	$Y = \beta_1 + \beta_2 \ln X$	$\Delta Y = \beta_2/100[100\Delta X/X]$	1 *per cent* change in X will induce a $\beta_2/100$ *unit* change in Y
Log-linear	$\ln Y = \beta_1 + \beta_2 X$	$100\Delta Y/Y = 100\beta_2 \Delta X$	1 *unit* change in X will induce a $100\beta_2$ *per cent* change in Y
Double-log	$\ln Y = \beta_1 + \beta_2 \ln X$	$100\Delta Y/Y = \beta_2[100\Delta X/X]$	1 *per cent* change in X will induce a β_2 *per cent* change in Y

and the double-log form:

$$\ln Y = \beta_1 + \beta_2 \ln X \tag{9.32}$$

then we cannot compare the two models with the use of R^2.

In such examples, we need to scale the Y variable in such a way that we will be able to compare the two models. The procedure is based on the work of Box and Cox (1964), and is usually known as the Box–Cox transformation. The procedure follows the following steps:

Step 1   Obtain the geometric mean of the sample Y values. This is:

$$\tilde{Y} = (Y_1 Y_2 Y_3 \cdots Y_n)^{1/n} = \exp\left(1/n \sum \ln Y_i\right) \tag{9.33}$$

Step 2   Transform the sample Y values by dividing each of them by $\tilde{Y}$ obtained above to get:

$$Y^* = Y_i/\tilde{Y} \tag{9.34}$$

Step 3   Estimate equations (9.31) and (9.32) substituting Y^* as the dependent variable in both of them. The *RSS* of the two equations are now directly comparable, and the equation with the lower *RSS* should be preferred.

Step 4   If we need to know whether one of the equations is significantly better than the other, then we have to calculate the following statistic:

$$\left(\frac{1}{2}n\right) \ln \left(\frac{RSS_2}{RSS_1}\right) \tag{9.35}$$

where RSS_2 is the *RSS* of the equation with the higher *RSS*, and RSS_1 of the other equation. The above statistic follows a χ^2 distribution with 1 degree of freedom. If χ^2-statistical exceeds the χ^2-critical value then we can say with confidence that the model with the lower *RSS* is superior at the level of significance for which the χ^2-critical is obtained.

Measurement errors

Up to this point our discussion has dealt with situations where explanatory variables are either omitted or included contrary to the correct model specification. However, another possibility exists that can create problems in the OLS coefficients. Sometimes in econometrics it is not possible to collect data on the variable that truly affects economic behaviour, or we might even collect data for which one or more variables are measured incorrectly. In such cases, variables used in the econometric analysis are different from the correct values and can therefore potentially create serious estimation problems.

Measurement error in the dependent variable

We begin our analysis by examining the case where there is a measurement error in the dependent variable only, and we assume that the true population equation is:

$$Y = \beta_1 + \beta_2 X_2 + \cdots + \beta_k X_k + u \tag{9.36}$$

which we further assume satisfies the assumptions of the CLRM, but we are unable to observe the actual values of Y. Not having information about the correct values of Y leads us to use available data on Y containing measurement errors.

The observed values of Y^* will differ from the actual relationship as follows:

$$Y^* = Y + w \tag{9.37}$$

where w denotes the measurement error in Y.

To obtain a model which can be estimated econometrically, we have that $Y = Y^* - w$ and we insert this into equation (9.36) obtaining:

$$Y^* = \beta_1 + \beta_2 X_2 + \cdots + \beta_k X_k + (u + w) \tag{9.38}$$

Therefore, we now have an error term $(u+w)$. Since $Y^*, X_2, \ldots, X_k$ are now observed, we can ignore the fact that Y^* is not a perfect measure of Y and estimate the model. The obtained OLS coefficients will be unaffected only if certain conditions about w occur. Firstly, we know from the CLRM assumptions that u has a zero mean and is uncorrelated with all Xs. If the measurement error w has a zero mean as well, then we get an unbiased estimator for the constant β_1 in the equation, if not then the OLS estimator for β_1 is biased, but this is rarely important in econometrics. Second, we need to have a condition for the relationship of w with the explanatory variables.

If the measurement error in Y is uncorrelated with the Xs then the OLS estimators for the slope coefficients are unbiased and consistent, and vice versa. As a final note, in case u and w are uncorrelated then $var(u + w) = \sigma_u^2 + \sigma_w^2 > \sigma_u^2$.

Therefore the measurement error leads to a larger residual variance which of course leads to larger variances of the OLS estimated coefficients. However, this is expected and there is nothing we can do to avoid it.

Measurement error in the explanatory variable

In this case we have as the true population equation:

$$Y = \beta_1 + \beta_2 X_2 + u \tag{9.39}$$

which satisfies the assumption of the CLRM and therefore OLS will provide unbiased and consistent estimators of both β_1 and β_2. Now with X_2 non-observed, we have only a measure of X_2, let's say X_2^*. The relationship between X_2 and X_2^* is:

$$X_2 = X_2^* - v \tag{9.40}$$

and inserting this into the population model gives:

$$Y = \beta_1 + \beta_2(X_2^* - v) + u \tag{9.41}$$

$$= \beta_1 + \beta_2 X_2^* + (u - \beta_2 v) \tag{9.42}$$

If it was the case that ε and v are uncorrelated with X_2^* and both have a zero mean, then the OLS estimators are consistent estimators for both β_1 and β_2. However, as shown below this is not generally the case. Also, again since ε and v are uncorrelated, the residual variance is $var(\varepsilon - \beta_2 v) = \sigma_\varepsilon^2 + \beta_2^2 \sigma_v^2$. Thus, only when $\beta_2 = 0$ does the measurement error not increase the variance, and the variances of β_1 and β_2 will be again higher.

Recall that the OLS slope estimator is given by:

$$\hat{\beta}_2 = \frac{\sum (X_2^* - \bar{X}_2^*)(Y - \bar{Y})}{\sum (X_2^* - \bar{X}_2^*)^2}$$

$$= \frac{\sum (X_2^* - \bar{X}_2^*)(\beta_1 + \beta_2 X_2^* + u - \beta_2 v) - \beta_1 - \beta_2 \bar{X}_2^* - \bar{u} + \beta_2 \bar{v}}{\sum (X_2^* - \bar{X}_2^*)^2}$$

$$= \frac{\sum (X_2^* - \bar{X}_2^*)(\beta_2(X_2^* - \bar{X}_2^*) + (u - \bar{u}) - \beta_2(v - \bar{v}))}{\sum (X_2^* - \bar{X}_2^*)^2} \tag{9.43}$$

For unbiasedness we want $E(\hat{\beta}_2) = \beta_2$. Taking the expected value of (9.43) we have:

$$E(\hat{\beta}_2) = \beta_2 + E\left(\frac{\sum (X_2^* - \bar{X}_2^*)(u - \bar{u})}{\sum (X_2^* - \bar{X}_2^*)^2} - \beta_2 \frac{\sum (X_2^* - \bar{X}_2^*)(v - \bar{v})}{\sum (X_2^* - \bar{X}_2^*)^2}\right)$$

$$= \beta_2 + E\left(\frac{Cov(X_2^*, u)}{Var(X_2^*)} - \beta_2 \frac{Cov(X_2^*, v)}{Var(X_2^*)}\right) \tag{9.44}$$

Therefore, we need to check whether these covariances are equal to zero or not. We have that:

$$Cov(X_2^*, u) = E(X_2^* u) - E(X_2^*) E(u) \tag{9.45}$$

But because $E(\varepsilon) = 0$ this reduces to:

$$Cov(X_2^*, u) = E(X_2^* u) = E[(X_2 + v)u] = E(X_2 u) + E(vu) \tag{9.46}$$

Since the actual X is uncorrelated with u, the first expectation in (9.46) equals zero. Also, assuming that the two errors (v and u) are independent, the second expectation is zero as well.

For the covariance of X_2^* with v we have:

$$Cov\left(X_2^*, v\right) = E\left(X_2^* v\right) - E\left(X_2^*\right) E(v) \tag{9.47}$$

$$= E\left[(X_2 + v)v\right] \tag{9.48}$$

$$= E(X_2 v) + E(v^2) = 0 + \sigma_v^2 \tag{9.49}$$

The term $E(X_2 v)$ is zero because the actual X_2 is independent of the measurement error. However, because $Cov(X_2^*, v) = \sigma_v^2$ which is non-zero, the observed X_2 (i.e. X_2^*) is correlated with its measurement error. Thus the slope coefficient is biased (because $E(\hat{\beta}_2) = \beta_2 + \sigma_v^2$). Finally, since its magnitude of bias is not affected by its sample size, the OLS estimator under measurement error in one of the explanatory variables is not only biased, but inconsistent as well.

Tests for misspecification

Normality of residuals

We mentioned before that one way of detecting misspecification problems is through observing the regression residuals. Recall also that one of the assumptions of the CLRM is that the residuals are normally distributed with a zero mean and a constant variance. Violation of this assumption leads to the inferential statistics of a regression model (i.e. t-stats, F-stats, etc.) not being valid. Therefore, it is quite essential to test for normality of residuals.

In order to test for this we first need to calculate the second, third and fourth moments of the residuals and then compute the Jarque–Berra (1990) JB statistic. The test can be done following the four simple steps presented below:

Step 1 Calculate the second, third and fourth moments (note that μ_3 is the skewness of the residuls and that μ_4 is the kurtosis of the residuals) of the residuals ($\hat{u}$) in the regression equation as:

$$\mu_2 = \frac{\sum \hat{u}^2}{n}; \quad \mu_3 = \frac{\sum \hat{u}^3}{n}; \quad \mu_4 = \frac{\sum \hat{u}^4}{n} \tag{9.50}$$

Step 2 Calculate the Jarque–Berra statistic by

$$JB = n\left[\frac{\mu_3^2}{6} + \frac{(\mu_4 - 3)^2}{24}\right] \tag{9.51}$$

which has a χ^2 distribution with 2 degrees of freedom.

Step 3 Find the $\chi^2(2)$ critical value from the tables of χ^2 distribution.

Step 4 If $JB > \chi^2$-critical we reject the null hypothesis of normality of residuals. Alternatively, if the p-value is less than 0.05 (for a 95% significance level), then we again reject the null hypothesis of normality.

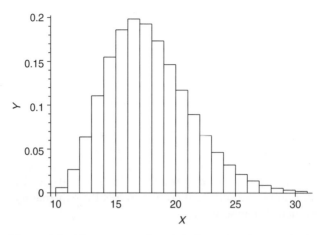

Figure 9.3   Histogram and statistic for regression residuals

The J-B normality test for residuals in EViews

To check for normality of residuals in a regression model we need to check on the histogram and the J-B statistic. To do this we first need to estimate the desired equation, either by typing the command for the equation estimation in the EViews command line, or by choosing **Quick/Estimate Equation**, then specify the equation and click <OK>. After the estimation the series RESID which is always in every EViews workfile will contain the residuals of this regression (note: the series RESID contains the residuals of the most recent estimated equation in EViews, so if another equation is estimated afterwards, the series RESID will change). To check for normality, we need to double-click on the RESID series and from the series object toolbar click on **View/Descriptive Statistics/Histogram and Stats**. This procedure will give us the graph and summary statistics shown in Figure 9.3.

From the histogram we can see that the residuals do not seem to be normally distributed. Also, at the lower right-hand corner of the figure we can see the value of the J-B statistic and its respective probability limit. The residuals come from a simple regression model that included only one explanatory variable and 38 observations. So, we can obtain the χ^2 critical value for 2 degree of freedom, $a = 0.05$ and $n = 38$, by the following command in EViews:

```
scalar chi_crit=@qchisq(.95,2)
```

This will create a scalar named chi_crit in our workfile, and the result of the scalar can be displayed in the status line at the bottom of the EViews main window, after double-clicking on the scalar. The value of the chi_crit is equal to 3.841, and since it is higher than the J-B statistic we cannot reject the null hypothesis that the residuals are normally distributed. Also, since the p-value is equal to 0.415 and greater than the chosen level of significance (0.05), we again conclude that we cannot reject the null hypothesis of normality.

The Ramsey RESET test for general misspecification

One of the most commonly used tests for general misspecification is Ramsey's (1969) Regressions Specification Error Test (RESET) as with many tests this has both an F-form and an LM form. Suppose that the 'true' population model is:

$$Y = \beta_1 + \beta_2 X_2 + \beta_3 X_2^2 + u \qquad (9.52)$$

and we wrongly estimate:

$$Y = \beta_1 + \beta_2 X_2 + \hat{u}^* \qquad (9.53)$$

where we omit X_2^2 because we do not actually know what the real nature of Y is.

The RESET test for such misspecification is based on the fitted values of Y obtained from regression (9.53) as:

$$\hat{Y} = \hat{\beta}_1 + \hat{\beta}_2 X_2 \qquad (9.54)$$

The RESET test involves including various powers of $\hat{Y}$ as proxies for X_2^2 that can capture possible non-linear relationships. Before implementing the test we need to decide how many terms we will include in the expanded regression. There is no formal answer to this question, but in general the squared and cubed terms have proven to be useful in most applications; so the expanded equation will be:

$$Y = \beta_1 + \beta_2 X_2 + \delta_1 \hat{Y}^2 + \delta_2 \hat{Y}^3 + \epsilon \qquad (9.55)$$

Then the situation boils down to a regular F-type test for the additional explanatory variables $\hat{Y}^2$ and $\hat{Y}^3$. If one or more of the coefficients are significant then this is evidence of general misspecification. A big drawback of the RESET test is that if we reject the null hypothesis of a correct specification, this merely indicates that the equation is misspecified in one way or another, without providing us with alternative models which are correct.

So, summing up, the RESET test can be performed step by step as follows:

Step 1 Estimate the model that we think is correct in describing the population equation, and obtain the fitted values of the dependent variable $\hat{Y}$.

Step 2 Estimate the model in step 1 again, this time including $\hat{Y}^2$ and $\hat{Y}^3$ as additional explanatory variables.

Step 3 The model in step 1 is the restricted model and that in step 2 is the unrestricted model. Calculate the F statistic for these two models.

Step 4 Find the F-critical value from the F tables for 2, $n - k - 3$ degrees of freedom.

Step 5 If F-statistic $> F$-critical we reject the null hypothesis of correct specification and conclude that our model is somehow misspecified. Alternatively, we can use the p-value approach. If the p-value for the F-stat is smaller than the required level of significance (usually 0.05), then we again reject the null

Table 9.3 Ramsey RESET test example

Dependent Variable: LCONS
Method: Least Squares
Date: 02/16/04 Time: 15:03
Sample: 1985:1 1994:2
Included observations: 38

Variable	Coefficient	Std. Error	t-Statistic	Prob.
C	2.717238	0.576652	4.712091	0.0000
LDISP	0.414366	0.126279	3.281340	0.0023

R-squared	0.230230	Mean dependent var	4.609274
Adjusted R-squared	0.208847	S.D. dependent var	0.051415
S.E. of regression	0.045732	Akaike info criterion	−3.280845
Sum squared resid	0.075291	Schwarz criterion	−3.194656
Log likelihood	64.33606	F-statistic	10.76719
Durbin–Watson stat	0.412845	Prob(F-statistic)	0.002301

hypothesis of correct specification. A Langrange multiplier test is also available and the χ^2 distribution will have 2 degrees of freedom.

The RESET test can also be calculated using the LM procedure described in chapter 5. To perform this we would take the residuals from the restricted model (9.53) and regress them on $\hat{Y}^2$ and $\hat{Y}^3$, TR^2 from this regression would give an LM test with a chi^2 distribution with 2 degrees of freedom.

Ramsey's RESET test in EViews

Assume that we estimated the following regression model from the file cons.wf1, by typing into the EViews command line:

```
ls lcons c ldisp
```

which regresses the logarithm of a consumer's expenditure on food (lcons) on the logarithm of disposable income (ldisp). The results obtained from this regression are shown in Table 9.3.

In order to test for general misspecification with Ramsey's RESET test we click on **View/Stability Tests/Ramsey RESET Test ...**, after which a new window opens (**RESET Specification**) which asks us to specify the number of fitted terms we want to use. If we choose 1 it will include only $\hat{Y}^2$, if we choose 2 it will include both $\hat{Y}^2$ and $\hat{Y}^3$, and so on. Let's assume that we choose only 1 and click <**OK**>. The results are shown in Table 9.4.

From the results we can see that F-stat is quite high. Even though we do not have F-critical, from the p-value we can see that because the p-value for the F-stat is smaller than the required level of significance (0.05), we can safely reject the null hypothesis of correct specification and conclude that our model is misspecified. Notice, as well, that the coefficient of the squared fitted term is statistically significant (t-stat = 4.66).

Ramsey's RESET test in Microfit

Microfit reports Ramsey's test in the regression results output under diagnostic tests, as test B, and it includes one fitted squared term. It reports statistical values and p-values of both the LM test and the F-type test described above. The interpretation is as usual with the use of the p-value approach as presented in the example above.

Tests for non-nested models

If we want to test models which are non-nested we cannot use the F-type test. By non-nested models we mean models in which neither equation is a special case of the other, in other words we do not have a restricted and an unrestricted model.

Suppose, for example, that we have the following two models:

$$Y = \beta_1 + \beta_2 X_2 + \beta_3 X_3 + u \tag{9.56}$$

$$Y = \beta_1 + \beta_2 \ln X_2 + \beta_3 \ln X_3 + \varepsilon \tag{9.57}$$

and that we want to test the first against the second, and vice versa. There are two different approaches.

The first is an approach proposed by Mizon and Richard (1986), who simply suggest the estimation of a comprehensive model of the form:

$$Y = \delta_1 + \delta_2 X_2 + \delta_3 X_3 + \delta_4 \ln X_2 + \delta_5 \ln X_3 + \epsilon \tag{9.58}$$

Table 9.4 Ramsey RESET test example (continued...)

Ramsey RESET Test:

F-statistic	**21.75213**	Probability	**0.000044**
Log likelihood ratio	18.36711	Probability	0.000018

Test Equation:
Dependent Variable: LCONS
Method: Least Squares
Date: 02/16/04 Time: 15:09
Sample: 1985:1 1994:2
Included observations: 38

Variable	Coefficient	Std. Error	t-Statistic	Prob.
C	−204.0134	44.32789	−4.602370	0.0001
LDISP	−204.4012	43.91503	−4.654471	0.0000
FITTED^2	53.74844	11.52431	**4.663919**	0.0000
R-squared	0.525270	Mean dependent var		4.609274
Adjusted R-squared	0.498142	S.D. dependent var		0.051415
S.E. of regression	0.036423	Akaike info criterion		−3.711559
Sum squared resid	0.046433	Schwarz criterion		−3.582275
Log likelihood	73.51961	F-statistic		19.36302
Durbin–Watson stat	0.795597	Prob(F-statistic)		0.000002

then applying an F test for significance of δ_2 and δ_3 having as the restricted model equation (9.57), or test for δ_4 and δ_5 having as an restricted model equation (9.56).

The second approach is proposed by Davidson and MacKinnon (1993), who suggest that if model (9.56) is true, then the fitted values of (9.57) should be insignificant in (9.56) and vice versa. Therefore, in order to test (9.56) we need to first estimate (9.57) and take the fitted values of this model, which we may call $\widetilde{Y}$. The test is then based on the t statistic on $\widetilde{Y}$ in the following equation:

$$Y = \beta_1 + \beta_2 X_2 + \beta_3 X_3 + \zeta \widetilde{Y} + v \tag{9.59}$$

where a significant ζ coefficient will suggest, of course, rejection of (9.56). A drawback of this test is that the comprehensive equation (9.58) may not make sense from an economic theory point of view.

The case is exactly the opposite if we want to test (9.57) against (9.56). There are some drawbacks with these testing techniques:

1 It is not necessary to have results that clearly suggest which model is better. Both models may be rejected or neither model may be rejected. If the case is that neither is rejected we choose the one with the higher $\bar{R}^2$.

2 Rejecting (9.56) does not necessarily mean that (9.57) is the correct alternative.

3 The situation is even more difficult if the two competing models also have different dependent variables. Tests have been proposed to deal with this problem but they are beyond the scope of this text and will not be presented here.

Example: the Box–Cox transformation in EViews

This example looks at the relationship between income and consumption, proposing two functional forms and using the Box–Cox transformation to decide which of the two is preferable. A Ramsey RESET test is also performed.

We use data for income, consumption and the consumer price index, in quarterly frequency from 1985 q^1 up to 1994 q^1 and q^2. The file name is box_cox.wf1 and the variable names are *inc*, *cons* and *cpi* respectively.

We can specify the consumption function in two ways:

$$C_t = \beta_{11} + \beta_{12} Y_t + u_{1t} \tag{9.60}$$

or

$$\ln C_t = \beta_{21} + \beta_{22} \ln Y_t + u_{2t} \tag{9.61}$$

where C_t is real consumption (adjusted for inflation), β_{11}, β_{12}, β_{21} and β_{22} are coefficients to be estimated, Y_t is real income (adjusted for inflation) and u_{1t} and u_{2t} are the disturbance terms for the two alternative specifications.

We therefore need to restate the nominal data into real terms for both equations, and to create the log of the variables in order to estimate equation (9.61). We can use *cpi* to remove the effects of price inflation, as follows:

$$X_{real} = X_{nominal} * \left(\frac{CPI_{base}}{CPI_t} \right) \tag{9.62}$$

In EViews, we use the following commands:

```
scalar cpibase=102.7
genr consreal=cons*(cpibase/cpi)
gern increal=inc*(cpibase/cpi)
```

And we can transform the logarithm of the variables *consreal* and *inc* real in EViews using the commands:

```
gern lincr=log(increal)
genr lconsr=log(consreal)
```

We now have all of our data sets in place for the Box–Cox transformation. First we need to obtain the geometric mean which can be calculated as:

$$\widetilde{Y} = (Y_1 Y_2 Y_3 \cdots Y_n)^{1/n} = \exp \left(1/n \sum \ln Y_i \right) \tag{9.63}$$

In EViews, the first step is to prepare the sum of the logs of the dependent variable, to do which we type the following command in the EViews command line:

```
scalar scons = @sum(lconsr)
```

In order to view a scalar value in EViews we need to double click on the scalar and its value will appear at the lower right-hand corner. We observe that the sum of the logs is calculated as 174.704. The command to find the geometric mean of the dependent variable, with $n = 38$ observations, is:

```
scalar constilda=exp((1/38)*scons)
```

and we need to transform the sample Y values, i.e. *lconsr*, by dividing each by *constilda* to generate a new series *constar*. In EViews the command is:

```
genr constar=lconsr/constilda
```

The new series *constar* can now be substituted as the dependent variable in equations (9.60) and (9.61) above to provide the following new equations:

$$C_t^* = \beta_{11} + \beta_{12} Y_t + u_{1t} \tag{9.64}$$

and

$$C_t^* = \beta_{21} + \beta_{22} \ln Y_t + u_{2t} \tag{9.65}$$

Table 9.5   Regression model for the Box–Cox test

Dependent Variable: CONSTAR
Method: Least Squares
Date: 02/25/04 Time: 16:56
Sample: 1985:1 1994:2
Included observations: 38

Variable	Coefficient	Std. Error	t-Statistic	Prob.
C	−0.025836	0.008455	−3.055740	0.0042
LINCR	0.015727	0.001842	8.536165	0.0000

R-squared	0.669319	Mean dependent var	0.046330
Adjusted R-squared	0.660133	S.D. dependent var	0.001096
S.E. of regression	0.000639	Akaike info criterion	−11.82230
Sum squared resid	1.47E−05	Schwarz criterion	−11.73611
Log likelihood	226.6238	F-statistic	72.86612
Durbin–Watson stat	0.116813	Prob(F-statistic)	0.000000

To run these two regression in EViews, the commands are:

```
ls constar c increal
ls constar c lincr
```

the results of which are presented in Tables 9.5 and 9.6 respectively. Summarized results are presented in Table 9.7. From the summarized results we see that the constant and income terms in both functional forms are significant; the R^2 values are similar at 65–67%.

The residual sums of squares (*RSS*) of the regressions are 1.54E − 05 and 1.47E − 05 for the linear (9.64) and the double-log model (9.65) respectively. Thus equation (9.65) has the lower *RSS*, and would be the preferred option. In order to test this result, we can calculate the Box–Cox test statistic which is given by the following equation:

$$\left(\frac{1}{2}n\right)\ln\left(\frac{RSS_2}{RSS_1}\right) \tag{9.66}$$

$$= (0.5 * 38) * ln(1.54 * 10^{-5}/1.47 * 10^{-5}) \tag{9.67}$$

$$= 19 * ln(1.0476) = 0.8839 \tag{9.68}$$

where RSS_2 is the higher *RSS* value, obtained from the linear function (9.64).

The critical value, taken from the Chi-square distribution with one degree of freedom (one independent variable) and 0.05 level of significance, is 3.841. Thus the test statistic is less than the critical value and so we cannot conclude that the log function is superior to the linear function at a 5% level of significance.

Table 9.6 Regression model for the Box–Cox test (continued...)

Dependent Variable: CONSTAR
Method: Least Squares
Date: 02/25/04 Time: 16:56
Sample: 1985:1 1994:2
Included observations: 38

Variable	Coefficient	Std. Error	t-Statistic	Prob.
C	0.030438	0.001928	15.78874	0.0000
INCREAL	0.000161	1.95E−05	8.255687	0.0000

R-squared	0.654366	Mean dependent var	0.046330
Adjusted R-squared	0.644765	S.D. dependent var	0.001096
S.E. of regression	0.000653	Akaike info criterion	−11.77808
Sum squared resid	1.54E−05	Schwarz criterion	−11.69189
Log likelihood	225.7835	F-statistic	68.15636
Durbin–Watson stat	0.117352	Prob(F-statistic)	0.000000

Table 9.7 Summary of OLS results for the Box–Cox test

Variables	Linear Model	Log-Log Model
Constant	0.0304	−0.025836
	(15.789)	(−3.056)
Income	0.000161	0.015727
	(8.256)	(8.536)
R^2	0.654366	0.669319
Sample size (n)	38	38

Approaches in choosing an appropriate model

The traditional view: average economic regression

In the past, the traditional approach to econometric modelling was to start by formulating the simplest possible model to obey the underlying economic theory, and after estimating that model to perform various tests in order to determine whether or not it was satisfactory.

A satisfactory model in that sense would be: (a) one having significant coefficients (i.e. high t ratios), and coefficients whose signs correspond with the theoretical predictions, (b) one with a good fit (i.e. high R^2), and (c) one having residuals that do not suffer from autocorrelation or heteroskedasticity.

If one or more of these points are violated, then researchers try to find better methods of estimation (i.e. the Cochrane–Orcutt iterative method of estimation for the case of serial correlation), or to check other possible cases of bias such as whether important variables have been omitted from the model, or whether redundant variables have been included in the model, or to consider alternative forms of functional forms, and so on.

This approach, which essentially starts with a simple model and then 'builds up' the models as the situation demands, is called the 'simple to specific approach' or the 'average economic regression (AER)', a term coined by Gilbert (1986) because this was the method that most traditional econometric research was following in practice.

The AER approach has received major criticisms:

1 One obvious criticism is the fact that the procedure followed in the AER approach suffers from data mining. Since, usually, only the final model is presented by the researcher, we do not have any information regarding the number of variables that were actually used in the model before obtaining the 'final' model results.

2 Another criticism is that the alterations to the original model are carried out in an arbitrary manner based mainly on the beliefs of the researcher. It is, therefore, quite possible for two different researchers examining the same case to come up with totally different conclusions.

3 By definition the initial starting model is incorrect as it has omitted variables. This will mean that all the diagnostic tests on this model are incorrect. So we may find that important variables are insignificant and exclude them.

The Hendry 'general to specific approach'

Following from these two major criticisms against the AER, an alternative approach has been developed which is called the 'general to specific approach' or the Hendry approach, because it was mainly developed by Professor Hendry of the London School of Economics (see Hendry and Richard, 1983). The approach is to start with a general model that contains – nested within it as special cases – other simpler models. Let us use an example to understand this better. Assume that we have a variable Y that can be affected by two explanatory variables X and Z: the general to specific approach proposes as a starting point the estimation of the following regression equation:

$$Y_t = a + \beta_0 X_t + \beta_1 X_{t-1} + \beta_2 X_{t-2} + \cdots + \beta_m X_{t-m}$$
$$+ \gamma_0 Z_t + \gamma_1 Z_{t-1} + \gamma_2 Z_{t-2} + \cdots + \gamma_m Z_{t-m}$$
$$+ \delta_1 Y_{t-1} + \delta_2 Y_{t-2} + \cdots + \delta_m Y_{t-m} + u_t \qquad (9.69)$$

That is, to regress Y_t on contemporaneous and lagged terms X_t and Z_t as well as lagged values of Y_t. This model is called an autoregressive (because lagged values of the dependent variable appear as regressors as well) distributed lag (because the effect of X and Z on Y is spread over a period of time from $t - m$ to t) model (ARDL). Also, models like (9.69) are known as dynamic models because they examine the behaviour of a variable over time.

The procedure then is, after estimating the model, to apply appropriate tests and to narrow down the model to simpler ones which are always nested to the previously estimated model.

Let us consider the above example for $m = 2$ to see how we may proceed in practice with this approach. We have the original model:

$$Y_t = a + \beta_0 X_t + \beta_1 X_{t-1} + \beta_2 X_{t-2}$$
$$+ \gamma_0 Z_t + \gamma_1 Z_{t-1} + \gamma_2 Z_{t-2} + \delta_1 Y_{t-1} + \delta_2 Y_{t-2} + u_t \qquad (9.70)$$

where one restriction may be that all the Xs are non-important in the determination of Y. Then for this we have hypothesis $H_0: \beta_0 = \beta_1 = \beta_2 = 0$; and if we accept that, we have a simpler model such as the one below:

$$Y_t = a\gamma_0 Z_t + \gamma_1 Z_{t-1} + \gamma_2 Z_{t-2} + \delta_1 Y_{t-1} + \delta_2 Y_{t-2} + u_t \qquad (9.71)$$

Another possible restriction may be that the second lagged term of each variable is insignificant; i.e. hypothesis $H_0: \beta_2 = \gamma_2 = \delta_2 = 0$. Accepting this restriction will give the following model:

$$Y_t = a + \beta_0 X_t + \beta_1 X_{t-1} + \gamma_0 Z_t + \gamma_1 Z_{t-1} + \delta_1 Y_{t-1} + u_t \qquad (9.72)$$

It should be clear by now that models (9.71) and (9.72) are both nested models of the initial (9.70) model; but (9.72) is not a nested model of (9.71), and therefore, we cannot proceed to (9.72) after estimating (9.71).

An important question when we are proceeding from the general to the more specific model, is how do we know what the final simplified model should be. To answer this question, Hendry and Richard (1983) suggested that the simplified model should:

1 be data admissible;

2 be consistent with the theory;

3 use regressors that are not correlated with u_t;

4 exhibit parameter constancy;

5 exhibit data coherency, i.e. have residuals that are purely random (white noise); and

6 be encompassing, meaning to include all possible rival models in the sense that it allows us to interpret their results.

Exercises

Exercise 9.1

The file wages_01.wf1 contains data for monthly wage rates (measured in UK pounds) and IQ scores of a large number of City University graduates, after five years of employment:

(a) Find summary statistics for the above mentioned variables and discuss them.

(b) Estimate a functional form that will show how a one-point increase in the IQ score will change the respective wage rate by a constant amount measured in UK pounds. What is the change in the wage rate for a 10-point increase in the IQ score?

(c) Estimate a functional form that will show how a one-point increase in the IQ score will have a percentage change effect on the wage rate. What is the percentage change in the wage rate for a 10-point increase in the IQ score?

(d) Use the Box–Cox transformation to decide which of the two models is more appropriate.

Part

IV

Topics in Econometrics

10 Dummy Variables

Introduction: the nature of qualitative information

So far, we have examined equation specifications that are utilized in econometric analysis, as well as techniques in order to obtain estimates of the parameters in an equation and procedures for assessing the significance, accuracy and precision of those estimates. An assumption implicitly made so far has been that we can always obtain a set of numerical values for all the variables we want to use in our models. However, it is easy to understand that there are variables that can play a very important role in the explanation of an econometric model that are not numerical or easy to quantify. Examples of these could be the following:

(a) gender may play a very important role in determining salaries earned from employment;

(b) different ethnic groups may follow different patterns regarding consumption and savings;

(c) educational levels can definitely affect earnings from employment; and /or

(d) being a member of a labour union may imply different treatment/attitudes than not belonging to the union, and so on.

All these are cases for cross-sectional analysis.

Not easily quantifiable (or in general qualitative) information could also be a case of a time-series econometric framework. Consider the following examples:

(a) changes in a political regime may affect production processes, employment conditions, and so on;

(b) a war can have an impact on all aspects of economic activity;

(c) certain days in a week or certain months in a year can have different effects in the fluctuations of stock prices; and

(d) seasonal effects are quite often observed in the demand of particular products, i.e. ice cream in summer, furs during winter etc.

The aim of this chapter is to show the methods that should be used to include information from qualitative variables into econometric models. This is possible by what are known as dummy or dichotomous variables. The next section presents the possible effects of qualitative variables in regression equations and the methods required to use them. We then present special cases of dummy variables and the Chow test for structural stability.

The use of dummy variables

Intercept dummy variables

Consider the following cross-sectional regression equation:

$$Y_i = \beta_1 + \beta_2 X_{2i} + u_i \tag{10.1}$$

The constant term (β_1) in this equation measures the mean value of Y_i when X_{2i} is equal to zero. The important thing here is that this regression equation assumes that the value of β_0 will be the same for all the observations in our data set. However, the coefficient might be different depending on different aspects regarding our data set. For example, regional differences might exist in the values of Y_i; Y_i might represent the growth of GDP for EU countries for instance. Differences in growth rates are quite possible between core countries and peripheral countries. The question now is how can we quantify this information in order to enter it in the regression equation and check for the validity or not of this possible difference? The answer to this question is: with the use of a special type of variable – a dummy (or fake) variable that captures qualitative effects by coding the different possible outcomes with numerical values.

This can usually be done by simply dichotomizing the possible outcomes and by arbitrarily assigning the values of 0 and 1 to the two different possibilities. So, for the EU countries example we can have a new variable, D, which can take the following values:

$$D = \begin{cases} 1 & \text{for core country} \\ 0 & \text{for peripheral country} \end{cases} \tag{10.2}$$

Note that the choice of which of the two different outcomes is to be assigned the value of 1 does not alter the results in an important way, as we will show later.

Thus, entering this dummy variable in regression model (10.1) we get:

$$Y_i = \beta_1 + \beta_2 X_{2i} + \beta_3 D_i + u_i \tag{10.3}$$

and in order to get the interpretation of D_i, consider the two possible values of D, and how those will affect the specification of equation (10.3). For $D = 0$ we will have:

$$Y_i = \beta_1 + \beta_2 X_{2i} + \beta_3(0)_i + u_i \tag{10.4}$$
$$= \beta_1 + \beta_2 X_{2i} + u_i \tag{10.5}$$

which is the same as for the initial model. Whilst for $D = 1$ we will have:

$$Y_i = \beta_1 + \beta_2 X_{2i} + \beta_3(1)_i + u_i \tag{10.6}$$
$$= (\beta_1 + \beta_3) + \beta_2 X_{2i} + u_i \tag{10.7}$$

where now the constant is different from β_1 and is equal to $(\beta_1 + \beta_3)$. So, we can see that by including the dummy variable, the value of the intercept has changed, shifting the function (and therefore the regression line) up or down; depending on whether the observation in question corresponds to a core or a peripheral country.

Graphically this can be depicted in Figures 10.1 and 10.2 where we have two cases for β_3: (a) the first being positive and shifting the regression line up, suggesting that (if X_{2i} is investment rates) the mean GDP growth for core countries is bigger than for peripheral countries for any level of investment; and (b) the second being negative, suggesting exactly the opposite result.

Once the regression equation (10.3) is estimated, the coefficient β_3 will be tested in the usual way with the t statistic. Only if β_3 is significantly different from zero can we conclude that we have a relationship such as depicted by Figures 10.1 and 10.2.

For other examples we could consider Y as the salary level and X the years of experience of various individuals, with a dummy variable being the sex of each individual (male $= 1$, female $= 0$); or, in the time-series framework we might have dummy variables for certain periods (like war dummies that take the value of 1 for the

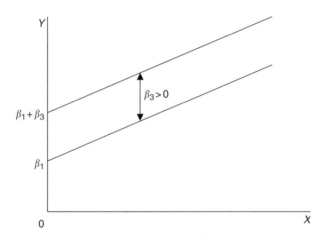

Figure 10.1   The effect of a dummy variable on the constant of the regression line

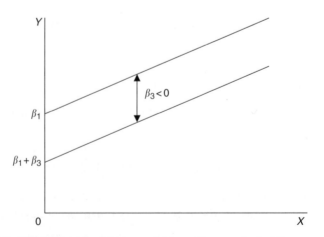

Figure 10.2   The effect of a dummy variable on the constant of the regression line

period during the war and zero otherwise), or for certain events (like dummy variables for oil price shocks, etc.).

Slope dummy variables

In the previous section, we examined how qualitative information can affect the regression model, and we saw that only the constant in the relationship is allowed to change. The implicit assumption underlying this was that the relationships between Y and the Xs were not affected by the inclusion of the qualitative dummy variable.

The relationship between Y and the Xs is represented by the derivative (or slope) of the function in the simple linear regression model, and by the partial derivatives in the multiple regression model. Sometimes, however, it could be the case that slope coefficients might be affected by differences regarding dummy variables.

Consider, for example, the Keynesian consumption function model, relating consumer expenditure (Y_t) to disposable income (X_{2t}). This simple regression model has the following form:

$$Y_t = \beta_1 + \beta_2 X_{2t} + u_t \tag{10.8}$$

The slope coefficient (β_2) of this regression is the marginal propensity to consume given by:

$$\frac{dY_t}{dX_{2t}} = \beta_2 \tag{10.9}$$

and shows the percentage of the disposable income that will be consumed. Assume that we have time-series observations for total consumer expenditure and disposable income from 1970 until 1999 for the UK economy. Assume, further, that we think that a change in the marginal propensity to consume occurred in 1982 due to the oil price shock that generally affected the economic environment. In order to test this, we need to construct a dummy variable (D_t) that will take the following values:

$$D = \begin{cases} 0 & \text{for years from 1970--81} \\ 1 & \text{for years from 1982--99} \end{cases} \tag{10.10}$$

This dummy variable, because we assume that it affected the slope parameter, must be included in the model in the following multiplicative way:

$$Y_t = \beta_1 + \beta_2 X_{2t} + \beta_3 D_t X_{2t} + u_t \tag{10.11}$$

The effect of the dummy variable can be dichotomized again according to two different outcomes. For $D_t = 0$ we will have:

$$Y_t = \beta_1 + \beta_2 X_{2t} + \beta_3 (0) X_{2t} + u_t \tag{10.12}$$

$$= \beta_1 + \beta_2 X_{2t} + u_t \tag{10.13}$$

which is the same as with the initial model, and for $D = 1$ we will have:

$$Y_t = \beta_1 + \beta_2 X_{2t} + \beta_3(1)X_{2t} + u_t \qquad (10.14)$$

$$= \beta_1 + (\beta_2 + \beta_3)X_{2i} + ut \qquad (10.15)$$

So, before 1982 the marginal propensity to consume is given by β_2, and after 1982 it is $\beta_2 + \beta_3$ (higher if β_3 is higher and lower if β_3 is lower). To illustrate the effect better, see Figures 10.3 and 10.4 for the cases where $\beta_3 > 0$ and $\beta_3 < 0$ respectively.

The combined effect of intercept and slope dummies

It is now simple to understand what the outcome will be when using a dummy variable that is allowed to affect both the intercept and the slope coefficients. Consider the model:

$$Y_t = \beta_1 + \beta_2 X_{2t} + u_t \qquad (10.16)$$

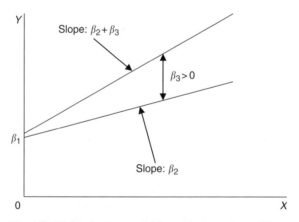

Figure 10.3   The effect of a dummy variable on the constant of the regression line

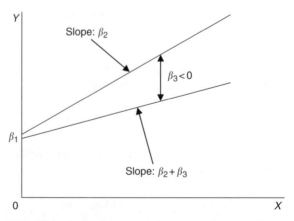

Figure 10.4   The effect of a dummy variable on the constant of the regression line

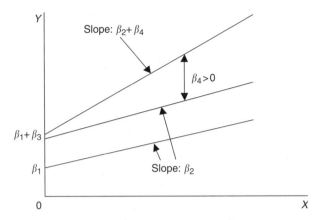

Figure 10.5 The effect of a dummy variable on the constant of the regression line

and let's assume that we have a dummy variable defined as follows:

$$D = \begin{cases} 0 & \text{for } t = 1, \ldots, s \\ 1 & \text{for } t = s+1, \ldots, T \end{cases} \qquad (10.17)$$

Then, using the dummy variable to examine its effects on both the constant and the slope coefficients we will have:

$$Y_t = \beta_1 + \beta_2 X_{2t} + \beta_3 D_t + \beta_4 D_t X_{2t} + u_t \qquad (10.18)$$

and the different outcomes will be, for $D_t = 0$:

$$Y_t = \beta_1 + \beta_2 X_{2t} + u_t \qquad (10.19)$$

which is the same as for the initial model, and for $D = 1$:

$$Y_t = (\beta_1 + \beta_3) + (\beta_2 + \beta_4)X_{2t} + u_t \qquad (10.20)$$

The effects are shown graphically in Figure 10.5.

Computer example of the use of dummy variables

The file dummies.wf1 contains data on wages (*wage*) and IQ levels (*iq*) of 935 individuals. It also includes various dummy variables for specific characteristics of the 935 individuals. One is the dummy variable *male*, which takes the value of 1 when the individual is a male and the value of 0 if the individual is female.

We want to see the possible effects of the *male* dummy on the wage rates (i.e. to examine whether males get different wages than females). First, we regress only wages on the IQ levels and a constant, to examine whether IQ plays a score in the wage

Table 10.1 The relationship between wages and IQ

Dependent Variable: WAGE
Method: Least Squares
Date: 03/30/04 Time: 14:20
Sample: 1 935
Included observations: 935

Variable	Coefficient	Std. Error	t-Statistic	Prob.
C	116.9916	85.64153	1.366061	0.1722
IQ	8.303064	0.836395	9.927203	0.0000

R-squared	0.095535	Mean dependent var	957.9455
Adjusted R-squared	0.094566	S.D. dependent var	404.3608
S.E. of regression	384.7667	Akaike info criterion	14.74529
Sum squared resid	1.38E+08	Schwarz criterion	14.75564
Log likelihood	−6891.422	F-statistic	98.54936
Durbin–Watson stat	0.188070	Prob(F-statistic)	0.000000

determination. The results are obtained by using the following command in EViews:

```
ls wage c iq
```

and they are presented in Table 10.1.

From these results we understand that IQ is indeed an important determinant (its *t* statistic is highly significant), and because our model is linear we also have that a 1-unit increase in the IQ level corresponds to an 8.3-units increase in the wage rate of the individual. Independent of the IQ level, the wage rate is 116.9 units.

Using a constant dummy

Including the male dummy as a dummy affecting only the constant, we find the regression results (shown in Table 10.2). The command in EViews for this estimation is the following:

```
ls wage c iq male
```

From these results we can now see that, independent of the IQ, if the individual is a female she will have a wage of 224.8 units, while if the individual is a male he will have a wage of 722.8 units (224.8 + 498.0). This interpretation is of course based on the fact that the coefficient of the dummy variable is highly statistically significant, reflecting the fact that, indeed, males get higher wages than females.

Using a slope dummy

Continuing, we want to check whether the marginal effect is also affected by the sex. In other words, we want to see whether, on average, an increase in the IQ level of men will mean higher wage increases than for women. To do this we estimate a regression

Table 10.2 Wages and IQ and the role of sex (using a constant dummy)

Dependent Variable: WAGE
Method: Least Squares
Date: 03/30/04 Time: 14:21
Sample: 1 935
Included observations: 935

Variable	Coefficient	Std. Error	t-Statistic	Prob.
C	224.8438	66.64243	3.373884	0.0008
IQ	5.076630	0.662354	7.664527	0.0000
MALE	498.0493	20.07684	24.80715	0.0000

R-squared	0.455239	Mean dependent var	957.9455
Adjusted R-squared	0.454070	S.D. dependent var	404.3608
S.E. of regression	298.7705	Akaike info criterion	14.24043
Sum squared resid	83193885	Schwarz criterion	14.25596
Log likelihood	−6654.402	F-statistic	389.4203
Durbin–Watson stat	0.445380	Prob(F-statistic)	0.000000

Table 10.3 Wages and IQ and the role of sex (using a slope dummy)

Dependent Variable: WAGE
Method: Least Squares
Date: 03/30/04 Time: 14:21
Sample: 1 935
Included observations: 935

Variable	Coefficient	Std. Error	t-Statistic	Prob.
C	412.8602	67.36367	6.128825	0.0000
IQ	3.184180	0.679283	4.687559	0.0000
MALE * IQ	4.840134	0.193746	24.98181	0.0000

R-squared	0.458283	Mean dependent var	957.9455
Adjusted R-squared	0.457120	S.D. dependent var	404.3608
S.E. of regression	297.9346	Akaike info criterion	14.23483
Sum squared resid	82728978	Schwarz criterion	14.25036
Log likelihood	−6651.782	F-statistic	394.2274
Durbin–Watson stat	0.455835	Prob(F-statistic)	0.000000

in EViews that includes a multiplicative slope dummy (*male* * *iq*), using the command:

```
ls wage c iq male*iq
```

The results of which are presented in Table 10.3. We observe that the slope dummy is statistically significant indicating that there is a difference in the slope coefficient for different sexes. Particularly, we have that the marginal effect for women is 3.18 while that for men is equal to $3.18 + 4.84 = 8.02$.

Using both dummies together

Finally, we can examine the above relationship further by using both dummies at the same time to see the difference in the results. The results of this model are presented

Table 10.4 Wages and IQ and the role of sex (using both constant and slope dummies)

Dependent Variable: WAGE
Method: Least Squares
Date: 03/30/04 Time: 14:23
Sample: 1 935
Included observations: 935

Variable	Coefficient	Std. Error	t-Statistic	Prob.
C	357.8567	84.78941	4.220535	0.0000
IQ	3.728518	0.849174	4.390756	0.0000
MALE	149.1039	139.6018	1.068066	0.2858
MALE*IQ	3.412121	1.350971	2.525680	0.0117

R-squared	0.458946	Mean dependent var	957.9455
Adjusted R-squared	0.457202	S.D. dependent var	404.3608
S.E. of regression	297.9121	Akaike info criterion	14.23574
Sum squared resid	82627733	Schwarz criterion	14.25645
Log likelihood	−6651.210	F-statistic	263.2382
Durbin–Watson stat	0.450852	Prob(F-statistic)	0.000000

in Table 10.4 and suggest that only the effect on the slope is now significant, and the effect on the constant is equal to zero.

Special cases of the use of dummy variables

Using dummy variables with multiple categories

A dummy variable might have more than two categories. Consider for example a model of wage determination where Y_i is the wage rate of a number of individuals and X_{2i} is the years of experience of each individual in the sample. It is logical to assume that the educational attainment level will affect the wage rate of each individual as well. Therefore, in this case we can have several dummies defined for the highest level of educational attainment of each individual, given by:

$$D_1 = \begin{cases} 1 & \text{if primary only} \\ 0 & \text{otherwise} \end{cases} \tag{10.21}$$

$$D_2 = \begin{cases} 1 & \text{if secondary only} \\ 0 & \text{otherwise} \end{cases} \tag{10.22}$$

$$D_3 = \begin{cases} 1 & \text{if BSc only} \\ 0 & \text{otherwise} \end{cases} \tag{10.23}$$

$$D_4 = \begin{cases} 1 & \text{if MSc only} \\ 0 & \text{otherwise} \end{cases} \tag{10.24}$$

So, we can have a wage equation of the following form:

$$Y_i = \beta_1 + \beta_2 X_{2i} + a_2 D_{2i} + a_3 D_{3i} + a_4 D_{4i} + u_i \tag{10.25}$$

Note that we did not use all four dummy variables. This is because if we use all four dummy variables we will have exact multicollinearity since $D_1 + D_2 + D_3 + D_4$ will always be equal to 1, and therefore they will form an exact linear relationship with the constant β_1. This known as the *dummy variable trap*. To avoid this, the rule is that the number of dummy variables that we use will always be one less than the total number of possible categories. The dummy variables that will be omitted will define a reference group, as will become clear in the interpretation of the dummies on the model.

The wage equation can be separated according to the use of the dummies as follows. If $D_2 = 1$; $D_3 = D_4 = 0$ and then:

$$Y_i = \beta_1 + \beta_2 X_{2i} + a_2 D_{2i} + u_i \tag{10.26}$$
$$= (\beta_1 + a_2) + \beta_2 X_{2i} + u_i \tag{10.27}$$

so, the constant for the case of secondary education is $(\beta_1 + a_2)$. If $D_3 = 1$; $D_2 = D_4 = 0$ and:

$$Y_i = \beta_1 + \beta_2 X_{2i} + a_3 D_{3i} + u_i \tag{10.28}$$
$$= (\beta_1 + a_3) + \beta_2 X_{2i} + u_i \tag{10.29}$$

so that the constant for the case of BSc degree holders is $(\beta_1 + a_3)$. If $D_4 = 1$; $D_2 = D_3 = 0$, then:

$$Y_i = \beta_1 + \beta_2 X_{2i} + a_3 D_{4i} + u_i \tag{10.30}$$
$$= (\beta_1 + a_4) + \beta_2 X_{2i} + u_i \tag{10.31}$$

so that the constant for the case of MSc degree holders is $(\beta_1 + a_4)$. While if $D_2 = D_3 = D_4 = 0$, then:

$$Y_i = \beta_1 + \beta_2 X_{2i} \tag{10.32}$$

and for this case the constant for the primary education is equal to the constant of the original model, β_1.

So, in fact we don't need all four variables to depict all four outcomes. Taking as reference variable primary education, coefficients a_2, a_3 and a_4 measure the expected wage differential that workers with secondary, BSc and MSc degrees will have compared to those with primary education only.

It is important to note that, mathematically, it does not matter which dummy variable is omitted. We will leave this as an exercise for the reader to understand why this is the case. However, the choice of the D_1 dummy to be used as the reference dummy variable is a convenient one, because it is the lowest level of education and therefore we expect the lowest wage rates to correspond to this category.

In terms of graphical depiction, the effect of the multiple dummy variable 'educational level' is shown in Figure 10.6.

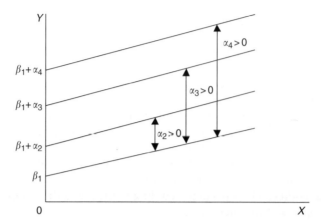

Figure 10.6   The effect of a dummy variable on the constant of the regression line

The dummy variable trap is a quite serious mistake and should be avoided by all means. Fortunately, computer softwares will signal to the researcher a message that OLS estimation is not possible, suggesting that there is a possibility of committing exact multicollinearity due to the dummy variable trap by mistake (for more about exact multicollinearity see Chapter 6).

Using more than one dummy variable

The dummy variable analysis can be easily extended to cases of more than one dummy variable, some of which may have more than one category. In cases like this, the interpretation of the dummy variables, although following the regular form, might appear more complicated and the researcher should take care using them.

To illustrate this, consider the previous model, hypothesizing that apart from the educational level there are other qualitative aspects determining the wage rate, such as age, gender and category of occupation. In this case we can have the following model:

$$Yi = \beta_1 + \beta_2 X_{2i} + \beta_3 EDUC_{2i} + \beta_4 EDUC_{3i} + \beta_5 EDUC_{4i}$$
$$+ \beta_6 SEXM_i + \beta_7 AGE_{2i} + \beta_8 AGE_{3i}$$
$$+ \beta_9 OCUP_{2i} + \beta_{10} OCUP_{3i} + \beta_{11} OCUP_{4i} + u_i \qquad (10.33)$$

where we have the following dummies:

$$EDUC_1 = \begin{cases} 1 & \text{if primary only} \\ 0 & \text{otherwise} \end{cases} \qquad (10.34)$$

$$EDUC_2 = \begin{cases} 1 & \text{if secondary only} \\ 0 & \text{otherwise} \end{cases} \qquad (10.35)$$

$$EDUC_3 = \begin{cases} 1 & \text{if BSc only} \\ 0 & \text{otherwise} \end{cases} \tag{10.36}$$

$$EDUC_4 = \begin{cases} 1 & \text{if MSc only} \\ 0 & \text{otherwise} \end{cases} \tag{10.37}$$

and $EDUC_1$ defines the reference group.

$$SEXM = \begin{cases} 1 & \text{if male} \\ 0 & \text{if female} \end{cases} \tag{10.38}$$

$$SEXF = \begin{cases} 1 & \text{if female} \\ 0 & \text{if male} \end{cases} \tag{10.39}$$

and *SEXF* defines the reference group.

$$AGE_1 = \begin{cases} 1 & \text{for less than 30} \\ 0 & \text{otherwise} \end{cases} \tag{10.40}$$

$$AGE_2 = \begin{cases} 1 & \text{for 30 to 40} \\ 0 & \text{otherwise} \end{cases} \tag{10.41}$$

$$AGE_3 = \begin{cases} 1 & \text{for more than 40} \\ 0 & \text{otherwise} \end{cases} \tag{10.42}$$

and AGE_1 is the reference group. And finally:

$$OCUP_1 = \begin{cases} 1 & \text{if unskilled} \\ 0 & \text{otherwise} \end{cases} \tag{10.43}$$

$$OCUP_2 = \begin{cases} 1 & \text{if skilled} \\ 0 & \text{otherwise} \end{cases} \tag{10.44}$$

$$OCUP_3 = \begin{cases} 1 & \text{if clerical} \\ 0 & \text{otherwise} \end{cases} \tag{10.45}$$

$$OCUP_4 = \begin{cases} 1 & \text{if self-employed} \\ 0 & \text{otherwise} \end{cases} \tag{10.46}$$

with $OCUP_1$ being the reference group in this case.

Using seasonal dummy variables

In the analysis of time series data, seasonal effects might play a very important role, and the seasonal variations can be easily examined with the use of dummy variables.

So, for example, for quarterly time series data we can introduce four dummy variables as follows:

$$D_1 = \begin{cases} 1 & \text{for the first quarter} \\ 0 & \text{otherwise} \end{cases} \qquad (10.47)$$

$$D_2 = \begin{cases} 1 & \text{for the second quarter} \\ 0 & \text{otherwise} \end{cases} \qquad (10.48)$$

$$D_3 = \begin{cases} 1 & \text{for the third quarter} \\ 0 & \text{otherwise} \end{cases} \qquad (10.49)$$

$$D_4 = \begin{cases} 1 & \text{for the fourth quarter} \\ 0 & \text{otherwise} \end{cases} \qquad (10.50)$$

and in a regression model we can use them as:

$$Y_t = \beta_1 + \beta_2 X_{2t} + a_2 D_{2t} + a_3 D_{3t} + a_4 D_{4t} + u_t \qquad (10.51)$$

and can analyse (using the procedure described above) the effects on the average level of Y of each of these dummies. Note that we have used only 3 of the 4 dummies in order to avoid the dummy variable trap described above. Similarly, it will be easy for the reader to understand that for monthly data sets we will have 12 dummy variables, while if we use the constant as well we need to use only 11, keeping one as a reference group. An illustrative example is given below using the January-effect hypothesis for monthly stock returns.

Computer example of dummy variables with multiple categories

Using again the data in the file dummies.wf1 we can examine the case of dummy variables with multiple categories. In order to see the effect we can use, for example, the educational level variable which has four different classifications as defined in the previous section. The command to examine the effect of educational levels, in EViews, is the following:

```
ls wage c educ2 educ3 educ4
```

Note that we do not use all four dummies, because we have the constant and therefore we shouldn't include them all in order to avoid the dummy variable trap. The results are given in Table 10.5.

The results provide statistically significant estimates for all coefficients, so we can proceed with the interpretation. The effect on wages if an individual has finished only primary education is given by the constant and is equal to 774.2. An individual who has finished secondary education will have a wage of 88.4 units higher than that of those with primary education only, an individual with a BSc will have 221.4 units more than

Table 10.5 Dummy variables with multiple categories

Dependent Variable: WAGE
Method: Least Squares
Date: 03/30/04 Time: 14:48
Sample: 1 935
Included observations: 935

Variable	Coefficient	Std. Error	t-Statistic	Prob.
C	774.2500	40.95109	18.90670	0.0000
EDUC2	88.42176	45.30454	1.951719	0.0513
EDUC3	221.4167	48.88677	4.529174	0.0000
EDUC4	369.1184	47.69133	7.739739	0.0000

R-squared	0.100340	Mean dependent var	957.9455
Adjusted R-squared	0.097441	S.D. dependent var	404.3608
S.E. of regression	384.1553	Akaike info criterion	14.74424
Sum squared resid	1.37E+08	Schwarz criterion	14.76495
Log likelihood	−6888.932	F-statistic	34.61189
Durbin–Watson stat	0.166327	Prob(F-statistic)	0.000000

Table 10.6 Changing the reference dummy variable

Dependent Variable: WAGE
Method: Least Squares
Date: 03/30/04 Time: 14:58
Sample: 1 935
Included observations: 935

Variable	Coefficient	Std. Error	t-Statistic	Prob.
C	1143.368	24.44322	46.77651	0.0000
EDUC1	−369.1184	47.69133	−7.739739	0.0000
EDUC2	−280.6967	31.19263	−8.998812	0.0000
EDUC3	−147.7018	36.19938	−4.080229	0.0000

R-squared	0.100340	Mean dependent var	957.9455
Adjusted R-squared	0.097441	S.D. dependent var	404.3608
S.E. of regression	384.1553	Akaike info criterion	14.74424
Sum squared resid	1.37E+08	Schwarz criterion	14.76495
Log likelihood	−6888.932	F-statistic	34.61189
Durbin–Watson stat	0.166327	Prob(F-statistic)	0.000000

that of primary, and finally an individual with an MSc will have 369.1 more units of wage than primary only. So the final effects can be summarized as follows:

Primary	774.2
Secondary	862.6
BSc	995.6
MSc	1,143.3

It is easy to show that if we change the reference variable the results will remain unchanged. Consider the following regression equation model, which uses as a reference category the *educ*4 dummy (the command in EViews is: ls wage c educ1 educ2 educ3), and of which the results are presented in Table 10.6. We leave it for the reader to do the simple calculations and see that the final effects are identical to those of the previous case. Thus, changing the reference dummy does not affect our results at all.

Table 10.7   Using more than one dummies together

Dependent Variable: WAGE
Method: Least Squares
Date: 03/30/04 Time: 15:03
Sample: 1 935
Included observations: 935

Variable	Coefficient	Std. Error	t-Statistic	Prob.
C	641.3229	41.16019	15.58115	0.0000
EDUC2	19.73155	35.27278	0.559399	0.5760
EDUC3	112.4091	38.39894	2.927402	0.0035
EDUC4	197.5036	37.74860	5.232077	0.0000
AGE2	−17.94827	29.59479	−0.606467	0.5444
AGE3	71.25035	30.88441	2.307001	0.0213
MALE	488.0926	20.22037	24.13865	0.0000

R-squared	0.462438	Mean dependent var	957.9455
Adjusted R-squared	0.458963	S.D. dependent var	404.3608
S.E. of regression	297.4286	Akaike info criterion	14.23568
Sum squared resid	82094357	Schwarz criterion	14.27192
Log likelihood	−6648.182	F-statistic	133.0523
Durbin–Watson stat	0.451689	Prob(F-statistic)	0.000000

The reader can check that changing the reference category to *educ2* or *educ3* yields the same results.

Finally, we may have an example using three different dummies (*educ*, *age* and *male*) together in the same equation (we will use *educ1*, *age1* and *female* as reference dummies to avoid the dummy variable trap) and we will leave this as an exercise for the reader to try and interpret the results of this model. The results are presented in Table 10.7.

Application: the January effect in emerging stockmarkets

Asteriou and Kavetsos (2003) examined the efficient market hypothesis (in terms of the presence or not of the 'January effect' for eight transition economies, namely the Czech Republic, Hungary, Lithuania, Poland, Romania, Russia, Slovakia and Slovenia. (For more details regarding the January effect see Gultekin and Gultekin, 1983, and Jaffe and Westerfield, 1989.) In their analysis they used a monthly data set from 1991 to the early months of 2003 using monthly time series data, for the stockmarkets of each of the aforementioned countries. The test for January effects is strongly based on the use of seasonal dummy variables. In practice what needs to be done is to create 12 dummies (one for each month) that take the following values:

$$D_{it} = \begin{cases} 1 & \text{if the return at time } t \text{ corresponds to month } i \\ 0 & \text{otherwise} \end{cases} \qquad (10.52)$$

Table 10.8 Tests for seasonal effects

Variables	Czech Rep. coef	t-stat	Hungary coef	t-stat	Lithuania coef	t-stat	Poland coef	t-stat
D1	0.016	0.631	**0.072**	**2.471**	−0.008	−0.248	**0.072**	**1.784**
D2	0.004	0.146	−0.008	−0.280	0.018	0.543	0.033	0.826
D3	−0.001	−0.031	0.017	0.626	0.041	1.220	−0.026	−0.650
D4	0.001	0.023	0.022	0.800	−0.014	−0.421	0.041	1.024
D5	−0.013	−0.514	−0.005	−0.180	−0.036	−1.137	0.049	1.261
D6	−0.041	−1.605	0.004	0.126	**−0.071**	**−2.106**	−0.051	−1.265
D7	0.036	1.413	0.017	0.583	−0.013	−0.381	0.033	0.814
D8	−0.022	−0.849	0.007	0.245	−0.009	−0.264	0.014	0.341
D9	−0.029	−1.127	−0.027	−0.926	**−0.086**	**−2.547**	−0.034	−0.842
D10	−0.014	−0.532	0.011	0.387	−0.014	−0.420	0.025	0.611
D11	−0.039	−1.519	−0.002	−0.058	0.048	1.427	0.012	0.287
D12	0.033	1.294	**0.060**	**2.083**	−0.011	−0.325	0.061	1.528
R^2(OLS)	0.105		0.070		0.196		0.070	
B-G Test	12.934 (0.374)		12.409 (0.413)		34.718 (0.001)		34.591 (0.001)	
LM(1) Test	0.351 (0.553)		0.039 (0.843)		4.705 (0.030)		2.883 (0.090)	

	Romania coef	t-stat	Russia coef	t-stat	Slovakia coef	t-stat	Slovenia coef	t-stat
D1	0.088	1.873	0.034	0.581	0.044	1.223	**0.061**	**2.479**
D2	0.007	0.154	0.065	1.125	**0.081**	**2.274**	−0.012	−0.482
D3	−0.064	−1.367	0.089	1.536	−0.012	−0.327	−0.023	−0.934
D4	0.036	0.846	0.078	1.347	−0.048	−1.329	−0.013	−0.537
D5	0.009	0.218	0.027	0.471	−0.034	−0.939	0.011	0.455
D6	0.034	0.727	0.067	1.100	−0.012	−0.313	−0.028	−1.089
D7	−0.032	−0.689	−0.025	−0.404	0.002	0.044	**0.048**	**1.854**
D8	−0.023	−0.499	−0.041	−0.669	0.032	0.846	**0.045**	**1.855**
D9	−0.041	−0.877	−0.056	−0.919	−0.024	−0.631	0.006	0.232
D10	0.007	0.147	0.047	0.810	−0.012	−0.340	0.033	1.336
D11	0.002	0.033	0.035	0.599	−0.018	−0.501	0.006	0.243
D12	−0.005	−0.103	0.086	1.487	0.037	1.028	0.007	0.305
R^2(OLS)	0.141		0.075		0.103		0.155	
B-G Test	16.476 (0.170)		17.014 (0.149)		24.517 (0.017)		27.700 (0.006)	
LM(1) Test	1.355 (0.244)		0.904 (0.342)		13.754 (0.000)		0.612 (0.434)	

From the methodology point of view, to test for seasonal effects in general corresponds to estimating the following equation:

$$R_{it} = a_1 D_{1t} + a_2 D_{2t} + a_3 D_{3t} + \cdots + a_{12} D_{12t} + u_t \tag{10.53}$$

where R_t indicates the stockmarket return at time t, a_i is the average return of month i, D_{it} are the seasonal dummy variables as defined above, and u_t is an iid (ideally independently distributed) error term. The null hypothesis to be tested is that the coefficients a_i are equal. If they are equal there are no seasonal effects, and vice versa.

Then, to explicitly test for January effects, the regression model is modified as follows:

$$R_{it} = c + a_2 D_{2t} + a_3 D_{3t} + \cdots + a_{12} D_{12t} + u_t \tag{10.54}$$

Table 10.9   Tests for the January effect

Variables	Czech Rep.		Hungary		Lithuania		Poland	
	coef	t-stat	coef	t-stat	coef	t-stat	coef	t-stat
C	0.016	0.631	**0.072**	**2.471**	−0.008	−0.248	**0.072**	**1.784**
D2	−0.012	−0.327	−0.079	−1.976	0.027	0.559	−0.039	−0.677
D3	−0.017	−0.455	−0.054	−1.348	0.050	1.038	−0.098	−1.721
D4	−0.015	−0.416	−0.049	−1.227	−0.006	−0.123	−0.031	−0.537
D5	−0.029	−0.809	−0.077	−1.906	−0.027	−0.591	−0.023	−0.413
D6	−0.057	−1.581	−0.068	−1.658	−0.063	−1.314	−0.123	−2.156
D7	0.020	0.553	−0.055	−1.335	−0.005	−0.094	−0.039	−0.686
D8	−0.038	−1.046	−0.064	−1.574	−0.001	−0.012	−0.058	−1.020
D9	−0.045	−1.243	**−0.098**	**−2.402**	−0.078	−1.626	**−0.106**	**−1.856**
D10	−0.030	−0.822	−0.060	−1.474	−0.006	−0.122	−0.047	−0.829
D11	−0.055	−1.520	**−0.073**	**−1.788**	0.057	1.184	−0.060	−1.058
D12	0.017	0.469	−0.011	−0.274	−0.003	−0.055	−0.010	−0.181
R^2(OLS)	0.105		0.070		0.196		0.070	
B-G Test	12.934 (0.374)		12.409 (0.413)		34.718 (0.001)		34.591 (0.001)	
LM(1) Test	0.351 (0.553)		0.039 (0.843)		4.705 (0.030)		2.883 (0.090)	

	Romania		Russia		Slovakia		Slovenia	
	coef	t-stat	coef	t-stat	coef	t-stat	coef	t-stat
C	**0.088**	**1.873**	0.034	0.581	0.044	1.223	**0.061**	**2.479**
D2	−0.081	−1.215	0.031	0.385	0.038	0.743	**−0.072**	**−2.094**
D3	**−0.152**	**−2.290**	0.055	0.676	−0.055	−1.096	**−0.084**	**−2.413**
D4	−0.052	−0.813	0.044	0.542	**−0.091**	**−1.805**	**−0.074**	**−2.133**
D5	−0.078	−1.236	−0.006	−0.077	−0.077	−1.529	−0.050	−1.431
D6	−0.054	−0.810	0.034	0.402	−0.056	−1.069	**−0.089**	**−2.489**
D7	−0.120	−1.811	−0.058	−0.693	−0.042	−0.810	−0.012	−0.339
D8	−0.111	−1.677	−0.074	−0.885	−0.012	−0.228	−0.015	−0.441
D9	**−0.129**	**−1.944**	−0.090	−1.067	−0.068	−1.300	−0.055	−1.589
D10	−0.081	−1.220	0.013	0.162	−0.056	−1.105	−0.028	−0.808
D11	−0.086	−1.301	0.001	0.013	−0.062	−1.219	−0.055	−1.581
D12	−0.093	−1.397	0.052	0.641	−0.007	−0.138	−0.053	−1.537
R^2(OLS)	0.141		0.075		0.103		0.155	
B-G Test	16.476 (0.170)		17.014 (0.149)		24.517 (0.017)		27.700 (0.006)	
LM(1) Test	1.355 (0.244)		0.904 (0.342)		13.754 (0.000)		0.612 (0.434)	

where R_t again indicates stockmarket returns, the intercept c represents the mean return for January, and in this case the coefficients a_i, represent the difference between the return of January and month i.

The null hypothesis to be tested in this case is that all dummy variable coefficients are equal to zero. A negative value of a dummy coefficient would be proof of a January effect. The estimation of the coefficients in equation (10.54) will specify which months have lower average returns than those obtained in January.

The summarized results obtained from Asteriou and Kavetsos (2003) for equation (10.54) are presented in Table 10.8, while those for the January effect are presented in Table 10.9. From these results we see, first, that there are significant seasonal effects for five out of the eight countries in the sample (note that bold indicates that the coefficients are significant in Table 10.8), while they also found evidence in favour of the January effect (bold indicates coefficients in Table 10.9) for Hungary, Poland,

Romania, Slovakia and Slovenia. For more details regarding the interpretation of these results see Asteriou and Kavetsos (2003).

Tests for structural stability

The dummy variable approach

The use of dummy variables can be considered as a test for stability of the estimated parameters in a regression equation. When an equation includes both a dummy variable for the intercept and a multiplicative dummy variable for each of the explanatory variables, the intercept and each partial slope is allowed to vary, implying different underlying structures for the two conditions (0 and 1) associated with the dummy variable.

Therefore, using dummy variables is like conducting a test for structural stability. In essence, two different equations are being estimated from the coefficients of a single equation model. Individual t statistics are used to test the significance of each term, including a dummy variable, while the statistical significance for the entire equation can be established by a Wald test as described in Chapter 5.

The advantages of using the dummy variable approach when testing for structural stability are the following:

(a) a single equation is used to provide the set of the estimated coefficients for two or more structures;

(b) only one degree of freedom is lost for every dummy variable used in the equation;

(c) a larger sample is used for the estimation of the model (than the Chow test case that we will describe below), improving the precision of the estimated coefficients; and

(d) it provides us with information regarding the exact nature of the parameter instability (i.e. whether or not it affects the intercept and one or more of the partial slope coefficients).

The Chow test for structural stability

An alternative way to test for structural stability is provided by the Chow test (Chow, 1960). The test consists of breaking the sample into two (or more according to the case) structures, estimating the equation for each of them, and then comparing the *SSR* from the separate equations with that of the whole sample.

To illustrate this, consider the case of the Keynesian consumption function for the UK data set, examined with the use of dummy variables. In order to apply the Chow test the following steps are followed:

Step 1 Estimate the basic regression equation:

$$Y_t = \beta_1 + \beta_2 X_{2t} + u_t \tag{10.55}$$

for three different data sets:

(a) the whole sample (n),

(b) the period before the oil shock (n_1), and

(c) the period after the oil shock (n_2).

Step 2 Obtain the *SSR* for each of the three subsets and label them as SSR_n, SSR_{n_1} and SSR_{n_2} respectively as above.

Step 3 Calculate the following F statistic:

$$F = \frac{(SSR_n - (SSR_{n_1} + SSR_{n_2}))/k}{(SSR_{n_1} + SSR_{n_2})/(n_1 + n_2 + 2k)} \qquad (10.56)$$

where k is the number of parameters estimated in the equation of step 1 (for this case $k = 2$).

Step 4 Compare the F statistic obtained above with the critical $F_{(k, n_1 + n_2 + 2k)}$ for the required significance level. If F-statistical $> F$-critical then we reject the hypothesis H_0 that the parameters are stable for the entire data set, and conclude that there is evidence of structural instability.

Note that while the Chow test might suggest that there is parameter instability, it does not give us any information regarding which parameters are affected. For this reason dummy variables provide a better and more direct way of examining structural stability.

Questions

Questions

1 Explain how we can use dummy variables to quantify qualitative information in a regression model. Use appropriate examples from the economic theory.

2 Show what is the combined effect of the use of a dichotomous dummy variable on the constant and the slope coefficient (both graphically and mathematically) of the simple regression model.

3 Provide an example of economic theory where the use of seasonal dummy variables is required. Explain why when there is a constant included in the model, we cannot use all dummies together but need to exclude one dummy that will be the reference dummy. What is the meaning of a reference dummy variable?

4 Describe the steps involved in conducting the Chow test for structural stability. Is the Chow test preferable to the dummy variables approach? Explain why or why not.

11 Dynamic Econometric Models

Although many econometric models are formulated in static terms, it is quite possible in time series models to have relationships where the concept of time plays a more central role. So, for example, we might find ourselves with a model that has the following form:

$$Y_t = a + \beta_0 X_t + \beta_1 X_{t-1} + \beta_2 X_{t-2} + \cdots + \beta_p X_{t-p} + u_t \qquad (11.1)$$

In this model we have that Y_t is not depending on the current value of X_t only, but also on past (lagged) values of X_t. There are various reasons why lags might need to be introduced in a model. Consider, for example, an exogenous shock stimulating the purchase of capital goods. It is unavoidable that some time will elapse from the moment the shock occurred till the firm's knowledge of the situation. This can be either because (a) it requires some time to get the relevant statistical information, (b) it takes time for the firm's managers to draw up plans for the new capital project, or (c) the firm might want to obtain different prices from competing suppliers of capital equipment, among various other reasons. Therefore, lagged effects will occur and dynamic models which can capture the effects of the time paths of exogenous variables and/or disturbances on the time path of the endogenous variables are needed.

In general there are two types of dynamic models:

(1) **distributed lag** models that include lagged terms of the independent (or explanatory variables), and

(2) **autoregressive** models that include lagged terms of the dependent variable.

These two types of model are described in this chapter.

Distributed lag models

Consider the model:

$$Y_t = \alpha + \beta_0 X_t + \beta_1 X_{t-1} + \beta_2 X_{t-2} + \cdots + \beta_p X_{t-p} + u_t$$

$$= \alpha + \sum_{i=0}^{p} \beta_i X_{t-i} + u_t \qquad (11.2)$$

in which the βs are coefficients of the lagged X terms. With this model the reaction to Y_t after a change in X_t is distributed over a number of time periods. In the model we have p lagged terms and the current X_t term, so, it takes $p+1$ periods for the full effect of a change in X_t to influence Y_t.

It is interesting to examine the effect of the βs:

(a) The coefficient β_0 is the weight attached to the current X (X_t) given by $\Delta Y_t / \Delta X_t$. It therefore, shows how much the average change in Y_t will be when X_t changes by one unit. β_0 is for this reason called the impact multiplier.

(b) β_i is similarly given by $\Delta Y_t / \Delta X_{t-i}$ and shows the average change in Y_t for a unit increase in X_{t-i}, i.e. for a unit increase in X made i periods prior to t. For this reason the β_is are called the interim multipliers of order i.

(c) The total effect is given by the sum of the effects on all periods:

$$\sum_{i=0}^{p} \beta_i = \beta_0 + \beta_1 + \beta_2 + \cdots + \beta_p \qquad (11.3)$$

This is also called the long-run equilibrium effect when the economy is at the steady state (equilibrium) level. In the long-run:

$$X^* = X_t = X_{t-1} = \cdots = X_{t-p} \qquad (11.4)$$

and therefore:

$$Y_t^* = \alpha + \beta_0 X^* + \beta_1 X^* + \beta_2 X^* + \cdots + \beta_p X^* + u_t$$

$$= \alpha + X^* \sum_{i=0}^{p} \beta_i + u_t \qquad (11.5)$$

Distributed lag models can be estimated by simple OLS and the estimators of the βs are BLUE. The question here is how many lags are required in order to have a correctly specified equation? Or, in other words, what is the optimal lag-length?

One way to resolve this is to use a relatively large value for p, estimate the model for $p, p-1, p-2, \ldots$ lags and choose the model with the lowest value of AIC, SBC or any other criterion. However, this approach generates two considerable problems:

(a) it can suffer from severe multicollinearity problems, because of close relationships between $X_t, X_{t-1}, X_{t-2}, \ldots, X_{t-p}$; and

(b) a large number of p means a considerable loss of degrees of freedom because we can use only the $p+1$ to n observations.

Therefore, an alternative approach is needed to provide methods that can resolve these difficulties. The typical approach is to impose restrictions regarding the structure of the βs and then reduce from $p+1$ to only a few the number of parameters to be estimated. Two of the most popular methods to do this are the Koyck (geometrical lag) and the Almon (polynomial lag) transformations which are presented below.

The Koyck transformation

Koyck (1954) proposed a geometrically declining scheme for the βs. To understand this consider again the distributed lag model:

$$Y_t = \alpha + \beta_0 X_t + \beta_1 X_{t-1} + \beta_2 X_{t-2} + \cdots + \beta_p X_{t-p} + u_t \qquad (11.6)$$

Koyck made two assumptions:

(a) all the βs have the same sign; and

(b) the βs decline geometrically as in the following equation:

$$\beta_i = \beta_0 \lambda^i \tag{11.7}$$

where λ takes values among 0 and 1 and $i = 0, 1, 2, \ldots$

It is easy to see that it is declining. Since λ is positive and less than one and all the β_i have the same sign, then $\beta_0 \lambda^1 > \beta_0 \lambda^2 > \beta_0 \lambda^3$ and so on; and therefore $\beta_1 > \beta_2 > \beta_3$ and so on (for a graphical depiction of this see Figure 11.1).

Let us say that we have an infinite distributed lag model:

$$Y_t = \alpha + \beta_0 X_t + \beta_1 X_{t-1} + \beta_2 X_{t-2} + \cdots + u_t \tag{11.8}$$

Substituting $\beta_i = \beta_0 \lambda^i$ we have:

$$Y_t = \alpha + \beta_0 \lambda^0 X_t + \beta_0 \lambda^1 X_{t-1} + \beta_0 \lambda^2 X_{t-2} + \cdots + u_t \tag{11.9}$$

For this infinite lag model the immediate impact is given by β_0 (because $\lambda^0 = 1$), while the long-run effect will be the sum of an infinite geometric series. Koyck transforms this model to a much simpler one as follows:

Step 1   Lag both sides of equation (11.9) one period to get:

$$Y_{t-1} = \alpha + \beta_0 \lambda^0 X_{t-1} + \beta_0 \lambda^1 X_{t-2} + \beta_0 \lambda^2 X_{t-3} + \cdots + u_{t-1} \tag{11.10}$$

Step 2   Multiply both sides of (11.10) by λ to get:

$$\lambda Y_{t-1} = \lambda \alpha + \beta_0 \lambda^1 X_{t-1} + \beta_0 \lambda^2 X_{t-2} + \beta_0 \lambda^3 X_{t-3} + \cdots + \lambda u_{t-1} \tag{11.11}$$

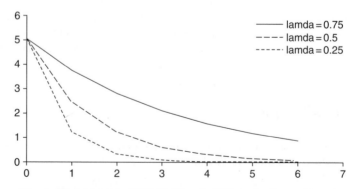

Figure 11.1   Koyck distributed lag for different values of lamda

Step 3 Subtract (11.11) from (11.9) to obtain:

$$Y_t - \lambda Y_{t-1} = \alpha(1 - \lambda) + \beta_0 X_t + u_t - \lambda u_{t-1} \tag{11.12}$$

or

$$Y_t = \alpha(1 - \lambda) + \beta_0 X_t + \lambda Y_{t-1} + v_t \tag{11.13}$$

where $v_t = u_t - \lambda u_{t-1}$. In this case the immediate effect is β_0 and the long-run effect is $\beta_0/(1 - \lambda)$ (consider again that in the long run we have $Y^* = Y_t = Y_{t-1} = \cdots$). So equation (11.13) is now enough to give us both the immediate and long-run coefficients very easily.

The Almon transformation

An alternative procedure is provided by Almon (1965). Almon assumes that the coefficients β_i can be approximated by polynomials in i, such as:

$$\beta_i = f(i) = a_0 i^0 + a_1 i^1 + a_2 i^2 + a_3 i^3 + \cdots + a_r i^r \tag{11.14}$$

The Almon procedure requires prior selection of the degree of the polynomial (r) as well as of the largest lag to be used in the model (p). Therefore, unlike the Koyck transformation, where the distributed lag is infinite, the Almon procedure must be finite.

Suppose we choose $r = 3$ and $p = 4$; then we have:

$$\beta_0 = f(0) = a_0$$
$$\beta_1 = f(1) = a_0 + a_1 + a_2 + a_3$$
$$\beta_2 = f(2) = a_0 + 2a_1 + 4a_2 + 8a_3$$
$$\beta_3 = f(3) = a_0 + 3a_1 + 9a_2 + 27a_3$$
$$\beta_4 = f(4) = a_0 + 4a_1 + 16a_2 + 64a_3$$

Substituting these into the distributed lag model of order $p = 4$ we have:

$$\begin{aligned} Y_t = \alpha &+ (a_0)X_t + (a_0 + a_1 + a_2 + a_3)X_{t-1} \\ &+ (a_0 + 2a_1 + 4a_2 + 8a_3)X_{t-2} \\ &+ (a_0 + 3a_1 + 9a_2 + 27a_3)X_{t-3} \\ &+ (a_0 + 4a_1 + 16a_2 + 64a_3)X_{t-4} + u_t \end{aligned} \tag{11.15}$$

and factorizing the a_is we get:

$$\begin{aligned} Y_t = \alpha &+ a_0(X_t + X_{t-1} + X_{t-2} + X_{t-3} + X_{t-4}) \\ &+ a_1(X_{t-1} + 2X_{t-2} + 3X_{t-3} + 4X_{t-4}) \end{aligned}$$

$$+ a_2(X_{t-1} + 4X_{t-2} + 9X_{t-3} + 16X_{t-4})$$

$$+ a_3(X_{t-1} + 8X_{t-2} + 27X_{t-3} + 64X_{t-4}) + u_t \qquad (11.16)$$

Therefore what is required is to apply appropriate transformations of the Xs such as the ones given in parentheses. If α_3 is not statistically significant, then a second-degree polynomial might be preferable. If we want to include additional terms we can easily do that as well. The best model will be either the one that maximizes R^2 (for different model combinations regarding r and p), or the one that minimizes AIC, SBC or any other criteria.

Other models of lag structures

There are several other models for reducing the number of parameters in a distributed lag model. Some of the most important ones are the Pascal lag, the gamma lag, the LaGuerre lag and the Shiller lag. For a full explanation of these models see Kmenta (1986).

Autoregressive models

Autoregressive models are models that simply include lagged dependent (or endogenous) variables as regressors. In the Koyck transformation discussed earlier, we saw that Y_{t-1} appears as a regressor, so it can be considered as a case of a distributed lag model that was transformed to an autoregressive model. There are two more specifications involving lag-dependent variables:

(a) the partial adjustment model; and

(b) the adaptive expectations model.

We will examine these two models in detail below.

The partial adjustment model

Suppose that the adjustment of the actual value of a variable Y_t to its optimal (or desired) level (denoted by Y_t^*) needs to be modelled. One way to do this is through the partial adjustment model which assumes that the change in actual Y_t $(Y_t - Y_{t-1})$ will be equal to a proportion of the optimal change $(Y_t^* - Y_{t-1})$ or:

$$Y_t - Y_{t-1} = \lambda(Y_t^* - Y_{t-1}) \qquad (11.17)$$

where λ is the adjustment coefficient, which takes values from 0 to 1, and $1/\lambda$ denotes the speed of adjustment.

Consider the two extreme cases: (a) if $\lambda = 1$ then $Y_t = Y_t^*$ and therefore the adjustment to the optimal level is instantaneous; whilst (b) if $\lambda = 0$ then $Y_t = Y_{t-1}$

which means that there is no adjustment of the Y_t. Therefore, the closer λ is to unity, the faster the adjustment will be. To understand this better, we can use a model from economic theory. Suppose Y_t^* is the desired level of inventories for a firm i, and that this depends on the level of the sales of the firm X_t:

$$Y_t^* = \beta_1 + \beta_2 X_t \tag{11.18}$$

Because there are 'frictions' in the market, there is bound to be a gap among the actual level of inventories and the desired one. Suppose also that only a part of the gap can be closed each period. Then the equation that will determine the actual level of inventories will be given by:

$$Y_t = Y_{t-1} + \lambda(Y_t^* - Y_{t-1}) + u_t \tag{11.19}$$

That is, the actual level of inventories is equal to that at time $t - 1$ plus an adjustment factor and a random component.

Combining (11.18) and (11.19):

$$
\begin{aligned}
Y_t &= Y_{t-1} + \lambda(\beta_1 + \beta_2 X_t - Y_{t-1}) + u_t \\
&= \beta_1 \lambda + (1 - \lambda)Y_{t-1} + \beta_2 \lambda X_t + u_t
\end{aligned}
\tag{11.20}
$$

From this model we have the following:

(a) the short-run reaction of Y to a unit change in X is $\beta_2\lambda$;

(b) the long-run reaction is given by β_1; and

(c) an estimate of β_1 can be obtained by dividing the estimate of $\beta_2\lambda$ by one minus the estimate of $(1 - \lambda)$, i.e. $\beta_1 = \beta_2\lambda/[1 - (1 - \lambda)]$.

Here, it is useful to note that the error correction model is also an adjustment model. However, we provide a full examination of these kind of models in Chapter 17.

A computer example of the partial adjustment model

Consider the money demand function:

$$M_t^* = aY_t^{b_1} R_t^{b_2} e^{u_t} \tag{11.21}$$

where the usual notation applies. Taking logarithms of this equation we get:

$$\ln M_t^* = \ln a + b_1 \ln Y_t + b_2 \ln R_t + u_t \tag{11.22}$$

The partial adjustment hypothesis can be written as:

$$\frac{M_t}{M_{t-1}} = \left(\frac{M_t^*}{M_{t-1}}\right)^{\lambda} \tag{11.23}$$

where if we take logarithms we get:

$$\ln M_t - \ln M_{t-1} = \lambda \left(\ln M_t^* - \ln M_{t-1} \right) \tag{11.24}$$

Substituting (11.22) into (11.24) we get:

$$\ln M_t - \ln M_{t-1} = \lambda \left(\ln a + b_1 \ln Y_t + b_2 \ln R_t + u_t - \ln M_{t-1} \right) \tag{11.25}$$

$$\ln M_t = \lambda \ln a + \lambda b_1 \ln Y_t + \lambda b_2 \ln R_t + (1 - \lambda) \ln M_{t-1} + \lambda u_t \tag{11.26}$$

or

$$\ln M_t = \gamma_1 + \gamma_2 \ln Y_t + \gamma_3 \ln R_t + \gamma_4 \ln M_{t-1} + v_t \tag{11.27}$$

We will use EViews in order to obtain OLS results for this model using data for the Italian economy. We will use data for gross domestic product (*GDP*), the consumer price index (cpi) the M2 monetary aggregate (*M2*) and the official discount interest rate (*R*) of the Italian economy. The data are quarterly observations from 1975q1 until 1997q4. First we need to divide both *GDP* and *M2* by the consumer price index in order to obtain real GDP and real money balances. We do this by creating the following variables:

```
genr lm2_p=log(m2/cpi)
genr lgdp_p=log(gdp/cpi)
```

Then we need to calculate the logarithm of the interest rate (*R*). We can do that with the following command:

```
genr lr=log(r)
```

Now we are able to estimate the model given in equation (11.27) by OLS by typing the following command on the command line:

```
ls lm2_p c lgdp_p lr lm2_p(-1)
```

the results of which are given in Table 11.1.

The coefficients have their expected (according to economic theory) signs and all are significantly different from zero. The R^2 is very high (0.93) but this is mainly because one of the explanatory variables is the lagged dependent variable. We leave it as an exercise for the reader to test for possible serial correlation for this model (see Chapter 8 and note the inclusion of the lagged dependent variable).

From the obtained results we can obtain an estimate for the adjustment coefficient (λ) by using the fact that $\gamma_4 = 1 - \lambda$. So, we have that $1 - 0.959 = 0.041$. This tells us that 4.1% of the difference between the desired and actual demand for money is eliminated in each quarter, or that 16.4% of the difference is eliminated each year.

The estimated coefficients in Table 11.1 are of the short-run demand for money and they are the short-run elasticities with respect to *GDP* and *R* respectively. The short-run income elasticity is 0.026 and the short-run interest rate elasticity is −0.017.

The long-run demand for money was given by equation (11.22). Estimates of these long-run parameters can be obtained by dividing each of the short-run coefficients by

Table 11.1 Results for the Italy Money Supply Example

Dependent Variable: LM2_P
Method: Least Squares
Date: 03/02/04 Time: 17:17
Sample (adjusted): 1975:2 1997:4
Included observations: 91 after adjusting endpoints

Variable	Coefficient	Std. Error	t-Statistic	Prob.
C	0.184265	0.049705	3.707204	0.0004
LGDP_P	0.026614	0.010571	2.517746	0.0136
LR	−0.017358	0.005859	−2.962483	0.0039
LM2_P(−1)	0.959451	0.030822	31.12873	0.0000
R-squared	0.933470	Mean dependent var		1.859009
Adjusted R-squared	0.931176	S.D. dependent var		0.059485
S.E. of regression	0.015605	Akaike info criterion		−5.439433
Sum squared resid	0.021187	Schwarz criterion		−5.329065
Log likelihood	251.4942	F-statistic		406.8954
Durbin–Watson stat	1.544176	Prob (F-statistic)		0.000000

the estimate of the adjustment coefficient ($\lambda = 0.041$). So, we have that the long-run function is:

$$\ln M_t^* = 4.487 + 0.634 \ln Y_t - 0.414 \ln R_t + u_t \tag{11.28}$$

Note that these are the quarterly elasticities. If we want the yearly elasticities we should multiply the respective coefficients by 4.

The adaptive expectations model

The second of the autoregressive models is the adaptive expectations model, which is based on the adaptive expectations hypothesis formulated by Cagan (1956). Before understanding the model it is crucial to have a clear picture of the adaptive expectations hypothesis. So, consider an agent who forms expectations of a variable X_t. If we denote by the superscript e expectations, then X_{t-1}^e is the expectation formed at time $t-1$ for X in t.

The adaptive expectations hypothesis assumes that agents make errors in their expectations (given by $X_t - X_{t-1}^e$) and also that they revise their expectations by a constant proportion of the most recent error. Thus:

$$X_t^e - X_{t-1}^e = \theta(X_t - X_{t-1}^e) \quad 0 < \theta \le 1 \tag{11.29}$$

where θ is the adjustment parameter.
If we consider again the two extreme cases we have that:

(a) if $\theta = 0$ then $X_t^e = X_{t-1}^e$ and no revision in the expectations is made; while

(b) if $\theta = 1$ then $X_t^e = X_t$ and we have an instantaneous adjustment in the expectations.

The adaptive expectations hypothesis can now be incorporated in an econometric model. Suppose that we have the following model:

$$Y_t = \beta_1 + \beta_2 X_t^e + u_t \tag{11.30}$$

where, for example, we can think of Y_t as consumption and of X_t^e as expected income. Assume, then, that for the specific model the expected income follows the adaptive expectations hypothesis, so that:

$$X_t^e - X_{t-1}^e = \theta(X_t - X_{t-1}^e) \tag{11.31}$$

If actual X in period $t-1$ exceeds the expectations, then we would expect agents to revise their expectations upwards. Equation (11.31) then becomes:

$$X_t^e = \theta X_t + (1 - \theta)X_{t-1}^e \tag{11.32}$$

Substituting (11.32) into (11.30) we obtain:

$$Y_t = \beta_1 + \beta_2(\theta X_t + (1 - \theta)X_{t-1}^e) + u_t$$
$$= \beta_1 + \beta_2\theta X_t + \beta_2(1 - \theta)X_{t-1}^e + u_t \tag{11.33}$$

In order to estimate the X_{t-1}^e variable from equation (11.33) to obtain an estimable econometric model, we need to follow the following procedure:
Lagging equation (11.30) one period we get:

$$Y_{t-1} = \beta_1 + \beta_2 X_{t-1}^e + u_{t-1} \tag{11.34}$$

Multiplying both sides of (11.34) by $(1 - \theta)$ we get:

$$(1 - \theta)Y_{t-1} = (1 - \theta)\beta_1 + (1 - \theta)\beta_2 X_{t-1}^e + (1 - \theta)u_{t-1} \tag{11.35}$$

Subtracting (11.35) from (11.33) we get:

$$Y_t - (1 - \theta)Y_{t-1} = \beta_1 - (1 - \theta)\beta_1 + \beta_2\theta X_t + u_t - (1 - \theta)u_{t-1} \tag{11.36}$$

or

$$Y_t = \beta_1\theta + \beta_2\theta X_t + (1 - \theta)Y_{t-1} + u_t - (1 - \theta)u_{t-1} \tag{11.37}$$

and finally:

$$Y_t = \beta_1^* + \beta_2^* X_t + \beta_3^* Y_{t-1} + v_t \tag{11.38}$$

where $\beta_1^* = \beta_1\theta$, $\beta_2^* = \beta_2\theta$, $\beta_3^* = (1 - \theta)$ and $v_t = u_t - (1 - \theta)u_{t-1}$. Once estimates of the β^*s have been obtained, β_1, β_2 and θ can be estimated as follows:

$$\hat{\theta} = 1 - \beta_3^*, \quad \hat{\beta}_1 = \frac{\beta_1^*}{\theta} \quad \text{and} \quad \hat{\beta}_2 = \frac{\beta_2^*}{\theta} \tag{11.39}$$

Here, it is interesting to mention that through this procedure we are able to obtain an estimate of the marginal propensity to consume out of expected income, although we do not have data for expected income.

Tests of autocorrelation in autoregressive models

It is of very high importance to test for autocorrelation in models with lagged dependent variables. In Chapter 8 we mentioned that in such cases the DW test statistic is not appropriate and Durbin's h test should be used instead, or alternatively the LM test for autocorrelation. Both tests were presented analytically in Chapter 8.

Exercises

Exercise 11.1

Show how we might obtain an estimate of the marginal propensity to consume out of expected income, although we do not have data for expected income, using the adaptive expectations autoregressive model.

Exercise 11.2

Derive the Almon polynomial transformation for $p = 5$ and $r = 4$. Explain how to proceed with the estimation of this model.

Exercise 11.3

Explain how we can test for serial correlation in autoregressive models.

Exercise 11.4

Show how the Koyck transformation transforms an infinite distributed lag model to an autoregressive model. Explain the advantages of this transformation.

Exercise 11.5

Assume we have the following distributed lag model:

$$Y_t = 0.847 + 0.236X_t + 0.366X_{t-1} + 0.581X_{t-2}$$
$$+ 0.324X_{t-3} + 0.145X_{t-4} \tag{11.40}$$

find (a) the impact effect, and (b) the long-run effect of a unit change in X on Y.

Table 11.2   Results for an adaptive expectations model

Dependent Variable: CE
Method: Least Squares
Date: 03/02/04 Time: 18:00
Sample (adjusted): 1976:1 1997:4
Included observations: 88 after adjusting endpoints

Variable	Coefficient	Std. Error	t-Statistic	Prob.
C	−7.692041	3.124125	−2.462146	0.0310
YD	0.521338	0.234703	2.221233	0.0290
CE(−1)	0.442484	0.045323	9.762089	0.0000

R-squared	0.958482	Mean dependent var	1.863129
Adjusted R-squared	0.588722	S.D. dependent var	0.055804
S.E. of regression	0.032454	Akaike info criterion	−3.650434
Sum squared resid	0.148036	Schwarz criterion	−3.565979
Log likelihood	161.6191	F-statistic	49.58733
Durbin–Watson stat	0.869852	Prob (F-statistic)	0.000000

Exercise 11.6

The model:

$$C_t = \beta_1 + \beta_2 Y_t + \beta_3 C_{t-1} + v_t \tag{11.41}$$

(where CE = aggregate consumer expenditure and YD = personal disposable income) was estimated by simple OLS using data for the UK economy. The results are given in Table 11.2. Is this model a satisfactory one? Explain (using the adaptive expectations hypothesis) the meaning of each of the estimated coefficients.

Exercise 11.7

The file cons_us.wf1 contains data of consumption expenditure (CE) and personal disposable income (PDI) (measured in constant prices) for the US economy.

(a) Estimate the partial adjustment model for CE by OLS.

(b) Provide an interpretation of the estimated coefficients.

(c) Calculate the implied adjustment coefficient.

(d) Test for serial correlation using Durbin's h method and the LM test.

12 Simultaneous Equation Models

Introduction: basic definitions

All econometric models covered so far have dealt with a single dependent variable and estimations of single equations. However, in modern world economics, interdependence is very commonly encountered. Several dependent variables are determined simultaneously, therefore appearing both as dependent and explanatory variables in a set of different equations. For example, in the single equation case that we have examined so far, we had equations such as demand functions of the following form:

$$Q_t^d = \beta_1 + \beta_2 P_t + \beta_3 Y_t + u_t \tag{12.1}$$

where Q_t^d is quantity demanded, P_t is the relative price of the commodity, and Y_t is income. However, economic analysis suggests that price and quantity are typically determined simultaneously by the market processes, and therefore a full market model is not captured by a single equation but consists of a set of three different equations: the demand function, the supply function, and the condition for equilibrium in the market of the product. So, we have:

$$Q_t^d = \beta_1 + \beta_2 P_t + \beta_3 Y_t + u_{1t} \tag{12.2}$$

$$Q_t^s = \gamma_1 + \gamma_1 P_t + u_{2t} \tag{12.3}$$

$$Q_t^d = Q_t^s \tag{12.4}$$

where of course Q_t^s denotes the quantity supplied.

Equations (12.2), (12.3) and (12.4) are called *structural equations* of the simultaneous equations model, and the coefficients β and γ are called *structural parameters*.

Because price and quantity are jointly determined, they are both *endogenous variables*, and because income is not determined by the specified model, income is characterized as an *exogenous variable*. Note, here, that in the single-equation models, we were using the terms exogenous variable and explanatory variable interchangeably, but this is no longer possible in simultaneous equations models. So, we have price as an explanatory variable but not as an exogenous variable as well.

Equating (12.3) to (12.2) and solving for P_t we get:

$$P_t = \frac{\beta_1 - \gamma_1}{\beta_2 - \gamma_2} + \frac{\beta_3}{\beta_2 - \gamma_2} Y_t + \frac{u_{1t} - u_{2t}}{\beta_2 - \gamma_2} \tag{12.5}$$

which can be rewritten as:

$$P_t = \pi_1 + \pi_2 Y_t + v_{1t} \tag{12.6}$$

If we substitute (12.6) into (12.3) we get:

$$\begin{aligned} Q &= \gamma_1 + \gamma_2 (\pi_1 + \pi_2 Y_t + v_{1t}) + u_{1t} \\ &= \gamma_1 + \gamma_2 \pi_1 + \gamma_2 \pi_2 Y_t + \gamma_2 v_{1t} + u_{2t} \\ &= \pi_3 + \pi_4 Y_t + v_{2t} \end{aligned} \tag{12.7}$$

So, now we have that equations (12.3) and (12.7) specify each of the endogenous variables in terms only of the exogenous variables, the parameters of the model and the stochastic error terms. These two equations are known as *reduced form equations* and the πs are known as *reduced form parameters*. In general reduced form equations can be obtained by solving for each of the endogenous variables in terms of the exogenous variables, the unknown parameters and the error terms.

Consequences of ignoring simultaneity

One of the assumptions of the CLRM states that the error term of an equation should be uncorrelated with each of the explanatory variables in this equation. If such a correlation exists, then the OLS regression equation is biased. It should be evident from the reduced form equations that in cases of simultaneous equation models such a bias exists. Recall that the new error terms v_{1t} and v_{2t} depend on u_{1t} and u_{2t}. However, to show this more clearly consider the following general form of a simultaneous equation model:

$$Y_{1t} = a_1 + a_2 Y_{2t} + a_3 X_{1t} + a_4 X_{3t} + e_{1t} \tag{12.8}$$

$$Y_{2t} = \beta_1 + \beta_2 Y_{1t} + \beta_3 X_{3t} + \beta_4 X_{2t} + e_{2t} \tag{12.9}$$

In this model we have two structural equations, with two endogenous variables (Y_{1t} and Y_{2t}) and three exogenous variables (X_{1t}, X_{2t} and X_{3t}). Let us see what happens if one of the error terms increases, assuming everything else in the equations to be held constant:

(a) if e_{1t} increases, this cause Y_{1t} to increase due to equation (12.8), then

(b) if Y_{1t} increases (assuming that β_2 is positive) Y_{2t} will then also increase due to the relationship in equation (12.9), but

(c) if Y_{2t} increases in (12.9) it also increases in (12.8) where it is an explanatory variable.

Therefore, an increase in the error term of one equation causes an increase in an explanatory variable in the same equation. So the assumption of no correlation among the error term and the explanatory variables is violated leading to biased estimates.

The identification problem

Basic definitions

We saw before that the reduced form equations express the endogenous variables as functions of the exogenous variables only. Therefore, it is possible to apply OLS to these equations in order to obtain consistent and efficient estimations of the reduced form parameters (the πs).

A question here is whether we can obtain consistent estimates (the βs and the γs), by going back and solving for those parameters. The answer is that there are three possible situations:

(1) it is not possible to go back from the reduced form to the structural form;
(2) it is possible to go back in a unique way; or
(3) there is more than one way to go back.

This problem of being or not being able to go back and determine estimates of the structural parameters from estimators of the reduced form coefficients is called the identification problem.

The first situation (not possible to go back) is called *underidentification*, the second situation (the unique case) is called *exact identification* and the third situation (where there is more than one way) is called *overidentification*.

Conditions for identification

There are two conditions required for an equation to be identified: the order condition and the rank condition. First, we state the two conditions and then we use examples to illustrate their use.

The order condition

Let's define as G the number of endogenous variables in the system, and as M the number of variables that are missing from the equation under consideration (these can be either endogenous, exogenous or lagged endogenous variables). Then the order condition states that:

(a) if $M < G - 1$ the equation is underidentified;
(b) if $M = G - 1$ the equation is exactly identified; and
(c) if $M > G - 1$ the equation is overidentified.

The order condition is necessary but not sufficient. By this we mean that if this condition does not hold, then the equation is not identified, but if it does hold then we cannot be certain that it is identified, thus we still need to use the rank condition to conclude.

The rank condition

For the rank condition we first need to construct a table with a column for each variable and a row for each equation. Then, for each equation we need to put a $\sqrt{}$ in the column if the variable that corresponds to this column is included in the equation, otherwise we put a 0. This gives us an array of $\sqrt{}$s and 0s for each equation. Then, for a particular equation, we need to do the following:

(a) delete the row of the equation that is under examination;
(b) write out the remaining elements of each column for which there is a zero in the equation under examination; and

(c) consider the resulting array: if there are at least $G - 1$ rows and columns which are not all zeros, then the equation is identified, otherwise it is not identified.

The rank condition is necessary and sufficient, but we first need the order condition to tell us whether the equation is exactly identified or overidentified.

Example of the identification procedure

Consider the demand and supply model described in equations (12.2), (12.3) and (12.4). We first form a table with a column for each variable and a row for each of the three equations:

	Q^d	Q^s	P	Y
Equation 1	✓	0	✓	✓
Equation 2	0	✓	✓	0
Equation 3	✓	✓	0	0

Here we have three endogenous variables (Q^d, Q^s and P), so $G = 3$ and $G - 1 = 2$.

Now consider the order condition. For the demand function we have that the number of excluded variables is 1, so $M = 1$, and because $M < G - 1$ then the demand function is not identified. For the supply function we have that $M = 1$ and because $M = G - 1$ then the supply function is exactly identified.

Proceeding with the rank condition we need to check only for the supply function (because we saw that the demand is not identified). The array we have (after deleting the Q^s and P columns and the Equation 2 line) will be given by:

	Q^d	Q^s	P	Y
Equation 1	✓	0	✓	✓
Equation 2	0	✓	✓	0
Equation 3	✓	✓	0	0

	Q^d	Y
Equation 1	✓	✓
Equation 3	✓	0

The question is, are there at least $G - 1 = 2$ rows and columns that are not all zeros? The answer is yes, and therefore the rank condition is satisfied and we have that the supply function is indeed exactly identified.

A second example: the macroeconomic model of a closed economy

Consider the simple macroeconomic model for a closed economy described by the equations below:

$$C_t = \beta_1 + \beta_2 Y_t \tag{12.10}$$

$$I_t = \gamma_1 + \gamma_1 Y_t + \gamma_3 R_t \tag{12.11}$$

$$Y_t = C_t + I_t + G_t \tag{12.12}$$

where C_t denotes consumption, Y_t is GDP, I_t is investments, R_t denotes the interest rate and G_t is government expenditure. Here we have that C_t, I_t and Y_t are endogenous variables, while R_t and G_t are exogenous. First we form a table with five columns (one for each variable) and three rows (one for each equation):

	C	Y	I	R	G
Equation 1	✓	✓	0	0	0
Equation 2	0	✓	✓	✓	0
Equation 3	✓	✓	✓	0	✓

From the table we have that for equation 1, $M = 3$ (I, R and G are excluded) while $G = 3$ and therefore, $M > G - 1$ so the consumption function appears to be overidentified. Similarly, for equation 2 we have that $M = G - 1$ and therefore it appears to be exactly identified.

Employing the rank condition for the consumption function, we have (after excluding the C and Y columns and the Equation 1 row) the following table:

	I	R	G
Equation 2	✓	✓	0
Equation 3	✓	0	✓

So, there are $G - 1 = 2$ rows and columns with no all-zero elements and therefore it is overidentified. For the investment function (after excluding the I, Y and R columns and the Equation 2 row) we have:

	C	G
Equation 1	✓	0
Equation 3	✓	✓

and again there are $G - 1 = 2$ rows and columns with no all-zero elements so the rank condition is again satisfied and we conclude that the investment function is indeed identified.

Estimation of simultaneous equation models

The question of identification is closely related to the problem of estimating the structural parameters in a simultaneous equation model. Thus, when an equation is not identified, such an estimation is not possible. In cases, though, of exact or overidentification there are procedures that allow us to obtain estimates of the structural parameters. These procedures are different from simple OLS in order to avoid the simultaneity bias we presented before.

In general, in cases of exact identification the appropriate method is the so-called method of *indirect least squares* (ILS), while in cases of overidentified equations the *two-stage least squares* (TSLS) method is the most commonly used. The next two sections briefly present those procedures.

Estimation of an exactly identified equation: the method of indirect least squares

This method can be used only when the equations of the simultaneous equation model are found to be exactly identified. The procedure of the ILS involves the following three steps:

Step 1 Find the reduced form equations,

Step 2 Estimate the reduced form parameters by applying simple OLS to the reduced form equations, and

Step 3 Obtain unique estimates of the structural parameters from the estimates of the parameters of the reduced form equation in step 2.

The OLS estimates of the reduced form parameters are unbiased, but when transformed the structural parameter estimates they provide are only consistent. In the rare case where all of the structural form equations are exactly identified then ILS provides estimates that are consistent, asymptotic-efficient and asymptotically normal.

The ILS method is not commonly used for two reasons:

(1) Most simultaneous equations models tend to be overidentified.

(2) If the system has several equations, solving for the reduced form and then for the structural form can be very tedious. An alternative is the TSLS method.

Estimation of an overidentified equation: the method of two-stage least squares

The basic idea behind the TSLS method is to replace the stochastic endogenous regressor (which is correlated with the error term and causes the bias) with one that is non-stochastic and consequently independent of the error term. This involves the following two stages (hence two-stage least squares):

Stage 1 Regress each endogenous variable which is a regressor as well, on all of the endogenous and lagged endogenous variables in the entire system by using simple OLS (that is equivalent to estimating the reduced form equations) and obtain the fitted values of the endogenous variables of these regressions ($\hat{Y}$).

Stage 2 Use the fitted values from stage 1 as proxies or instruments for the endogenous regressors in the original (structural form) equations.

One requirement is that the R^2s of the estimate equations in stage 1 should be relatively high. This is in order to ensure that $\hat{Y}$ and Y are highly correlated and therefore $\hat{Y}$ is a good instrument for Y. One advantage of the TSLS method is that for equations that are exactly identified, they will yield estimates identical to those obtained from the ILS, while TSLS is also appropriate even for overidentified equations.

Example: the IS-LM model

Consider the following IS-LM model:

$$R_t = \beta_{11} + \beta_{12}M_t + \beta_{13}Y_t + \beta_{14}M_{t-1} + u_{1t} \qquad (12.13)$$

$$Y_t = \beta_{21} + \beta_{22}R_t + \beta_{23}I_t + u_{1t} \qquad (12.14)$$

where R denotes the interest rate, M denotes the money stock, Y is GDP and I is investment expenditure. In this model R and Y are the endogenous variables and M and I are the exogenous variables. We will leave it as an exercise for the reader to prove that equation (12.13) is exactly identified and equation (12.14) is overidentified.

We want to estimate the model and, because the second equation is overidentified, we will have to use the TSLS method. The data for this example are in the file simult.wf1 and are annual time series data from 1972q1 to 1998q3 for the UK economy.

In order to estimate an equation with TSLS, we can either go to **Quick/Estimate Equation** and in the **Equation Specification** window change the method from the default **LS – Least Squares (NLS and ARMA)** to **TSLS – Two-stage Least Squares (TSNLS and ARMA)** and then specify the equation that we want to estimate in the first box and the list of instruments in the second; or type the following command in EViews:

```
tsls r c m y m(-1) @ c m i m(-1)
```

where before the @ symbol is the equation we want to estimate and after the @ symbol we include the variable names that we want to use as instruments. The results of this method are given in Table 12.1.

The interest rate equation can be viewed as the LM relationship. The coefficient of Y is very small and positive (but insignificant), suggesting that the LM function is very flat, while increases in the money stock reduce the rate of interest. Also, R^2 is very small, suggesting that there are variables missing from our equation.

Table 12.1 TSLS estimation of the R (LM) equation

Dependent Variable: R
Method: Two-Stage Least Squares
Date: 03/02/04 Time: 23:52
Sample(adjusted): 1972:1 1998:3
Included observations: 107 after adjusting endpoints
Instrument list: C M I M(−1)

Variable	Coefficient	Std. Error	t-Statistic	Prob.
C	9.069599	5.732089	1.582250	0.1167
M	−0.008878	0.002614	−3.396474	0.0010
Y	4.65E−05	6.44E−05	0.722214	0.4718
M(−1)	0.008598	0.002566	3.350368	0.0011

R-squared	0.182612	Mean dependent var		9.919252
Adjusted R-squared	0.158805	S.D. dependent var		3.165781
S.E. of regression	2.903549	Sum squared resid		868.3518
F-statistic	8.370503	Durbin–Watson stat		0.362635
Prob(F-statistic)	0.000049			

Table 12.2 TSLS estimation of the *Y* (IS) equation

Dependent Variable: Y
Method: Two-Stage Least Squares
Date: 03/02/04 Time: 23:56
Sample(adjusted): 1972:1 1998:3
Included observations: 107 after adjusting endpoints
Instrument list: C M I M(−1)

Variable	Coefficient	Std. Error	t-Statistic	Prob.
C	72538.68	14250.19	5.090368	0.0000
R	−3029.112	921.8960	−3.285742	0.0014
I	4.258678	0.266492	15.98049	0.0000

R-squared	0.834395	Mean dependent var	145171.7
Adjusted R-squared	0.831210	S.D. dependent var	24614.16
S.E. of regression	10112.50	Sum squared resid	1.06E+10
F-statistic	294.8554	Durbin–Watson stat	0.217378
Prob(F-statistic)	0.000000		

Table 12.3 The first stage of the TSLS method

Dependent Variable: Y
Method: Least Squares
Date: 03/03/04 Time: 00:03
Sample(adjusted): 1969:3 1998:3
Included observations: 117 after adjusting endpoints

Variable	Coefficient	Std. Error	t-Statistic	Prob.
C	60411.05	1561.051	38.69896	0.0000
M	6.363346	1.912864	3.326607	0.0012
I	1.941795	0.102333	18.97519	0.0000
M(−1)	−3.819978	1.921678	−1.987835	0.0492

R-squared	0.992349	Mean dependent var	141712.3
Adjusted R-squared	0.992146	S.D. dependent var	26136.02
S.E. of regression	2316.276	Akaike info criterion	18.36690
Sum squared resid	6.06E+08	Schwarz criterion	18.46133
Log likelihood	−1070.464	F-statistic	4885.393
Durbin–Watson stat	0.523453	Prob(F-statistic)	0.000000

Estimating the second equation (which can be viewed as the IS relationship) we need to type the following command:

```
TSLS y c r i @ c m i m(-1)
```

the results of which are presented in Table 12.2.

Interpreting these results, we can say that income and the rate of interest are negatively related, according to the theoretical prediction, and income is quite sensitive to changes in the rate of interest. Also, a change in investments would cause the function to shift to the right, again as theory suggests. The R^2 of this specification is quite high.

To better understand the two-stage least squares method we can carry out the estimation stage by stage. We will do so for the second equation only. The first stage

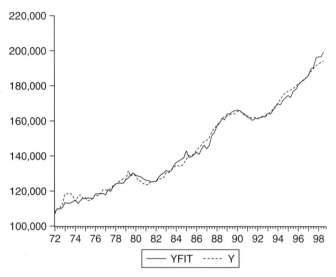

Figure 12.1 Actual and fitted values of *Y*

Table 12.4 The second stage of the TSLS method

Dependent Variable: YFIT
Method: Least Squares
Date: 03/03/04 Time: 00:14
Sample(adjusted): 1972:1 1998:3
Included observations: 107 after adjusting endpoints

Variable	Coefficient	Std. Error	t-Statistic	Prob.
C	75890.95	8497.518	8.930955	0.0000
RFIT	−3379.407	549.7351	−6.147337	0.0000
I	4.252729	0.158912	26.76155	0.0000

R-squared	0.942570	Mean dependent var	144905.9
Adjusted R-squared	0.941466	S.D. dependent var	24924.47
S.E. of regression	6030.176	Akaike info criterion	20.27458
Sum squared resid	3.78E + 09	Schwarz criterion	20.34952
Log likelihood	−1081.690	F-statistic	853.4572
Durbin–Watson stat	0.341516	Prob(F-statistic)	0.000000

involves regressing Y on a constant M, I and $M(-1)$, so we need to type the following command:

```
ls y c m i m(-1)
```

the results of which are presented in Table 12.3. A positive result here is that R^2 is very high, so the fitted Y variable is a very good proxy for Y.

Next we need to obtain the fitted values of this regression equation. This can be done by subtracting the residuals of the model from the actual Y variable. The EViews command is as follows:

```
genr yfit=y-resid
```

Plotting these two variables together by the command:

```
plot y yfit
```

we see (Figure 12.1) that they are moving very closely together.

We should do the same for R in order to get the rfit variable and then as the second stage estimate the model with the fitted endogenous variables instead of the actual Y and R. The command for this is:

```
ls yfit c rfit i
```

and the results are reported in Table 12.4.

Part

V Time Series Econometrics

13 ARIMA Models and the Box–Jenkins Methodology

An introduction to time series econometrics

In this section we discuss single equation estimation techniques in a different way from Parts II and III of the text. In those parts we were trying to analyse the behaviour and variability of a dependent variable by regressing it on a number of different regressors or explanatory variables. In the time series econometrics framework, the starting point is to exploit the information that we can get from a variable that is available through the variable itself. An analysis of a single time series is called a univariate time series, and this is the topic of this chapter. In time series econometrics we can also have multivariate time series models which will be the topic of discussion in later chapters. In general, the purpose of time series analysis is to capture and examine the dynamics of the data.

As we have mentioned before, traditional econometricians have emphasized the use of economic theory and the study of contemporaneous relationships in order to explain relationships among dependent and explanatory variables. (From here on we use the term traditional econometrics to differentiate the econometric analysis examined in Parts II and III from the new ('modern') developments of time series econometrics.) Lagged variables were sometimes introduced but not in any systematic way, or at least not in a way to attempt to analyse the dynamics or the temporal structure of the data. There are various aspects to time series analysis but one common theme to them all is to fully exploit the dynamic structure in the data, by this we mean that we extract as much information as possible from the past history of the series. The two principle types of time series analysis are time series forecasting and dynamic modelling. Time series forecasting is unlike most other econometrics in that it is not concerned with building structural models, understanding the economy or testing hypothesis. All that it is concerned with is building efficient models, which forecast well. This is usually done by exploiting the dynamic inter-relationship, which exists over time for any single variable. Dynamic modelling on the other hand is still concerned with understanding the structure of the economy and testing hypothesis however it starts from the view that most economic series are slow to adjust to any shock and so to understand the process we must fully capture the adjustment process which may be long and complex. Over the past couple of decades the techniques developed in the time series forecasting literature have become increasingly useful in econometrics generally. Hence we begin this chapter with an account of the basic 'work horse' of time series forecasting, the ARIMA model.

ARIMA models

Box and Jenkins (1976) first introduced ARIMA models, the term deriving from:

AR = autoregressive
I = integrated
MA = moving average.

In the next sections we will present all the different versions of ARIMA models and introduce the concept of stationarity, which will be extensively analysed. After defining stationarity, we will proceed with the simplest model, the autoregressive of order one model, and then continue with our survey of the ARIMA models. Finally, we will briefly present the Box–Jenkins approach for model selection and forecasting.

Stationarity

A key concept underlying time series processes is that of stationarity. A time series is covariance stationary when it has the following three characteristics:

(a) exhibits mean reversion in that it fluctuates around a constant long-run mean;

(b) has a finite variance that is time-invariant; and

(c) has a theoretical correlogram that diminishes as the lag length increases.

In its simplest terms a time series Y_t is said to be stationary if:

(a) $E(Y_t) = $ constant for all t;

(b) $Var(Y_t) = $ constant for all t; and

(c) $Cov(Y_t, Y_{t+k}) = $ constant for all t and all $k \neq 0$,
    or if its mean, its variance and its covariances remain constant over time.

Thus, these quantities would remain the same whether observations for the time series were, for example, from 1975 to 1985 or from 1985 to 1995. Stationarity is important because if the series is non-stationary then all the typical results of the classical regression analysis are not valid. Regressions with non-stationary series may have no meaning and are therefore called 'spurious'. (We will examine and analyse the concepts of spurious regressions more analytically in Chapter 16.)

Shocks to a stationary time series are necessarily temporary; over time, the effects of the shocks will dissipate and the series will revert to its long-run mean level. As such, long-term forecasts of a stationary series will converge to the unconditional mean of the series.

Autoregressive time series models

The AR(1) model

The simplest, purely statistical time series model is the autoregressive of order one model, or AR(1) model, which is given below:

$$Y_t = \phi Y_{t-1} + u_t \tag{13.1}$$

where, for simplicity, we do not include a constant and $|\phi| < 1$ and u_t is a gaussian (white noise) error term. The implication behind the AR(1) model is that the time series behaviour of Y_t is largely determined by its own value in the preceding period. So, what will happen in t is largely dependent on what happened in $t - 1$, or alternatively what will happen in $t + 1$ will be determined by the behaviour of the series in the current time t.

Condition for stationarity

Equation (13.1) introduces the constraint $|\phi| < 1$, in order to guarantee stationarity as defined in the previous section. If we have $|\phi| > 1$, then Y_t will tend to get bigger and bigger each period and so we would have an explosive series. To illustrate this, consider the following example in EViews.

Example of stationarity in the AR(1) model

Open EViews and create a new workfile by choosing **File/New Workfile**. In the **workfile range** choose **undated or irregular** and define the **start observation** as 1 and the **end observation** as 500. To create a stationary time series process type the following commands in the EViews command line (the bracketed comments provide a description of each command):

`smpl 1 1`	[sets the sample to be the first observation only]
`genr yt=0`	[generates a new variable yt with the value of 0]
`smpl 2 500`	[sets the sample to be from the 2nd to the 5 hundredth observation]
`genr  yt = 0.4*yt(−1)+nrnd`	[creates yt as an AR(1) model with $\phi = 0.4$]
`smpl 1 500`	[sets the sample back to the full sample]
`plot yt`	[provides a plot of the yt series]

The plot of the Y_t series will look like that shown in Figure 13.1. We can see clearly that this series has a constant mean and a constant variance, which are the first two characteristics of a stationary series.

If we obtain the correlogram of the series we will see that it indeed diminishes as the lag length increases. To do this in EViews, first double click on yt to open it in a new window and then go to **View/Correlogram** and click <**OK**>.

Continuing, if we want to create a time series (say X_t) which has $|\phi| > 1$, we type the following commands:

```
smpl 1 1
genr xt=1
smpl 2 500
genr xt = 1.2*xt(−1) + nrnd
smpl 1 200
plot xt
```

And with the final command we obtain Figure 13.2, where we can see that the series is exploding. Note that we specified the sample to be from 1 to 200. This is because the explosive behaviour is so big that EViews cannot plot all 500 data values in one graph.

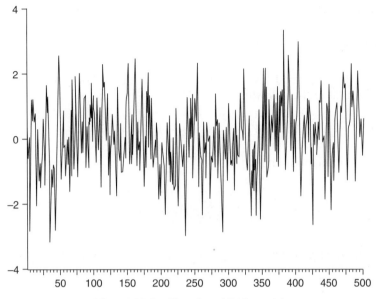

Figure 13.1 Plot of an AR(1) model

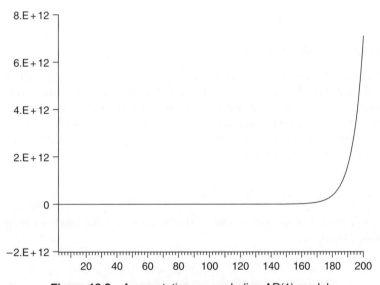

Figure 13.2 A non-stationary, exploding AR(1) model

The AR(p) model

A generalization of the AR(1) model is the AR(p) model; the number in parenthesis denotes the order of the autoregressive process and therefore the number of lagged dependent variables that the model will have. For example, the AR(2) model will be an autoregressive model of order two, and will have the form:

$$Y_t = \phi_1 Y_{t-1} + \phi_2 Y_{t-2} + u_t \qquad (13.2)$$

Similarly, the AR(p) model will be an autoregressive model of order p, and will have p lagged terms as in the following:

$$Y_t = \phi_1 Y_{t-1} + \phi_2 Y_{t-2} + \cdots + \phi_p Y_{t-p} + u_t \qquad (13.3)$$

or using the summation symbol:

$$Y_t = \sum_{i=1}^{p} \phi_i Y_{t-i} + u_t \qquad (13.4)$$

Finally, using the lag operator L (the lag operator L has the property: $L^n Y_t = Y_{t-n}$) we can write the AR(p) model as:

$$Y_t(1 - \phi_1 L - \phi_2 L^2 - \cdots - \phi_p L^p) = u_t \qquad (13.5)$$

$$\Phi(L)Y_t = u_t \qquad (13.6)$$

where $\Phi(L)Y_t$, is a polynomial function of Y_t.

Stationarity in the AR(p) model

The condition for stationarity of an AR(p) process is guaranteed only if the p roots of the polynomial equation $\Phi(z) = 0$ are greater than 1 in absolute value, where z is a real variable. (This can be alternatively expressed with the following terminology: the solutions of the polynomial equation $\Phi(z) = 0$, should lie outside the unit circle.) To see this consider the AR(1) process. The condition for the AR(1) process according to the polynomial notation reduces to:

$$(1 - \phi z) = 0 \qquad (13.7)$$

being greater than 1 in absolute value. If this is so, and if the first root is equal to λ, then the condition is:

$$|\lambda| = \left| \frac{1}{\phi} \right| > 1 \qquad (13.8)$$

$$|\phi| < 1 \qquad (13.9)$$

Also, a necessary but not sufficient requirement for the AR(p) model to be stationary is that the summation of the p autoregressive coefficients should be less than 1:

$$\sum_{i=1}^{p} \phi_i < 1 \qquad (13.10)$$

Properties of the AR models

We start by defining the unconditional mean and the variance of the AR(1) process, which are given by:

$$E(Y_t) = E(Y_{t-1}) = E(Y_{t+1}) = 0$$

where $Y_{t+1} = \phi Y_t + u_{t+1}$. Substituting repeatedly for lagged Y_t we have:

$$Y_{t+1} = \phi^t Y_0 + \left(\phi^t u_1 + \phi^{t-1} u_2 + \cdots + \phi^0 u_{t+1}\right)$$

and since $|\phi| < 1$, ϕ^t will be close to zero for large t. Thus, we have that:

$$E(Y_{t+1}) = 0 \tag{13.11}$$

and

$$Var(Y_t) = Var(\phi Y_{t-1} + u_t) = \phi^2 \sigma_Y^2 + \sigma_u^2 = \frac{\sigma_u^2}{1 - \phi^2 \sigma_Y^2} \tag{13.12}$$

Time series are also characterized by the autocovariance and the autocorrelation functions. The covariance among two random variables X_t and Z_t is defined to be:

$$Cov(X_t, Z_t) = E\{[X_t - E(X_t)][Z_t - E(Z_t)]\} \tag{13.13}$$

Thus for two elements of the Y_t process, let's say Y_t and Y_{t-1}, we will have:

$$Cov(Y_t, Y_{t-1}) = E\{[Y_t - E(Y_t)][Y_{t-1} - E(Y_{t-1})]\} \tag{13.14}$$

which is called the autocovariance function. For the AR(1) model the autocovariance function will be given by:

$$
\begin{aligned}
Cov(Y_t, Y_{t-1}) &= E\{[Y_t Y_{t-1}] - [Y_t E(Y_{t-1})] - [E(Y_t) Y_{t-1}] \\
&\quad + [E(Y_t) E(Y_{t-1})]\} \\
&= E[Y_t Y_{t-1}]
\end{aligned}
$$

where $E(Y_t) = E(Y_{t-1}) = E(Y_{t+1}) = 0$. This leads to:

$$
\begin{aligned}
Cov(Y_t, Y_{t-1}) &= E[(\phi Y_{t-1} + u_t) Y_{t-1}] \\
&= E(\phi Y_{t-1} Y_{t-1}) + E(u_t Y_{t-1}) \\
&= \phi \sigma_Y^2
\end{aligned} \tag{13.15}
$$

We can easily show that:

$$Cov(Y_t, Y_{t-2}) = E(Y_t Y_{t-2})$$
$$= E[(\phi Y_{t-1} + u_t) Y_{t-2}]$$
$$= E[(\phi(\phi Y_{t-2} + u_{t-1}) + u_t) Y_{t-2}]$$
$$= E(\phi^2 Y_{t-2} Y_{t-2})$$
$$= \phi^2 \sigma_Y^2 \qquad (13.16)$$

and in general:

$$Cov(Y_t, Y_{t-k}) = \phi^k \sigma_Y^2 \qquad (13.17)$$

The autocorrelation function will be given by:

$$Cor(Y_t, Y_{t-k}) = \frac{Cov(Y_t, Y_{t-k})}{\sqrt{Var(Y_t) Var(Y_{t-k})}} = \frac{\phi^k \sigma_Y^2}{\sigma_Y^2} = \phi^k \qquad (13.18)$$

So, for an AR(1) series the autocorrelation function (ACF) (and the graph of it which plots the values of $Cor(Y_t, Y_{t-k})$ against k and is called correlogram) will decay exponentially as k increases.

Finally, the partial autocorrelation function (PACF) involves plotting the estimated coefficient Y_{t-k} from an OLS estimate of an AR(k) process, against k. If the observations are generated by an AR(p) process then the theoretical partial autocorrelations will be high and significant for up to p lags and then zero for lags beyond p.

Moving average models

The MA(1) model

The simplest moving average model is that of order one, or the MA(1) model, which has the form:

$$Y_t = u_t + \theta u_{t-1} \qquad (13.19)$$

Thus, the implication behind the MA(1) model is that Y_t depends on the value of the immediate past error, which is known at time t.

The MA(q) model

The general form of the MA model is an MA(q) model of the form:

$$Y_t = u_t + \theta_1 u_{t-1} + \theta_2 u_{t-2} + \cdots + \theta_q u_{t-q} \qquad (13.20)$$

which can be rewritten as:

$$Y_t = u_t + \sum_{j=1}^{q} \theta_j u_{t-j} \tag{13.21}$$

or, using the lag operator:

$$Y_t = \left(1 + \theta_1 L + \theta_2 L^2 + \cdots + \theta_q L^q\right) u_t \tag{13.22}$$

$$= \Theta(L) u_t \tag{13.23}$$

Because any MA(q) process is, by definition, an average of q stationary white-noise processes, it follows that every moving average model is stationary, as long as q is finite.

Invertibility in MA models

A property often discussed in connection with the moving average processes is that of invertibility. A time series Y_t is invertible if it can be represented by a finite-order MA or convergent autoregressive process. Invertibility is important because the use of the ACF and PACF for identification implicitly assumes that the Y_t sequence can be well-approximated by an autoregressive model. For an example consider the simple MA(1) model:

$$Y_t = u_t + \theta u_{t-1} \tag{13.24}$$

Using the lag operator this can be rewritten as:

$$Y_t = (1 + \theta L) u_t$$

$$u_t = \frac{Y_t}{(1 + \theta L)} \tag{13.25}$$

If $|\theta| < 1$, then the left-hand side of (13.25) can be considered as the sum of an infinite geometric progression:

$$u_t = Y_t (1 - \theta L + \theta^2 L^2 - \theta^3 L^3 + \cdots) \tag{13.26}$$

(To understand this consider the MA(1) process:

$$Y_t = u_t - \theta u_{t-1}$$

Lagging this relationship one period and solving for u_t we have:

$$u_{t-1} = Y_{t-1} - \theta u_{t-2}$$

Substituting this into the original expression we have:

$$Y_t = u_t - \theta(Y_{t-1} - \theta u_{t-2}) = u_t - \theta Y_{t-1} + \theta^2 u_{t-2}$$

Lagging the above expression one period and solving for u_{t-2} and resubstituting we get:

$$Y_t = u_t - \theta Y_{t-1} + \theta^2 Y_{t-2} - \theta^3 u_{t-3}$$

And repeating this an infinite number of times we finally get the expression (13.26).)
Thus, the MA(1) process has been inverted into an infinite order AR process with
geometrically declining weights. Note that for the MA(1) process to be invertible it
is necessary that $|\theta| < 1$.

In general the MA(q) processes are invertible if the roots of the polynomial

$$\Theta(z) = 0 \tag{13.27}$$

are greater than 1 in absolute value.

Properties of the MA models

The mean of the MA process will be clearly equal to zero as it is the mean of white noise
error terms. The variance will be (for the MA(1) model) given by:

$$Var(Y_t) = Var(u_t + \theta u_{t-1}) = \sigma_u^2 + \theta^2 \sigma_u^2 = \sigma_u^2(1 + \theta^2) \tag{13.28}$$

The autocovariance will be given by:

$$Cov(Y_t, Y_{t-1}) = E[(u_t + \theta u_{t-1})(u_{t-1} + \theta u_{t-2})] \tag{13.29}$$

$$= E(u_t u_{t-1}) + \theta E(u_{t-1}^2) + \theta^2 E(u_{t-1} u_{t-2}) \tag{13.30}$$

$$= \theta \sigma_u^2 \tag{13.31}$$

And since u_t is serially uncorrelated it is easy to see that:

$$Cov(Y_t, Y_{t-k}) = 0 \quad \text{for } k > 1 \tag{13.32}$$

From this we can understand that for the MA(1) process the autocorrelation function
will be:

$$Cor(Y_t, Y_{t-k}) = \frac{Cov(Y_t, Y_{t-k})}{\sqrt{Var(Y_t)Var(Y_{t-k})}} = \begin{cases} \dfrac{\theta \sigma_u^2}{\sigma_u^2(1+\theta^2)} = \dfrac{\sigma_u^2}{1+\theta^2} & \text{for } k=1 \\ 0 & \text{for } k>1 \end{cases} \tag{13.33}$$

So, if we have an MA(q) model we will expect the correlogram (the graph of the
ACF) to have q spikes for $k = q$, and then go down to zero immediately. Also, since
any MA process can be represented as an AR process with geometrically declining
coefficients, the partial autocorrelation function (or the PACF) for an MA process should
decay slowly.

ARMA models

After presenting the AR(p) and the MA(q) processes, it should be clear to the reader that we can have combinations of the two processes to give a new series of models called ARMA(p, q) models. The general form of the ARMA(p, q) models is the following:
The general form of the ARMA model is an ARMA(p, q) model of the form:

$$Y_t = \phi_1 Y_{t-1} + \phi_2 Y_{t-1} + \cdots + \phi_p Y_{t-p} + u_t$$
$$+ \theta_1 u_{t-1} + \theta_2 u_{t-2} + \cdots + \theta_q u_{t-q} \tag{13.34}$$

which can be rewritten, using the summations, as:

$$Y_t = \sum_{i=1}^{p} \phi_i Y_{t-i} + u_t + \sum_{j=1}^{q} \theta_j u_{t-j} \tag{13.35}$$

or, using the lag operator:

$$Y_t(1 - \phi_1 L - \phi_2 L^2 - \cdots - \phi_p L^p) = (1 + \theta_1 L + \theta_2 L^2 + \cdots + \theta_q L^q) u_t \tag{13.36}$$

$$\Phi(L) Y_t = \Theta(L) u_t \tag{13.37}$$

In the ARMA(p, q) models the condition for stationarity has to deal with the AR(p) part of the specification only. Therefore, we have that the p roots of the polynomial equation $\Phi(z) = 0$ should lie outside the unit circle. Similarly, the property of invertibility for the ARMA(p, q) models will have to do only with the MA(q) part of the specification and it will be that the roots of the $\Theta(z)$ polynomial should lie outside the unit circle as well. In the next section we will talk about integrated processes and explain the I part of the ARIMA models. Here it is useful to note that the ARMA(p, q) model can also be denoted as an ARIMA(p,0,q) model. To give an example consider the ARMA(2,3) model, which is equivalent to the ARIMA(2,0,3) model and is given below:

$$Y_t = \phi_1 Y_{t-1} + \phi_2 Y_{t-1} + \phi_2 Y_{t-2} + u_t$$
$$+ \theta_1 u_{t-1} + \theta_2 u_{t-2} + \theta_3 u_{t-3} \tag{13.38}$$

Integrated processes and the ARIMA models

An integrated series

ARMA models can only be made on time series Y_t that are stationary. This means that the mean, variance and covariance of the series are constant over time. However, most economic and financial time series show trends over time, and so the mean of Y_t during one year will be different from its mean in another year. Thus the mean of most economic and financial time series is not constant over time, which means that the series are non-stationary. In order to avoid this problem, and in order to induce stationarity, we need to detrend the raw data through a process called differencing. The first differences of a series Y_t are given by the equation:

$$\Delta Y_t = Y_t - Y_{t-1} \tag{13.39}$$

As most economic and financial time series show trends to some degree, we nearly always end up taking first differences of the input series. If, after first differencing, a series is stationary then the series is also called integrated to order one, and denoted I(1) – which completes the abbreviation ARIMA. If the series, even after first differencing is not stationary, then we need to take second differences by the equation:

$$\Delta\Delta Y_t = \Delta^2 Y_t = \Delta Y_t - \Delta Y_{t-1} \tag{13.40}$$

If the series becomes stationary after second differences, then it is integrated of order two and denoted by I(2). In general if we difference a series d times in order to induce stationarity, the series is called integrated of order d and is denoted by I(d). Thus the general ARIMA model is called an ARIMA(p, d, q), with p being the number of lags of the dependent variable (the AR terms), d being the number of differences required to take in order to make the series stationary, and q being the number of lagged terms of the error term (the MA terms).

ARIMA models

To give an example of an ARIMA(p, d, q) model, we can say that in general an integrated series of order d must be differenced d times before it can be represented by a stationary and invertible ARMA process. If this ARMA representation is of order (p, q) then the original, undifferenced series is following an ARIMA(p, d, q) representation. Alternatively, if a process Y_t has an ARIMA(p, d, q) representation, then the $\Delta^d Y_t$ has an ARMA(p, q) representation as presented by the equation below:

$$\Delta^d Y_t (1 - \phi_1 L - \phi_2 L^2 - \cdots - \phi_p L^p) = (1 + \theta_1 L + \theta_2 L^2 + \cdots + \theta_q L^q) u_t \tag{13.41}$$

Box–Jenkins model selection

A fundamental idea in the Box–Jenkins approach is the principle of *parsimony*. Parsimony (meaning sparseness or stinginess) should come as second nature to economists and financial analysts. Incorporating additional coefficients will necessarily increase the fit of the regression equation (i.e. the value of the R^2 will increase), but the cost will be a reduction of the degrees of freedom. Box and Jenkins argue that parsimonious models produce better forecasts than overparametrized models. In general Box and Jenkins popularized a three-stage method aimed at selecting an appropriate (parsimonious) ARIMA model for the purpose of estimating and forecasting a univariate time series. The three stages are: (a) identification, (b) estimation, and (c) diagnostic checking and are presented below.

We have seen above that a low-order MA model is equivalent to a high-order AR model, and similarly a low-order AR model is equivalent to a high-order MA model.

This gives rise to the main difficulty in using ARIMA models, which is called the identification problem. The essence of this is that any model may be given more than one (and in most cases many) different representations, which are essentially equivalent. How then should we choose the best one and how should we estimate it? Defining the 'best' representation is fairly easy and here we use the principle of parsimony, this simply means that we pick the form of the model with the smallest number of parameters to be estimated. The trick is finding this model. You might think that we could simply start with a high-order ARMA model and simply remove the insignificant coefficients. Unfortunately this does not work because within this high-order model will be many equivalent ways of representing the same model and the estimation process cannot choose between them. We therefore have to know the form of the model before we can estimate it. In this context this is known as the identification problem and it represents the first stage of the Box–Jenkins procedure.

Identification

In the identification stage (this identification should not be confused with the identification procedure explained in the simultaneous equations chapter), the researcher visually examines the time plot of the series autocorrelation function, and partial correlation function. Plotting each observation of the Y_t sequence against t provides useful information concerning outliers, missing values, and structural breaks in the data. We have mentioned before that most economic and financial time series are trended and therefore non-stationary. Typically, non-stationary variables have a pronounced trend (increasing or declining) or appear to meander without a constant long-run mean or variance. Missing values and outliers can be corrected at this point. At one time, the standard practice was to first-difference any series deemed to be non-stationary.

A comparison of the sample ACF and PACF to those of various theoretical ARIMA processes may suggest several plausible models. In theory, if the series is non-stationary the ACF of the series will not die down or show signs of decay at all. If this is the case then we need to transform the series in order to make them stationary. As we said before, a common stationarity-inducing transformation is to take logarithms and then first differences of the series.

Once we have achieved stationarity, the next step is to identify the p and q orders of the ARIMA model. For a pure MA(q) process, the ACF will tend to show estimated autocorrelations which are significantly different from zero up to lag q and then it will die down immediately after the qth lag. The PACF for MA(q) will tend to die down quickly either by an exponential decay or by a damped sinewave.

Contrary to the MA processes, the pure AR(p) process will have an ACF which will tend to die down quickly either by an exponential decay or by a damped sinewave, while the PACF will tend to show spikes (significant autocorrelations) for lags up to p and then it will die down immediately.

If neither the ACF or the PACF show a definite cut off, then a mixed process is suggested. In this case it is difficult to identify the AR and MA orders but not impossible. The idea is that we should think of the ACF and PACF of pure AR and MA processes as being superimposed onto one another. For example, if both ACF and PACF show signs of

Table 13.1 ACF and PACF patterns for possible ARMA(p, q) models

Model	ACF	PACF
Pure white noise	All autocorrelations are zero	All partial autocorrelations are zero
MA(1)	Single positive spike at lag 1	Damped sinewave or exponential decay
AR(1)	Damped sinewave or exponential decay	Single positive spike at lag 1
ARMA(1,1)	Decay (exp. or sinewave) beginning at lag 1	Decay (exp. or sinewave) beginning at lag 1
ARMA(p, q)	Decay (exp. or sinewave) beginning at lag q	Decay (exp. or sinewave) beginning at lag p

slow exponential decay, then an ARMA(1,1) process may be identified. Similarly, if the ACF shows three significant spikes at lags one, two and three and then an exponential decay, and the PACF spikes at the first lag and then shows an exponential decay, then an ARMA(3,1) process should be considered. Table 13.1 reports some possible combinations of ACF and PACF forms that allow us to detect the order of ARMA processes. In general, it is difficult to identify mixed processes, so sometimes more than one ARMA(p, q) model might be estimated. This is why the estimation and the diagnostic checking stages are important and necessary.

Estimation

In the estimation stage, each of the tentative models is estimated and the various coefficients are examined. In this second stage, the estimated models are compared using the Akaike information criterion (AIC) and the Schwartz Bayesian criterion (SBC). We want a parsimonious model, so we will choose the model with the smallest AIC and SBC values. Of the two criteria, the SBC is preferable. Also at this stage we have to be aware of the common factor problem. The Box–Jenkins approach necessitates that the series is stationary and the model invertible.

Diagnostic checking

In the diagnostic checking stage we examine the goodness of fit of the model. The standard practice at this stage is to plot the residuals and look for outliers and evidence of periods in which the model does not fit the data well. We must be careful here to avoid overfitting (the procedure of adding another coefficient in an appropriate model). The special statistics that we use here are the Box–Pierce statistic (BP) and the Ljung–Box (LB) Q-statistic (see Ljung and Box, 1979), which serve to test for autocorrelations of the residuals.

The Box–Jenkins approach step by step

The Box–Jenkins approach involves the following steps:

Step 1   Calculate the ACF and PACF of the raw data, and check whether the series is stationary or not. If the series are stationary go to step 3, if not go to step 2.

Step 2   Take the logarithm and the first differences of the raw data and calculate the ACF and PACF for the first logarithmic differenced series.

Step 3   Examine the graphs of the ACF and PACF and determine which models would be good starting points.

Step 4   Estimate those models.

Step 5   For each of these estimated models:

   (a) check to see if the parameter of the longest lag is significant. If not, then you probably have too many parameters, and should decrease the order of p and/or q.

   (b) check the ACF and PACF of the errors. If the model has at least enough parameters, then all error ACFs and PACFs will be insignificant.

   (c) check the AIC and SBC together with the adj-R^2 of the estimated models to detect which model is the parsimonious one (i.e. the one that minimizes AIC and SBC and has the highest adj-R^2).

Step 6   If changes in the original model are needed, go back to step 4.

Example: the Box–Jenkins approach

The file ARIMA.wf1 contains quarterly data observations for the consumer price index (*cpi*) and gross domestic product (*gdp*) of the UK economy. We will try to identify the underlying ARMA model for the *gdp* variable.

Step 1   As a first step we need to calculate the ACF and PACF of the raw data. To do this we need to double click on the cpi variable in order to open the variable in a new EViews window. We can then calculate the ACF and PACF and view their respective graphs by clicking on **View/Correlogram** in the window that contains the *gdp* variable. This will give us Figure 13.3.

From Figure 13.3 we can see that the ACF does not die down at all for all lags (see also the plot of *gdp* to see that it is clearly trended), which clearly suggests that the series is integrated and that we need to proceed with taking logarithms and first differences of the series.

Step 2   We take logs and then first differences of the *gdp* series by typing the following commands in the EViews command line:

```
genr lgdp = log(gdp)
genr dlgdp = lgdp − lgdp(−1)
```

Date: 02/26/04   Time: 15:31
Sample: 1980:1 1998:2
Included observations: 74

Autocorrelation	Partial Correlation		AC	PAC	Q-Stat	Prob
. |*******|	. |*******|	1	0.963	0.963	71.464	0.000
. |*******|	.*| . |	2	0.922	−0.079	137.85	0.000
. |*******|	. | . |	3	0.878	−0.049	198.98	0.000
. |****** |	. | . |	4	0.833	−0.047	254.74	0.000
. |****** |	. | . |	5	0.787	−0.038	305.16	0.000
. |****** |	. | . |	6	0.740	−0.021	350.47	0.000
. |***** |	. | . |	7	0.695	−0.002	391.06	0.000
. |***** |	. | . |	8	0.650	−0.040	427.05	0.000
. |***** |	. | . |	9	0.604	−0.029	458.63	0.000
. |**** |	. | . |	10	0.559	−0.026	486.05	0.000

Figure 13.3   ACF and PACF of GDP

Date: 02/26/04   Time: 15:43
Sample: 1980:1 1998:2
Included observations: 73

Autocorrelation	Partial Correlation		AC	PAC	Q-Stat	Prob
. |*** |	. |*** |	1	0.454	0.454	15.645	0.000
. |** |	. |*. |	2	0.288	0.104	22.062	0.000
. |** |	. |*. |	3	0.312	0.187	29.661	0.000
. |** |	. | . |	4	0.242	0.037	34.303	0.000
. |*. |	. | . |	5	0.130	−0.049	35.664	0.000
. |** |	. |*. |	6	0.238	0.174	40.287	0.000
. | . |	.*| . |	7	0.055	−0.187	40.536	0.000
.*| . |	.*| . |	8	−0.085	−0.141	41.149	0.000
. | . |	. | . |	9	−0.010	−0.032	41.158	0.000
. | . |	. | . |	10	−0.020	−0.026	41.193	0.000

Figure 13.4   ACF and PACF of DLGDP

and then double click on the newly created *dlgdp* (log-differenced series) and click again on **View/Correlogram** to obtain the correlogram of the *dlgdp* series.

Step 3   From step 2 above we obtain the ACF and PACF of the *dlgdp* series, provided in Figure 13.4. From this correlogram we can see that there are 2 to 3 spikes on the ACF, and then all are zero, while there is also one spike in the PACF which then dies down to zero quickly. This suggests that we might have up to MA(3) and AR(1) specifications. So, the possible models are the ARMA(1,3), ARMA(1,2) or ARMA(1,1) models.

Step 4   We then estimate the three possible models. The command for estimating the ARMA(1,3) model is:

```
ls dlgdp c ar(1) ma(1) ma(2) ma(3)
```

similarly, for the ARMA(1,2) it is:

```
ls dlgdp c ar(1) ma(1) ma(2)
```

and for the ARMA(1,1) it is:

```
ls dlgdp c ar(1) ma(1)
```

The results are presented in Tables 13.2, 13.3 and 13.4 respectively.

Step 5 Finally, we have to check the diagnostics of the three alternative models to see which model is more appropriate. Summarized results of all three specifications are provided in Table 13.5, from which we see that in terms of significance of estimated coefficients, the model that is more appropriate is probably ARMA(1,3). ARMA(1,2) has one insignificant term (the coefficient of the MA(2) term which should be dropped), but when we include both MA(2) and MA(3), the MA(3) term is highly significant and the MA(2) term is significant at the 90% level. In terms of AIC and SBC we have contradictory results. The AIC suggests the ARMA(1,3) model, but the SBC suggests the ARMA(1,1) model. The adj-R^2 is higher for the ARMA(1,3) model as well. So, evidence here suggests that the ARMA(1.3) model is probably the most appropriate one. Remember that we need a parsimonious model, so there might be a problem of overfitting here. For this we also check the Q-statistics of the correlograms of the residuals for lags 8, 16 and 24. We see that only the ARMA(1,3) model has insignificant lags for all three different cases, while the other two models have significant (for 90%) lags for the 8th and the

Table 13.2 Regression results of an ARMA(1,3) model

Dependent Variable: DLGDP
Method: Least Squares
Date: 02/26/04 Time: 15:50
Sample(adjusted): 1980:3 1998:2
Included observations: 72 after adjusting endpoints
Convergence achieved after 10 iterations
Backcast: 1979:4 1980:2

Variable	Coefficient	Std. Error	t-Statistic	Prob.
C	0.006817	0.001541	4.423742	0.0000
AR(1)	0.710190	0.100980	7.032979	0.0000
MA(1)	−0.448048	0.146908	−3.049866	0.0033
MA(2)	−0.220783	0.123783	−1.783625	0.0790
MA(3)	0.323663	0.113301	2.856665	0.0057

R-squared	0.340617	Mean dependent var		0.005942
Adjusted R-squared	0.301251	S.D. dependent var		0.006687
S.E. of regression	0.005590	Akaike info criterion		−7.468887
Sum squared resid	0.002093	Schwarz criterion		−7.310785
Log likelihood	273.8799	F-statistic		8.652523
Durbin–Watson stat	1.892645	Prob(F-statistic)		0.000011

Inverted AR Roots	.71		
Inverted MA Roots	.55+.44i	.55 −.44i	−.65

Table 13.3   Regression results of an ARMA(1,2) model

Dependent Variable: DLGDP
Method: Least Squares
Date: 02/26/04 Time: 16:00
Sample(adjusted): 1980:3 1998:2
Included observations: 72 after adjusting endpoints
Convergence achieved after 32 iterations
Backcast: 1980:1 1980:2

Variable	Coefficient	Std. Error	t-Statistic	Prob.
C	0.006782	0.001387	4.890638	0.0000
AR(1)	0.722203	0.114627	6.300451	0.0000
MA(1)	−0.342970	0.171047	−2.005128	0.0489
MA(2)	−0.124164	0.130236	−0.953374	0.3438

R-squared	0.286174	Mean dependent var		0.005942
Adjusted R-squared	0.254681	S.D. dependent var		0.006687
S.E. of regression	0.005773	Akaike info criterion		−7.417330
Sum squared resid	0.002266	Schwarz criterion		−7.290849
Log likelihood	271.0239	F-statistic		9.087094
Durbin–Watson stat	2.023172	Prob(F-statistic)		0.000039

Inverted AR Roots	.72			
Inverted MA Roots	.56		−.22	

Table 13.4   Regression results of an ARMA(1,1) model

Dependent Variable: DLGDP
Method: Least Squares
Date: 02/26/04 Time: 16:03
Sample(adjusted): 1980:3 1998:2
Included observations: 72 after adjusting endpoints
Convergence achieved after 9 iterations
Backcast: 1980:2

Variable	Coefficient	Std. Error	t-Statistic	Prob.
C	0.006809	0.001464	4.651455	0.0000
AR(1)	0.742291	0.101186	7.335927	0.0000
MA(1)	−0.471431	0.161407	−2.920758	0.0047

R-squared	0.279356	Mean dependent var		0.005942
Adjusted R-squared	0.258468	S.D. dependent var		0.006687
S.E. of regression	0.005758	Akaike info criterion		−7.435603
Sum squared resid	0.002288	Schwarz criterion		−7.340742
Log likelihood	270.6817	F-statistic		13.37388
Durbin–Watson stat	1.876198	Prob(F-statistic)		0.000012

Inverted AR Roots	.74			
Inverted MA Roots	.47			

16th lag, suggesting that the residuals are serially correlated. So, again here the ARMA(1,3) model seems to be the most appropriate. As an alternative specification someone might want to go back to step 4 (as step 6 suggests) and reestimate a model with an AR(1) term and MA(1) and MA(3) terms only to see what happens to the diagnostics. We will leave this as an exercise for the reader.

Table 13.5 Summary results of alternative ARMA(p, q) models

	ARMA(1,3)	ARMA(1,2)	ARMA(1,1)
Degrees of freedom	68	69	70
SSR	0.002093	0.002266	0.002288
ϕ (t-stat in parenthesis)	0.71 (7.03)	0.72 (6.3)	0.74 (7.33)
θ_1 (t-stat in parenthesis)	−0.44 (−3.04)	−0.34 (−2.0)	−0.47 (−2.92)
θ_2 (t-stat in parenthesis)	−0.22 (−1.78)	−0.12 (0.9)	—
θ_3 (t-stat in parenthesis)	0.32 (2.85)	—	—
AIC/SBC	−7.4688/−7.3107	−7.4173/−7.2908	−7.4356/−7.3407
Adj R^2	0.301	0.254	0.258
Ljung–Box statistics for residuals (sig levels in parentheses)	$Q(8) = 5.65(0.22)$ $Q(16) = 14.15(0.29)$ $Q(24) = 19.48(0.49)$	$Q(8) = 9.84(0.08)$ $Q(16) = 20.66(0.08)$ $Q(24) = 24.87(0.25)$	$Q(8) = 11.17(0.08)$ $Q(16) = 19.81(0.07)$ $Q(24) = 28.58(0.15)$

Questions and exercises

Questions

1 Explain what is the implication behind the AR and MA models by giving examples of each.

2 Define the concepts stationarity and invertibility and state which are the conditions for stationarity in the AR models and invertibility for the MA models.

3 Define and explain the concepts of stationarity and invertibility. Why are they important in the analysis of time series data? Present examples of stationary and non-stationary, invertible and non-invertible processes.

4 Discuss analytically the three stages that are involved in the Box–Jenkins process for ARIMA model selection.

Exercise 13.1

Show that an MA(1) process can be expressed as an infinite AR process.

Exercise 13.2

The file ARIMA.wf1 contains quarterly data for the consumer price index (*cpi*) and gross domestic product (*gdp*) of the UK economy. Follow the steps described in the Example for the Box–Jenkins approach regarding *gdp* for the *cpi* variable.

14

Modelling the Variance: ARCH–GARCH Models

Introduction

Recent developments in financial econometrics require the use of models and techniques that are able to model the attitude of investors not only towards expected returns, but towards risk (or uncertainty) as well. This fact requires models that are capable of dealing with the volatility (variance) of the series. Such models are the ARCH-family of models which we present and analyse in this chapter.

Conventional econometric analysis views the variance of the disturbance terms as constant over time (the homoskedasticity assumption that we analysed in Chapter 7). However, mainly financial but also many economic time series exhibit periods of unusually high volatility followed by more tranquil periods of low volatility ('wild' and 'calm' periods as some financial analysts like to call them).

Even from a quick look at financial data (see for example Figure 14.1 that plots daily returns of the FTSE-100 from 1 Jan 1990 up to 31 Dec 1999) we can see that there are certain periods that have higher volatility (and therefore are riskier) than others. This means that the expected value of the magnitude of the disturbance terms can be greater at certain periods compared to others. Additionally, these riskier times seem to be concentrated and followed by periods of lower risk (lower volatility) that are again concentrated. In other words, we observe that large changes in stock returns seem to be followed by other large changes and vice versa. This phenomenon is what financial analysts call volatility clustering. In terms of the graph it is clear that there are subperiods of higher volatility, while it is also clear that after 1997 the volatility of the series is much higher than what it used to be in the past.

Therefore, in such cases it is clear that the assumption of homoskedasticity (or constant variance) is very limiting, and in such instances it is preferable to examine patterns that allow the variance to depend upon its history. Or, to use more appropriate terminology, better to examine not the unconditional variance (which is the long-run forecast of the variance and can be still treated as constant) but the conditional variance, based on our best model of the variable under consideration.

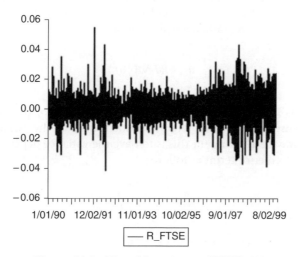

Figure 14.1 Plot of the returns of FTSE-100

To understand this better, consider an investor who is planning to buy an asset at time t and sell it at time $t + 1$. For this investor, the forecast of the rate of return of this asset alone will not be enough. She/he would be interested in what the variance of the return over the holding period will be. Therefore, the unconditional variance is of no use either; the investor will want to examine the behaviour of the conditional variance of the series to estimate the riskiness of the asset at a certain period of time.

This chapter will focus on the modelling of the behaviour of conditional variance, or more appropriately of conditional heteroskedasticity (from which comes the CH part of the ARCH models). The next section presents the first model that proposed the concept of autoregressive conditional heteroskedasticity (ARCH) developed by Robert F. Engle in his seminal paper 'Autoregressive Conditional Heteroskedasticity with Estimates of the Variance of United Kingdom Inflation' published in *Econometrica* in 1982, and which started a whole new era in applied econometrics with lots of ARCH variations, extensions and applications we shall then present the generalized ARCH (GARCH) model, followed by an alternative specification. Finally, illustrations of ARCH/GARCH models are presented using examples from financial and economic time series.

The ARCH model

The first ARCH model was presented by Engle (1982). The model suggests that the variance of the residuals at time t depends on the squared error terms from past periods. Engle simply suggested that it is better to simultaneously model the mean and the variance of a series when we suspect that the conditional variance is not constant.

Let's see this in a more detailed way. Consider the simple model:

$$Y_t = a + \beta' X_t + u_t \tag{14.1}$$

where X_t is a $k \times 1$ vector of explanatory variables and β is a $k \times 1$ vector of coefficients. Normally, we assume that u_t is independently distributed with a zero mean and a constant variance σ^2, or in mathematical notation:

$$u_t \sim iid\ N(0, \sigma^2) \tag{14.2}$$

Engle's idea starts from the fact that he allows the variance of the residuals (σ^2) to depend on past history, or to have heteroskedasticity because the variance will change over time. One way of allowing for this is to have the variance depend on one lagged period of the squared error terms as follows:

$$\sigma_t^2 = \gamma_0 + \gamma_1 u_{t-1}^2 \tag{14.3}$$

which is the basic ARCH(1) process.

The ARCH(1) model

Following on, the ARCH(1) model will simultaneously model the mean and the variance of the series with the following specification:

$$Y_t = a + \beta' X_t + u_t \tag{14.4}$$

$$u_t | \Omega_t \sim iid \ N(0, h_t)$$

$$h_t = \gamma_0 + \gamma_1 u_{t-1}^2 \tag{14.5}$$

where Ω_t is the information set. Here equation (14.4) is called the mean equation and equation (14.5) is called the variance equation. Note that we have changed the notation of the variance from σ_t^2 to h_t. This is in order to keep the same notation from now on, throughout this chapter. (The reason that it is better to use h_t instead of σ_t^2 will become clear to the reader through the more mathematical explanation provided later in the chapter.)

The ARCH(1) model says that when a big shock happens in period $t - 1$, it is more likely that the value of u_t (in absolute terms because of the squares) will be bigger as well. That is, when u_{t-1}^2 is large/small, the variance of the next innovation u_t is also large/small. The estimated coefficient of γ_1 has to be positive for positive variance.

The ARCH(q) model

In fact, the conditional variance can depend not only on one lagged realization but more than one, for each case producing a different ARCH process. For example the ARCH(2) process will be:

$$h_t = \gamma_0 + \gamma_1 u_{t-1}^2 + \gamma_2 u_{t-2}^2 \tag{14.6}$$

the ARCH(3) will be given by:

$$h_t = \gamma_0 + \gamma_1 u_{t-1}^2 + \gamma_2 u_{t-2}^2 + \gamma_3 u_{t-3}^2 \tag{14.7}$$

and in general the ARCH(q) process will be given by:

$$h_t = \gamma_0 + \gamma_1 u_{t-1}^2 + \gamma_2 u_{t-2}^2 + \cdots + \gamma_q u_{t-q}^2$$

$$= \gamma_0 + \sum_{j=1}^{q} \gamma_j u_{t-j}^2 \tag{14.8}$$

Therefore, the ARCH(q) model will simultaneously examine the mean and the variance of a series according to the following specification:

$$Y_t = a + \beta'X_t + u_t \tag{14.9}$$

$$u_t | \Omega_t \sim iid \; N(0, h_t)$$

$$h_t = \gamma_0 + \sum_{j=1}^{q} \gamma_j u_{t-j}^2 \tag{14.10}$$

Again, the estimated coefficients of the γs have to be positive for positive variance.

Testing for ARCH effects

Before estimating ARCH(q) models it is important to check for the possible presence of ARCH effects in order to know which models require the ARCH estimation method instead of the OLS. Testing for ARCH effects was extensively examined in Chapter 7, but a short version of the test for qth order autoregressive heteroskedasticity is provided here as well. The test can be done along the lines of the Breusch–Pagan test, which entails estimation of the mean equation:

$$Y_t = a + \beta'X_t + u_t \tag{14.11}$$

by OLS as usual (note that the mean equation can have as explanatory variables in the x_t vector, autoregressive terms of the dependent variable as well), to obtain the residuals $\hat{u}_t$, and then run an auxiliary regression of the squared residuals ($\hat{u}_t^2$) upon the lagged squared terms ($\hat{u}_{t-1}^2, \ldots, \hat{u}_{t-q}^2$) and a constant as in:

$$\hat{u}_t^2 = \gamma_0 + \gamma_1 \hat{u}_{t-1}^2 + \cdots + \gamma_q \hat{u}_{t-q}^2 + w_t \tag{14.12}$$

and then compute the R^2 times T. Under the null hypothesis of heteroskedasticity ($\gamma_0 = \gamma_1 = \cdots = \gamma_q$) the resulting test statistic follows a χ^2 distribution with q degrees of freedom. Rejection of the null suggests evidence of ARCH(q) effects.

Estimation of ARCH models by iteration

The presence of ARCH effects in a regression model does not completely invalidate the use of OLS estimation, the coefficients will still be consistent estimates, they will not however be fully efficient and the estimate of the covariance matrix of the parameters will be biased leading to invalid 't' statistics. A fully efficient estimator with a valid covariance matrix can however be calculated by setting up a model which explicitly recognizes the presence of the ARCH effects. However this model can no longer be estimated using a simple technique such as OLS, which has an analytical solution. Instead we must solve a non-linear maximization problem, which requires an iterative computer algorithm to search for the solution to the problem. The method used to estimate ARCH models is a special case of a general estimation strategy known as the maximum-likelihood approach. A formal exposition of this approach is beyond the scope of this book (see Cuthbertson, Hall and Taylor, 1992), but we will give an intuitive account of how this is done here. We assume that we have the correct model and we know the distribution of the error process, we then select a set of values for the parameters to be estimated, we can then in principle calculate the probability that the set of endogenous variables, which we have observed in our dataset, would actually occur. We then select a set of parameters for our model, which maximize this probability. These are then called the maximum-likelihood parameters and they have the general property that they are consistent and efficient (under the full set of CLRM assumptions OLS is a maximum-likelihood estimator). Except in certain rare cases finding the parameters which maximize this likelihood function requires the computer to search over the parameter space and hence the computer will perform a number of steps (or iterations) as it searches for the best set of parameters. Packages such as EViews or Microfit include routines, which do this very efficiently, although sometimes if the problem becomes too complex the programme may fail to find a true maximum and there are switches within the software to help convergence by adjusting a range of options. The following section explains step by step how to use EViews for estimating ARCH models, providing different examples.

Estimating ARCH models in EViews

The file ARCH.wf1 contains daily data for the logarithmic returns FTSE-100 (named *r_ftse*) and three more stocks of the UK stockmarket (named *r_stock1*, *r_stock2* and *r_stock3* respectively). We first consider the behaviour of *r_ftse* alone. The first step is to check whether the series is characterized by ARCH effects. From the time plot of the series (Figure 14.1) we saw clearly that there are periods with larger and smaller volatility in the sample, so the possibility of ARCH effects is quite high.

The first step in our analysis is to estimate an AR(1) model (having this as the mean equation for simplicity) for *r_ftse* using simple OLS. To do this click **Quick/Estimate Equation**, to open the **Equation Specification** window. In this window we need to specify the equation that we want to estimate (by typing it in the white box of the **Equation Specification** window). Our equation for an AR(1) model will be:

```
r_ftse c r_ftse(-1)
```

We then click <**OK**> to obtain the results shown in Table 14.1.

These results do not interest us by themselves. What we care about is whether there are ARCH effects in the residuals of this model, and in order to test for such effects we use the Breusch–Pagan ARCH test. In EViews from the equation results window we click on **View/Residuals Tests/ARCH LM Test** ... EViews asks us to specify the number of lagged terms to include, which is simply the q term in the ARCH(q) processes. If we want to test for an ARCH(1) process we type 1, and for higher orders the number that we need to specify for q. Testing for ARCH(1) (by typing 1 and pressing <**OK**>) we get the results of Table 14.2.

The $T * R^2$ statistic (or Obs*R-squared as EViews presents it) is 46.05 and has a probability limit of 0.000. This clearly suggests that we reject the null hypothesis of

Table 14.1   A simple AR(1) model for the FTSE-100

Dependent Variable: R_FTSE
Method: Least Squares
Date: 12/26/03 Time: 15:16
Sample: 1/01/1990 12/31/1999
Included observations: 2610

Variable	Coefficient	Std. Error	t-Statistic	Prob.
C	0.000363	0.000184	1.975016	0.0484
R_FTSE(−1)	0.070612	0.019538	3.614090	0.0003

R-squared	0.004983	Mean dependent var	0.000391
Adjusted R-squared	0.004602	S.D. dependent var	0.009398
S.E. of regression	0.009376	Akaike info criterion	−6.500477
Sum squared resid	0.229287	Schwarz criterion	−6.495981
Log likelihood	8485.123	F-statistic	13.06165
Durbin–Watson stat	1.993272	Prob(F-statistic)	0.000307

Table 14.2   Testing for ARCH(1) effects in the FTSE-100

ARCH Test:

F-statistic	46.84671	Probability	0.000000
Obs*R-squared	46.05506	Probability	0.000000

Test Equation:
Dependent Variable: RESID^2
Method: Least Squares
Date: 12/26/03 Time: 15:27
Sample(adjusted): 1/02/1990 12/31/1999
Included observations: 2609 after adjusting endpoints

Variable	Coefficient	Std. Error	t-Statistic	Prob.
C	7.62E−05	3.76E−06	20.27023	0.0000
RESID^2(−1)	0.132858	0.019411	6.844466	0.0000

R-squared	0.017652	Mean dependent var	8.79E−05
Adjusted R-squared	0.017276	S.D. dependent var	0.000173
S.E. of regression	0.000171	Akaike info criterion	−14.50709
Sum squared resid	7.64E−05	Schwarz criterion	−14.50260
Log likelihood	18926.50	F-statistic	46.84671
Durbin–Watson stat	2.044481	Prob(F-statistic)	0.000000

homoskedasticity, or that ARCH(1) effects are present. Testing for higher-order ARCH effects (for example order 6) we get the results shown in Table 14.3.

This time the $T * R^2$ statistic is even higher (205.24) suggesting a massive rejection of the null hypothesis. Observe also that the lagged squared residuals are all highly statistically significant. It is therefore clear for this equation specification that an ARCH model will provide better results.

In order to estimate an ARCH model we can click on **Estimate** in our equation results window (or in a new workfile by clicking on **Quick/Estimate Equation**, to open the **Equation Specification** window) to go back to the **Equation Specification** window, and this time change the estimation method by clicking on the down

Table 14.3 Testing for ARCH(6) effects in the FTSE-100

ARCH Test:

F-statistic	37.03529	Probability	0.000000
Obs*R-squared	205.2486	Probability	0.000000

Test Equation:
Dependent Variable: RESID^2
Method: Least Squares
Date: 12/26/03 Time: 15:31
Sample(adjusted): 1/09/1990 12/31/1999
Included observations: 2604 after adjusting endpoints

Variable	Coefficient	Std. Error	t-Statistic	Prob.
C	4.30E−05	4.46E−06	9.633006	0.0000
RESID^2(−1)	0.066499	0.019551	3.401305	0.0007
RESID^2(−2)	0.125443	0.019538	6.420328	0.0000
RESID^2(−3)	0.097259	0.019657	4.947847	0.0000
RESID^2(−4)	0.060954	0.019658	3.100789	0.0020
RESID^2(−5)	0.074990	0.019539	3.837926	0.0001
RESID^2(−6)	0.085838	0.019551	4.390579	0.0000

R-squared	0.078821	Mean dependent var	8.79E−05
Adjusted R-squared	0.076692	S.D. dependent var	0.000173
S.E. of regression	0.000166	Akaike info criterion	−14.56581
Sum squared resid	7.16E−05	Schwarz criterion	−14.55004
Log likelihood	18971.68	F-statistic	37.03529
Durbin–Watson stat	2.012275	Prob(F-statistic)	0.000000

arrow in the method setting and choosing the **ARCH-Autoregressive Conditional Heteroskedasticity** option. In this new window, the upper part is devoted to the mean equation specification and the lower part to the ARCH specification, or the variance equation specification. At the moment in this window there will be some things that are not clear to the reader, but they will soon become clear after continuing with the rest of this chapter. In order to estimate a simple ARCH(1) model, assuming that the mean equation as before follows an AR(1) process, in the mean equation specification we type:

```
r_ftse c rftse(-1)
```

also making sure that the **ARCH-M** part selects **None** which is the default EViews case. For the ARCH specification we need to click on **GARCH (symmetric)**, which is again the default EViews case, and in the small boxes type 1 for the **Order ARCH** and 0 for the **GARCH**. Then by clicking <OK> we get the results shown in Table 14.4.

Note that it took 10 iterations to reach convergence in estimating this model. The model can be written as:

$$Y_t = 0.0004 + 0.0751Y_{t-1} + u_t \tag{14.13}$$
$$(2.25) \quad (3.91)$$

$$u_t|\Omega_t \sim iid\ N(0, h_t)$$

$$h_t = 0.000007 + 0.1613u_{t-1}^2 \tag{14.14}$$
$$(35.97) \quad (7.97)$$

Table 14.4   An ARCH(1) model for the FTSE-100

Dependent Variable: R_FTSE
Method: ML–ARCH
Date: 12/26/03 Time: 15:34
Sample: 1/01/1990 12/31/1999
Included observations: 2610
Convergence achieved after 10 iterations

	Coefficient	Std. Error	z-Statistic	Prob.
C	0.000401	0.000178	2.257832	0.0240
R_FTSE(−1)	0.075192	0.019208	3.914538	0.0001
		Variance Equation		
C	7.39E−05	2.11E−06	35.07178	0.0000
ARCH(1)	0.161312	0.020232	7.973288	0.0000
R-squared	0.004944	Mean dependent var		0.000391
Adjusted R-squared	0.003799	S.D. dependent var		0.009398
S.E. of regression	0.009380	Akaike info criterion		−6.524781
Sum squared resid	0.229296	Schwarz criterion		−6.515789
Log likelihood	8518.839	F-statistic		4.316204
Durbin–Watson stat	2.001990	Prob(F-statistic)		0.004815

with values of z statistics in parentheses. Note that the estimate of γ_1 is highly significant and positive, which is consistent with the finding from the ARCH test above. The estimates of a and β from the simple OLS model have changed slightly and become more significant.

In order to estimate a higher-order ARCH model, like the ARCH(6) that we examined above, we can again click on **Estimate** and this time change the **Order ARCH** to 6 (by typing 6 in the small box) leaving 0 for the **GARCH**. The results for this model are presented in Table 14.5.

Again we have that all the γs are statistically significant and positive, which is consistent with our findings above. After estimating ARCH models in EViews we can create the conditional standard deviation series by clicking on the estimation results window **View/Conditional SD Graph**. The conditional standard deviation graph for the ARCH(6) model is shown in Figure 14.2.

We can also obtain the variance series from EViews by clicking on **Procs/Make GARCH Variance Series**. EViews automatically gives names like GARCH01, GARCH02 and so on for each of the series. We renamed our obtained variance series as ARCH1 for the ARCH(1) series model and ARCH6 for the ARCH(6) model. A plot of these two series together is presented in Figure 14.3.

From this graph we can see that the ARCH(6) model provides a conditional variance series which is much smoother than that obtained from the ARCH(1) model. We will discuss this more fully later. In order to obtain the conditional standard deviation series which was plotted above, we can take the square root of the conditional variance series with the following command:

```
genr sd_arch1=arch1^(1/2)      [for the series of the ARCH(1) model]
genr sd_arch6=arch6^(1/2)      [for the series of the ARCH(6) model]
```

Table 14.5 An ARCH(6) model for the FTSE-100

Dependent Variable: R_FTSE
Method: ML–ARCH
Date: 12/26/03 Time: 15:34
Sample: 1/01/1990 12/31/1999
Included observations: 2610
Convergence achieved after 12 iterations

	Coefficient	Std. Error	z-Statistic	Prob.
C	0.000399	0.000162	2.455417	0.0141
R_FTSE(−1)	0.069691	0.019756	3.527551	0.0004
Variance Equation				
C	3.52E−05	2.58E−06	13.64890	0.0000
ARCH(1)	0.080571	0.014874	5.416946	0.0000
ARCH(2)	0.131245	0.024882	5.274708	0.0000
ARCH(3)	0.107555	0.022741	4.729525	0.0000
ARCH(4)	0.081088	0.022652	3.579805	0.0003
ARCH(5)	0.089852	0.022991	3.908142	0.0001
ARCH(6)	0.123537	0.023890	5.171034	0.0000
R-squared	0.004968	Mean dependent var		0.000391
Adjusted R-squared	0.001908	S.D. dependent var		0.009398
S.E. of regression	0.009389	Akaike info criterion		−6.610798
Sum squared resid	0.229290	Schwarz criterion		−6.590567
Log likelihood	8636.092	F-statistic		1.623292
Durbin–Watson stat	1.991483	Prob(F-statistic)		0.112922

A plot of the conditional standard deviation series for both models is presented in Figure 14.4.

A more mathematical approach

Consider the simple stationary model of the conditional mean of a series Y_t:

$$Y_t = a + \beta' \mathbf{X_t} + u_t \tag{14.15}$$

It is typical to treat the variance of the error term $Var(u_t) = \sigma^2$ as a constant, but we can allow the variance to change over time. To see this better let's decompose the u_t term, in a systematic component and a random component as:

$$u_t = z_t \sqrt{h_t} \tag{14.16}$$

where z_t follows a standard normal distribution with zero mean and variance one, and h_t is a scaling factor.
In the basic ARCH(1) model we assume that:

$$h_t = \gamma_0 + \gamma_1 u_{t-1}^2 \tag{14.17}$$

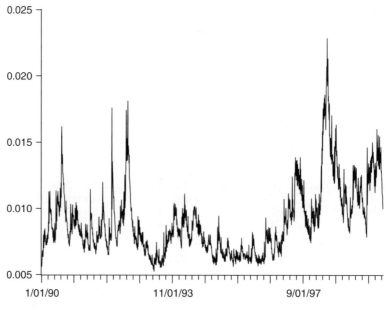

Figure 14.2   Conditional standard deviation graph for an ARCH(6) model of the FTSE-100

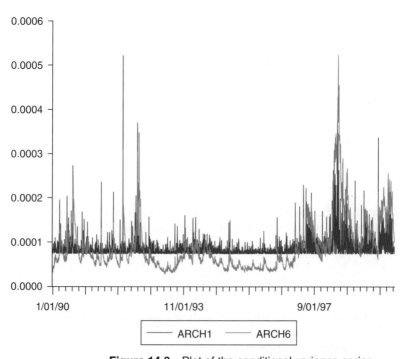

Figure 14.3   Plot of the conditional variance series

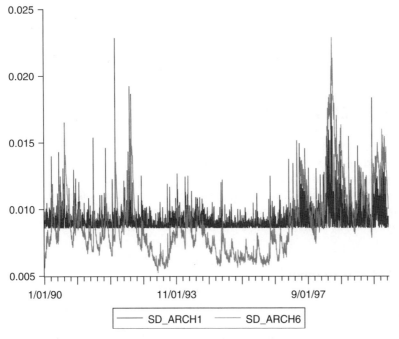

Figure 14.4   Plot of the conditional standard deviation series

The process then for y_t is now given by:

$$y_t = a + \beta'\mathbf{x_t} + z_t\sqrt{\gamma_0 + \gamma_1 u_{t-1}^2} \tag{14.18}$$

And from this expression it is easy to see that the mean of the residuals will be zero $(E(u_t) = 0)$, because $E(z_t) = 0$. Additionally, the unconditional (long-run) variance of the residuals will be given by:

$$Var(u_t) = E\left(z_t^2\right)E(h_t) = \frac{\gamma_0}{1 - \gamma_1} \tag{14.19}$$

which means that we simply need to impose the constraints $\gamma_0 > 0$ and $0 < \gamma_1 < 1$ in order to have stationarity.

The intuition behind the ARCH(1) model is that the conditional (short-run) variance (or volatility) of the series is a function of the immediate past values of the squared error term. Therefore, the effect of each new shock z_t depends on the size of the shock in one lagged period.

An easy way to extend the ARCH(1) process is to add additional, higher-order lagged parameters as determinants of the variance of the residuals to change (14.17) to:

$$h_t = \gamma_0 + \sum_{j=1}^{q} \gamma_j u_{t-j}^2 \tag{14.20}$$

which denotes an ARCH(q) process. ARCH(q) models are useful when the variability of the series is expected to change more slowly than in the ARCH(1) model. However, ARCH(q) models are quite often difficult to estimate, because they often yield negative estimates of the γ_js. To resolve this issue, Bollerslev (1986) came up with the idea of the generalized ARCH (GARCH) model that we will examine in the next section.

The GARCH model

One of the drawbacks of the ARCH specification, according to Engle (1995), was that it looked more like a moving average specification than an autoregression. From this, a new idea was born which was to include the lagged conditional variance terms as autoregressive terms. This idea was worked out by Tim Bollerslev, who in 1986 published a paper entitled 'Generalised Autoregressive Conditional Heteroskedasticity' in *Journal of Econometrics*, starting a new family of GARCH models.

The GARCH(p, q) model

The general GARCH(p, q) model has the following form:

$$Y_t = a + \boldsymbol{\beta}' \mathbf{X_t} + u_t \tag{14.21}$$

$$u_t | \Omega_t \sim iid\ N(0, h_t)$$

$$h_t = \gamma_0 + \sum_{i=1}^{p} \delta_i h_{t-i} + \sum_{j=1}^{q} \gamma_j u_{t-j}^2 \tag{14.22}$$

which says that the value of the variance scaling parameter h_t now depends both on past values of the shocks, which are captured by the lagged squared residual terms, and on past values of itself, which are captured by lagged h_t terms.

It should be clear to the reader by now that for $p = 0$ the model reduces to ARCH(q). The simplest form of the GARCH(p,q) model is the GARCH(1,1) model for which the variance equation has the form:

$$h_t = \gamma_0 + \delta_1 h_{t-1} + \gamma_1 u_{t-1}^2 \tag{14.23}$$

This model specification usually performs very well and is easy to estimate because it has only three unknown parameters γ_0, γ_1 and δ_1.

The GARCH(1,1) as an infinite ARCH(p) process

To show that the GARCH(1,1) is a parsimonious alternative to an infinite ARCH(q) process consider equation (14.23). Successive substitution into the right-hand side of (14.23) gives:

$$h_t = \gamma_0 + \delta h_{t-1} + \gamma_1 u_{t-1}^2$$

$$= \gamma_0 + \delta \left(\gamma_0 + \delta h_{t-2} + \gamma_1 u_{t-2}^2 \right) + \gamma_1 u_{t-1}^2$$

$$= \gamma_0 + \gamma_1 u_{t-1}^2 + \delta\gamma_0 + \delta^2 h_{t-2} + \delta\gamma_1 u_{t-2}^2$$

$$= \gamma_0 + \gamma_1 u_{t-1}^2 + \delta\gamma_0 + \delta^2 \left(\gamma_0 + \delta h_{t-3} + \gamma_1 u_{t-3}^2\right) + \delta\gamma_1 u_{t-2}^2$$

$$\cdots$$

$$= \frac{\gamma_0}{1-\delta} + \gamma_1 \left(u_{t-1}^2 + \delta u_{t-2}^2 + \delta^2 \gamma_1 u_{t-3}^2 + \cdots\right)$$

$$= \frac{\gamma_0}{1-\delta} + \gamma_1 \sum_{j=1}^{\infty} \delta^{j-1} u_{t-j}^2 \tag{14.24}$$

which shows that the GARCH(1,1) specification is equivalent to an infinite order ARCH model with coefficients that decline geometrically. For this reason, it is essential to estimate GARCH(1,1) models as alternatives to high-order ARCH models because with the GARCH(1,1) we have less parameters to estimate and therefore lose fewer degrees of freedom.

Estimating GARCH models in EViews

Consider again the r-ftse series from the ARCH.wf1 file. In order to estimate a GARCH model we click on **Quick/Estimate Equation**, to open the **Equation Specification** window, and again change the estimation method by clicking on the down arrow in the method setting and choosing the **ARCH-Autoregressive Conditional Heteroskedasticity** option. In this new **Equation Specification** window, the upper part is for the mean equation specification while the lower part is for the ARCH/GARCH specification or the variance equation. In order to estimate a simple GARCH(1,1) model, assuming that the mean equation as before follows an AR(1) process, in the mean equation specification we type:

```
r_ftse c rftse(-1)
```

making sure that within the **ARCH-M** part **None** is selected, which is the default in EViews. For the ARCH/GARCH specification we need to click on **GARCH (symmetric)**, which is again the default EViews case, and in the small boxes type 1 for the **Order ARCH** and 1 for the **GARCH**. It is obvious that for higher orders, for example a GARCH(4,2) model, we would have to change the number in the small boxes by typing 2 for the **Order ARCH** and 4 for the **GARCH**. After specifying the number of ARCH and GARCH and clicking <**OK**> we get the required results. Table 14.6 presents the results for a GARCH(1,1) model.

Note that it took only five iterations to reach convergence in estimating this model. The model can be written as:

$$Y_t = 0.0004 + 0.0644 Y_{t-1} + \hat{u}_t \tag{14.25}$$
$$\quad\;\; (2.57) \quad\;\; (3.05)$$

$$u_t | \Omega_t \sim iid\ N(0, h_t)$$

$$h_t = 0.0000002 + 0.893 h_{t-1} + 0.084 \hat{u}_{t-1}^2 \tag{14.26}$$
$$\quad (4.049) \quad\;\; (59.43) \quad\;\; (7.29)$$

Table 14.6   A GARCH(1,1) model for the FTSE-100

Dependent Variable: R_FTSE
Method: ML–ARCH
Date: 12/26/03 Time: 18:52
Sample: 1/01/1990 12/31/1999
Included observations: 2610
Convergence achieved after 5 iterations

	Coefficient	Std. Error	z-Statistic	Prob.
C	0.000409	0.000158	2.578591	0.0099
R_FTSE(−1)	0.064483	0.021097	3.056426	0.0022
Variance Equation				
C	2.07E − 06	5.10E−07	4.049552	0.0001
ARCH(1)	0.084220	0.011546	7.294102	0.0000
GARCH(1)	0.893243	0.015028	59.43780	0.0000

R-squared	0.004924	Mean dependent var	0.000391
Adjusted R-squared	0.003396	S.D. dependent var	0.009398
S.E. of regression	0.009382	Akaike info criterion	−6.645358
Sum squared resid	0.229300	Schwarz criterion	−6.634118
Log likelihood	8677.192	F-statistic	3.222895
Durbin–Watson stat	1.981507	Prob(F-statistic)	0.011956

with values of z statistics in parentheses. Note that the estimate of δ is highly significant and positive as well as the coefficient of the γ_1 term. Taking the variance series for the GARCH(1,1) model (by clicking on **Procs/Make GARCH Variance Series**) we have renamed it GARCH11 and plotted this series together with the ARCH6 series to obtain the results shown in Figure 14.5.

From this we observe that the two series are quite similar (if not identical) which is just because the GARCH term captures a high-order of ARCH terms as we have proved before. Therefore, again we say that it is better to estimate a GARCH instead of a high-order ARCH model due to its easier estimation and the least possible loss of degrees of freedom.

Changing the values in the boxes of the ARCH/GARCH specification to 6 in order to estimate a GARCH(6,6) model we obtain the results shown in Table 14.7, where the insignificance of all the parameters apart from the ARCH(1) term suggest that it is not an appropriate model.

Similarly, estimating a GARCH(1,6) model gives the results in Table 14.8 where now only the ARCH(1) and the GARCH(1) term are significant, while also now some of the ARCH lagged terms have a negative sign. Comparing all the models from both the ARCH and the GARCH alternative specifications, we conclude that the GARCH(1,1) is preferred for the reasons we have discussed.

Alternative specifications

There are many alternative specifications that could be analysed to model conditional volatility, and some of the more important variants are presented briefly in this section. (Berra and Higgins (1993) and Bollerslev, Engle and Nelson (1994) provide very good

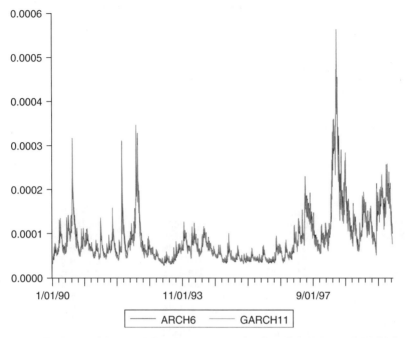

Figure 14.5   Plots of the conditional variance series for ARCH(6) and GARCH(1,1)

reviews of these alternative specifications, while Engle (1995) collects some of the most important papers in the ARCH/GARCH literature.)

The GARCH in mean or GARCH-M model

GARCH-M models allow the conditional mean to depend on its own conditional variance. Consider, for example, investors that are risk-averse and therefore require a premium as a compensation in order to hold a risky asset. That premium is clearly a positive function of the risk (i.e. the higher the risk the higher the premium should be). If the risk is captured by the volatility or by the conditional variance, then the conditional variance may enter the conditional mean function of Y_t.

Therefore, the GARCH-M(p,q) model has the following form:

$$Y_t = a + \beta' X_t + \theta h_t + u_t \tag{14.27}$$

$$u_t | \Omega_t \sim iid\ N(0, h_t)$$

$$h_t = \gamma_0 + \sum_{i=1}^{p} \delta_i h_{t-i} + \sum_{j=1}^{q} \gamma_j u_{t-j}^2 \tag{14.28}$$

Another variant of the GARCH-M type models is to capture risk not by the variance series but using the standard deviation of the series having the following specification

Table 14.7 A GARCH(6,6) model for the FTSE-100

Dependent Variable: R_FTSE
Method: ML–ARCH
Date: 12/26/03 Time: 19:05
Sample: 1/01/1990 12/31/1999
Included observations: 2610
Convergence achieved after 18 iterations

	Coefficient	Std. Error	z-Statistic	Prob.
C	0.000433	0.000160	2.705934	0.0068
R_FTSE(−1)	0.065458	0.020774	3.150930	0.0016
		Variance Equation		
C	1.70E−06	7.51E−06	0.227033	0.8204
ARCH(1)	0.038562	0.015717	2.453542	0.0141
ARCH(2)	0.070150	0.113938	0.615692	0.5381
ARCH(3)	0.022721	0.269736	0.084234	0.9329
ARCH(4)	−0.017544	0.181646	−0.096585	0.9231
ARCH(5)	0.011091	0.077074	0.143905	0.8856
ARCH(6)	−0.017064	0.063733	−0.267740	0.7889
GARCH(1)	0.367407	3.018202	0.121730	0.9031
GARCH(2)	0.116028	1.476857	0.078564	0.9374
GARCH(3)	0.036122	1.373348	0.026302	0.9790
GARCH(4)	0.228528	0.819494	0.278864	0.7803
GARCH(5)	0.217829	0.535338	0.406900	0.6841
GARCH(6)	−0.092748	0.979198	−0.094719	0.9245
R-squared	0.004904	Mean dependent var		0.000391
Adjusted R-squared	−0.000465	S.D. dependent var		0.009398
S.E. of regression	0.009400	Akaike info criterion		−6.643400
Sum squared resid	0.229305	Schwarz criterion		−6.609681
Log likelihood	8684.637	F-statistic		0.913394
Durbin–Watson stat	1.983309	Prob(F-statistic)		0.543473

for the mean and the variance equation:

$$Y_t = a + \beta' X_t + \theta \sqrt{h_t} + u_t \qquad (14.29)$$

$$u_t | \Omega_t \sim iid\ N(0, h_t)$$

$$h_t = \gamma_0 + \sum_{i=1}^{p} \delta_i h_{t-i} + \sum_{j=1}^{q} \gamma_j u_{t-j}^2 \qquad (14.30)$$

GARCH-M models can be linked with asset-pricing models like the Capital Asset Pricing Models (CAPM) with lots of financial applications (for more see Campbell, Lo and MacKinley, 1997; Hall, Miles and Taylor, 1990).

Estimating GARCH-M models in EViews

In order to estimate a GARCH-M model in EViews first click **Quick/Estimate Equation** to open the **Estimation Window**. We then change the estimation method by clicking on the down arrow in the method setting and choosing the **ARCH-Autoregressive**

Table 14.8 A GARCH(1,6) model for the FTSE-100

Dependent Variable: R_FTSE
Method: ML–ARCH
Date: 12/26/03 Time: 19:34
Sample: 1/01/1990 12/31/1999
Included observations: 2610
Convergence achieved after 19 iterations

	Coefficient	Std. Error	z-Statistic	Prob.
C	0.000439	0.000158	2.778912	0.0055
R_FTSE(−1)	0.064396	0.020724	3.107334	0.0019
		Variance Equation		
C	9.12E−07	2.79E−07	3.266092	0.0011
ARCH(1)	0.040539	0.013234	3.063199	0.0022
ARCH(2)	0.048341	0.025188	1.919235	0.0550
ARCH(3)	−0.027991	0.031262	−0.895354	0.3706
ARCH(4)	−0.037356	0.028923	−1.291542	0.1965
ARCH(5)	0.016418	0.028394	0.578219	0.5631
ARCH(6)	0.015381	0.023587	0.652097	0.5143
GARCH(1)	0.934786	0.011269	82.95460	0.0000

R-squared	0.004883	Mean dependent var	0.000391
Adjusted R-squared	0.001438	S.D. dependent var	0.009398
S.E. of regression	0.009391	Akaike info criterion	−6.646699
Sum squared resid	0.229310	Schwarz criterion	−6.624220
Log likelihood	8683.943	F-statistic	1.417557
Durbin–Watson stat	1.981261	Prob(F-statistic)	0.174540

Conditional Heteroskedasticity option. In this new **Equation Specification** window, the upper part is again for the mean equation specification while the lower part is for the ARCH/GARCH specification or the variance equation. In order to estimate a GARCH-M(1,1) model, assuming that the mean equation as before follows an AR(1) process, in the mean equation specification we type:

```
r_ftse c rftse(−1)
```

and this time click on either **Std.Dev** or the **Var** selections from the **ARCH-M** part for versions (14.29) and (14.27) of the mean equation respectively.

For the ARCH/GARCH specification we need to click on **GARCH (symmetric)**, which is again the default EViews case, and in the small boxes we specify by typing the number of the q lags $(1, 2, \ldots, q)$ for the **Order ARCH** and the number of p lags $(1, 2, \ldots, p)$ for the **GARCH**. Table 14.9 below presents the results for a GARCH-M(1,1) model based on the specification that uses the variance series to capture risk in the mean equation as given by (14.27).

Note that the variance term (GARCH) in the mean equation is slightly significant but its inclusion substantially increases the significance of the GARCH term in the variance equation. Reestimating the above model but this time clicking on the Std.Dev from the ARCH-M part, to include the conditional standard deviation in the mean equation, we got the results presented in Table 14.10, where this time the conditional

Table 14.9 A GARCH-M(1,1) model for the FTSE-100

Dependent Variable: R_FTSE
Method: ML – ARCH
Date: 12/26/03 Time: 19:32
Sample: 1/01/1990 12/31/1999
Included observations: 2610
Convergence achieved after 13 iterations

	Coefficient	Std. Error	z-Statistic	Prob.
GARCH	6.943460	4.069814	1.706088	0.0880
C	−2.39E−05	0.000311	−0.076705	0.9389
R_FTSE(−1)	0.061006	0.020626	2.957754	0.0031

Variance Equation				
C	7.16E-07	2.22E−07	3.220052	0.0013
ARCH(1)	0.049419	0.006334	7.801997	0.0000
GARCH(1)	0.942851	0.007444	126.6613	0.0000

R-squared	0.004749	Mean dependent var	0.000391
Adjusted R-squared	0.002838	S.D. dependent var	0.009398
S.E. of regression	0.009385	Akaike info criterion	−6.648319
Sum squared resid	0.229341	Schwarz criterion	−6.634831
Log likelihood	8682.056	F-statistic	2.485254
Durbin–Watson stat	1.974219	Prob(F-statistic)	0.029654

Table 14.10 A GARCH-M(1,1) for the FTSE-100 (using the standard deviation)

Dependent Variable: R_FTSE
Method: ML – ARCH
Date: 12/26/03 Time: 19:36
Sample: 1/01/1990 12/31/1999
Included observations: 2610
Convergence achieved after 13 iterations

	Coefficient	Std. Error	z-Statistic	Prob.
SQR(GARCH)	0.099871	0.080397	1.242226	0.2142
C	−0.000363	0.000656	−0.553837	0.5797
R_FTSE(−1)	0.063682	0.020771	3.065923	0.0022

Variance Equation				
C	9.23E-07	2.72E−07	3.394830	0.0007
ARCH(1)	0.055739	0.007288	7.647675	0.0000
GARCH(1)	0.934191	0.008832	105.7719	0.0000

R-squared	0.005128	Mean dependent var	0.000391
Adjusted R-squared	0.003218	S.D. dependent var	0.009398
S.E. of regression	0.009383	Akaike info criterion	−6.648295
Sum squared resid	0.229253	Schwarz criterion	−6.634807
Log likelihood	8682.025	F-statistic	2.684559
Durbin–Watson stat	1.980133	Prob(F-statistic)	0.019937

standard deviation (or SQR(GARCH)) coefficient is not significant, suggesting that if there is an effect of the risk on the mean return this is captured better by the variance.

The threshold GARCH (TGARCH) model

A major restriction of the ARCH and GARCH specifications above is the fact that they are symmetric. By this we mean that what matters is only the absolute value of the innovation and not its sign (because the residual term is squared). Therefore, in ARCH/GARCH models a big positive shock will have exactly the same effect in the volatility of the series as a big negative shock of the same magnitude. However, for equities it has been observed that negative shocks (or 'bad news') in the market have a larger impact on volatility than positive shocks (or 'good news') of the same magnitude.

The threshold GARCH model was introduced by the works of Zakoian (1990) and Glosten, Jaganathan and Runkle (1993). The main target of this model is to capture asymmetries in terms of negative and positive shocks. To do that it simply adds into the variance equation a multiplicative dummy variable to check whether there is statistically significant difference when shocks are negative.

The specification of the conditional variance equation (for a TGARCH(1,1)) is given by:

$$h_t = \gamma_0 + \gamma u_{t-1}^2 + \vartheta u_{t-1}^2 d_{t-1} + \delta h_{t-1} \qquad (14.31)$$

where d_t takes the value of 1 for $u_t < 0$, and 0 otherwise. So 'good news' and 'bad news' have a different impact. Good news has an impact γ, while bad news has an impact of $\gamma + \theta$. If $\theta > 0$ we conclude that there is asymmetry, while if $\theta = 0$ the news impact is symmetric. TARCH models can be extended to higher order specifications by including more lagged terms as follows:

$$h_t = \gamma_0 + \sum_{i=1}^{q} (\gamma_i + v_i d_{t-i}) u_{t-i}^2 + \sum_{j=1}^{q} \delta_j h_{t-j} \qquad (14.32)$$

Estimating TGARCH models in EViews

In order to estimate a TGARCH model in EViews first click **Quick/Estimate Equation** to open the **Estimation Window**. Then change the estimation method, by clicking on the down arrow in the method setting, to choose the **ARCH-Autoregressive Conditional Heteroskedasticity** option. In this new **Equation Specification** window we again have the upper part for the mean equation specification and the lower part for the ARCH/GARCH specification or the variance equation. To estimate a TGARCH(p,q) model, assuming that the mean equation follows an AR(1) process as before, we type in the mean equation specification:

```
r_ftse c rftse(-1)
```

Table 14.11   A TGARCH(1,1) model for the FTSE-100

Dependent Variable: R_FTSE
Method: ML–ARCH
Date: 12/27/03 Time: 15:04
Sample: 1/01/1990 12/31/1999
Included observations: 2610
Convergence achieved after 11 iterations

	Coefficient	Std. Error	z-Statistic	Prob.
C	0.000317	0.000159	1.999794	0.0455
R_FTSE(–1)	0.059909	0.020585	2.910336	0.0036

Variance Equation				
C	7.06E – 07	1.90E – 07	3.724265	0.0002
ARCH(1)	0.015227	0.006862	2.218989	0.0265
(RESID<0)*ARCH(1)	0.053676	0.009651	5.561657	0.0000
GARCH(1)	0.950500	0.006841	138.9473	0.0000

R-squared	0.004841	Mean dependent var	0.000391
Adjusted R-squared	0.002930	S.D. dependent var	0.009398
S.E. of regression	0.009384	Akaike info criterion	−6.656436
Sum squared resid	0.229320	Schwarz criterion	−6.642949
Log likelihood	8692.649	F-statistic	2.533435
Durbin–Watson stat	1.972741	Prob(F-statistic)	0.026956

ensuring also that we clicked on **None** in the **ARCH-M** part of the mean equation specification.

For the ARCH/GARCH specification we need to click on **TARCH (asymmetric)**, and in the small boxes specify the number of the q lags $(1, 2, \ldots, q)$ for the **Order ARCH** and the number of p lags $(1, 2, \ldots, p)$ for the **GARCH**. Table 14.11 presents the results for a TGARCH(1,1) model.

Note that because the coefficient of the (RESID < 0)*ARCH(1) term is positive and statistically significant, that indeed for the FTSE-100 there are asymmetries in the news. Specifically, bad news has larger effects on the volatility of the series than good news.

The exponential GARCH (EGARCH) model

The exponential GARCH or EGARCH model was first developed by Nelson (1991), and the variance equation for this model is given by:

$$\log(h_t) = \gamma + \sum_{j=1}^{q} \zeta_j \left| \frac{u_{t-j}}{\sqrt{h_{t-j}}} \right| + \sum_{j=1}^{q} \xi_j \frac{u_{t-j}}{\sqrt{h_{t-j}}} + \sum_{i=1}^{p} \delta_i \log(h_{t-i}) \tag{14.33}$$

where γ, the ζs, ξs and δs are parameters to be estimated. Note that the left-hand side is the log of the variance series. This makes the leverage effect exponential instead of quadratic, and therefore the estimates of the conditional variance are guaranteed to be non-negative. The EGARCH model allows for the testing of asymmetries as well as the TARCH. To test for asymmetries the parameters of importance are the ξs. If

$\xi_1 = \xi_2 = \cdots = 0$, then the model is symmetric. When $\xi_j < 0$, then positive shocks (good news) generate less volatility than negative shocks (bad news).

Estimating EGARCH models in EViews

In order to estimate an EGARCH model in EViews first click **Quick/Estimate Equation** to open the **Estimation Window**. Then change the estimation method by clicking the down arrow in the method setting to choose the **ARCH-Autoregressive Conditional Heteroskedasticity** option. In this new **Equation Specification** window we again have the upper part for the mean equation specification, while the lower part is for the ARCH/GARCH specification or the variance equation. In order to estimate an EGARCH(p,q) model, assuming that the mean equation as before follows an AR(1) process, we type in the mean equation specification:

```
r_ftse c rftse(-1)
```

again making sure we clicked on **None** in the **ARCH-M** part of the mean equation specification.

For the ARCH/GARCH specification we now click on **EGARCH**, and in the small boxes specify the number of the q lags $(1, 2, \ldots, q)$ for the **Order ARCH** and the number of p lags $(1, 2, \ldots, p)$ for the **GARCH**. Table 14.12 presents the results for an EGARCH(1,1) model.

Table 14.12   An EGARCH(1,1) model for the FTSE-100

Dependent Variable: R_FTSE
Method: ML–ARCH
Date: 12/26/03 Time: 20:19
Sample: 1/01/1990 12/31/1999
Included observations: 2610
Convergence achieved after 17 iterations

	Coefficient	Std. Error	z-Statistic	Prob.
C	0.000306	0.000156	1.959191	0.0501
R_FTSE(−1)	0.055502	0.020192	2.748659	0.0060
Variance Equation				
C	−0.154833	0.028461	−5.440077	0.0000
|RES|/SQR[GARCH](1)	0.086190	0.012964	6.648602	0.0000
RES/SQR[GARCH](1)	−0.044276	0.007395	−5.987227	0.0000
EGARCH(1)	0.990779	0.002395	413.7002	0.0000
R-squared	0.004711	Mean dependent var		0.000391
Adjusted R-squared	0.002800	S.D. dependent var		0.009398
S.E. of regression	0.009385	Akaike info criterion		−6.660033
Sum squared resid	0.229350	Schwarz criterion		−6.646545
Log likelihood	8697.343	F-statistic		2.465113
Durbin-Watson stat	1.964273	Prob(F-statistic)		0.030857

Note that because the coefficient of the RES/SQR[GARCH](1) term is negative and statistically significant, that indeed for the FTSE-100 bad news has larger effects on the volatility of the series than good news.

Adding explanatory variables in the mean equation

ARCH/GARCH models may be quite sensitive to the specification of the mean equation. Consider, for example, again the FTSE-100 return series we examined above. In all our analyses we assumed (quite restrictively and without prior information) that a good specification for the mean equation would be a simple AR(1) model. It is quite obvious that, using daily data, AR models of a higher order would be more appropriate. Also it might be more appropriate to use MA terms together with the AR terms. Estimating an ARCH(1) and a GARCH(1,1) model for the FTSE-100 returns assuming that it follows an ARMA(1,1) specification, in both cases gives results for the mean equation that are statistically insignificant. (We leave this as an exercise for the reader. To the mean equation specification, type: r_ftse c AR(1) MA(1), and then arrange the number of ARCH(q) and GARCH(p) terms.) It should be clear that results, or even convergence of iterations, might be highly affected by wrong specifications of the mean equation, and if research using GARCH models is to be undertaken, the researcher has to be very careful in first identifying the correct specification.

Adding explanatory variables in the variance equation

GARCH models also allow us to add explanatory variables in the specification of the conditional variance equation. We can have an augmented GARCH(q,p) specification such as the following:

$$h_t = \gamma_0 + \sum_{i=1}^{p} \delta_i h_{t-i} + \sum_{j=1}^{q} \gamma_j u_{t-j}^2 + \sum_{k=1}^{m} \mu_k X_k \qquad (14.34)$$

where x_k is a set of explanatory variables that might help to explain the variance. As an example consider the case of the FTSE-100 returns again, and let's assume that we suspect that the Gulf War (which took place in 1994) affected the FTSE-100 returns making them more volatile. We can test this by constructing a dummy variable, named *Gulf*, that will take the value of 1 for observations during 1994 and 0 for the rest of the period. Then in the estimation of the GARCH model, apart from specifying as always the mean equation and the order of q and p in the variance equation, we can add the dummy variable in the box where EViews allows us to enter variance regressors, by typing the name of the variable there. Estimation of a GARCH(1,1) model with the dummy variable in the variance regression gave the results shown in Table 14.13, where we can see that the dummy variable is statistically insignificant, so that we can reject the hypothesis that the Gulf War affected the volatility of the FTSE-100 returns. Other examples with dummy and regular explanatory variables are given in

Table 14.13 A GARCH(1,1) with an explanatory variable in the variance equation

Dependent Variable: R_FTSE
Method: ML–ARCH
Date: 12/27/03 Time: 17:25
Sample: 1/01/1990 12/31/1999
Included observations: 2610
Convergence achieved after 10 iterations

	Coefficient	Std. Error	z-Statistic	Prob.
C	0.000400	0.000160	2.503562	0.0123
R_FTSE(−1)	0.068514	0.021208	3.230557	0.0012
Variance Equation				
C	2.22E−06	6.02E−07	3.687964	0.0002
ARCH(1)	0.083656	0.013516	6.189428	0.0000
GARCH(1)	0.891518	0.016476	54.11098	0.0000
GULF	−4.94E−07	5.96E−07	−0.829246	0.4070
R-squared	0.004964	Mean dependent var		0.000391
Adjusted R-squared	0.003054	S.D. dependent var		0.009398
S.E. of regression	0.009384	Akaike info criterion		−6.644526
Sum squared resid	0.229291	Schwarz criterion		−6.631039
Log likelihood	8677.107	F-statistic		2.598278
Durbin–Watson stat	1.989232	Prob(F-statistic)		0.023694

the empirical illustration section below for the GARCH model of the UK GDP and the effect of sociopolitical instability.

Empirical illustrations of ARCH/GARCH models

A GARCH model of UK GDP and the effect of socio-political instability

Asteriou and Price (2001) used GARCH models to capture the effects of socio-political instability in UK GDP. In order to approximate and quantify socio-political instability, they constructed indices which summarize various variables capturing phenomena of social unrest, for the case of the UK and for the period 1960–97 using quarterly time series data. Specifically, their indices were constructed by applying the method of principal components to the following variables: *TERROR*, the number of terrorist activities which caused mass violence; *STRIKES*, the number of strikes which were caused by political reasons; *ELECT*, the number of elections; *REGIME*, a dummy variable which takes the value of one for government changes to different political parties, zero otherwise; *FALKL*, a dummy variable which takes the value of 1 for the period of the Falkland's war (1982; q1–q4), zero otherwise; and finally *GULF*, a dummy variable which takes the value of 1 for the period of the gulf war (1991; q1–q4), zero otherwise. Their main results are presented below.

Table 14.14   GARCH estimates of GDP growth with political uncertainty proxies

dependent variable: $\Delta \ln(Y_t)$; sample: 1961q2 1997q4

Parameter	1	2	3	4
constant	0.003 (3.49)	0.005 (3.78)	0.004 (3.80)	0.006 (5.66)
$\Delta \ln(Y_{t-3})$	0.135 (1.36)	0.194 (1.99)	0.186 (1.87)	0.270 (3.42)
$\Delta \ln(Y_{t-4})$	0.131 (1.23)	0.129 (1.22)	0.122 (1.48)	0.131 (1.29)
$\Delta \ln(I_{t-2})$	0.180 (2.25)	0.132 (1.48)	0.162 (1.92)	
Regime		−0.012 (−4.91)		−0.012 (−5.63)
Terror		−0.004 (−2.72)		−0.005 (−2.66)
Strikes		−0.011 (−2.58)		−0.015 (−3.44)
PC1			−0.005 (−4.33)	
PC2			−0.003 (−2.02)	
		Variance Equation		
constant	0.00001 (1.83)	0.00001 (1.66)	0.000006 (1.16)	0.00006 (1.71)
ARCH(1)	0.387 (3.27)	0.314 (2.44)	0.491 (4.18)	0.491 (4.46)
GARCH(1)	0.485 (2.95)	0.543 (3.14)	0.566 (6.21)	0.566 (3.36)
R^2	0.006	0.099	0.030	0.104
S.E. of d.v.	0.010	0.010	0.010	0.010
S.E. of Reg.	0.010	0.010	0.010	0.010

Results from GARCH models

Asteriou and Price (2001) estimated the following model:

$$\Delta \ln(Y_t) = a_0 + a_{1i} \sum_{i=0}^{4} \Delta \ln(Y_{t-i}) + a_{2i} \sum_{i=0}^{4} \Delta \ln(I_{t-i}) + \sum_{j=1}^{6} d_j X_{jt} + u_t \qquad (14.35)$$

$$u_t \sim N(0, h_t) \qquad (14.36)$$

$$h_t = b_1 e_{t-1}^2 + b_2 h_{t-1} \qquad (14.37)$$

That is, the growth rate of GDP (denoted by $\Delta \ln(Y_t)$) is modelled as an $AR(4)$ process, including the growth and four lags of investments (denoted by $\Delta \ln(I_t)$) plus the political instability proxies (X_{jt}), where the variance is conditioned on the lagged variance and lagged squared residuals.

Table 14.14, model 1, presents results of a GARCH(1,1) model for GDP growth or reference without including political dummies. (In each case the model has been first estimated with four lagged terms of GDP per capita and four lagged terms of the rate of growth of investment, and after that reduced down to a parsimonious model, including only the significant regressors.) Despite the low R^2, the variance part of the model is well-fitting.

Continuing, Asteriou and Price reestimated the above model including in equation (14.35) the political dummies. All the dummies entered the equation with the expected negative sign while three of them were statistically significant. The results of the parsimonious model are shown in Table 14.14 model 2, and from these we observe that regime, terror and strikes are highly significant and negative. The variance equation is improved and R^2, while it remains relatively low, is increased compared to the previous specification.

The results from the alternative specification, with the inclusion of the PCs in the place of the political instability variables (Table 14.14 model 3) are similar to the previous model. Negative and significant coefficients were obtained for the first and the third components.

Asteriou and Price (2001) also estimated all the above specifications without including the investment terms. The results for the case of the political uncertainty dummies are presented in the same table, model 4, and show clearly that the strong negative direct impact remains. Thus, the impact of political uncertainty on growth does not appear to operate through investment growth, leaving open the possibility of political uncertainty affecting the *level* of investment.

Results from GARCH-M models

Asteriou and Price (2001) mainly argued that it is political instability which affects uncertainty and thereby growth. So it was of considerable interest for them to allow uncertainty to affect growth directly. In order to do this they used the GARCH-M class of models, first to test whether uncertainty in GDP (conditioned by the 'in mean' term of the GARCH-M model) affects GDP growth, and second whether political instability (conditioned by the political dummies and by the *PCs* in the variance equation) affects GDP growth separately.

The GARCH-M model they estimated may be presented as follows:

$$\Delta \ln(Y_t) = a_0 + \sum_{i=0}^{4} a_{1i} \Delta \ln(Y_{t-i}) + \sum_{i=0}^{4} a_{2i} \Delta \ln(I_{t-i}) + \gamma h_t + u_t \tag{14.38}$$

$$e_t \sim N(0, h_t) \tag{14.39}$$

$$h_t = b_1 u_{t-1}^2 + b_2 h_{t-1} + \sum_{i=1}^{6} b_{3i} X_{it} \tag{14.40}$$

That is, the growth rate of GDP is modelled as an *AR* process, including four lags of the growth rate of investments and the variance of the error term. Equation (14.39) defines h_t as the variance of the error term in (14.38), and (14.40) states that the variance of the error term is in turn a function of the lagged variance and lagged squared residuals as well as the political instability proxies X_{it}. In order to accept the first hypothesis it would be necessary that γ is non-zero, while in order to accept the second hypothesis there should be evidence of positive statistically significant estimates for the coefficients of the political instability proxies (b_{3i}).

Table 14.15 report the results of estimating a GARCH-M(1,1) model without political instability proxies (Table 14.15, model 1). (Again, as in the previous section, the reported results are only from the parsimonious models.) The model is satisfactory given that the parameters (b_1, b_2) are strongly significant. The inclusion of the 'in mean' specification turns out to be redundant as γ is insignificant, suggesting that GDP uncertainty does not itself affect GDP growth. However, this turns out to be misleading and follows from the fact that political factors are ignored.

In estimating a GARCH-M(1,1) model including in the variance equation the political dummies (see Table 14.15, model 2), Asteriou and Price observed that all the political instability variables – with the exception of *REGIME* – entered the equation with the expected positive sign, indicating that political uncertainty increases the variance of GDP growth. All variables were statistically significant. The 'in mean' term is in this

Table 14.15   GARCH-M(1,1) estimates with political uncertainty proxies

Parameter	1	2	3
dependent variable: $\Delta \ln(Y_t)$; *sample: 1961q2 1997q4*			
constant	0.008 (2.67)	0.009 (4.22)	0.007 (4.33)
$\Delta \ln(Y_{t-3})$	0.154 (1.59)	0.175 (1.15)	0.161 (2.10)
$\Delta \ln(Y_{t-4})$	0.128 (1.24)	0.089 (0.81)	0.141 (1.84)
$\Delta \ln(Iv_{t-2})$	0.136 (1.69)	0.132 (1.33)	0.126 (1.84)
SQR(GARCH)	−0.498 (−1.40)	−0.674 (−3.07)	−0.444 (−2.42)
Variance Equation			
constant	0.00001 (1.68)	0.00005 (1.21)	0.000002 (0.80)
ARCH(1)	0.335 (3.07)	0.133 (1.33)	0.460 (4.05)
GARCH(1)	0.554 (3.53)	0.650 (4.00)	0.580 (6.64)
Elect		0.007 (3.11)	
Regime		0.006 (2.84)	
Faukl		0.002 (5.11)	
Strikes		0.066 (2.91)	
PC1			0.000047 (1.45)
PC2			0.000002 (0.09)
PC3			0.000031 (3.20)
R^2	0.054	0.053	0.064
S.E. of d.v.	0.010	0.0106	0.0106
S.E. of Reg.	0.010	0.0108	0.0107

case highly significant and negative. The results from the alternative specification, with the inclusion of the *PCs* in the place of the political instability variables (Table 14.15, model 3) are similar to the previous one, with the exception that positive and significant coefficients were obtained only for the fifth component.

Continuing, Asteriou and Price estimated more general GARCH-M(1,1) models, first including the political dummies and the *PCs* in the growth equation, and second including political dummies and *PCs* in both the growth and the variance equation.

With the first version of the model they wanted to test whether the inclusion of the dummies in the growth equation would affect the significance of the 'in mean' term which captures the uncertainty of GDP. Their results, presented in Table 14.16, showed that GDP growth was significantly affected only by the political uncertainty, captured either by the dummies or by the *PCs*, denoting the importance of political factors other than the GARCH process. (We report here only the results from the model with the political uncertainty dummies. The results with the *PCs* are similar but are not presented here for economy of space. Tables and results are available from the authors upon request.)

The final and most general specification was used to capture both effects stemming from political uncertainty, namely the effect of political uncertainty on GDP growth, and its effect on the variance of GDP together. Asteriou and Price's results are presented in Table 14.17. After the inclusion of the political dummies in the variance equation, the model was improved (the political dummies significantly altered the variance of GDP), but the effect on GDP growth came only from the political uncertainty proxies that were included in the growth equation. The 'in mean' term was negative but insignificant.

Table 14.16 GARCH-M(1,1) estimates with political proxies

dependent variable: $\Delta \ln(Y_t)$; *sample: 1961q2 1997q4*

Parameter	Estimate	Std. error	t-statistic
constant	0.009	0.003	2.964
$\Delta \ln(Y_{t-3})$	0.206	0.093	2.203
$\Delta \ln(Y_{t-4})$	0.123	0.102	1.213
$\Delta \ln(I_{t-4})$	0.109	0.088	1.241
SQR(GARCH)	−0.447	0.365	−1.304
Regime	−0.012	0.002	−5.084
Terror	−0.005	0.001	−3.018
Strikes	−0.012	0.004	−2.753
Variance Equation			
constant	0.00001	0.000008	1.648
ARCH(1)	0.285	0.120	2.380
GARCH(1)	0.575	0.161	3.553
R^2	0.124		
S.E. of d.v.	0.0106		
S.E. of Reg.	0.0103		

Table 14.17 GARCH-M(1,1) estimates with political proxies

dependent variable: $\Delta \ln(Y_t)$; *sample: 1961q2 1997q4*

Parameter	Estimate	Std. error	t-statistic
constant	0.005	0.001	3.611
$\Delta \ln(Y_{t-3})$	0.172	0.095	1.799
$\Delta \ln(Y_{t-4})$	0.123	0.090	1.353
$\Delta \ln(I_{t-4})$	0.181	0.089	2.023
SQR(GARCH)	−0.169	0.254	−0.667
Regime	−0.013	0.006	−1.925
Gulf	−0.007	0.003	−1.899
Strikes	−0.020	0.006	−3.356
Variance Equation			
constant	0.00002	0.00001	2.013
ARCH(1)	0.265	0.126	2.091
GARCH(1)	0.527	0.171	3.076
Elect	0.00004	0.00001	2.608
Regime	0.0001	0.0001	1.131
Falkl	0.00002	0.00002	1.326
R^2	0.141		
S.E. of d.v.	0.0106		
S.E. of Reg.	0.0103		

The final conclusion of Asteriou and Price (2001) was that political instability has two identifiable effects. First, some measures impact on the variance of GDP growth, while others directly affect growth itself. Instability has a direct impact on growth and does not operate indirectly via the conditional variance of growth.

Questions and exercises

Questions

1 Explain what is the meaning of ARCH and GARCH models showing how each of the two is a form of heteroskedasticity.

2 Explain how we can test for the presence of ARCH(q) effects in a simple OLS estimation framework.

3 Explain how we may estimate models with ARCH and GARCH effects.

4 What is meant by the comment that 'GARCH(1,1) is an alternative parsimonious process for an infinite ARCH(q) process'. Prove this mathematically.

5 Explain the meaning of symmetries in news, and provide appropriate specifications for GARCH models that can capture those effects.

6 What should we be very careful of in estimating ARCH/GARCH models?

7 Provide a GARCH-M(q,p) model and explain the intuition behind this model.

8 Explain the effect of the dummy variable in the TARCH model. Why does it enter the variance equation in a multiplicative form and what is the rationale behind this?

Exercise 14.1

The file arch.wf1 contains daily data for the logarithmic returns FTSE-100 (named *r_ftse*) and three more stocks of the UK stockmarket (name *r_stock1*, *r_stock2* and *r_stock3* respectively). For each of the stock series do the following:

(a) Estimate an AR(1) up to AR(15) model and test the individual and joint significance of the estimated coefficients.

(b) Compare AIC and SBC values of the above models and, along with the results for the significance of the coefficients, conclude which will be the most appropriate specification.

(c) Reestimate this specification using OLS and test for the presence of ARCH(p) effects. Choose several alternative values for p.

(d) For the preferred specification of the mean equation, estimate an ARCH(p) model and compare your results with the previous OLS results.

(e) Obtain the conditional variance and conditional standard deviations series and rename them with names that will show from which model they were obtained (e.g. SD_ARCH6 for the conditional standard deviation of an ARCH(6) process).

(f) Estimate a GARCH(q,p) model, obtain the conditional variance and standard deviation series (rename them again appropriately) and plot them against the series you have obtained before. What do you observe?

(g) Estimate a TGARCH(q,p) model. Test the significance of the TARCH coefficient. Is there any evidence of asymmetric effects?

(h) Estimate an EGARCH(q,p) model. How does this affect your results?

(i) Summarize all models in one table and comment on your results.

Exercise 14.2

You are working in a financial institution and your boss proposes to upgrade the financial risk-management methodology that the company uses. In particular, in order to model the FTSE-100 index your boss suggests estimation using an ARCH(1) process. You disagree and wish to convince your boss that a GARCH(1,1) process is better.

(a) Explain, intuitively first, why a GARCH(1,1) process will fit the returns of FTSE-100 better than an ARCH(1) process. (Hint: You will need to refer to the stylized facts of the behaviour of stock indices.)

(b) Prove your point with the use of mathematics. (Hint: You will need to mention ARCH(q) processes here.)

(c) Estimate both models and try to analyse them in such a way that you can convince your boss about the preferability of the model you are proposing. Check the conditional standard deviation and conditional variance series as well. (Hint: Check the number of iterations and talk about computational efficiency.)

15 Vector Autoregressive (VAR) Models and Causality Tests

Vector autoregressive (VAR) models

It is quite common in economics to have models where some variables are not only explanatory variables for a given dependent variable, but they are also explained by the variables that they are used to determine. In those cases we have models of simultaneous equations, in which it is necessary to clearly identify which are the endogenous and which are the exogenous or predetermined variables. The decision regarding such a differentiation among variables was heavily criticized by Sims (1980).

According to Sims (1980), if there is simultaneity among a number of variables, then all these variables should be treated in the same way. In other words there should be no distinction between endogenous and exogenous variables. Therefore, once this distinction is abandoned, all variables are treated as endogenous. This means that in its general reduced form each equation has the same set of regressors which leads to the development of the VAR models.

The VAR model

So, when we are not confident that a variable is really exogenous, we have to treat each variable symmetrically. Take for example the time series y_t that is affected by current and past values of x_t and, simultaneously, the time series x_t to be a series that is affected by current and past values of the y_t series. In this case we will have the simple bivariate model given by:

$$y_t = \beta_{10} - \beta_{12}x_t + \gamma_{11}y_{t-1} + \gamma_{12}x_{t-1} + u_{yt} \tag{15.1}$$

$$x_t = \beta_{20} - \beta_{21}y_t + \gamma_{21}y_{t-1} + \gamma_{22}x_{t-1} + u_{xt} \tag{15.2}$$

where we assume that both y_t and x_t are stationary and u_{yt} and u_{xt} are uncorrelated white-noise error terms. Equations (15.1) and (15.2) constitute a first-order VAR model, because the longest lag length is unity. These equations are not reduced-form equations since y_t has a contemporaneous impact on x_t (given by $-\beta_{21}$), and x_t has a contemporaneous impact on y_t (given by $-\beta_{12}$). Rewriting the system with the use of matrix algebra, we get:

$$\begin{bmatrix} 1 & \beta_{12} \\ \beta_{21} & 1 \end{bmatrix} \begin{bmatrix} y_t \\ x_t \end{bmatrix} = \begin{bmatrix} \beta_{10} \\ \beta_{20} \end{bmatrix} + \begin{bmatrix} \gamma_{11} & \gamma_{12} \\ \gamma_{21} & \gamma_{21} \end{bmatrix} \begin{bmatrix} y_{t-1} \\ x_{t-1} \end{bmatrix} + \begin{bmatrix} u_{yt} \\ u_{xt} \end{bmatrix} \tag{15.3}$$

or

$$\mathbf{B}z_t = \mathbf{\Gamma}_0 + \mathbf{\Gamma}_1 z_{t-1} + u_t \tag{15.4}$$

where

$$\mathbf{B} = \begin{bmatrix} 1 & \beta_{12} \\ \beta_{21} & 1 \end{bmatrix}, \quad z_t = \begin{bmatrix} y_t \\ x_t \end{bmatrix}, \quad \mathbf{\Gamma}_0 = \begin{bmatrix} \beta_{10} \\ \beta_{20} \end{bmatrix},$$

$$\mathbf{\Gamma}_1 = \begin{bmatrix} \gamma_{11} & \gamma_{12} \\ \gamma_{21} & \gamma_{21} \end{bmatrix} \quad \text{and} \quad u_t = \begin{bmatrix} u_{yt} \\ u_{xt} \end{bmatrix}.$$

Multiplying both sides by $\mathbf{B}^{-1}$ we obtain:

$$\mathbf{z}_t = \mathbf{A}_0 + \mathbf{A}_1 \mathbf{z}_{t-1} + \mathbf{e_t} \qquad (15.5)$$

where $\mathbf{A}_0 = \mathbf{B}^{-1}\mathbf{\Gamma}_0$, $\mathbf{A}_1 = \mathbf{B}^{-1}\mathbf{\Gamma}_1$ and $\mathbf{e_t} = \mathbf{B}^{-1}\boldsymbol{u}_t$.

For purposes of notational simplification we can denote as a_{i0} the ith element of the vector $\mathbf{A}_0$, a_{ij} the element in row i and column j of the matrix $\mathbf{A}_1$ and e_{it} as the ith element of the vector $\mathbf{e_t}$. Using this we can rewrite the VAR model as:

$$y_t = a_{10} + a_{11}y_{t-1} + a_{12}x_{t-1} + e_{1t} \qquad (15.6)$$

$$x_t = a_{20} + a_{21}y_{t-1} + a_{22}x_{t-1} + e_{2t} \qquad (15.7)$$

To distinguish between the original VAR model and the system we have just obtained, we call the first a structural or primitive VAR system and the second a VAR in standard (or reduced) form. It is important to note that the new error terms, e_{1t} and e_{2t}, are composites of the two shocks u_{yt} and u_{xt}. Since $\mathbf{e_t} = \mathbf{B}^{-1}\boldsymbol{u}_t$ we can obtain e_{1t} and e_{2t} as:

$$e_{1t} = (u_{yt} + \beta_{12}u_{xt})/(1 - \beta_{12}\beta_{21}) \qquad (15.8)$$

$$e_{2t} = (u_{xt} + \beta_{21}u_{yt})/(1 - \beta_{12}\beta_{21}) \qquad (15.9)$$

Since u_{yt} and u_{xt} are white-noise processes, it follows that both e_{1t} and e_{2t} are white-noise processes as well.

Pros and cons of the VAR models

The VAR model approach has some very good characteristics. First, it is very simple. The econometrician does not have to worry about which variables are endogenous or exogenous. Second, estimation is very simple as well, in the sense that each equation can be estimated with the usual OLS method separately. Third, forecasts obtained from VAR models are in most cases better than those obtained from the far more complex simultaneous equation models (see Mahmoud, 1984; McNees, 1986).

However, on the other hand the VAR models have faced severe criticism on various different points. First, they are a-theoretic since they are not based on any economic theory. Since initially there are no restrictions on any of the parameters under estimation, in effect 'everything causes everything'. However, statistical inference is often used in the estimated models so that some coefficients that appear to be insignificant can be dropped, in order to lead to models that might have an underlying consistent theory. Such inference is normally carried out using what are called causality tests which are presented in the next section.

A second criticism concerns the loss of degrees of freedom. If we suppose that we have a three-variable VAR model and we decide to include 12 lags for each variable in each equation, this will entail estimation of 36 parameters in each equation plus the equation constant. If the sample size is not sufficiently large, estimating that large a number of parameters will consume many degrees of freedom, creating problems in estimation.

Finally, the obtained coefficients of the VAR models are difficult to interpret since they totally lack any theoretical background. In order to overcome this criticism, the advocates of VAR models estimate so-called impulse response functions. The impulse response function examines the response of the dependent variable in the VAR to shocks in the error terms. The difficult issue here however is defining the shocks. The general view is that we would like to shock the structural errors, that is the errors in (15.1) or (15.2) which we can interpret easily as a shock to a particular part of the structural model. However, we only observe the reduced form errors in (15.6) and (15.7) and these are each made up of a combination of the structural errors. So we have to disentangle the structural errors in some way and this is known as the identification problem (this is quie different from the Box-Jenkins identification problem mentioned earlier). There are a variety of ways of doing this although we are not going to explore these in this text. We would stress however that the different methods can give rise to quite different results and there is no objective statistical criteria for choosing between these different methods.

Causality tests

We said before that one of the good features of VAR models is that they allow us to test for the direction of causality. Causality in econometrics is somewhat different to the concept in everyday use; it refers more to the ability of one variable to predict (and therefore cause) the other. Suppose two variables, say y_t and x_t, affect each other with distributed lags. The relationship between those variables can be captured by a VAR model. In this case it is possible to have that (a) y_t causes x_t, (b) x_t causes y_t, (c) there is a bi-directional feedback (causality among the variables), and finally (d) the two variables are independent. The problem is to find an appropriate procedure that allows us to test and statistically detect the cause and effect relationship among the variables.

Granger (1969) developed a relatively simple test that defined causality as follows: a variable y_t is said to Granger-cause x_t, if x_t can be predicted with greater accuracy by using past values of the y_t variable rather than not using such past values, all other terms remaining unchanged.

The next section presents the Granger causality test, and will be followed by an alternative causality test developed by Sims (1972).

The Granger causality test

The Granger causality test for the case of two stationary variables y_t and x_t, involves as a first step the estimation of the following VAR model:

$$y_t = a_1 + \sum_{i=1}^{n} \beta_i x_{t-i} + \sum_{j=1}^{m} \gamma_j y_{t-j} + e_{1t} \tag{15.10}$$

$$x_t = a_2 + \sum_{i=1}^{n} \theta_i x_{t-i} + \sum_{j=1}^{m} \delta_j y_{t-j} + e_{2t} \tag{15.11}$$

where it is assumed that both ε_{yt} and ε_{xt} are uncorrelated white-noise error terms. In this model we can have the following different cases:

Case 1 The lagged x terms in (15.10) may be statistically different from zero as a group, and the lagged y terms in (15.11) not statistically different from zero. In this case we have that x_t causes y_t.

Case 2 The lagged y terms in (15.11) may be statistically different from zero as a group, and the lagged x terms in (15.10) not statistically different from zero. In this case we have that y_t causes x_t.

Case 3 Both sets of x and y terms are statistically different from zero in (15.10) and (15.11), so that we have bi-directional causality.

Case 4 Both sets of x and y terms are not statistically different from zero in (15.10) and (15.11), so that x_t is independent of y_t.

The Granger causality test, then, involves the following procedure. First, estimate the VAR model given by equations (15.10) and (15.11). Then check the significance of the coefficients and apply variable deletion tests first in the lagged x terms for equation (15.10), and then in the lagged y terms in equation (15.11). According to the result of the variable deletion tests we may conclude about the direction of causality based upon the four cases mentioned above.

More analytically, and for the case of one equation (we will examine equation (15.10), it is intuitive to reverse the procedure in order to test for equation (15.11)), we perform the following steps:

Step 1 Regress y_t on lagged y terms as in the following model:

$$y_t = a_1 + \sum_{j=1}^{m} \gamma_j y_{t-j} + e_{1t} \tag{15.12}$$

and obtain the *RSS* of this regression (which is the restricted one) and label it as RSS_R.

Step 2 Regress y_t on lagged y terms plus lagged x terms as in the following model:

$$y_t = a_1 + \sum_{i=1}^{n} \beta_i x_{t-i} + \sum_{j=1}^{m} \gamma_j y_{t-j} + e_{1t} \tag{15.13}$$

and obtain the *RSS* of this regression (which now is the unrestricted one) and label it as RSS_U.

Step 3 Set the null and the alternative hypotheses as below:

$$H_0: \sum_{i=1}^{n} \beta_i = 0 \text{ or } x_t \text{ does not cause } y_t$$

$$H_1: \sum_{i=1}^{n} \beta_i \neq 0 \text{ or } x_t \text{ does cause } y_t$$

Step 4 Calculate the F statistic for the normal Wald test on coefficient restrictions given by:

$$F = \frac{(RSS_R - RSS_U)/m}{RSS_U/(n - k)}$$

which follows the $F_{m,n-k}$ distribution. Here $k = m + n + 1$.

Step 5 If the computed F value exceeds the F-critical value, reject the null hypothesis and conclude that x_t causes y_t.

The Sims causality test

Sims (1980) proposed an alternative test for causality making use of the fact that in any general notion of causality it is not possible for the future to cause the present. Therefore, when we want to check whether a variable y_t causes x_t, Sims suggests estimating the following VAR model:

$$y_t = a_1 + \sum_{i=1}^{n} \beta_i x_{t-i} + \sum_{j=1}^{m} \gamma_j y_{t-j} + \sum_{\rho=1}^{k} \zeta_\rho x_{t+\rho} + e_{1t} \tag{15.14}$$

$$x_t = a_2 + \sum_{i=1}^{n} \theta_i x_{t-i} + \sum_{j=1}^{m} \delta_j y_{t-j} + \sum_{\rho=1}^{k} \xi_\rho y_{t+\rho} + e_{2t} \tag{15.15}$$

The new approach here is that apart from lagged values of x and y, there are also leading values of x included in the first equation (and similarly leading values of y in the second equation).

Examining only the first equation, if y_t causes x_t then we will expect that there is some relationship between y and the leading values of x. Therefore, instead of testing for the lagged values of x_t we test for $\sum_{\rho=1}^{k} \zeta_\rho = 0$. Note that if we reject the restriction then the causality runs from y_t to x_t, and not vice versa, since the future cannot cause the present.

To carry out the test we simply estimate a model with no leading terms (which is the restricted version) and then the model as appears in (15.14) (which is the unrestricted model), and then obtain the F statistic as in the Granger test above.

It is unclear which version of the two tests is preferable, and most researchers use both. The Sims test, however, using more regressors (due to the inclusion of the leading terms), leads to a bigger loss of degrees of freedom.

Computer example: financial development and economic growth, what is the causal relationship?

The aim here is to investigate the effects of financial and stockmarket development on the process of economic growth in the UK. (This section is heavily based on Asteriou and

Price, 2000a.) The importance of the relationship between financial development and economic growth has been well recognized and emphasized in the field of economic development (see e.g., Gurley and Shaw, 1955; Goldsmith, 1969, among others). However, whether the financial system (with emphasis on stockmarkets) is important for economic growth more generally is not clear. One line of research stresses the importance of the financial system in mobilizing savings, allocating capital, exerting corporate control and easing risk management, while, in contrast, a different line of research does not mention at all the role of the financial system in economic growth. We discuss the above points and test these questions empirically using the Granger causality test for the case of the UK.

Following standard practice in empirical studies (e.g. Roubini and Sala-i-Martin, 1992; King and Levine, 1993a,b) our indicator for economic development is real GDP per capita.

The existing literature suggests as a proxy for financial development ratios of a broad measure of money, often M2, to the level of nominal GDP or GNP. This ratio directly measures the extent of monetization, rather than financial deepening. It is possible that this ratio may be increasing because of the monetization process rather than increased financial intermediation. An alternative is to deduct active currency in circulation from M2 or to use the ratio of domestic bank credit to nominal GDP. In our analysis, two alternative proxies of financial development are employed based on two different definitions of money. The first is the currency ratio, the ratio of currency to the narrow definition of money (M0) (the sum of currency and demand deposits). The second is the monetization ratio given by a broader definition of money (M4) over nominal GDP, the inverse of velocity. The first variable is a proxy for the complexity of the financial market; a decrease in the currency ratio will accompany real growth in the economy, especially in its early stages, as there exists more diversification of financial assets and liabilities and more transactions will be carried out in the form of non-currency. The monetization variable is designed to show the real size of the financial sector. We would expect to see the ratio increase (decrease) over time if the financial sector develops faster (slower) than the real sector.

A third measure of financial development is constructed in order to provide more direct information on the extent of financial intermediation. This is the ratio of bank claims on the private sector to nominal GDP (the 'claims ratio'). As it is the supply of credit to the private sector which, according to the McKinnon/Shaw inside model, is ultimately responsible for the quantity and the quality of investment and, in turn, for economic growth, this variable may be expected to exert a causal influence on real GDP per capita (Demetriades and Hussein, 1996).

In order to examine the connection between growth and the stockmarket, we have to construct individual indicators of stockmarket development. One important aspect of stockmarket development is liquidity (see Bencivenga, Smith and Starr, 1996, and Holmstrom and Tirole, 1993), which can be measured in two ways. The first is to compute the ratio of the total value of trades of the capital market over nominal GDP. The second is to compute the 'turnover ratio', defined as the value of trades of the capital market over the market capitalization, where market capitalization equals the total value of all listed shares in the capital market.

Finally, we need data for employment and for the stock of capital in order to construct the capital/labour ratio of an implicit Cobb–Douglas productivity function. The data for the stock of capital are available for the UK only on a yearly basis. Assuming that capital depreciates with a constant annual depreciation rate of δ, we applied the implicit annual rate to an initial value of the stock of capital for the first quarter of 1970 using the quarterly time series for gross fixed capital formation. This enabled us to simulate a quarterly time series for the stock of capital.

The data set used in estimation and testing consists of quarterly observations from the UK and the sample period spans from the first quarter of 1970 to the first quarter of 1997, with the exception of the turnover ratio which covers the period 1983:q1–1997:q1. The data were drawn from the UK's National Income and Expenditure Accounts and from Datastream.

The conventional Granger causality test involves the testing of the null hypothesis 'x_t does not cause y_t', simply by running the following two regressions:

$$y_t = \sum_{i=1}^{m} a_i y_{t-i} + \sum_{j=1}^{n} b_j x_{t-j} + e_t \qquad (15.16)$$

$$y = \sum_{i=1}^{m} a_i y_{t-i} + e_t \qquad (15.17)$$

and testing $b_i = 0$ for every i.

The testing procedure for the identification of causal directions becomes, however, more complex when, as is common in macroeconomic time series, the variables have unit roots. In such a case – after testing for the existence of cointegration – it is useful to reparametrize the model in the equivalent ECM form (see Hendry *et al.*, 1984; Johansen, 1988) as follows:

$$\Delta y_t = \alpha_0 + \alpha_{1i} \sum_{i}^{m} \Delta x_{t-i} + \alpha_{2k} \sum_{k}^{n} \Delta z_{t-k} + \alpha_3 \upsilon_{t-1} + u_t \qquad (15.18)$$

where $\upsilon_{t-1} = y_{t-1} - \alpha_1 x_{t-1} - \alpha_2 z_{t-1}$ is the residual of the cointegration equation. (This might seem difficult at the moment, but it will become clearer to the reader after studying Chapters 16 and 17 that deal with the integration and cointegration of time series.)

The null hypothesis, now, that x does not Granger-cause y, given z, is $H_0(\alpha_1 = \alpha_3 = 0)$. This means that there are two sources of causation for y, either through the lagged terms Δx or through the lagged cointegrating vector. This latter source of causation is not detected by a standard Granger causality test. The null hypothesis can be rejected if either one or more of these sources affects y (i.e. the parameters are different from zero). The hypothesis is again tested using a standard F test. Following Granger and Lin (1995), the conventional Granger causality test is not valid, because two integrated series cannot cause each other in the long run unless they are cointegrated. We therefore test for causality among the variables that are found to be cointegrated, using the VECM representations for the cointegrated variables. Results of those causality tests are presented in Table 15.1.

Causality in the long run exists only when the coefficient of the cointegrating vector is statistically significant and different from zero (Granger and Lin, 1995). In our analysis we apply variable deletion (F-type) tests for the coefficient of the cointegrating vector and for the lagged values of the financial proxies for the GDP per capital VECM

Table 15.1 Testing for long-run Granger causality

Model: $\Delta y_t = \alpha_0 + \alpha_{1i} \sum_i^m \Delta x_{t-i} + \alpha_{2k} \sum_k^n \Delta z_{t-k} + \alpha_3 \upsilon_{t-1} + u_t$
where $y = $ (GDP per capita); $x = $ (turnover, monetization); $z = $ (K/L ratio)

x-variable	F-statistic		Lags	Causality relationship
turnover (ΔT)	$a_3 = 0$	$F(1, 71) = 20.26^*$	1	$cv_{t-1} \rightarrow \Delta Y$
	$a_{2k} = 0$	$F(1, 71) = 3.73^*$	1	$\Delta T \rightarrow \Delta Y$
monetization (ΔM)	$a_3 = 0$	$F(1, 74) = 23.60^*$	6	$cv_{t-1} \rightarrow \Delta Y$
	$a_{2k} = 0$	$F(6, 74) = 7.30^*$	6	$\Delta M \rightarrow \Delta Y$

Model: $\Delta y_t = \alpha_0 + \alpha_{1i} \sum_i^m \Delta x_{t-i} + \alpha_{2k} \sum_k^n \Delta z_{t-k} + \alpha_3 \upsilon_{t-1} + u_t$
where $y = $ (Turnover, Monetization); $x = $ (GDP per capita); $z = $ (K/L ratio)

y-variable	F-statistic		Lags	Causality relationship
turnover (ΔT)	$a_3 = 0$	$F(1, 71) = 5.88^*$	1	$cv_{t-1} \rightarrow \Delta Y$
	$a_{2k} = 0$	$F(1, 71) = 1.07$	1	$\Delta T - / \rightarrow \Delta Y$
monetization (ΔM)	$a_3 = 0$	$F(1, 74) = 12.81^*$	6	$cv_{t-1} \rightarrow \Delta Y$
	$a_{2k} = 0$	$F(6, 74) = 0.836^*$	6	$\Delta M - / \rightarrow \Delta Y$

* Denotes the rejection of the null hypothesis of no causality.

and vice versa (testing for the validity of the supply-leading and demand-following hypotheses respectively). The results reported in Table 15.1, show that there is strong evidence in favour of the supply-leading hypothesis. In both cases (turnover ratio and monetization ratio) the causality direction runs from the financial proxy variable to GDP per capita, while the opposite hypothesis – that GDP per capita causes financial development – is strongly rejected. Also, we observe in all cases that the coefficients of the cointegrating vectors are statistically significant and the F-type tests reject the hypothesis that those coefficients are equal to zero, suggesting that in all cases there is a long bi-directional causality relationship.

16 Non-Stationarity and Unit-Root Tests

As we saw in Chapter 13, there are important differences between stationary and non-stationary time series. In stationary time series, shocks will be temporary and over time their effects will be eliminated as the series revert to their long-run mean values. On the other hand, non-stationary time series will necessarily contain permanent components. Therefore, the mean and/or the variance of a non-stationary time series will depend on time, which leads to cases where a series (a) has no long-run mean to which the series returns, and (b) the variance will depend on time and will approach infinity as time goes to infinity.

We have also discussed ways of identifying non-stationary series. In general, we said that a stationary series will follow a theoretical correlogram that will die out quickly as the lag-length increases, while the theoretical correlogram of a non-stationary time series will not die out (diminish or tend to zero) for increasing lag length. However, this method is bound to be imprecise because a near unit-root process will have the same shape of autocorrelation function (ACF) with that of a real unit-root process. Thus, what might appear as a unit root for one researcher may appear as a stationary process for another.

The point of this discussion is that formal tests for identifying non-stationarity (or, differently stated, the presence of unit roots) are needed. The next section explains what a unit root is and discusses the problems regarding the existence of unit roots in regression models. We then present formal tests for the existence of unit roots followed by a discussion of how we can obtain results for the above tests using EViews and Microfit. Finally, results are presented from applications on various macroeconomic variables.

Unit roots and spurious regressions

What is a unit root?

Consider the AR(1) model:

$$y_t = \phi y_{t-1} + u_t \qquad (16.1)$$

where e_t is a white-noise process and the stationarity condition is $|\phi| < 1$.

In general we can have three possible cases:

Case 1 $|\phi| < 1$ and therefore the series is stationary. A graph of a stationary series for $\phi = 0.67$ is presented in Figure 16.1.

Case 2 $|\phi| > 1$ where in this case the series explodes. A graph of a series for $\phi = 1.26$ is given in Figure 16.2.

Case 3 $\phi = 1$ where in this case the series contains a unit root and is non-stationary. A graph of a series for $\phi = 1$ is given in Figure 16.3.

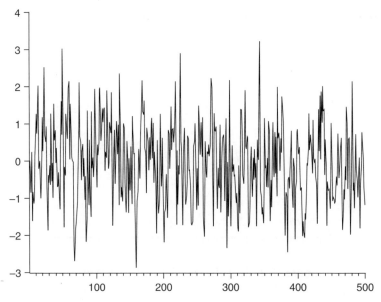

Figure 16.1 Plot of a stationary AR(1) model

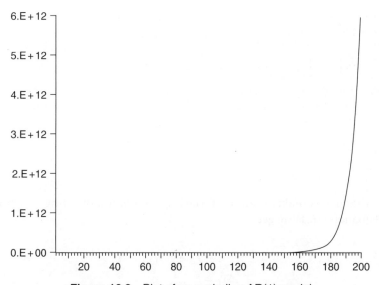

Figure 16.2 Plot of an exploding AR(1) model

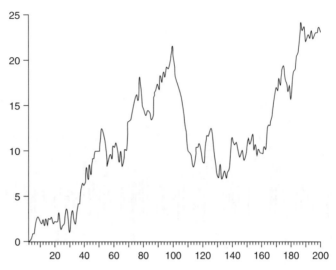

Figure 16.3   Plot of a non-stationary AR(1) model

In order to reproduce the graphs and the series which are stationary, exploding and non-stationary, we type the following commands in EViews (or in a program file and run the program):

```
smpl @first @first+1
genr y=0
genr x=0
genr z=0
smpl @first+1 @last
genr z=0.67*z(-1)+nrnd
genr y=1.16*y(-1)+nrnd
genr x=x(-1)+nrnd
plot y
plot x
plot z
```

So if $\phi = 1$ then y_t contains a unit root. Having $\phi = 1$ and subtracting y_{t-1} from both sides of equation (16.1) we get:

$$y_t - y_{t-1} = y_{t-1} - y_{t-1} + e_t$$

$$\Delta y_t = e_t \tag{16.2}$$

and because e_t is a white-noise process then we have that Δy_t is a stationary series. Therefore, after differencing y_t we obtained stationarity.

Definition 1   A series y_t is integrated of order one (denoted by $y_t \sim I(1)$) and contains a unit root, if y_t is non-stationary but Δy_t is stationary.

In general a non-stationary time series y_t might need to be differenced more than once before it becomes stationary. Then, a series y_t that becomes stationary after d numbers of differences is said to be integrated of order d.

> **Definition 2** A series y_t is integrated of order d (denoted by $y_t \sim I(d)$) if y_t is non-stationary but $\Delta^d y_t$ is stationary; where $\Delta y_t = y_t - y_{t-1}$ and $\Delta^2 y_t = \Delta(\Delta y_t) = \Delta y_t - \Delta y_{t-1}$, etc.

We can summarize the above information under a general rule:

$$\begin{pmatrix} \text{order of} \\ \text{integration} \\ \text{of a series} \end{pmatrix} \equiv \begin{pmatrix} \text{number of times the} \\ \text{series needs to be} \\ \text{differenced in order} \\ \text{to become stationary} \end{pmatrix} \equiv \begin{pmatrix} \text{number} \\ \text{of} \\ \text{unit roots} \end{pmatrix}$$

Spurious regressions

Most macroeconomic time series are trended and therefore in most cases are non-stationary (see for example time plots of the GDP, money supply and CPI for the UK economy). The problem with non-stationary or trended data is that the standard OLS regression procedures can easily lead to incorrect conclusions. It can be shown that in these cases the norm is to get very high values of R^2 (sometimes even higher than 0.95) and very high values of t-ratios (sometimes even higher than 4) while the variables used in the analysis have no interrelationships.

Many economic series typically have an underlying rate of growth, which may or may not be constant, for example GDP, prices or the money supply all tend to grow at a regular annual rate. Such series are not stationary as the mean is continually rising however they are also not integrated as no amount of differencing can make them stationary. This gives rise to one of the main reasons for taking the logarithm of data before subjecting it to formal econometric analysis. If we take the log of a series, which exhibits an average growth rate we will turn it into a series which follows a linear trend and which is integrated. This can be easily seen formally. Suppose we have a series x, which increases by 10% every period, thus;

$$x_t = 1.1 x_{t-1}$$

If we then take the log of this we get

$$\log(x_t) = \log(1.1) + \log(x_{t-1})$$

Now the lagged dependent variable has a unit coefficient and each period it increases by an absolute amount equal to $\log(1.1)$ which is of course constant. This series would now be $I(1)$.

More formally, consider the model:

$$y_t = \beta_1 + \beta_2 x_t + u_t \tag{16.3}$$

where constant u_t is the error term. The assumptions of the CLRM require both y_t and x_t to have a zero and constant variance (i.e. to be stationary). In the presence of non-stationarity then the results obtained from a regression of this kind are totally spurious (using the expression introduced by Granger and Newbold, 1974) and these regressions are called spurious regressions.

The intuition behind this is quite simple, over time we expect any non-stationary series to wander around, as in Figure 16.3, so over any reasonably long sample the series will either drift up or down. If we then consider two completely unrelated series which are both non stationary we would expect that either they will both go up or down together, or one will go up while the other goes down. If we then performed a regression of one series on the other we would then find either a significant positive relationship if they are going in the same direction or a significant negative one if they are going in opposite directions even though really they are both unrelated. This is the essence of a spurious regression.

A spurious regression usually has a very high R^2, t statistics that appear to provide significant estimates, but the results may have no economic meaning whatsoever. This is because the OLS estimates may not be consistent, and therefore the tests of statistical inference are not valid.

Granger and Newbold (1974) constructed a Monte Carlo analysis generating a large number of y_t and x_t series containing unit roots following the formulas:

$$y_t = y_{t-1} + e_{yt} \tag{16.4}$$

$$x_t = x_{t-1} + e_{xt} \tag{16.5}$$

where e_{yt} and e_{xt} aer artificially generated normal random numbers.

Since y_t and x_t are independent of each other, any regression between them should give insignificant results. However, when they regressed the various y_ts to the x_ts as shown in equation (16.3), they surprisingly found that they were unable to reject the null hypothesis of $\beta_2 = 0$ for approximately 75% of their cases. They also found that their regressions had very high R^2s and very low values of DW statistics.

To see the spurious regression problem we can type the following commands in EViews (or in a program file and run the program file several times) to see how many times we can reject the null of $\beta_2 = 0$. The commands are:

```
smpl @first @first+1
genr y=0
genr x=0
smpl @first+1 @last
genr y=y(-1)+nrnd
genr x=x(-1)+nrnd
scat(r) y x
smpl @first @last
ls y c x
```

An example of a scatter plot of y against x obtained in this way is shown in Figure 16.4. The estimated equation was:

$$y_t = -1.042 - 0.576x_t; \quad R^2 = 0.316; \quad DW = 0.118$$

$$(-1.743) \quad (-9.572)$$

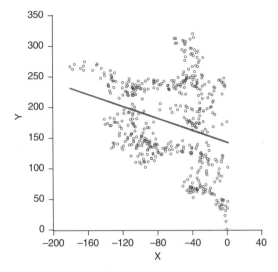

Figure 16.4   Scatter plot of a spurious regression example

Granger and Newbold (1974) proposed the following 'rule of thumb' for detecting spurious regressions: If $R^2 > DW$-statistic or if $R^2 \simeq 1$ then the regression 'must' be spurious.

To understand the problem of spurious regression better, it might be useful to use an example with real economic data. Consider a regression of the logarithm of real GDP (y) to the logarithm of real money supply (m) and a constant. The results obtained from such a regression are the following:

$$y_t = 0.042 + 0.453m_t; \quad R^2 = 0.945; \quad DW = 0.221$$
$$\quad (4.743) \quad (8.572)$$

Here we see very good t-ratios, with coefficients that have the right signs and more or less plausible magnitudes. The coefficient of determination is very high ($R^2 = 0.945$), but there is a high degree of autocorrelation ($DW = 0.221$). This shows evidence of the possible existence of spurious regression. In fact, this regression is totally meaningless because the money supply data are for the UK economy and the GDP figures are for the US economy. Therefore, although there should not be any significant relationship, the regression seems to fit the data very well, and this happens because the variables used in this example are, simply, trended (non-stationary).

So, the final point is that econometricians should be very careful when working with trended variables.

Explanation of the spurious regression problem

In a slightly more formal way the source of the spurious regression problem comes from the fact that if two variables, x and y, are both stationary then in general any linear combination of them will certainly be stationary. One important linear combination of them is of course the equations error, and so if both variables are stationary the error in the equation will also be stationary and have a well-behaved distribution. However when the variables become non-stationary then of course we can not guarantee that the errors will be stationary and in fact as a general rule (although not always) the error itself becomes non-stationary and when this happens we violate the basic assumptions of OLS. If the errors were non-stationary we would expect them to wander around and eventually get large. But OLS because it selects the parameters so as to make the sum of the squared errors as small as possible will select any parameter which gives the smallest error and so almost any parameter value can result.

The simplest way to examine the behaviour of u_t is to rewrite (16.3) as

$$u_t = y_t - \beta_1 - \beta_2 x_t \tag{16.6}$$

or, excluding the constant β_1 (which only affects the u_t sequence by rescaling it):

$$u_t = y_t - \beta_2 x_t \tag{16.7}$$

If y_t and x_t are generated by equations (16.4) and (16.5), then if we impose the initial conditions $y_0 = x_0 = 0$ we get that:

$$u_t = \sum_{i=1}^{t} e_{yi} - \beta_2 \sum_{i=1}^{t} e_{xi} \tag{16.8}$$

Explanation of equation (16.8)

This result comes from the solution by iteration of the difference equations given in (16.4) and (16.5). Consider the solution only for y. Since:

$$y_1 = y_0 + e_{y1}$$

then for y_2 we will have:

$$y_2 = y_1 + e_{y2} = y_0 + e_{y1} + e_{y2}$$

Continuing the process for y_3:

$$y_3 = y_2 + e_{y3} = y_0 + e_{y1} + e_{y2} + e_{y3}$$

and if we repeat the procedure t times we finally have that:

$$y_t = y_0 + \sum_{i=1}^{t} e_{yi}$$

The same holds for x_t.

From equation (16.8) we have that the variance of the error term will tend to become infinitely large as t increases. Moreover, the error term has a permanent component in that $E_t e_{t+1} = e_t$ for all $i > 0$. Hence, the assumptions of the CLRM are violated, and therefore any t test, F test or R^2 values are unreliable.

In terms of equation (16.3) there are four different cases to discuss:

Case 1 Both y_t and x_t are stationary and the CLRM is appropriate with OLS estimates being BLUE.

Case 2 y_t and x_t are integrated of different orders. In this case the regression equations are meaningless. Consider, for example, the case where x_t now follows the stationary process $x_t = \phi x_{t-1} + e_{xt}$ with $|\phi| < 1$. Then equation (16.8) is now $u_t = \sum e_{yi} - \beta_2 \sum \phi^i e_{xt-i}$. Although the expression $\sum_{i=1}^{t} \phi^i e_{xt-i}$ is convergent, the e_t sequence still contains a trend component.

Case 3 y_t and x_t are integrated of the same order and the u_t sequence contains a stochastic trend. In this case we have spurious regressions and it is often recommended to reestimate the regression equation in first differences or to re-specify it.

Case 4 y_t and x_t are integrated of the same order and the u_t sequence is stationary. In this special case, y_t and x_t are said to be cointegrated. We will examine cointegration in detail in the next chapter. For now it is sufficient to know that testing for non-stationarity is extremely important because regressions in the form of (16.3) are meaningless if cases 2 and 3 apply.

Testing for unit roots

Testing for the order of integration

A test for the order of integration is a test for the number of unit roots, and it follows the steps described below:

Step 1 Test y_t to see if it is stationary. If yes then $y_t \sim I(0)$; if no then $y_t \sim I(n)$; $n > 0$.

Step 2 Take first differences of y_t as $\Delta y_t = y_t - y_{t-1}$, and test Δy_t to see if it is stationary. If yes then $y_t \sim I(1)$; if no then $y_t \sim I(n)$; $n > 0$.

Step 3 Take second differences of y_t as $\Delta^2 y_t = \Delta y_t - \Delta y_{t-1}$, and test $\Delta^2 y_t$ to see if it is stationary. If yes then $y_t \sim I(0)$; if no then $y_t \sim I(n)$; $n > 0$. Etc... till we find that it is stationary and then we stop. So, for example if $\Delta^3 y_t \sim I(0)$, then $\Delta^2 y_t \sim I(1)$, and $\Delta y_t \sim I(2)$, and finally $y_t \sim I(3)$; which means that y_t needs to be differenced three times in order to become stationary.

The simple Dickey–Fuller test for unit roots

Dickey and Fuller (1979, 1981) devised a procedure to formally test for non-stationarity. The key insight of their test is that testing for non-stationarity is equivalent to testing for the existence of a unit root. Thus the obvious test is the following which is based on the simple AR(1) model of the form:

$$y_t = \phi y_{t-1} + u_t \tag{16.9}$$

What we need to examine here is whether ϕ is equal to 1 (unity and hence 'unit root'). Obviously, the null hypothesis is $H_0: \phi = 1$, and the alternative hypothesis is $H_1: \phi < 1$.

We can obtain a different (more convenient) version of the test by subtracting y_{t-1} from both sides of (16.9):

$$y_t - y_{t-1} = \phi y_{t-1} - y_{t-1} + u_t$$
$$\Delta y_{t-1} = (\phi - 1)y_{t-1} + u_t$$
$$\Delta y_{t-1} = \gamma y_{t-1} + u_t \tag{16.10}$$

where of course $\gamma = (\phi - 1)$. Then, now the null hypothesis is $H_0: \gamma = 0$ and the alternative hypothesis is $H_a: \gamma < 0$, where if $\gamma = 0$ then y_t follows a pure random-walk model.

Dickey and Fuller (1979) also proposed two alternative regression equations that can be used for testing for the presence of a unit root. The first contains a constant in the random-walk process as in the following equation:

$$\Delta y_{t-1} = \alpha_0 + \gamma y_{t-1} + u_t \tag{16.11}$$

This is an extremely important case, because such processes exhibit a definite trend in the series when $\gamma = 0$ (as we illustrated in Chapter 13), which is often the case for macroeconomic variables.

The second case is to also allow, a non-stochastic time trend in the model, so as to have:

$$\Delta y_{t-1} = \alpha_0 + a_2 t + \gamma y_{t-1} + u_t \tag{16.12}$$

The Dickey–Fuller test for stationarity is then simply the normal 't' test on the coefficient of the lagged dependent variable y_{t-1} from one of the three models (16.10, 16.11 or 16.12). This test does not however have a conventional 't' distribution and so we must use special critical values which were originally calculated by Dickey and Fuller.

MacKinnon (1991) tabulated appropriate critical values for each of the three above models and these are presented in Table 16.1.

In all cases the test concerns whether $\gamma = 0$. The DF-test statistic is the t statistic for the lagged dependent variable. If the DF statistical value is smaller in absolute terms

Table 16.1   Critical values for the DF test

Model	1%	5%	10%
$\Delta y_{t-1} = \gamma y_{t-1} + u_t$	−2.56	−1.94	−1.62
$\Delta y_{t-1} = \alpha_0 + \gamma y_{t-1} + u_t$	−3.43	−2.86	−2.57
$\Delta y_{t-1} = \alpha_0 + a_2 t + \gamma y_{t-1} + u_t$	−3.96	−3.41	−3.13
Standard critical values	−2.33	−1.65	−1.28

Note: Critical values are taken from MacKinnon (1991).

than the critical value then we reject the null hypothesis of a unit root and conclude that y_t is a stationary process.

The augmented Dickey–Fuller (ADF) test for unit roots

As the error term is unlikely to be white noise, Dickey and Fuller extended their test procedure suggesting an augmented version of the test which includes extra lagged terms of the dependent variable in order to eliminate autocorrelation. The lag length on these extra terms is either determined by the Akaike Information Criterion (AIC) or Schwartz Bayesian Criterion (SBC), or more usefully by the lag length necessary to whiten the residuals (i.e. after each case we check whether the residuals of the ADF regression are autocorrelated or not through LM tests and not the DW test).

The three possible forms of the ADF test are given by the following equations:

$$\Delta y_t = \gamma y_{t-1} + \sum_{i=1}^{p} \beta_i \Delta y_{t-i} + u_t \tag{16.13}$$

$$\Delta y_t = \alpha_0 + \gamma y_{t-1} + \sum_{i=1}^{p} \beta_i \Delta y_{t-i} + u_t \tag{16.14}$$

$$\Delta y_t = a_0 + \gamma y_{t-1} + a_2 t + \sum_{i=1}^{p} \beta_i \Delta y_{t-i} + u_t \tag{16.15}$$

The difference between the three regressions again concerns the presence of the deterministic elements a_0 and $a_2 t$. The critical values for the ADF tests are the same as those given in Table 16.1 for the DF test.

Unless the econometrician knows the actual data-generating process, there is a question concerning whether it is most appropriate to estimate (16.13), (16.14) or (16.15). Doldado, Jenkinson and Sosvilla-Rivero (1990) suggest a procedure which starts from the estimation of the most general model given by (16.15) and then answering a set of questions regarding the appropriateness of each model and moving to the next model. This procedure is illustrated in Figure 16.5. It needs to be stressed here that, although useful, this procedure is not designed to be applied in a mechanical fashion. Plotting the data and observing the graph is sometimes very useful because it can clearly indicate the presence or not of deterministic regressors. However, this procedure is the most sensible way to test for unit roots when the form of the data-generating process is unknown.

The Phillips–Perron test

The distribution theory supporting the Dickey–Fuller tests is based on the assumption that the error terms are statistically independent and have a constant variance. So, when using the ADF methodology we have to make sure that the error terms are uncorrelated and that they really have a constant variance. Phillips and Perron (1988) developed a generalization of the ADF test procedure that allows for fairly mild assumptions

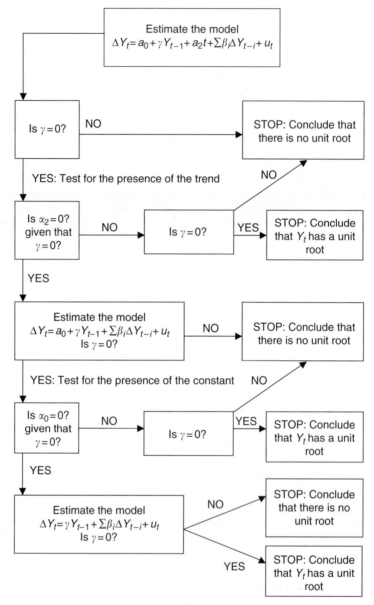

Figure 16.5 Procedure for testing for unit-root tests

Source: Enders (1995).

concerning the distribution of errors. The test regression for the Phillips–Perron (PP) test is the AR(1) process:

$$\Delta y_{t-1} = \alpha_0 + \gamma y_{t-1} + e_t \tag{16.16}$$

While the ADF test corrects for higher order serial correlation by adding lagged differenced terms on the right-hand side, the PP test makes a correction to the t statistic of the coefficient γ from the AR(1) regression to account for the serial correlation in e_t. So, the PP statistics are just modifications of the ADF t statistics that take into account the less restrictive nature of the error process. The expressions are extremely complex to derive and are beyond the scope of this text. However, since many statistical packages (one of them is EViews) have routines available to calculate these statistics, it is good for the researcher to test the order of integration of a series performing the PP test as well. The asymptotic distribution of the PP t statistic is the same as the ADF t statistic and therefore the MacKinnon (1991) critical values are still applicable. As with the ADF test, the PP test can be performed with the inclusion of a constant, a constant and linear trend, or neither in the test regression.

Unit-root tests in EViews and Microfit

Performing unit-root tests in EViews

The DF and ADF test

Step 1 Open the file gdp_uk.wf1 in EViews by clicking **File/Open/Workfile** and then choosing the file name from the appropriate path.

Step 2 Let's assume that we want to examine whether the series named GDP contains a unit root. Double click on the series named 'gdp' to open the series window and choose **View/Unit Root Test**... In the unit-root test dialog box that appears, choose the type of test (i.e. the Augmented Dickey–Fuller test) by clicking on it.

Step 3 We then have specify whether we want to test for a unit root in the level, first difference, or second difference of the series. We can use this option to determine the number of unit roots in the series. As we noted in the theory section, we first start with the level and if we fail to reject the test in levels we continue with testing for the first differences and so on. So here we first click on 'levels' in the dialog box to see what happens in the levels of the series and then continue, if appropriate, with the first and second differences.

Step 4 We also have to specify which model of the three ADF models we wish to use (i.e. whether to include a constant, a constant and linear trend, or neither in the test regression). For the model given by equation (16.13) click on 'none' in the dialog box; for the model given by equation (16.14) click on 'intercept'; and for the model given by equation (16.15) click on 'intercept and trend'. The choice of the model is very important since the distribution of the test statistic under the null hypothesis differs among these three cases.

Step 5 Finally, we have to specify the number of lagged dependent variables to be included in the model in order to correct for the presence of serial correlation.

Step 6 Having specified these options, click <**OK**> to carry out the test. EViews reports the test statistic together with the estimated test regression.

Step 7 We reject the null hypothesis of a unit root against the one-sided alternative if the ADF statistic is less than (lies to the left of) the critical value, and we conclude that the series is stationary.

Step 8 After running a unit-root test, we should examine the estimated test regression reported by EViews, especially if unsure about the lag structure or deterministic trend in the series. We may want to rerun the test equation with a different selection of right-hand variables (add or delete the constant, trend, or lagged differences) or lag order.

The PP test

Step 1 Open the file 'pp.wf1' in EViews by clicking **File/Open/Workfile** and then choosing the file name from the appropriate path.

Step 2 Let's assume that we want to examine whether the series GDP contains a unit root. Double click on the series named '*gdp*' to open the series window and choose **View/Unit Root Test**... In the unit-root test dialog box that appears, choose the type of test (i.e. the Phillips–Perron test) by clicking on it.

Step 3 We then have to specify whether we want to test for a unit root in the level, first difference, or second difference of the series. We can use this option to determine the number of unit roots in the series. As we said in the theory section we first start with the level and if we fail to reject the test in levels we continue with testing for the first differences and so on. So here we first click on 'levels' to see what happens in the levels of the series, and then continue, if appropriate, with the first and second differences.

Step 4 We also have to specify which model of the three we need to use (i.e. whether to include a constant, a constant and linear trend, or neither in the test regression). For the random walk model click on 'none' in the dialog box, for the random walk with drift model click on 'intercept', and for the random walk with drift and with deterministic trend model click on 'intercept and trend'.

Step 5 Finally, for the PP test we specify the lag truncation to compute the Newey–West heteroskedasticity and autocorrelation (HAC) consistent estimate of the spectrum at zero frequency.

Step 6 Having specified these options, click <**OK**> to carry out the test. EViews reports the test statistic together with the estimated test regression.

Step 7 We reject the null hypothesis of a unit root against the one-sided alternative if the ADF statistic is less than (lies to the left of) the critical value.

Performing unit-root tests in Microfit

The DF and ADF test

Step 1 Open the file 'exdaily.fit' in Microfit by clicking **File/Open** and then choosing the file name from the appropriate path.

Step 2 Let's assume that we want to examine whether the series named EUS (which is the US/UK exchange rate) contains a unit root. In the **process** editor type:

$$ADF\ EUS(12)$$

where the number in parenthesis specifies the maximum number of lagged dependent variables that we want our model to include. Click <**GO**>.

Step 3 Microfit presents two alternative panels of results. The first is for a model that includes an intercept but not a trend, which is the model given by equation (16.14). The second panel gives results for a model that includes both an intercept and a trend, which is the same as that given by equation (16.15). Microfit does not give results for the first model that does not include either an intercept or a trend.

Step 4 The reported results include DF and ADF statistics for $0, 1, 2, \ldots, 12$ lags. These are statistical values for 13 different cases depending on the number of lags included in each case. Apart from the DF and ADF test statistics, we also have results for the AIC and SBC. We can use those two criteria to specify the appropriate number of lags to be included by minimizing both AIC and SBC. If they contradict, usually the SBC is preferable.

Step 5 Having specified which model is appropriate to examine according to the lag structure, we then reject the null hypothesis of a unit root against the one-sided alternative if the DF/ADF statistic is less than (lies to the left of) the critical value, which is also reported by Microfit under each panel of results.

Note that although Microfit provides, very conveniently and quickly, results for 13 different cases of different numbers of lagged dependent variables (while in order to do that in EViews we have to repeat the procedure 13 times, each time specifying a different number of lags), Microfit does not give us any details about the regression equation estimated in order to obtain those statistics. It is something like a black box in terms of information regarding the equation, and therefore in some cases where we might suspect a close unit root it might be preferable to obtain the test manually by running each regression model in the **single** editor.

In case we need to do that, we first have to define the new variable Δeus_t by typing in the **process** editor:

$$deus = eus - eus(-1)$$

and then going to the single editor and specifying the regression by typing:

$$deus\ c\ eus(-1)deus\{1-4\}$$

which will give us a t statistic for $eus(-1)$ that will be equivalent to the ADF(4) statistic for the previous test.

There is no standard procedure for performing the PP test in Microfit.

Computer example: unit-root tests on various macroeconomic variables

The data used in this example (see file unionization.wf1) are mainly drawn from *International Historical Statistics* (Mitchell, 1998), where data on trade union membership, employment, unemployment rates, population, wages, prices, industrial production and GDP are available for most of the 1892–1997 period. We have also used some other sources (e.g. various issues of *Employment Gazette*, *Labour Market Trends* and OECD *Main Economic Indicators*) to amend and assure the quality of the data. (Data on capital stock were derived from the gross fixed capital formation series, assuming a rate of depreciation of 10% per year. The capital stock series is a little sensitive in respect of the initial value assumed, and for the period 1950–90 is highly correlated ($r = 0.9978$) with the UK capital stock series constructed by Nehru and Dhareshwar, 1993.) Our aim is to apply tests which will determine the order of integration of the variables. We will apply two asymptotically equivalent tests: the augmented Dickey–Fuller (ADF) test and the Phillips–Perron (PP) test.

We begin the ADF test procedure by examining the optimal lag length using Akaike's Final Prediction Error (FPE) criteria, before proceeding to identify the probable order of stationarity. The results of the tests for all the variables and for the three alternative models are presented in Table 16.2, first for their logarithmic levels (the unemployment and unionization rate variables are not logarithmed as they are expressed in percentages) and then (in cases where we found that the series contain a unit root) for their first differences, and so on. The results indicate that each of the series is non-stationary when the variables are defined in levels. But first-differencing the series removes the non-stationary components in all cases and the null hypothesis

Table 16.2 Augmented Dickey–Fuller test results

Model: $\Delta y_t = c_1 + b y_{t-1} + c_2 t + \sum_{k=1}^{p} d_k \Delta y_{t-k} + v_t; H_0: b = 0; H_a: b > 0$

Unit-root tests at logarithmic levels

Variables	Constant	Constant and trend	None	k
GDP per capita (y/l)	−0.905	−2.799	−0.789	4
Unionization rate (TUD)	−1.967	−1.246	−0.148	4
Unemployment (Un)	−2.435	−2.426	−1.220	4
Wages (w)	−1.600	−1.114	−3.087*	4
Employment (l)	−1.436	−2.050	−1.854	4
Capital/labour (k/l)	−0.474	−2.508	2.161*	4

Unit-root tests at first differences

Variables	Constant	Constant and trend	None	k
GDP per capita (Δ)(y/l)	−6.163*	−6.167*	−6.088*	4
Unionization rate (ΔTUD)	−3.102*	−3.425*	−3.086*	4
Unemployment (ΔUn)	−4.283	−4.223	−4.305*	4
Wages (Δw)	−3.294*	−3.854*	—	4
Employment (Δl)	−4.572*	−4.598*	−4.115*	4
Capital/labour (Δ(k/l))	−3.814*	−3.787*	—	4

Notes: * Denotes significance at the 5% level and the rejection of the null hypothesis of non-stationarity. Critical values obtained from Fuller (1976) are −2.88, −3.45 and −1.94 for the first, second and third model respectively. The optimal lag lengths k were chosen according to Akaike's FPE test.

Table 16.3 Phillips–Perron test results

Model: $\Delta y_t = \mu + \rho y_{t-1} + \varepsilon_t$; H_0: $\rho = 0$; H_a: $\rho > 0$

Unit-root tests at logarithmic levels

Variables	Constant	Constant and trend	k
GDP per capita (y, l)	−2.410	−2.851	4
Unionization rate (TUD)	−1.770	−0.605	4
Unemployment (Un)	−2.537	−2.548	4
Wages (w)	2.310	−0.987	4
Employment (l)	−1.779	−2.257	4
Capital/labour (k/l)	−0.199	−2.451	4

Unit-root tests at first differences

Variables	Constant	Constant and trend	k
GDP per capita ($\Delta(y/l)$)	−11.107*	−11.050*	4
Unionization rate (ΔTUD)	−5.476*	−5.637*	4
Unemployment (ΔUn)	−8.863*	−8.824*	4
Wages (Δw)	−4.621*	−5.071*	4
Employment (Δl)	−7.958*	−7.996*	4
Capital/labour ($\Delta(k/l)$)	−10.887*	−10.849*	4

Notes: * Denotes significance at the 5% level and the rejection of the null hypothesis of non-stationarity. Critical values obtained from Fuller (1976) are −2.88, −3.45 and −1.94 for the first, second and third model respectively. The optimal lag lengths k were chosen according to Akaike's FPE test.

of non-stationarity is clearly rejected at the 5% significance level suggesting that all our variables are integrated of order one, as was expected. (There is an exception for the more restricted model and for the wages and capital/labour variables, where the tests indicate that they are I(0). However, the robustness of the two first models allows us to treat the variables as I(1) and proceed with cointegration analysis.)

The results of the Phillips–Perron tests are reported in Table 16.3, and are not fundamentally different from the respective ADF results. (The lag truncations for the Bartlett kernel were chosen according to the Newey and West, 1987, suggestions.) Analytically the results from the tests in the levels of the variables clearly point to the presence of a unit root in all cases. The results after first-differencing the series robustly reject the null hypothesis of the presence of a unit root, suggesting therefore that the series are integrated of order one.

Computer example: unit-root tests for the financial development and economic growth example

Consider again the data we described in the Computer Example of the previous chapter for the Granger causality tests. Here we report results of tests for unit roots and orders of integration of all the variables (see file finance.wf1).

We begin the ADF test procedure by examining the optimal lag length using Akaike's FPE criteria; then we proceed to identify the probable order of stationarity. The results of the tests for all the variables and for the three alternative models are presented in

Table 16.4 Augmented Dickey–Fuller test results

Model: $\Delta y_t = c_1 + by_{t-1} + c_2 t + \sum_{k=1}^{p} d_k \Delta y_{t-k} + v_t$; $H_0: b = 0$; $H_a: b > 0$

Unit-root tests at logarithmic levels

Variables	Constant	Constant and trend	None	k
GDP per capita (Y)	−0.379	−2.435	3.281*	1
Monetization ratio (M)	−0.063	−1.726	1.405	4
Currency ratio (CUR)	−1.992	1.237	1.412	9
Claims ratio (CL)	−2.829	−2.758	1.111	7
Turnover ratio (T)	−1.160	−2.049	−1.84	2
Capital/labour (K)	−0.705	−2.503	−2.539	2

Unit-root tests at first differences

Variables	Constant	Constant and trend	None	k
GDP per capita (ΔY)	−6.493*	−6.462*	—	1
Monetization ratio (ΔM)	−3.025*	−4.100*	−2.671*	4
Currency ratio (ΔCUR)	−3.833*	−4.582*	2.585*	5
Claims ratio (ΔCL)	−6.549*	−6.591*	−6.596*	3
Turnover ratio (ΔT)	−6.196*	−6.148*	−5.452*	2
Capital/labour (ΔK)	−2.908*	−3.940*	—	2

Notes: * Denotes significance at the 5% level and the rejection of the null hypothesis of non-stationarity. Critical values obtained from Fuller (1976) are −2.88, −3.45 and −1.94 for the first, second and third model respectively. The optimal lag lengths k were chosen according to Akaike's FPE test.

Table 16.5 Phillips–Perron test results

Model: $\Delta y_t = \mu + \rho y_{t-1} + \varepsilon_t$; $H_0: \rho = 0$; $H_a: \rho > 0$

Unit-root tests at logarithmic levels

Variables	Constant	Constant and trend	k
GDP per capita (Y)	−0.524	−2.535	4
Monetization ratio (M)	−0.345	−1.180	4
Currency ratio (CUR)	−2.511	−0.690	4
Claims ratio (CL)	−4.808*	−4.968*	4
Turnover ratio (T)	−0.550	−3.265	3
Capital/labour (K)	−1.528	−2.130	4

Unit-root tests at first differences

Variables	Constant	Constant and trend	k
GDP per capita (ΔY)	−8.649*	−8.606*	4
Monetization ratio (ΔM)	−7.316*	−7.377*	4
Currency ratio (ΔCUR)	−11.269*	−11.886*	4
Claims ratio (ΔCL)	—	—	—
Turnover ratio (ΔT)	−11.941*	−11.875*	3
Capital/labour (ΔK)	−4.380*	−4.301*	4

Notes: * Denotes significance at the 5% level and the rejection of the null hypothesis of non-stationarity. Critical values obtained from Fuller (1976) are −2.88, −3.45 and −1.94 for the first, second and third model respectively. The optimal lag lengths k were chosen according to Akaike's FPE test.

Table 16.4, first for their logarithmic levels and then (in cases where we found that the series contain a unit root) for their first differences, and so on. The results indicate that each of the series in non-stationary when the variables are defined in levels. But first-differencing the series removes the non-stationary components in all cases and the null hypothesis of non-stationarity is clearly rejected at the 5% significance level, suggesting that all our variables are integrated of order one, as was expected.

The results of the Phillips–Perron tests are reported in Table 16.5, and are not fundamentally different from the respective ADF results. (The lag truncations for the Bartlett kernel were chosen according to Newey and West's (1987) suggestions.) Analytically, the results from the tests on the levels of the variables clearly point to the presence of a unit root in all cases except the claims ratio, which appears to be integrated of order zero. The results after first-differencing the series robustly reject the null hypothesis of the presence of a unit root, suggesting therefore that the series are integrated of order one.

Questions and exercises

Questions

1 Explain why it is important to test for stationarity.

2 Describe how someone can test for stationarity.

3 Explain the term spurious regression and provide an example from economic time-series data.

Exercise 16.1

The file gdp_uk.wf1 contains data for the UK GDP in quarterly frequency from 1955 until 1998. Check for the possible order of integration of the GDP variable using both the ADF and the PP tests following the steps described in Figure 16.5.

Exercise 16.2

The file Korea.wf1 contains data from various macroeconomic indicators of the Korean economy. Check for the order of integration of all the variables using both the ADF and PP tests. Summarize your results in a table and comment on them.

Exercise 16.3

The file Nelson_Ploser.wf1 contains data from various macroeconomic indicators of the US economy. Check for the order of integration of all the variables using both the ADF and PP tests. Summarize your results in a table and comment on them.

17 Cointegration and Error-Correction Models

Introduction: what is cointegration?

Cointegration: a general approach

The main message from Chapter 16 was that trended time series can potentially create major problems in empirical econometrics due to spurious regressions. We have also said before that most macroeconomic variables are trended and therefore the spurious regression problem is highly likely to be present in most macroeconometric models. One way of resolving this is to difference the series successively until stationarity is achieved and then use the stationary series for regression analysis. However, this solution is not ideal. There are two main problems with using first differences. If the model is correctly specified as a relationship between y and x (for example) and we difference both variables then implicitly we are also differencing the error process in the regression. This would then produce a non-invertible moving average error process and would present serious estimation problems. The second problem is that if we difference the variables the model can no longer give a unique long run solution. By this we mean that if we pick a particular value for x then regardless of the initial value for y the dynamic solution for y will eventually converge on a unique value. So, for example, if $y = 0.5x$ and we set $x = 10$ then $y = 5$. But if we have the model in differences, $y_t - y_{t-1} = 0.5(x_t - x_{t-1})$ then even if we know that $x = 10$ we cannot solve for y without knowing the past value of y and x and so the solution for y is not unique given x. The desire to have models which combine both short-run and long-run properties, and which at the same time maintain stationarity in all of the variables, has led to a reconsideration of the problem of regression using variables that are measured in their levels.

The basic idea behind this chapter follows from our explanation of spurious regression in Chapter 16 and in particular equation (16.8) which showed that if the two variables are non-stationary then we can represent the error as a combination of two cumulated error processes. These cumulated error processes are often called stochastic trends and normally we would expect that they would combine to produce another non-stationary process. However in the special case that X and Y are really related then we would expect them to move together and so the two stochastic trends would be very similar to each other and when we combine them together it should be possible to find a combination of them which eliminates the non-stationarity. In this special case we say that the variables are cointegrated. In theory, this should only happen when there is really a relationship linking the two variables together and so cointegration becomes a very powerful way of detecting the presence of economic structures.

Cointegration then becomes an over-riding requirement for any economic model using non-stationary time series data. If the variables do not cointegrate then we have the problems of spurious regression and econometric work becomes almost meaningless. On the other hand if the stochastic trends do cancel then we have cointegration and, as we shall see later, everything works even more effectively than we previously would have thought.

The key point here is that if there really is a genuine long-run relationship between Y_t and X_t, then although the variables will rise over time (because they are trended), there will be a common trend that links them together. For an equilibrium, or long-run relationship to exist, what we require, then, is a linear combination of Y_t and X_t that is a stationary variable (an $I(0)$ variable). A linear combination of Y_t and X_t can be directly taken from estimating the following regression:

$$Y_t = \beta_1 + \beta_2 X_t + u_t \tag{17.1}$$

and taking the residuals:

$$\hat{u}_t = Y_t - \hat{\beta}_1 - \hat{\beta}_2 X_t \tag{17.2}$$

If $\hat{u}_t \sim I(0)$ then the variables Y_t and X_t are said to be cointegrated.

Cointegration: a more mathematical approach

To put it differently, consider a set of two variables $\{Y, X\}$ that are integrated of order
1 (i.e. $\{Y, X\} \sim I(1)$) and suppose that there is a vector $\{\theta_1, \theta_2\}$ which gives a linear
combination of $\{Y, X\}$ which is stationary, denoted by:

$$\theta_1 Y_t + \theta_2 X_t = u_t \tilde{\ } I(0) \tag{17.3}$$

then the variable set $\{Y, X\}$ is called the cointegration set, and the coefficients vector
$\{\theta_1, \theta_2\}$ is called the cointegration vector. What we are interested in is the long-run
relationship, which for Y_t is:

$$Y_t^* = \beta X_t \tag{17.4}$$

In order to see how this comes from the cointegration method, we can normalize (17.3)
for Y_t to give:

$$Y_t = -\frac{\theta_2}{\theta_1} X_t + e_t \tag{17.5}$$

where now $Y^* = -(\theta_2/\theta_1)X_t$, which can be interpreted as the long-run or equilibrium
value of Y_t (conditional on the values of X_t). We will come back to this point when
discussing the error-correction mechanism later in the chapter.

For bivariate economic $I(1)$ time series processes cointegration often manifests itself
by more or less parallel plots of the series involved. As we have said before, we are
interested in detecting long-run or equilibrium relationships and this is mainly what
the concept of cointegration allows.

The concept of cointegration was first introduced by Granger (1981) and elaborated
further by Engle and Granger (1987), Engle and Yoo (1987), Phillips and Ouliaris
(1990), Stock and Watson (1988), Phillips (1986 and 1987) and Johansen (1988, 1991,
1995a), among others. Working in the context of a bivariate system with at most
one cointegrating vector, Engle and Granger (1987) give the formal definition of
cointegration among two variables as follows:

Definition 1   Time series Y_t and X_t are said to be cointegrated of order d, b where
$d \geq b \geq 0$, written as $Y_t, X_t \sim CI(d, b)$, if (a) both series are integrated
of order d, (b) there exists a linear combination of these variables,

say $\beta_1 Y_t + \beta_2 X_t$ which is integrated of order $d - b$. The vector $\{\beta_1, \beta_2\}$ is called the cointegrating vector.

A straightforward generalization of the above definition can be made for the case of n variables as follows:

> **Definition 2**   If Z_t denotes an $n \times 1$ vector of series $Z_{1t}, Z_{2t}, Z_{3t}, \ldots, Z_{nt}$ and (a) each Z_{it} is $I(d)$; (b) there exists an $n \times 1$ vector β such that $Z_t'\beta \sim I(d - b)$ then $Z_t \tilde{\ } CI(d, b)$.

For empirical econometrics, the most interesting case is where the series transformed with the use of the cointegrating vector become stationary, that is when $d = b$, and the cointegrating coefficients can be identified as parameters in the long-run relationship between the variables. The next sections of this chapter will deal with these cases.

Cointegration and the error-correction mechanism (ECM): a general approach

The problem

We said before that when we have non-stationary variables in a regression model then we may get results that are spurious. So if we have Y_t and X_t that are both $I(1)$, then if we regress:

$$Y_t = \beta_1 + \beta_2 X_t + u_t \tag{17.6}$$

we will not generally get satisfactory estimates of $\hat{\beta}_1$ and $\hat{\beta}_2$.

One way of resolving this is to difference the data in order to ensure stationarity of our variables. Therefore, after that we will have that $\Delta Y_t \sim I(0)$ and $\Delta X_t \sim I(0)$, and the regression model will be:

$$\Delta Y_t = a_1 + a_2 \Delta X_t + \Delta u_t \tag{17.7}$$

In this case the regression model may give us correct estimates of the $\hat{a}_1$ and $\hat{a}_2$ parameters and the spurious equation problem has been resolved. However, what we have from equation (17.7) is only the short-run relationship between the two variables. Remember that in the long-run:

$$Y_t^* = \beta_1 + \beta_2 X_t \tag{17.8}$$

so ΔY_t is bound to give us no information about the long-run behaviour of our model. Knowing that economists are mainly interested in long-run relationships this constitutes a big problem, and in order to resolve this the concept of cointegration and the ECM are very useful.

Cointegration (again)

We said before that Y_t and X_t are both $I(1)$. In the special case that there is a linear combination of Y_t and X_t, that is $I(0)$, then Y_t and X_t are cointegrated. Thus, if this is the case the regression of equation (17.6) is no longer spurious, and it also provides us with the linear combination:

$$\hat{u}_t = Y_t - \hat{\beta}_1 - \hat{\beta}_2 X_t \qquad (17.9)$$

that connects Y_t and X_t in the long run.

The error-correction model (ECM)

If, then, Y_t and X_t are cointegrated, by definition $\hat{u}_t \sim I(0)$. Thus, we can express the relationship between Y_t and X_t with an ECM specification as:

$$\Delta Y_t = a_0 + b_1 \Delta X_t - \pi \hat{u}_{t-1} + Y_t \qquad (17.10)$$

which will now have the advantage of including both long-run and short-run information. In this model, b_1 is the impact multiplier (the short-run effect) that measures the immediate impact that a change in X_t will have on a change in Y_t. On the other hand π is the feedback effect, or the adjustment effect, and shows how much of the disequilibrium is being corrected, i.e. the extent to which any disequilibrium in the previous period effects any adjustment in Y_t. Of course $\hat{u}_{t-1} = Y_{t-1} - \hat{\beta}_1 - \hat{\beta}_2 X_{t-1}$, and therefore from this equation we also have β_2 being the long-run response (note that it is estimated by equation (17.7)).

Equation (17.10) now emphasizes the basic approach of cointegration and error-correction models. The spurious regression problem arises because we are using non-stationary data but in equation (17.10) everything is stationary, the change in X and Y is stationary because they are assumed to be $I(1)$ variables and the residual from the levels regression (17.9) is also stationary by the assumption of cointegration. So equation (17.10) fully conforms to our set of assumptions about the classic linear regression model and OLS should perform well.

Advantages of the ECM

The ECM is important and popular for many reasons:

1 Firstly, it is a convenient model measuring the correction from disequilibrium of the previous period which has a very good economic implication.

2 Secondly, if we have cointegration ECMs are formulated in terms of first differences, which typically eliminate trends from the variables involved, they resolve the problem of spurious regressions.

3 A third very important advantage of ECMs is the ease with which they can fit into the general-to-specific approach to econometric modelling, which is in fact a search for the most parsimonious ECM model that best fits the given data sets.

4 Finally the fourth and most important feature of the ECM comes from the fact that the disequilibrium error term is a stationary variable (by definition of cointegration). Because of this, the ECM has important implications: the fact that the two variables are cointegrated implies that there is some adjustment process which prevents the errors in the long-run relationship becoming larger and larger.

Cointegration and the error-correction mechanism: a more mathematical approach

A simple model for only one lagged term of *X* and *Y*

The concepts of cointegration and the error-correction mechanism (ECM) are very closely related. To understand the ECM it is better to think first of the ECM as a convenient reparametrization of the general linear autoregressive distributed lag (ARDL) model.

Consider the very simple dynamic ARDL model describing the behaviour of Y in terms of X as follows:

$$Y_t = a_0 + a_1 Y_{t-1} + \gamma_0 X_t + \gamma_1 X_{t-1} + u_t \tag{17.11}$$

where the residual $u_t \sim iid(0, \sigma^2)$.

In this model the parameter γ_0 denotes the short-run reaction of Y_t after a change in X_t. The long-run effect is given when the model is in equilibrium where:

$$Y_t^* = \beta_0 + \beta_1 X_t^* \tag{17.12}$$

and for simplicity assume that

$$X_t^* = X_t = X_{t-1} = \cdots = X_{t-p} \tag{17.13}$$

Thus, it is given by:

$$Y_t^* = a_0 + a_1 Y_t^* + \gamma_0 X_t^* + \gamma_1 X_t^* + u_t$$
$$Y_t^*(1 - a_1) = a_0 + (\gamma_0 + \gamma_1)X_t^* + u_t$$
$$Y_t^* = \frac{a_0}{1 - a_1} + \frac{\gamma_0 + \gamma_1}{1 - a_1}X_t^* + u_t$$
$$Y_t^* = \beta_0 + \beta_1 X_t^* + u_t \tag{17.14}$$

So, the long-run elasticity between Y and X is captured by $\beta_1 = (\gamma_0 + \gamma_1)/(1 - a_1)$. Here, we need to make the assumption that $a_1 < 1$ in order that the short-run model (17.11) converges to a long-run solution.

We can then derive the ECM which is a reparametrization of the original (17.11) model:

$$\Delta Y_t = \gamma_0 \Delta X_t - (1-a)[Y_{t-1} - \beta_0 - \beta_1 X_{t-1}] + u_t \qquad (17.15)$$

$$\Delta Y_t = \gamma_0 \Delta X_t - \pi[Y_{t-1} - \beta_0 - \beta_1 X_{t-1}] + u_t \qquad (17.16)$$

Proof that the ECM is a reparametrization of the ARDL

To show that this is the same as the original model substitute the long-run solutions for $\beta_0 = a_0/(1-a_1)$ and $\beta_1 = (\gamma_0 + \gamma_1)/(1-a_1)$ to give:

$$\Delta Y_t = \gamma_0 \Delta X_t - (1-a)\left[Y_{t-1} - \frac{a_0}{1-a_1} - \frac{\gamma_0 + \gamma_1}{1-a_1} X_{t-1}\right] + u_t \quad (17.17)$$

$$\Delta Y_t = \gamma_0 \Delta X_t - (1-a)Y_{t-1} - a_0 + (\gamma_0 + \gamma_1)X_{t-1} + u_t \qquad (17.18)$$

$$Y_t - Y_{t-1} = \gamma_0 X_t - \gamma_0 X_{t-1} - Y_{t-1} + aY_{t-1} - a_0 - \gamma_0 X_{t-1} - \gamma_1 X_{t-1} + u_t \qquad (17.19)$$

and by rearranging and cancelling out terms that are added and subtracted at the same time we get:

$$Y_t = a_0 + a_1 Y_{t-1} + \gamma_0 X_t + \gamma_1 X_{t-1} + u_t \qquad (17.20)$$

which is the same as for the original model.

What is of importance here is that when the two variables Y and X are cointegrated, the ECM incorporates not only short-run but also long-run effects. This is because the long-run equilibrium $Y_{t-1} - \beta_0 - \beta_1 X_{t-1}$ is included in the model together with the short-run dynamics captured by the differenced term. Another important advantage is that all the terms in the ECM model are stationary and standard OLS is therefore valid. This is because if Y and X are $I(1)$, then ΔY and ΔX are $I(0)$, and by definition if Y and X are cointegrated then their linear combination $(Y_{t-1} - \beta_0 - \beta_1 X_{t-1}) \sim I(0)$.

A final very important point is that the coefficient $\pi = (1-a_1)$ provides us with information about the speed of adjustment in cases of disequilibrium. To understand this better, consider the long-run condition. When equilibrium holds, then $(Y_{t-1} - \beta_0 - \beta_1 X_{t-1}) = 0$. However, during periods of disequilibrium this term will no longer be zero and measures the distance the system is away from equilibrium. For example, suppose that due to a series of negative shocks in the economy (captured by the error term u_t) Y_t starts to increase less rapidly than is consistent with (17.14). This causes $(Y_{t-1} - \beta_0 - \beta_1 X_{t-1})$ to be negative because Y_{t-1} has moved below its long-run steady-state growth path. However, since $\pi = (1-a_1)$ is positive (and because of the minus sign in front of π) the overall effect is to boost ΔY_t back towards its long-run path as determined by X_t in equation (17.14). The speed of this adjustment to equilibrium is dependent upon the magnitude of $(1-a_1)$. We will discuss the magnitude of π in the next section.

A more general model for large numbers of lagged terms

Consider the following two-variable Y_t and X_t ARDL:

$$Y_t = \mu + \sum_{i=1}^{n} a_i Y_{t-i} + \sum_{i=0}^{m} \gamma_i X_{t-i} + u_t \qquad (17.21)$$

$$Y_t = \mu + a_1 Y_{t-1} + \cdots + a_n Y_{t-n} + \gamma_0 X_t + \gamma_1 X_{t-1} + \cdots + \gamma_m X_{t-m} + u_t \qquad (17.22)$$

We would like to obtain a long-run solution of the model, which would be defined as the point where Y_t and X_t settle down to constant steady-state levels Y^* and X^*, or more simply when:

$$Y^* = \beta_0 + \beta_1 X^* \qquad (17.23)$$

and again assume X^* is constant

$$X^* = X_t = X_{t-1} = \cdots = X_{t-m}$$

So, putting this condition into (17.21), we get the long-run solution as:

$$Y^* = \frac{\mu}{1 - \sum a_i} + \frac{\sum \gamma_i}{1 - \sum a_i} X^*$$

$$Y^* = \frac{\mu}{1 - a_1 - a_2 - \cdots - a_n} + \frac{(\gamma_1 + \gamma_2 + \cdots + \gamma_m)}{1 - a_1 - a_2 - \cdots - a_n} X^* \qquad (17.24)$$

or

$$Y^* = B_0 + B_1 X^* \qquad (17.25)$$

which means that we can define Y^* conditional on a constant value of X at time t as:

$$Y^* = B_0 + B_1 X_t \qquad (17.26)$$

Now, here there is an obvious link to the discussion of cointegration in the previous section. Defining e_t as the equilibrium error as in equation (17.4) before, we get that:

$$e_t \equiv Y_t - Y^* = Y_t - B_0 + B_1 X_t \qquad (17.27)$$

Therefore, what we need is to be able to estimate the parameters B_0 and B_1. Clearly B_0 and B_1 can be derived by estimating equation (17.21) by OLS and then calculating $A = \mu/(1 - \sum a_i)$ and $B = \sum \gamma_i/(1 - \sum a_i)$. However, the results obtained by this method are not transparent and calculating the standard errors will be very difficult. However, the ECM specification cuts through all these difficulties.

Take the following model which (although it looks quite different) is a reparametrization of (17.21):

$$\Delta Y_t = \mu + \sum_{i=1}^{n-1} a_i \Delta Y_{t-i} + \sum_{i=0}^{m-1} \gamma_i \Delta X_{t-i} + \theta_1 Y_{t-1} + \theta_2 X_{t-1} + u_t \qquad (17.28)$$

Note: For $n = 1$ the second term on the left-hand side of (17.28) disappears. From this equation we can see with a bit of mathematics that:

$$\theta_2 = \sum_{i=1}^{m} \gamma_i \qquad (17.29)$$

which is the numerator of the long-run parameter, B_1; and that:

$$\theta_1 = -\left(1 - \sum_{i=1}^{n} a_i\right) \qquad (17.30)$$

So, the long-run parameter B_0 is given by $B_0 = 1/\theta_1$ and the long-run parameter $B_1 = -\theta_2/\theta_1$. Therefore the level terms of Y_t and X_t in the ECM tell us exclusively about the long-run parameters. Given this, the most informative way to write the ECM is as follows:

$$Y_t = \mu + \sum_{i=1}^{n-1} a_i \Delta Y_{t-i} + \sum_{i=0}^{m-1} \gamma_i \Delta X_{t-i} + \theta_1\left(Y_{t-1} - \frac{1}{\theta_1} - \frac{\theta_2}{\theta_1}X_{t-1}\right) + u_t \qquad (17.31)$$

$$Y_t = \mu + \sum_{i=1}^{n-1} a_i \Delta Y_{t-i} + \sum_{i=0}^{m-1} \gamma_i \Delta X_{t-i} - \pi(Y_{t-1} - \hat{\beta}_0 - \hat{\beta}_1 x_{t-1}) + u_t \qquad (17.32)$$

where $\pi = 0$. Furthermore, knowing that $Y_{t-1} - \hat{\beta}_0 - \hat{\beta}_1 x_{t-1} = e_t$, our equilibrium error, we can rewrite (17.31) as:

$$\Delta Y_t = \mu + \sum_{i=1}^{n-1} a_i \Delta Y_{t-i} + \sum_{i=0}^{m-1} \gamma_i \Delta X_{t-i} - \pi \hat{e}_{t-1} + \varepsilon_t \qquad (17.33)$$

What is of major importance here is the interpretation of π. π is the error-correction coefficient and is also called the adjustment coefficient. In fact π tells us how much of the adjustment to equilibrium takes place each period, or how much of the equilibrium error is corrected. Consider the following cases:

(a) If $\pi = 1$ then 100% of the adjustment takes place within the period, or the adjustment is instantaneous and full.

(b) If $\pi = 0.5$ then 50% of the adjustment takes place each period.

(c) If $\pi = 0$ then there is no adjustment, and to claim that Y_t^* is the long-run part of Y_t does not make sense any more.

What is important is to connect this with the concept of cointegration. Because of cointegration, $\hat{e}_t \sim I(0)$ and therefore $\hat{e}_{t-1} \sim I(0)$ as well. Thus, in equation (17.33), which is the ECM representation, we have a regression that contains only $I(0)$ variables and allows us to use both long-run information and short-run disequilibrium dynamics, which is the most important feature of the ECM.

Testing for cointegration

Cointegration in single equations: the Engle–Granger approach

Granger (1981) introduced a remarkable link between non-stationary processes and the concept of long-run equilibrium; this link is the concept of cointegration defined above. Engle and Granger (1987) further formalized this concept by introducing a very simple test for the existence of cointegrating (i.e. long-run equilibrium) relationships.

In order to understand this approach (which is often called the EG approach) consider the following two series X_t and Y_t, and the following cases:

(a) If $Y_t \sim I(0)$ and $X_t \sim I(1)$, then every linear combination of those two series

$$\theta_1 Y_t + \theta_2 X_t \tag{17.34}$$

will result in a series that will always be $I(1)$ or non-stationary. This will happen because the behaviour of the non-stationary $I(1)$ series will dominate the behaviour of the $I(0)$ one.

(b) If we have that both X_t and Y_t are $I(1)$, then in general any linear combination of the two series, say

$$\theta_1 Y_t + \theta_2 X_t \tag{17.35}$$

will also be $I(1)$. However, although this is the more likely case, there are exceptions to this rule, and we might find in rare cases that there is a unique combination of the series as in (17.35) above that is $I(0)$. If this is the case then we say that X_t and Y_t are cointegrated of order $(1, 1)$.

Now the problem is how can we estimate the parameters of the long-run equilibrium relationship and make sure whether or not we have cointegration. Engle and Granger proposed a straightforward method which involves four steps:

Step 1: test the variables for their order of integration

By definition, cointegration necessitates that the variables be integrated of the same order. Thus the first step is to test each variable to determine its order of integration. The Dickey–Fuller and the augmented Dickey–Fuller tests can be applied in order to infer the number of unit roots (if any) in each of the variables. We can differentiate three cases which will either lead us to the next step or will suggest stopping:

(a) if both variables are stationary ($I(0)$), it is not necessary to proceed since standard time series methods apply to stationary variables (in other words we can apply classical regression analysis);

(b) if the variables are integrated of different order, it is possible to conclude that they are not cointegrated;

(c) if both variables are integrated of the same order then we proceed with step two.

Step 2: estimate the long-run (possible cointegrating) relationship

If the results of step 1 indicate that both X_t and Y_t are integrated of the same order (usually in economics $I(1)$), the next step is to estimate the long-run equilibrium relationship of the form:

$$Y_t = \beta_1 + \beta_2 X_t + e_t \tag{17.36}$$

and obtain the residuals of this equation.

If there is no cointegration, the results obtained will be spurious. However, if the variables are cointegrated, then OLS regression yields 'super-consistent' estimators for the cointegrating parameter $\hat{\beta}_2$.

Step 3: check for (cointegration) the order of integration of the residuals

In order to determine if the variables are actually cointegrated, denote the estimated residual sequence from this equation by $\hat{e}_t$. Thus, $\hat{e}_t$ is the series of the estimated residuals of the long-run relationship. If these deviations from long-run equilibrium are found to be stationary, then X_t and Y_t are cointegrated.

In fact we perform a DF test on the residual series to determine their order of integration. The form of the DF test is the following:

$$\Delta \hat{e}_t = a_1 \hat{e}_{t-1} + \sum_{i=1}^{n} \delta_i \Delta \hat{e}_{t-i} + v_t \tag{17.37}$$

Note that because $\hat{e}_t$ is a residual we do not include a constant nor a time trend. The critical values differ from the standard ADF values, being more negative (typically around -3.5). Critical values are provided in Table 17.1.

Obviously, if we find that $\hat{e}_t \sim I(0)$ then we can reject the null that the variables X_t and Y_t are not cointegrated. Similarly if we have a single equation with more than just one explanatory variable.

Step 4: estimate the error-correction model

If the variables are cointegrated, the residuals from the equilibrium regression can be used to estimate the error-correction model and to analyse the long-run and short-run effects of the variables as well as to see the adjustment coefficient, which is the coefficient of the lagged residual terms of the long-run relationship identified in step 2. At the end we always have to check for the adequacy of the model by performing diagnostic tests.

Table 17.1 Critical values for the null of no cointegration

	1%	5%	10%
No lags	−4.07	−3.37	−3.3
Lags	−3.73	−3.17	−2.91

Important note. It is of major importance to note that the critical values for the cointegration test (the ADF test on the residuals) are not the same as the standard critical values of the ADF test used for testing stationarity. In fact in order to have more robust conclusions regarding the evidence of cointegration, the critical values are more negative than the standard ADF ones. Engle and Granger (1987), in their seminal paper, performed their own Monte Carlo simulations in order to construct critical values for the cointegration tests, and these values are shown in Table 17.1. There are two sets of critical values; the first is for no lagged dependent variable terms in the augmentation term (i.e. for the simple DF test), and the second is for including lagged dependent variables (i.e. for the ADF test). A more comprehensive set of critical values may be found in Mackinnon (1991), which is now the primary source.

Drawbacks of the EG approach

One of the best features of the EG approach is that it is both very easy to understand and to implement. However, there are important shortcomings of the Engle–Granger methodology:

1 One very important issue has to do with the order of the variables. When estimating the long-run relationship, one has to place one variable in the left-hand side and use the others as regressors. The test does not say anything about which of the variables can be used as regressor and why. Consider, for example, the case of just two variables, X_t and Y_t. One can either regress Y_t on X_t (i.e. $Y_t = a + \beta X_t + u_{1t}$) or choose to reverse the order and regress X_t on Y_t (i.e. $X_t = a + \beta Y_t + u_{2t}$). It can be shown, with asymptotic theory, that as the sample goes to infinity the test for cointegration on the residuals of those two regressions is equivalent (i.e. there is no difference in testing for unit roots in u_{1t} and u_{2t}). However, in practice, in economics we rarely have very big samples and it is therefore possible to find that one regression exhibits cointegration while the other doesn't. This is obviously a very undesirable feature of the EG approach. The problem obviously becomes far more complicated when we have more than two variables to test.

2 A second problem is that when there are more than two variables there may be more than one cointegrating relationship, and the Engle–Granger procedure using residuals from a single relationship cannot treat this possibility. So, the most important problem is that it does not give us the number of cointegrating vectors.

3 A third and final problem is that it relies on a two-step estimator. The first step is to generate the residual series and the second step is to estimate a regression for this series in order to see if the series is stationary or not. Hence, any error introduced in the first step is carried into the second step.

All these problems are resolved with the use of the Johansen approach that we will examine later.

The EG approach in EViews and Microfit

The EG approach in EViews

The EG test is very easy to perform and does not require any more knowledge regarding the use of EViews. For the first step, ADF and PP tests on all variables are needed to determine the order of integration of the variables. If the variables (let's say X and Y) are found to be integrated of the same order, then the second step involves estimating the long-run relationship with simple OLS. So the command here is simply:

```
ls X c Y
```

or

```
ls Y c X
```

depending on the relationship of the variables (see the drawbacks of the EG approach). We then need to obtain the residuals of this relationship which are given by:

```
genr res_000=resid
```

where instead of 000 a different alphanumeric name can be entered to identify the residuals under question. The third step (the actual test for cointegration) is a unit-root test on the residuals, the command for which is:

```
adf res_000
```

for no lags, or

```
adf(4) res_000
```

for 4 lags in the augmentation term, and so on. A crucial point here is that the critical values for this test are not those reported in EViews, but the ones given in Table 17.1 in this text.

The EG approach in Microfit

In Microfit, after testing for the order of integration of the variables, for the second step we go to the **single** editor (by pressing the **single** button) and specify the equation we need to estimate and click **Start** to get the estimation results in the **results** window. Closing these results we go to the **Post Regression Menu** window and from this, after choosing **2. Move to Hypothesis Testing**, we choose choice **3. Unit Root Test on the Residuals**. Microfit asks us to determine the number of lags and then presents the ADF test results for this unit-root test. Again we have to remember to compare the test statistics with the appropriate critical values of Table 17.1.

Cointegration in multiple equations and the Johansen approach

It was mentioned before that if we have more than two variables in the model, then there is a possibility of having more than one cointegrating vector. By this we mean that the variables in the model might form several equilibrium relationships governing the joint evolution of all the variables. In general, for n number of variables we can have only up to $n - 1$ cointegrating vectors. Therefore, when $n = 2$, which is the simplest case, we can understand that if cointegration exists then the cointegrating vector is unique.

Having $n > 2$ and assuming that only one cointegrating relationship exists, where there are actually more than one, is a very serious problem that cannot be resolved by the EG single-equation approach. Therefore, an alternative to the EG approach is needed and this is the Johansen approach for multiple equations.

In order to present this approach, it is useful to extend the single-equation error-correction model to a multivariate one. Let's assume that we have three variables, Y_t, X_t and W_t which can all be endogenous, i.e. we have that (using matrix notation for $Z_t = [Y_t, X_t, W_t]$)

$$Z_t = A_1 Z_{t-1} + A_2 Z_{t-2} + \cdots + A_k Z_{t-k} + \mathbf{u}_t \tag{17.38}$$

which is comparable to the single-equation dynamic model for two variables Y_t and X_t given in (17.21). Thus, it can be reformulated in a vector error-correction model (VECM) as follows:

$$\Delta Z_t = \Gamma_1 \Delta Z_{t-1} + \Gamma_2 \Delta Z_{t-2} + \cdots + \Gamma_{k-1} \Delta Z_{t-k-1} + \Pi Z_{t-1} + \mathbf{u}_t \tag{17.39}$$

where $\Gamma_i = (I - A_1 - A_2 - \cdots - A_k)$ ($i = 1, 2, \ldots, k-1$) and $\Pi = -(I - A_1 - A_2 - \cdots - A_k)$. Here we need to carefully examine the 3×3 Π matrix. (The Π matrix is 3×3 due to the fact that we assume three variables in $Z_t = [Y_t, X_t, W_t]$.) The Π matrix contains information regarding the long-run relationships. We can decompose $\Pi = \alpha\beta'$ where α will include the speed of adjustment to equilibrium coefficients while β' will be the long-run matrix of coefficients.

Therefore the $\beta' Z_{t-1}$ term is equivalent to the error-correction term ($Y_{t-1} - \beta_0 - \beta_1 X_{t-1}$) in the single-equation case, except that now $\beta' Z_{t-1}$ contains up to $(n - 1)$ vectors in a multivariate framework.

For simplicity we assume that $k = 2$, so that we have only two lagged terms, and the model is then the following:

$$\begin{pmatrix} \Delta Y_t \\ \Delta X_t \\ \Delta W_t \end{pmatrix} = \Gamma_1 \begin{pmatrix} \Delta Y_{t-1} \\ \Delta X_{t-1} \\ \Delta W_{t-1} \end{pmatrix} + \Pi \begin{pmatrix} Y_{t-1} \\ X_{t-1} \\ W_{t-1} \end{pmatrix} + \mathbf{e}_t \tag{17.40}$$

or

$$\begin{pmatrix} \Delta Y_t \\ \Delta X_t \\ \Delta W_t \end{pmatrix} = \Gamma_1 \begin{pmatrix} \Delta Y_{t-1} \\ \Delta X_{t-1} \\ \Delta W_{t-1} \end{pmatrix} + \begin{pmatrix} a_{11} & a_{12} \\ a_{21} & a_{22} \\ a_{31} & a_{23} \end{pmatrix} \begin{pmatrix} \beta_{11} & \beta_{21} & \beta_{31} \\ \beta_{12} & \beta_{22} & \beta_{32} \end{pmatrix} \begin{pmatrix} Y_{t-1} \\ X_{t-1} \\ W_{t-1} \end{pmatrix} + \mathbf{e}_t \tag{17.41}$$

Let us now analyse only the error-correction part of the first equation (i.e. for ΔY_t on the left-hand side) which gives:

$$\Pi_1 Z_{t-1} = ([a_{11}\beta_{11} + a_{12}\beta_{12}] \quad [a_{11}\beta_{21} + a_{12}\beta_{22}]$$

$$[a_{11}\beta_{31} + a_{12}\beta_{32}]) \begin{pmatrix} Y_{t-1} \\ X_{t-1} \\ W_{t-1} \end{pmatrix} \qquad (17.42)$$

where Π_1 is the first row of the Π matrix.

Equation (17.42) can be rewritten as:

$$\Pi_1 Z_{t-1} = a_{11}(\beta_{11}Y_{t-1} + \beta_{21}X_{t-1} + \beta_{31}W_{t-1})$$

$$+ a_{12}(\beta_{12}Y_{t-1} + \beta_{22}X_{t-1} + \beta_{32}W_{t-1}) \qquad (17.43)$$

which shows clearly the two cointegrating vectors with their respective speed of adjustment terms a_{11} and a_{12}.

Advantages of the multiple equation approach

So, from the multiple equation approach we can obtain estimates for both cointegrating vectors (17.43), while with the simple equation we have only a linear combination of the two long-run relationships.

Also, even if there is only one cointegrating relationship (for example the first only) rather than two, with the multiple equation approach we can calculate all three differing speeds of adjustment coefficients $(a_{11} \quad a_{21} \quad a_{31})'$.

Only when $a_{21} = a_{31} = 0$, and only one cointegrating relationship exists, can we then say that the multiple equation method is the same (reduces to) as the single-equation approach, and therefore there is no loss from not modelling the determinants of ΔX_t and ΔW_t. Here, it is good to mention as well that when $a_{21} = a_{31} = 0$, is equivalent to X_t and W_t being weakly exogenous.

So, summarizing, only when all right-hand variables in a single equation are weakly exogenous does the single-equation approach provide the same result as a multivariate equation approach.

The Johansen approach (again)

Let us now go back and examine the behaviour of the Π matrix under different circumstances. Given that Z_t is a vector of non-stationary $I(1)$ variables, then ΔZ_{t-1} are $I(0)$ and ΠZ_{t-1} must also be $I(0)$ in order to have that $u_t \sim I(0)$ and therefore to have a well-behaved system.

In general there are three cases for ΠZ_{t-1} to be $I(0)$:

Case 1 When all the variables in Z_t are stationary. Of course this case is totally uninteresting since it implies that there is no problem of spurious regression and the simple VAR in levels model can be used to model this case.

Case 2 When there is no cointegration whatsoever and therefore the Π matrix is an $n \times n$ matrix of zeros because of no linear relationships among the Z_t. In this case the appropriate strategy is to use a VAR model in first differences with no long-run elements due to the non-existence of long-run relationships.

Case 3 When there exists up to $(n-1)$ cointegrating relationships of the form $\beta'Z_{t-1} \sim I(0)$. In this particular case, $r \leq (n-1)$ cointegrating vectors exist in β. This simply means that r columns of β form r linearly independent combinations of the variables in Z_t, each of which is stationary. Of course there will also be $(n-r)$ common stochastic trends underlying Z_t.

Recall that $\Pi = \alpha\beta'$ and so in case 3 above, although the Π matrix will always be dimensioned $n \times n$ the α and β matrices will be dimensioned $n \times r$. This therefore imposes a rank of r on the Π matrix which amounts to imposing that there are only r linearly independent rows to this matrix. So underlying the full size Π matrix is a restricted set of only r cointegrating vectors given by $\beta'Z_{t-1}$. Reduced rank regression, of this type, has been available in the statistics literature for many years but it was introduced into modern econometrics and linked with the analysis of non-stationary data by Johansen (1988).

Going back to the three different cases considered above regarding the rank of the matrix Π we have:

Case 1 When Π has a full rank (i.e. there are $r = n$ linearly independent columns) then the variables in Z_t are $I(0)$.

Case 2 When the rank of Π is zero (i.e. there are no linearly independent columns) then there are no cointegrating relationships.

Case 3 When Π has a reduced rank (i.e. there are $r \leq (n-1)$ linearly independent columns) and therefore there are $r \leq (n-1)$ cointegrating relationships.

Johansen (1988) developed a methodology that tests for the rank of Π and provides estimates of α and β through a procedure known as reduced-rank regression, but the actual procedure is quite complicated and beyond the scopes of this text [see Cuthbertson, Hall and Taylor (1992) for more details].

The steps of the Johansen approach in practice

Step 1: testing the order of integration of the variables

As with the EG approach, the first step in the Johansen approach is to test for the order of integration of the variables under examination. We said before that most economic time series are non-stationary and therefore integrated. Indeed the issue here is to have non-stationary variables in order to detect among them stationary cointegrating relationship(s) and avoid the problem of spurious regressions. It is clear that the most desirable case is when all the variables are integrated of the same order and then to proceed with the cointegration test. However, it is important to stress here that this is not always the case, and that even in cases where a mix of $I(0)$, $I(1)$ and $I(2)$ variables are present in the model, cointegrating relationships might well exist. The inclusion of these variables, though, will massively affect our results and more consideration should be applied in such cases.

Consider for example the inclusion of an $I(0)$ variable. In a multivariate framework for every $I(0)$ variable included in the model the number of cointegrating relationships will increase correspondingly. We said before that the Johansen approach amounts to testing for the rank of Π (i.e. finding the number of linearly independent columns in Π), and since each $I(0)$ variable is stationary by itself, it forms a cointegrating relationship by itself and therefore forms a linearly independent vector in Π.

Matters become more complicated when we include $I(2)$ variables. Consider for example a model with the inclusion of two $I(1)$ and two $I(2)$ variables. There is a possibility that the two $I(2)$ variables cointegrate down to an $I(1)$ relationship, and then this relationship may further cointegrate with one of the two $I(1)$ variables to form another cointegrating vector. In general, situations with variables in differing orders of integration are quite complicated, although the positive thing is that it is quite common in macroeconomics to have $I(1)$ variables. Those who are interested in further details regarding the inclusion of $I(2)$ variables can refer to Johansen's (1995b) paper that develops an approach to treat $I(2)$ models.

Step 2: setting the appropriate lag length of the model

The issue of finding the appropriate (optimal) lag length is very important because we want to have Gaussian error terms (i.e. standard normal error terms that do not suffer from non-normality, autocorrelation, heteroskedasticity etc.). Setting the value of the lag length is affected by the omission of variables that might affect only the short-run behaviour of the model. This is due to the fact that omitted variables instantly become part of the error term. Therefore, very careful inspection of the data and the functional relationship is necessary before proceeding with estimation in order to decide whether to include additional variables. It is quite common to use dummy variables to take into account short-run 'shocks' to the system, such as political events that had important effects on macroeconomic conditions.

The most common procedure in choosing the optimal lag length is to estimate a VAR model including all our variables in levels (non-differenced data). This VAR model should be estimated for a large number of lags, then reducing down by reestimating the model for one lag less until we reach zero lags (i.e. we estimate the model for 12 lags, then 11, then 10 and so on until we reach 0 lags).

In each of these models we inspect the values of the AIC and the SBC criteria, as well as the diagnostics concerning autocorrelation, heteroskedasticity, possible ARCH effects and normality of the residuals. In general the model that minimizes AIC and SBC is selected as the one with the optimal lag length. This model should also pass all the diagnostic checks.

Step 3: choosing the appropriate model regarding the deterministic components in the multivariate system

Another important aspect in the formulation of the dynamic model, is whether an intercept and/or a trend should enter either the short-run or the long-run model, or both models. The general case of the VECM including all the various options that can possibly happen is given by the following equation:

$$\Delta Z_t = \Gamma_1 \Delta Z_{t-1} + \cdots + \Gamma_{k-1} \Delta Z_{t-k-1} + \alpha \begin{pmatrix} \beta \\ \mu_1 \\ \delta_1 \end{pmatrix} (Z_{t-1} \quad 1 \quad t)$$

$$+ \mu_2 + \delta_2 t + u_t \tag{17.44}$$

And for this equation we can see the possible cases. We can have a constant (with coefficient μ_1) and/or a trend (with coefficient δ_1) in the long-run model (the cointegrating equation (CE)), and a constant (with coefficient μ_2) and/or a trend (with coefficient δ_2) in the short-run model (the VAR model).

In general five distinct models can be considered. Although the first and the fifth model are not that realistic, we present all of them for reasons of complementarity.

Model 1   No intercept or trend in CE or VAR ($\delta_1 = \delta_2 = \mu_1 = \mu_2 = 0$). In this case there are no deterministic components in the data or in the cointegrating relations. However, this is quite unlikely to occur in practice, especially as the intercept is generally needed in order to account for adjustments in the units of measurements of the variables in (Z_{t-1} 1 t).

Model 2   Intercept (no trend) in CE, no intercept or trend in VAR ($\delta_1 = \delta_2 = \mu_2 = 0$). This is the case where there are no linear trends in the data, and therefore the first differenced series have a zero mean. In this case the intercept is restricted to the long-run model (i.e. the cointegrating equation) to account for the unit of measurement of the variables in (Z_{t-1} 1 t).

Model 3   Intercept in CE and VAR, no trends in CE and VAR ($\delta_1 = \delta_2 = 0$). In this case there are no linear trends in the levels of the data, but we allow both specifications to drift around an intercept. In this case it is assumed that the intercept in the CE is cancelled out by the intercept in the VAR, leaving just one intercept in the short-run model.

Model 4   Intercept in CE and VAR, linear trend in CE, no trend in VAR ($\delta_2 = 0$). In this model we include a trend in the CE as a trend-stationary variable in order to take into account exogenous growth (i.e. technical progress). We also allow for intercepts in both specifications while there is no trend in the short-run relationship.

Model 5   Intercept and quadratic trend in the CE intercept and linear trend in VAR. This model allows for linear trends in the short-run model and thus quadratic trends in the CE. Thus, in this final model everything is unrestricted. However, this model is very difficult to interpret from an economics point of view, especially since the variables are entered as logs, because a model like this would imply an implausible ever-increasing or ever-decreasing rate of change.

So, the problem is which of the five different models is appropriate in testing for cointegration. We said before that the first and the last (fifth) model are not that likely to happen, and that they are also implausible in terms of economic theory, therefore the problem reduces to a choice of one of the three remaining models (models 2, 3 and 4). Johansen (1992) suggests that we need to test the joint hypothesis of both the rank order and the deterministic components, applying the so-called Pantula principle. The Pantula principle involves the estimation of all three models and the presentation of the results from the most restrictive hypothesis (i.e. $r =$ number of cointegrating relations $= 0$ and model 1) through the least restrictive hypothesis, i.e. $r =$ number of variables entering the VAR $- 1 = n - 1$ and model 4). The model-selection procedure then comprises moving from the most restrictive model, at each stage comparing the trace test statistic to its critical value, stopping only when we conclude for the first time that the null hypothesis of no cointegration is not rejected.

Step 4: determining the rank of Π or the number of cointegrating vectors

According to Johansen (1988) and Johansen and Juselius (1990), there are two methods (and corresponding test statistics) for determining the number of cointegrating relations, and both involve estimation of the matrix Π. This is a $k \times k$ matrix with rank r. The procedures are based on propositions about eigenvalues.

(a) One method tests the null hypothesis, that $Rank(\Pi) = r$ against the hypothesis that the rank is $r + 1$. So, the null in this case is that there is cointegrating vectors and that we have up to r cointegrating relationships, with the alternative suggesting that there is $(r + 1)$ vectors.

The test statistics are based on the characteristic roots (also called eigenvalues) obtained from the estimation procedure. The test consists of ordering the largest eigenvalues in descending order and considering whether they are significantly different from zero. To understand the test procedure, suppose we obtained n characteristic roots denoted by $\lambda_1 > \lambda_2 > \lambda_3 > \cdots > \lambda_n$. If the variables under examination are not cointegrated, the rank of Π is zero and all the characteristic roots will equal zero. Therefore $(1 - \hat{\lambda}_i)$ will be equal to 1 and since $\ln(1) = 0$, each one of the expressions will be equal to zero for no cointegration. On the other hand, if the rank of Π is equal to 1, then $0 < \lambda_1 < 1$ so that the first expression $(1 - \hat{\lambda}_i) < 0$, while all the rest will be equal to zero. To test how many of the numbers of the characteristic roots are significantly different from zero this test uses the following statistic:

$$\lambda_{\max}(r, r + 1) = -T \ln(1 - \hat{\lambda}_{r+1}) \tag{17.45}$$

As we said before, the test statistic is based on the *maximum eigenvalue* and because of that is called the *maximal eigenvalue statistic* (denoted by $\lambda_{\max}$).

(b) The second method is based on a likelihood ratio test about the trace of the matrix (and because of that it is called the *trace statistic*). The trace statistic considers whether the trace is increased by adding more eigenvalues beyond the rth eigenvalue. The null hypothesis in this case is that the number of cointegrating vectors is less than or equal to r. From the previous analysis it should be clear that when all $\hat{\lambda}_i = 0$, then the trace statistic is equal to zero as well. On the other hand, the closer the characteristic roots are to unity the more negative is the $\ln(1 - \hat{\lambda}_i)$ term and, therefore, the larger the trace statistic. This statistic is calculated by:

$$\lambda_{trace}(r) = -T \sum_{i=r+1}^{n} \ln(1 - \hat{\lambda}_{r+1}) \tag{17.46}$$

The usual procedure is to work downwards and stop at the value of r which is associated with a test statistic that exceeds the displayed critical value. Critical values for both statistics are provided by Johansen and Juselius (1990) (these critical values are directly provided from both EViews and Microfit after conducting a test for cointegration using the Johansen approach).

Step 5: testing for weak exogeneity

After determining the number of cointegrating vectors we need to proceed with tests of weak exogeneity. Remember that the Π matrix contains information about the long-run relationships, and that $\Pi = \alpha \beta'$, where α represents the speed of adjustment coefficients and β is the matrix of the long-run coefficients. From this it should be clear that when there are $r \leq n-1$ cointegrating vectors in β, then this automatically means that at least $(n - r)$ columns of α are equal to zero. Thus, once we have determined the number of cointegrating vectors, we should proceed with testing which of the variables are weakly exogenous.

A very useful feature of the Johansen approach for cointegration is that it allows us to test for restricted forms of the cointegrating vectors. Consider the case given by (17.40), and from this the following equation:

$$\begin{pmatrix} \Delta Y_t \\ \Delta X_t \\ \Delta W_t \end{pmatrix} = \Gamma_1 \begin{pmatrix} \Delta Y_{t-1} \\ \Delta X_{t-1} \\ \Delta W_{t-1} \end{pmatrix} + \begin{pmatrix} a_{11} & a_{12} \\ a_{21} & a_{22} \\ a_{31} & a_{23} \end{pmatrix} \begin{pmatrix} \beta_{11} & \beta_{21} & \beta_{31} \\ \beta_{12} & \beta_{22} & \beta_{32} \end{pmatrix} \begin{pmatrix} Y_{t-1} \\ X_{t-1} \\ W_{t-1} \end{pmatrix} + e_t \tag{17.47}$$

In this equation we can see that testing for weak exogeneity with respect to the long run parameters is equivalent to testing which of the rows of α are equal to zero. A variable Z is weakly exogenous if it is only a function of lagged variables and the parameters of the equation generating Z are independent of the parameters generating the other variables in the system. If we now think of the variable Y in (17.47), it is clearly a function of only lagged variables but in the general form above the parameters of the cointegrating vectors (β) are clearly common to all equations and so the parameters generating Y cannot be independent of those generating X and W as they are the same parameters. However if the first row of the α matrix were all zeros then the βs would drop out of the Y equation and it would be weakly exogenous. So a joint test that a particular row of α is zero is a test of the weak exogeneity of the corresponding variable. If a variable is found to be weakly exogenous we can drop it as an endogenous part of the system. This means that we can drop the whole equation for that variable although it will continue to feature on the right-hand side of the other equations.

Step 6: testing for linear restrictions in the cointegrating vectors

An important feature of the Johansen approach is that it allows us to obtain estimates of the coefficients of the matrices α and β, and then test for possible linear restrictions regarding those matrices. Especially for matrix β, the matrix that contains the long-run parameters, this is very important because it allows us to test specific hypotheses regarding various theoretical predictions from an economic theory point of view. So, for example, if we examine a money-demand relationship, we might be interested in testing restrictions regarding the long-run proportionality between money and prices, or the relative size of income and interest-rate elasticities of demand for money and so on. For more details regarding testing linear restrictions in the Johansen framework see Enders (1995) and Harris (1997).

The Johansen approach in EViews and Microfit

The Johansen approach in EViews

EViews has a specific command for testing for cointegration using the Johansen approach under group statistics. Consider the file money_ita.wf1, which has quarterly data from 1975q1 to 1997q4 for the Italian economy and for the following variables:

$lm2\_p$ = the log of the real money supply measured by the M2 definition

   deflated by the consumer price index (*cpi*);

$lgdp\_p$ = the log of real income (again deflated by the CPI); and

   r = the interest rate representing the opportunity cost of holding money.

The first step is to determine the order of integration of the variables. To do this we apply unit-root tests on all three variables that we want to test for cointegration. We apply the Doldado, Jenkinson and Sosvilla-Rivero (1990) procedure for choosing the appropriate model and we determine the number of lags according to the SBC criterion. For example, for M2 the model with constant and trend showed that the inclusion of the trend was not appropriate (because its coefficient was statistically insignificant), and we therefore estimated the model that includes only a constant. This model was found to be appropriate and we concluded from that model that there is a unit root in the series (because the ADF statistic was bigger than the 5% critical value). The results of all tests for levels and first differences are presented in Table 17.2.

The second step is to determine the optimal lag length. Unfortunately, EViews does not allow us to automatically detect the lag length (while Microfit does), so we need to estimate the model for a large number of lags and then reduce down to check for the optimal value of AIC and SBC (as described in step 1 of the Johansen approach). By doing this we found that the optimal lag length was 4 lags (not surprising for quarterly data).

We then need to apply the Pantula principle to decide which of the three models to choose in testing for cointegration. We therefore test each one of the three models for cointegration in Microfit by opening **Quick/Group Statistics/Cointegration Test**.

Table 17.2 Unit-root test results

Variables	Model	ADF-stat.	No. of lags
	ADF tests in the levels		
lm3_p	constant no trend	−2.43	2
lgdp_p	constant and trend	−2.12	4
r	constant and trend	−2.97	2
	ADF tests in first differences		
lm3_p	constant no trend	−4.45	2
lgdp_p	constant no trend	−4.37	4
R	constant and trend	−4.91	2

Table 17.3 Cointegration test results (model 2)

Date: 04/07/04 Time: 17:14
Sample(adjusted): 1976:2 1997:4
Included observations: 87 after adjusting endpoints
Trend assumption: No deterministic trend (restricted constant)
Series: LGDP_P LM2_P R
Lags interval (in first differences): 1 to 4
Unrestricted Cointegration Rank Test

Hypothesized No. of CE(s)	Eigenvalue	Trace statistic	5% critical value	1% critical value
None**	0.286013	51.38016	34.91	41.07
At most 1*	0.139113	22.07070	19.96	24.60
At most 2	0.098679	9.038752	9.24	12.97

*Note: *(**) denotes rejection of the hypothesis at the 5%(1%) level. Trace test indicates 2 cointegrating equation(s) at the 5% level and 1 cointegrating equation(s) at the 1% level.*

Then in the **series list** window we enter the names of the series to check for cointegration, for example:

```
lgdp_p lm2_p r
```

then press <OK>. The five alternative models explained in the theory are given under labels 1, 2, 3, 4 and 5. There is another option (option 6 in EViews) that compares all these models together. In our case we wish to estimate models 2, 3 and 4 (because as noted earlier models 1 and 5 occur only very rarely). To estimate model 2 we select that model, and specify the number of lags in the bottom-right corner box that has the (default by EViews) numbers '1 2' for inclusion of two lags. We change the '1 2' to '1 4' for four lags, and click <OK> to get the results. Note that there is another box that allows us to include (by typing their names) variables that will be treated as exogenous. Here we usually put variables that are either found to be $I(0)$ or dummy variables that possibly affect the behaviour of the model.

The results of this model are presented in Table 17.3 (we present only the results of the trace statistic needed for the Pantula principle; later on we will check all the results reported in the cointegration results window).

Doing the same for models 3 and 4 (in the **untitled group window** select **View/Cointegration Test** and simply change the model by clicking next to 3 or 4, we get the results reported in Tables 17.4 and 17.5.

Table 17.4 Cointegration test results (model 3)

Date: 04/07/04 Time: 17:27
Sample(adjusted): 1976:2 1997:4
Included observations: 87 after adjusting endpoints
Trend assumption: Linear deterministic trend
Series: LGDP_P LM2_P R
Lags interval (in first differences): 1 to 4
Unrestricted Cointegration Rank Test

Hypothesized No. of CE(s)	Eigenvalue	Trace statistic	5% critical value	1% critical value
None	0.166219	25.79093	29.68	35.65
At most 1	0.108092	9.975705	15.41	20.04
At most 2	0.000271	0.023559	3.76	6.65

Note: *(**) denotes rejection of the hypothesis at the 5%(1%) level. Trace test indicates no cointegration at both the 5% and 1% levels.

Table 17.5 Cointegration test results (model 4)

Date: 04/07/04 Time: 17:27
Sample(adjusted): 1976:2 1997:4
Included observations: 87 after adjusting endpoints
Trend assumption: Linear deterministic trend (restricted)
Series: LGDP_P LM2_P R
Lags interval (in first differences): 1 to 4

Unrestricted Cointegration Rank Test

Hypothesized No. of CE(s)	Eigenvalue	Trace statistic	5% critical value	1% critical value
None**	0.319369	52.02666	42.44	48.45
At most 1	0.137657	18.55470	25.32	30.45
At most 2	0.063092	5.669843	12.25	16.26

Note: *(**) denotes rejection of the hypothesis at the 5%(1%) level. Trace test indicates 1 cointegrating equation(s) at both the 5% and 1% levels.

Table 17.6 The Pantula principle test results

r	$n-r$	Model 2	Model 3	Model 4
0	3	51.38016	25.79093*	52.02666
1	2	22.0707	9.975705	18.5547
2	1	9.038752	0.023559	5.669843

Note: * Indicates the first time that the null cannot be rejected.

We then collect the trace statistics for all three models together as in Table 17.6 to choose which model is appropriate. We start with the smaller number of cointegrating vectors $r = 0$, and check whether the trace statistic for model 2 rejects the null, if yes we proceed to the right, checking whether the third model rejects the null, and so on. In our case, model 3 suggests that the trace statistic is smaller than the 5% critical value; so this model does not show cointegration, and we stop our analysis at this point.

For illustrative purposes for the use of EViews only, we consider the results from model 2 where only two cointegrating vectors were found to exist. From the full results (reported in Table 17.7) we see that both the trace and the maximal eigenvalue statistics suggest the existence of two cointegrating vectors. EViews then reports results regarding the coefficients of the α and β matrices, first unnormalized and then normalized. After establishing the number of cointegrating vectors, we proceed with the estimation of the ECM by clicking on **Procs/Make Vector Autoregression**. EViews here gives us two choices of VAR types; first, if there is no evidence of cointegration we can estimate the unrestricted VAR (by clicking on the corresponding button), or, if there is cointegration we can estimate the VECM. If we estimate the VECM we need to specify (by clicking on the **Cointegration** menu), which model we want and how many numbers of cointegrating vectors we want to have (determined from the previous step), and also to impose restrictions on the elements of the α and β matrices by clicking on the **VEC restrictions** menu. The restrictions are entered as $b(1, 1) = 0$ for the $\beta_{11} = 0$ restriction. More than one restriction can be entered and they should be separated by commas.

The Johansen approach in Microfit

In order to use the Johansen approach in Microfit, we first go to the **multi** window by pressing the **multi** button. Then from the **Multivariate Menu** we can choose **Unrestricted VAR** and specify the equation we want in the corresponding box. Here we enter the names of the variables we want to check for cointegration in order to determine the optimal lag length from the unrestricted VAR. After typing the names of the variables we click on **Start**, which takes us to the **Unrestricted VAR post estimation menu**. From this menu we choose option 4. **Hypothesis testing and lag order selection in the VAR**. Here we choose option 1. **Testing and selection criteria for order (lag-length) of the VAR** and obtain the results reported in Table 17.8.

In this table we see the AIC and SBC together with some other statistics regarding estimations of simple VARs for 13 different lag structures (from lags 12 to 0). The aim is to choose the model that minimizes AIC and SBC. In this particular case both statistics suggest a lag length of 6 as optimal (see bold values in the table).

In order to test for cointegration among the variables we now go to the **Multivariate Menu** and choose **Cointegrating VAR Menu**. Five different options are offered, corresponding to the models of the structure of deterministic components examined in the theoretical explanation of the Johansen approach above. In order to apply the Pantula principle, again all three models (models 2, 3 and 4; we leave out models 1 and 5) should be estimated. By choosing the model and clicking on **Start** we get the results for the maximal and the trace eigenvalue statistics together with their respective critical values. If the statistical values are bigger than the critical ones, we reject the null of no cointegration in favour of the alternative. After that we close the results and, following the **Cointegrating VAR post estimation menu**, specify the number of cointegrating relationships (that we determined by the trace and max statistics before) in choice 2, set the cointegrating vectors in choice 3 and so on, until choice 6 that leads us to the **Long Run Structural Modelling Menu** from which we can impose restrictions on the coefficients of the cointegrating vectors.

Table 17.7 Full results from the cointegration test (model 2)

Date: 04/07/04 Time: 17:41
Sample(adjusted): 1975:4 1997:4
Included observations: 89 after adjusting endpoints
Trend assumption: No deterministic trend (restricted constant)
Series: LGDP_P LM2_P R
Lags interval (in first differences): 1 to 2
Unrestricted Cointegration Rank Test

Hypothesized No. of CE(s)	Eigenvalue	Trace statistic	5% critical value	1% critical value
None**	0.219568	48.20003	34.91	41.07
At most 1**	0.193704	26.13626	19.96	24.60
At most 2	0.075370	6.974182	9.24	12.97

Note: *(**) denotes rejection of the hypothesis at the 5%(1%) level. Trace test indicates 2 cointegrating equation(s) at both the 5% and 1% levels.

Hypothesized No. of CE(s)	Eigenvalue	Max-Eigen statistic	5% critical value	1% critical value
None*	0.219568	22.06377	22.00	26.81
At most 1*	0.193704	19.16208	15.67	20.20
At most 2	0.075370	6.974182	9.24	12.97

Note: *(**) denotes rejection of the hypothesis at the 5%(1%) level. Max-eigenvalue test indicates 2 cointegrating equation(s) at the 5% level, and no cointegration at the 1% level.

Unrestricted Cointegrating Coefficients (normalized by b'*S11*b = I):

LGDP_P	LM2_P	R	C
−5.932728	4.322724	−0.226210	10.33096
4.415826	−0.328139	0.158258	−11.15663
0.991551	−17.05815	0.113204	27.97470

Unrestricted Adjustment Coefficients (alpha):

D(LGDP_P)	0.004203	0.001775	3.68E−05
D(LM2_P)	0.001834	−0.001155	0.003556
D(R)	0.228149	−0.399488	−0.139878

1 Cointegrating Equation(s):		Log likelihood	415.4267

Normalized cointegrating coefficients (std. err. in parentheses)

LGDP_P	LM2_P	R	C
1.000000	−0.728623	0.038129	−1.741351
	(0.61937)	(0.01093)	(1.17467)

Adjustment coefficients (std. err. in parentheses)

D(LGDP_P)	−0.024938
	(0.00583)
D(LM2_P)	−0.010881
	(0.00895)
D(R)	−1.353545
	(0.73789)

Continued

Table 17.7 Continued

2 Cointegrating Equation(s):		Log likelihood	425.0077

Normalized cointegrating coefficients (std. err. in parentheses)

LGDP_P	LM2_P	R	C
1.000000	0.000000	0.035579	−2.615680
		(0.01765)	(0.24340)
0.000000	1.000000	−0.003500	−1.199974
		(0.02933)	(0.40446)

Adjustment coefficients (std. err. in parentheses)

D(LGDP_P)	−0.017100	0.017588
	(0.00712)	(0.00417)
D(LM2_P)	−0.015981	0.008307
	(0.01112)	(0.00652)
D(R)	−3.117614	1.117312
	(0.86005)	(0.50413)

Table 17.8 Test statistics and choice criteria for selecting the order of the VAR model

Based on 258 observations from 1974M1 to 1995M6. Order of VAR = 12
List of variables included in the unrestricted VAR:
FF   ITL

Order	LL	AIC	SBC	LR test		Adjusted LR test	
12	−1326.9	−1354.9	−1460.2				
11	−1327.1	−1351.1	−1349.3	CHSQ (4) =	0.44302 [.979]	0.40181 [.982]	
10	−1328.1	−1348.1	−1339.2	CHSQ (8) =	2.4182 [.965]	2.1932 [.975]	
9	−1328.5	−1344.5	−1328.4	CHSQ (12) =	3.0913 [.995]	2.8037 [.997]	
8	−1332.1	−1354.1	−1320.9	CHSQ (16) =	10.2877 [.851]	9.3307 [.899]	
7	−1334.4	−1352.4	−1312.1	CHSQ (20) =	14.8836 [.783]	13.4991 [.855]	
6	−1335.7	**−1359.7**	**−1402.4**	CHSQ (24) =	17.6463 [.820]	16.0048 [.888]	
5	−1336.9	−1356.9	−1392.5	CHSQ (28) =	20.0586 [.862]	18.1927 [.921]	
4	−1337.2	−1353.2	−1381.6	CHSQ (32) =	20.5527 [.941]	18.6409 [.971]	
3	−1338.3	−1350.3	−1371.6	CHSQ (36) =	22.8243 [.957]	20.7011 [.981]	
2	−1341.0	−1349.0	−1363.2	CHSQ (40) =	28.1570 [.920]	25.5377 [.963]	
1	−1345.4	−1349.4	−1356.5	CHSQ (44) =	36.9251 [.766]	33.4902 [.875]	
0	−2836.3	−1336.3	−1336.3	CHSQ (48) =	3018.8 [.000]	2738.0 [.000]	

Note: AIC = Akaike information criterion; SBC = Schwarz Bayesian criterion.

Computer examples of cointegration

Here we again examine the test results from Asteriou and Price (2000a). The results for the order of integration of the variables included in their analysis were presented in the second computer example of Chapter 16. Once the stationarity order has been established, we can move to cointegration tests.

Table 17.9 reports the results from using the Engle–Granger (EG) (1987) cointegration methodology. We first regressed GDP per capita to the capital/labour ratio and to every financial development proxy (one at each specification). The test statistics presented in Table 17.9 are the augmented Dickey–Fuller tests relating to the hypothesis of a unit root in the cointegrating regression residuals of each specification. The results of the first method indicate that the hypothesis of the existence of a bivariate cointegrating relationship between the level of GDP per capita and each of the financial development proxies is clearly rejected in all cases (the critical value is −3.37, see Table 17.1).

Table 17.9 Engle–Granger cointegration tests

Variables in cointegrating vector	ADF statistic	k	n
Y, K, M	−2.6386	4	109
Y, K, CUR	−2.1290	6	109
Y, K, CL	−2.0463	4	104
Y, K, T	−3.3999	4	85

Note: k is the degree of augmentation of the ADF test, determined by the FPE test; n is the number of observations used in the first step of the Engle–Granger procedure.

However, as is well-known, the Engle–Granger procedure suffers from various shortcomings. One is that it relies on a two-step estimator; the first step is to generate the error series and the second is to estimate a regression for this series in order to see if the series is stationary or not. Hence, any error introduced by the researcher in the first step is carried into the second step, in particular the misspecification in the short-run dynamics. The Johansen (1988) maximum likelihood method circumvents the use of two-step estimators and, moreover, can estimate and test for the presence of multiple cointegrating vectors. The Johansen (1988) test also allows us to test restricted versions of the cointegrating vectors and speed of adjustment parameters.

Thus, we continue testing for cointegration with the Johansen method. First, we test for the presence of cointegrating vectors introducing in each case only one financial development proxy variable, then we proceed to include all four financial development proxies.

Monetization ratio

We want to test for the existence of cointegration relations among per capita GDP and the financial development variables. The first proxy variable for financial development is the monetization ratio. The Johansen method is known to be sensitive to the lag length (see Banerjee *et al.*, 1993), and we therefore estimate the VAR system comprising the monetization ratio, the capital/labour ratio and GDP per capita for various lag lengths and calculate the respective Akaike information criterion (AIC) and the Schwarz Bayesian criterion (SBC) in order to determine the appropriate lag length for the cointegration test. Nine alternative VAR(p), $p = 1, 2, \ldots, 9$, models were estimated over the same sample period, namely 1972q1 – 1997q1, and as to be expected the maximized values of the log-likelihood (LL) increase with p. Both criteria indicated that the optimal lag length is two. The results shown in Table 17.10 show that the log-likelihood ratio statistics suggest a VAR of order 7. By construct, both the AIC and the SBC suggest the use of two lags. Initially, we test for cointegration using only two lags in the VAR system.

We also need to determine the appropriate restrictions on the intercept and trends in the short- and long-run models. For this, we use the Pantula principle; that is, we estimate all three alternative models and move from the most restrictive model to the least restrictive model, comparing the trace or the maximal eigenvalue test statistic to its critical value, stopping (and therefore choosing the model) only when the null hypothesis is not rejected for the first time. The results from the three estimating models are presented in Table 17.11. The first time that the null hypothesis is not rejected is for the first model (restricted intercepts, no trends in the levels of the data) and we can

Table 17.10 Test statistics and choice criteria for selecting the order of the VAR

Based on 101 obs. from 1972q1 to 1997q1
Variables included in the unrestricted VAR: Y, K, M

Order	LL	AIC	SBC	LR test	Adjusted LR test
8	1092.2	1014.2	912.1	—	—
7	1089.4	1020.4	930.1	$\chi^2(9) = 5.62$ [.777]	4.17 [.900]
6	1068.0	1008.0	929.5	$\chi^2(18) = 48.33$ [.000]	35.89 [.007]
5	1064.1	1013.1	946.3	$\chi^2(27) = 56.21$ [.001]	41.74 [.035]
4	1060.7	1018.7	963.7	$\chi^2(36) = 62.97$ [.004]	46.76 [.0108]
3	1051.1	1018.1	974.9	$\chi^2(45) = 82.15$ [.001]	61.00 [.056]
2	1045.1	1021.1	989.7	$\chi^2(54) = 94.13$ [.001]	69.90 [.072]
1	938.8	968.8	949.2	$\chi^2(63) = 216.58$ [.000]	160.82 [.000]
0	284.5	275.5	270.7	$\chi^2(72) = 1615.1$ [.000]	1199.4 [.000]

Note: AIC = Akaike information criterion; SBC = Schwarz Bayesian criterion.

Table 17.11 The Pantula principle for the monetization ratio proxy variable, $k = 2$

H_0	r	n − r	Model 1	Model 2	Model 3
λ max test					
	0	3	40.68	19.96	31.21
	1	2	13.13*	4.56	13.65
	2	1	3.69	0.07	4.17
λ trace test					
	0	3	57.50	29.60	42.03
	1	2	4.56*	4.46	17.82
	2	1	0.07	0.07	4.17

Note: *Denotes the first time when the null hypothesis is not rejected for the 90% significance level.

see that both the trace and the maximal eigenvalue test statistics suggest the existence of one cointegrating relationship.

The results of the cointegration test are presented in Table 17.12. We observe one cointegration vector which is given in the last row of the table, and the monetization ratio and the capital/labour ratios show the expected positive signs. However, the model selected suggests that there is no constant in the cointegrating vector. This may be interpreted as evidence that the technological parameter in the production function is not significant, and that all the technological innovation is driven by the monetization ratio, but this is implausible. Also, the corresponding vector error-correction model (VECM) suffers from residual serial correlation and non-normality. This suggests that the lag length chosen may be too small and an alternative lag length might be used.

Thus, we reestimated the model for a lag-length of seven. (We also included intervention dummies for residual outliers to help accommodate non-normality.) The results in Table 17.13 indicate that the appropriate model this time has unrestricted intercepts and no trends, which is consistent with economic theory predictions; namely, that there is a stochastic trend in technical progress (see Greenslade, Hall and Henry, 1999).

Table 17.12   Cointegration test based on Johansen's max. likelihood method: $k = 2$

Null hypothesis	Alternative hypothesis		Critical values	
			95%	90%
λ_{max} rank tests		λ_{max} rank value		
$H_0 : r = 0$	$H_a : r > 0$	40.68*	22.04	19.86
$H_0 : r \leq 1$	$H_a : r > 1$	13.13	15.87	13.81
$H_0 : r \leq 2$	$H_a : r > 2$	3.69	9.16	7.53
λ_{trace} rank tests		λ_{trace} rank value		
$H_0 : r = 0$	$H_a : r = 1$	57.50*	34.87	31.39
$H_0 : r = 1$	$H_a : r = 2$	16.82	20.18	17.78
$H_0 : r = 2$	$H_a : r = 3$	3.69	9.16	7.53
Normalized ecm: $Y = 0.408*K + 0.286*M + 8.392$				

Note: 107 observations from 1970q3 to 1997q1. (*,**) denote rejection of the null hypothesis for the 5% and 10% significance levels respectively. Critical values from Ostervald–Lenum (1992).

Table 17.13   The Pantula principle for the monetization ratio proxy variable, $k = 7$

H_0	r	$n - r$	Model 1	Model 2	Model 3
λ max test					
	0	3	32.29	29.20	42.60
	1	2	27.27	8.76*	12.80
	2	1	8.58	0.19	8.61
λ trace test					
	0	3	69.32	38.17	64.02
	1	2	36.35	8.96*	21.41
	2	1	8.58	0.13	8.61

Note: * Denotes the first time when the null hypothesis is not rejected for the 90% significance level.

Table 17.14   Cointegration test based on Johansen's max. likelihood method: $k = 7$

Null hypothesis	Alternative hypothesis		Critical values	
			95%	90%
λ_{max} rank tests		λ_{max} rank value		
$H_0 : r = 0$	$H_a : r > 0$	29.20*	21.12	19.02
$H_0 : r \leq 1$	$H_a : r > 1$	8.76	14.88	12.98
$H_0 : r \leq 2$	$H_a : r > 2$	0.19	8.07	6.50
λ_{trace} rank tests		λ_{trace} rank value		
$H_0 : r = 0$	$H_a : r = 1$	38.17*	31.54	28.78
$H_0 : r = 1$	$H_a : r = 2$	8.96	17.86	15.75
$H_0 : r = 2$	$H_a : r = 3$	0.19	8.07	6.50
Normalized ecm: $Y = 0.376*K + 0.335*M$				

Notes: 102 observations from 1971q1 to 1997q1. (*,**) denote rejection of the null hypothesis for the 5% and 10% significance levels respectively. Critical values from Ostervald–Lenum (1992).

The results for the cointegration tests are presented in Table 17.14. Again we conclude that there exists one cointegrating relationship (as in the case with the two lags) which is reported in the last row of the table. We observe a strong positive relationship between the monetization ratio and the GDP per capita, which provides evidence in favour of the hypothesis that there is a link between financial development and economic growth.

Table 17.15 Summary results from the VECMs and diagnostic tests

	ΔY	ΔK	ΔM
constant	0.904 (4.507)	−0.141 (−1.488)	−0.908 (−2.775)
ecm(−1)	−0.208 (−4.49)	0.004 (1.54)	0.280 (2.78)
R^2	0.79	0.75	0.79
S.E. of regression	0.006	0.002	0.01
$\chi^2_{S.C.}(4)$	0.639	2.748	8.195
$\chi^2_{Norm}(2)$	0.776	5.995	5.585
$\chi^2_{Het}(1)$	2.511	0.067	2.993
$\chi^2_{Arch}(4)$	1.445	4.781	3.239

Note: * Rejects null hypothesis at 5% significance level. *t* statistics in parentheses.

Table 17.15 reports summary results from the VECMs and the basic diagnostics about the residuals of each error-correction equation. Namely, we present the coefficients and the corresponding *t* statistics for the ecm_{t-1} component which in our case have the expected signs and are statistically significant in the equations of *Y* and *M*. The insignificance of the ECM component for the capital/labour variable indicates that this ratio is weakly exogenous to the model. The diagnostic tests involve χ^2 tests for the hypothesis that there is no serial correlation; that the residual follow the normal distribution; that there is no heteroskedasticity; and lastly that there is no autoregressive conditional heteroskedasticity. In all equations the diagnostics suggest that the residuals are Gaussian as the Johansen method presupposes.

Turnover ratio

Continuing, we proceed with the next financial development proxy variable which is the turnover ratio. The results of the tests for the lag length of this model (which includes GDP per capita, turnover ratio, capital/labour ratio, intercept and various structural dummy variables) are reported in Table 17.16 and indicate a lag length of order 2. All three alternative measures of the order of lag length agree for this choice. In this case the selected model is the one with the unrestricted intercept but not trend in the levels of the data, consistent with our expectations (see Table 17.17). The results of the cointegration test are presented in Table 17.18. We observe one cointegration vector reported in the same table with the expected signs, indicating that there exists a positive long-run relationship between GDP per capita and the turnover ratio. Again the diagnostics reported in Table 17.19 show that the error terms are Gaussian. The ECM coefficients have the expected signs and are statistically significant and different from zero. However, the low coefficient on capital is hard to interpret.

Claims and currency ratios

Extending our analysis to the other two financial development proxy variables (claims and currency ratios) we found in both cases that the suitable model was the second

Table 17.16 Test statistics and choice criteria for selecting the order of the VAR

Based on 77 obs. from 1978q1 to 1997q1
List of variables included in the unrestricted VAR: Y, K, T

Order	LL	AIC	SBC	LR test	Adjusted LR test
8	692.6	614.6	523.2	—	—
7	685.3	616.3	535.4	$\chi^2(9) = 14.54$ [.104]	9.63 [.381]
6	679.9	619.9	549.6	$\chi^2(18) = 25.24$ [.118]	16.72 [.542]
5	672.0	621.0	561.2	$\chi^2(27) = 41.17$ [.040]	27.26 [.449]
4	667.2	625.2	576.0	$\chi^2(36) = 50.80$ [.052]	33.64 [.581]
3	664.4	631.4	592.7	$\chi^2(45) = 56.42$ [.118]	37.37 [.783]
2	649.4	625.3	597.2	$\chi^2(54) = 86.55$ [.003]	57.32 [.353]
1	606.8	591.8	574.3	$\chi^2(63) = 171.48$ [.000]	113.58 [.000]
0	170.4	164.4	157.3	$\chi^2(72) = 1044.4$ [.000]	691.75 [.000]

Note: AIC = Akaike information criterion; SBC = Schwarz Bayesian criterion.

Table 17.17 The Pantula principle for the turnover ratio proxy variable

H_0	r	n − r	Model 1	Model 2	Model 3
λ max test					
	0	3	49.86	24.11	27.76
	1	2	23.74	8.67*	17.96
	2	1	7.34	0.55	0.43
λ trace test					
	0	3	49.86	33.43	54.19
	1	2	23.74	9.23*	26.43
	2	1	7.34	0.55	8.46

Note: * Denotes the first time when the null hypothesis is not rejected for the 90% significance level.

Table 17.18 Cointegration test based on Johansen's max. likelihood method

Null hypothesis	Alternative hypothesis		Critical values	
			95%	90%
λ_{max} rank tests		λ_{max} rank value		
$H_0 : r = 0$	$H_a : r > 0$	24.11*	21.12	19.02
$H_0 : r \leq 1$	$H_a : r > 1$	8.67	14.88	12.98
$H_0 : r \leq 2$	$H_a : r > 2$	0.55	8.07	6.50
λ_{trace} rank tests		λ_{trace} rank value		
$H_0 : r = 0$	$H_a : r = 1$	33.43*	31.54	28.78
$H_0 : r = 1$	$H_a : r = 2$	9.23	17.86	15.75
$H_0 : r = 2$	$H_a : r = 3$	0.55	8.07	6.50

Normalised ecm: $Y = 0.376^*K + 0.335^*M$

Note: 83 observations from 1976q3 to 1997q1. (*,**) denote rejection of the null hypothesis for the 5% and 10% significance levels respectively. Critical values form Ostervald–Lenum (1992).

(unrestricted intercept, no trends), but there is no cointegration relationship among those variables and the GDP per capita (see Tables 17.20 and 17.21).

Thus, with the Johansen procedure we found strong evidence of cointegration between two of the four financial development proxies (monetization and the turnover ratio) and GDP per capita.

Table 17.19 Summary results from the VECMs and diagnostic tests

	ΔY	ΔK	ΔT
ecm(-1)	-0.025 (-4.29)	0.006 (2.283)	0.44 (2.61)
R^2	0.59	0.77	0.42
S.E. of Regression	0.005	0.0027	0.171
$\chi^2_{S.C.}(4)$	6.48	5.56	3.03
$\chi^2_{Norm}(2)$	0.18	3.01	4.40
$\chi^2_{Het}(1)$	0.93	0.06	1.04
$\chi^2_{Arch}(4)$	3.89	11.45	1.88

Note: * Rejects null hypothesis at 5% significance level. *t* statistics in parentheses.

Table 17.20 The Pantula principle for the claims ratio proxy variable

H_0	r	$n-r$	*Model 1*	*Model 2*	*Model 3*
λ max test					
	0	3	39.60	13.27*	31.73
	1	2	11.04	9.60	12.88
	2	1	7.60	0.24	9.34
λ trace test					
	0	3	58.25	23.12*	53.96
	1	2	18.65	9.58	22.22
	2	1	0.06	0.24	9.34

Note: * Denotes the first time when the null hypothesis is not rejected for the 90% significance level.

Table 17.21 The Pantula principle for the currency ratio proxy variable

H_0	r	$n-r$	*Model 1*	*Model 2*	*Model 3*
λ max test					
	0	3	39.11	11.20*	32.00
	1	2	7.70	7.51	10.87
	2	1	6.13	0.09	7.37
λ trace test					
	0	3	52.95	18.81*	50.25
	1	2	13.84	7.60	18.25
	2	1	6.13	0.09	7.37

Note: * Denotes the first time when the null hypothesis is not rejected for the 90% significance level.

A model with more than one financial development proxy variable

In this section we examine a specification which includes more than one financial development proxy. First we estimated a model including all four proxy variables; the selected lag length was two (see Table 17.22) and the appropriate model includes unrestricted intercepts but no trends in the VECMs (Table 17.23).

The results for the cointegration test are reported in Table 17.24. This time we have two cointegrating vectors, which is consistent with the previous findings of cointegration among monetization and GDP per capita, and turnover and GDP per capita. The results from the VECM for all those variables are reported in Table 17.25, and indicate that the claims ratio and the currency

Table 17.22 Test statistics and choice criteria for selecting the order of the VAR

Based on 77 obs. from 1978q1 to 1997q1
List of variables included in the unrestricted VAR: Y, K, T, M, CL, CUR

Order	LL	AIC	SBC	LR test	Adjusted LR test
8	1421.4	1121.4	769.8	—	—
7	1363.1	1099.1	789.7	$\chi^2(36) = 16.67$ [.000]	40.91 [.264]
6	1312.6	1084.6	817.4	$\chi^2(72) = 17.67$ [.000]	76.32 [.341]
5	1287.0	1095.0	869.9	$\chi^2(108) = 268.94$ [.000]	94.30 [.823]
4	1254.7	1098.7	915.8	$\chi^2(144) = 333.54$ [.000]	116.95 [.952]
3	1225.3	1105.3	964.6	$\chi^2(180) = 392.33$ [.000]	137.57 [992]
2	1190.3	1106.3	1007.9	$\chi^2(216) = 462.23$ [.000]	162.08 [.998]
1	1129.5	1081.5	1025.2	$\chi^2(252) = 583.96$ [.000]	204.76 [.987]
0	90.47	378.4	364.4	$\chi^2(288) = 2061.9$ [.000]	723.01 [.000]

Note: AIC = Akaike information criterion; SBC = Schwarz Bayesian criterion.

Table 17.23 The Pantula principle for all the financial dev. ratio proxy variables

H_0	r	n − r	Model 1	Model 2	Model 3
λ max test					
	0	6	51.37	51.12	56.60
	1	5	41.90	34.65	47.95
	2	4	29.81	18.37*	24.86
	3	3	17.37	10.80	17.20
	4	2	7.50	5.79	10.80
	5	1	5.70	0.86	5.76
λ trace test					
	0	6	153.68	121.99	163.23
	1	5	102.31	70.86	106.23
	2	4	60.40	36.20*	58.67
	3	3	30.58	17.46	33.80
	4	2	13.21	6.66	16.60
	5	1	5.70	0.86	5.79

Note: * Denotes the first time when the null hypothesis is not rejected for the 90% significance level.

ratio should be treated as weakly exogenous variables in the cointegrating model. Therefore, we reestimated treating those two proxies as exogenous variables. However, while the results then clearly indicated the existence of one cointegrating vector with the correct – according to the theory – signs of the coefficients for the capital/labour ratio and the financial proxies, we were in all cases unable to accept the exogeneity test conducted after that.

Thus, we finally estimated a model including the financial development proxies, which we found are cointegrated with per capita GDP (namely the turnover and the monetization ratio). The results of the test for cointegration of this model are presented in Table 17.26. It is clear that we have one cointegrating vector which is reported in the same table. From these results, we observe a positive relationship between GDP per capita and the capital/labour ratio with a higher coefficient than from the previous cases, and also positive relationships between the dependent variable and the two financial development ratios. We do not wish to claim too much about the results of this final specification, but it seems to capture some of the implications of the underlying economic theory and at least is consistent with the previous findings of the tests for cointegration for each variable reflecting financial development separately.

Table 17.24 Cointegration test based on Johansen's max. likelihood method

Null hypothesis	Alternative hypothesis		Critical values	
			95%	90%
λ_{max} rank tests		λ_{max} rank value		
$H_0 : r = 0$	$H_a : r > 0$	51.12*	39.83	36.84
$H_0 : r \leq 1$	$H_a : r > 1$	34.65*	33.64	31.02
$H_0 : r \leq 2$	$H_a : r > 2$	18.37	27.42	24.99
$H_0 : r \leq 3$	$H_a : r > 3$	10.80	21.12	19.02
$H_0 : r \leq 4$	$H_a : r > 4$	5.79	14.88	12.98
$H_0 : r \leq 5$	$H_a : r > 5$	0.86	8.07	6.50
λ_{trace} rank tests		λ_{trace} rank value		
$H_0 : r = 0$	$H_a : r = 1$	121.99*	95.87	91.40
$H_0 : r = 1$	$H_a : r = 2$	70.86*	70.49	66.23
$H_0 : r = 2$	$H_a : r = 3$	36.20	48.88	45.70
$H_0 : r = 3$	$H_a : r = 4$	17.46	31.54	28.78
$H_0 : r = 4$	$H_a : r = 5$	6.66	17.86	15.75
$H_0 : r = 5$	$H_a : r = 6$	0.86	8.07	6.50

Normalised ecm1: $Y = 0.138^*K + 0.130^*M + 0.252^*CUR + 0.098^*CL + 0.058^*T$
Normalised ecm2: $Y = 0.231^*K + 0.200^*M + 0.279^*CUR + 0.007^*CL + 0.089^*T$

Notes: 83 observations from 1976q3 to 1997q1. (*,**) denote rejection of the null hypothesis for the 5% and 10% significance levels respectively. Critical values form Ostervald–Lenum (1992).

Table 17.25 Summary results from the VECMs and diagnostic tests

	ΔY	ΔK	ΔM	ΔCUR	ΔCL	ΔT
constant	1.27(4.88)	−0.26(−1.93)	−0.01(−0.32)	−0.14(−0.35)	−0.01(−1.14)	−29.3(−2.57)
ecm1(−1)	0.007(1.2)	−0.007(−0.2)	0.01(1.79)	−0.01(−1.14)	−1.52(−5.91)	0.03(0.18)
ecm2(−1)	−0.03(−5.18)	0.007(2.27)	0.01(1.80)	−0.004(−0.44)	−0.33(−1.31)	0.35(1.78)
R^2	0.59	0.70	0.52	0.40	0.52	0.23
S.E. of Regression	0.005	0.003	0.1	0.009	0.25	0.19
$\chi^2_{S.C.}(4)$	3.95	8.69	13.95*	3.43	15.18*	22.29*
$\chi^2_{Norm}(2)$	0.52	3.32	15.53*	7.31*	69.74*	1.49
$\chi^2_{Het}(1)$	0.85	0.08	0.0001	0.62	0.004	0.64
$\chi^2_{Arch}(4)$	5.43	1.71	3.16	2.32	2.54	0.89

Table 17.26 Cointegration test based on Johansen's max. likelihood method

Null hypothesis	Alternative hypothesis		Critical values	
			95%	90%
λ_{max} rank tests		λ_{max} rank value		
$H_0 : r = 0$	$H_a : r > 0$	30.24*	27.42	24.99
$H_0 : r \leq 1$	$H_a : r > 1$	14.29	21.12	19.02
$H_0 : r \leq 2$	$H_a : r > 2$	5.07	14.88	12.98
$H_0 : r \leq 3$	$H_a : r > 3$	0.02	8.07	6.50
λ_{trace} rank tests		λ_{trace} rank value		
$H_0 : r = 0$	$H_a : r = 1$	49.63*	48.88	45.70
$H_0 : r = 1$	$H_a : r = 2$	19.39	31.54	28.78
$H_0 : r = 2$	$H_a : r = 3$	5.09	17.86	15.75
$H_0 : r = 3$	$H_a : r = 4$	0.02	8.07	6.50

Normalised ecm: $Y = 0.122^*K + 0.110^*M + 0.073^*T$

Notes: 83 observations from 1976q3 to 1997q1. (*,**) denote rejection of the null hypothesis for the 5% and 10% significance levels respectively. Critical values form Ostervald–Lenum (1992).

Questions and exercises

Questions

1 Explain the meaning of cointegration. Why is it so important for economic analysis?

2 Why is it necessary to have series that are integrated of the same order in order to possibly have cointegration? Give examples.

3 What is the error-correction model? Prove that the ECM is a reparametrization of the ARDL model.

4 What are the good features of the ECM that make it so popular in modern econometric analysis?

5 Explain step by step how can one test for cointegration using the EG approach.

6 State the drawbacks of the Engle–Granger (EG) approach, and discuss these drawbacks in face of its alternative (i.e. the Johansen approach).

7 Is it possible to have two I(1) variables and two I(2) variables, in a Johansen test for cointegration, and find that the I(2) variables are cointegrated with the I(1)? Explain analytically.

Exercise 17.1

The file korea_phillips.wf1 contains data for wages and unemployment for the Korean economy. Test for cointegration among those two variables with the EG approach and comment on the validity of the Phillips curve theory for the Korean economy.

Exercise 17.2

The file cointegration.wf1 contains data on three variables (x, y and z). Test the variables for their order of integration and then apply the EG approach for the three different pairs of variables. In which of the pairs do you find cointegration?

Exercise 17.3

Use the file in exercise 2 and verify your results by using the Johansen approach. Include all three variables in a multivariate Johansen cointegration test. What is your result? Can you identify the cointegrating vector(s)?

Exercise 17.4

The files Norway.wf1, Sweden.wf1 and Finland.wf1 contain data for gross domestic product and various financial proxies as in the computer example for the UK case presented in this chapter. For each of these countries test for cointegration among the pairs of the variables applying both the EG and the Johansen approach as in the computer example. After determining whether or not cointegration exists, estimate the respective ECMs.

Part

VI Panel Data Econometrics

18 Traditional Panel Data Models

Introduction: the advantages of panel data

Panel data estimation is often considered to be an efficient analytical method in handling econometric data. Panel data analysis has become popular among social scientists because it allows the inclusion of data for N cross-sections (e.g., countries, households, firms, individuals, etc.) and T time periods (e.g., years, quarters, months, etc.). The combined panel data matrix set consists of a time series for each cross-sectional member in the data set, and offers a variety of estimation methods. In this case, the number of observations available increases by including developments over time.

A dataset which consists only of observations of N individuals at the same point in time is referred to as a cross section dataset. Some cross section datasets also exist over time so that we may have a number of cross section samples taken at different points in time. These datasets do not however constitute a panel dataset as we can not generally follow the same individual member though time. Examples of such datasets would be household surveys which are repeated every year but where different households are surveyed each year and so we cannot follow the same household through time. A true panel dataset would allow us to follow each individual in the panel over a number of periods.

If the panel has the same number of time observations for every variable and every individual it is known as a balanced panel. Often we work with unbalanced panels where we have different numbers of time observations for some of the individuals. When a panel is unbalanced this does not cause any major conceptual problems but the data handling from a computer point of view may become a little more complex.

The basic idea behind panel data analysis comes from the notion that the individual relationships will all have the same parameters. This is sometimes known as the pooling assumption as we are in effect pooling all the individual together into one dataset and imposing a common set of parameters across them. If the pooling assumption is correct then panel data estimation can offer some considerable advantages. (a) The sample size can be increased considerably by using a panel and hence much better estimates can be obtained. (b) Under certain circumstances the problem of omitted variables which might cause biased estimates in a single individual regression may not occur in a panel context. Of course the disadvantage of panel estimation is that if the pooling assumption is not correct then we may have problems. Although even in this case, which is often referred to as a heterogeneous panel (because the parameters are different across the individuals) we would normally expect the panel data estimator to give some representative average estimate of the individual parameters. However, we would warn that there are certain circumstances in which this may not happen and panel techniques can give quite biased results.

A common problem of time-series estimations is that while estimating samples with very few observations, it is difficult for the analyst to obtain significant t-ratios or F-statistics from regressions. This problem is common with annual data estimations, since there are very few annual series which extend more than 50 years. An efficient solution to the problem is to 'pool' the data into a 'panel' of time series from different cross-sectional units. This pooling of the data generates differences among the different cross-sectional or time-series observations that can actually be captured with the inclusion of dummy variables. This use of dummies to capture systematic differences among panel observations results in what is known as a *fixed-effects model*, the easiest way of dealing with pooled data. An alternative method is called the *random-effects model*.

The linear panel data model

A panel data set is formulated by a sample that contains N cross-sectional units (i.e. countries) that are observed at different T time periods. Consider for example a simple linear model with one explanatory variable as given by:

$$Y_{it} = a + \beta X_{it} + u_{it} \tag{18.1}$$

where the variables Y and X have both i and t subscripts for $i = 1, 2, \ldots, N$ sections and $t = 1, 2, \ldots, T$ time periods. If our sample set consists of a constant T for all cross-sectional units, or in other words if we obtain a full nest of data both across countries and across time, then the data set is called *balanced*. Otherwise when observations are missing for the time periods of some of the cross-sectional units then the panel is called *unbalanced*.

In this simple panel the coefficients a and β do not have any subscripts, suggesting that they will be the same for all units and for all years. We can introduce some degree of heterogeneity in this panel by relaxing the fact that the constant a should be identical for all cross-sections. To understand this consider a case where in our sample we have different countries (for example high and low-income, OECD and non-OECD, and so on), and that we expect differences in their behaviour. Thus our model becomes:

$$Y_{it} = a_i + \beta X_{it} + u_{it} \tag{18.2}$$

where, a_i can now differ for each country in the sample. At this point someone may wonder whether the β coefficient should also vary across different countries. However, this would require a separate analysis for each one of the N cross-sectional units and this is the pooling assumption which is the basis of panel data estimation.

Different methods of estimation

In general, simple linear panel data models can be estimated using three different methods: (a) with a common constant as in equation (18.1), (b) allowing for fixed effects, and (c) allowing for random effects.

The common constant method

The common constant method (also called the pooled OLS method) of estimation presents results under the principal assumption that there are no differences among the data matrices of the cross-sectional dimension (N). In other words the model estimates a common constant a for all cross-sections (common constant for countries). Practically, the common constant method implies that there are no differences between the estimated cross-sections and it is useful under the hypothesis that the data set is *a priori* homogeneous (e.g. we have a sample of only high-income countries, or EU-only countries, etc). However, this case is quite restrictive and cases of more interest involve the inclusion of fixed and random effects in the method of estimation.

The fixed effects method

In the fixed effects method the constant is treated as group (section)-specific. This means that the model allows for different constants for each group (section). So the model is similar to that of (18.1). The fixed effects estimator is also known as the least-squares dummy variables (LSDV) estimator because in order to allow for different constants for each group, it includes a dummy variable for each group. To understand this better consider the following model:

$$Y_{it} = a_i + \beta_1 X_{1it} + \beta_2 X_{2it} + \cdots + \beta_k X_{kit} + u_{it} \tag{18.3}$$

which can be rewritten in a matrix notation as:

$$Y = D\alpha + X\beta' + u \tag{18.4}$$

where we have:

$$Y = \begin{pmatrix} Y_1 \\ Y_2 \\ \vdots \\ Y_N \end{pmatrix}_{NT \times 1}, \quad D = \begin{pmatrix} i_T & 0 & \cdots & 0 \\ 0 & i_T & & 0 \\ \vdots & \vdots & & \vdots \\ 0 & 0 & & i_T \end{pmatrix}_{NT \times N},$$

$$X = \begin{pmatrix} x_{11} & x_{12} & \cdots & x_{1k} \\ x_{21} & x_{22} & & x_{2k} \\ \vdots & \vdots & & \vdots \\ x_{N1} & x_{N2} & & x_{Nk} \end{pmatrix}_{NT \times k} \tag{18.5}$$

and

$$\alpha = \begin{pmatrix} a_1 \\ a_2 \\ \vdots \\ a_N \end{pmatrix}_{N \times 1}, \quad \beta' = \begin{pmatrix} \beta_1 \\ \beta_2 \\ \vdots \\ \beta_k \end{pmatrix}_{k \times 1} \tag{18.6}$$

where the dummy variable is the one that allows us to take different group-specific estimates for each of the constants for every different section.

Before assessing the validity of the fixed effects method, we need to apply tests to check whether fixed effects (i.e. different constants for each group) should indeed be included in the model. To do this the standard F-test can be used to check fixed effects against the simple common constant OLS method. The null hypothesis is that all the constants are the same (homogeneity), and that therefore the common constant method is applicable:

$$H_0: \quad a_1 = a_2 = \cdots = a_N \tag{18.7}$$

The *F* statistic is:

$$F = \frac{\left(R_{FE}^2 - R_{CC}^2\right)/(N-1)}{\left(1 - R_{FE}^2\right)/(NT - N - k)} \sim F(N-1, NT - N - k) \qquad (18.8)$$

where R_{FE}^2 is the coefficient of determination of the fixed effects model and R_{CC}^2 is the coefficient of determination of the common constant model. If *F*-statistical is bigger than the *F*-critical then we reject the null.

The fixed effects model has the following properties:

(1) It essentially captures all effects which are specific to a particular individual and which do not vary over time. So if we had a panel of countries the fixed effects would take full account of things such as geographical factors, natural endowments and any other of the many basic factors which vary between countries but not over time. Of course this means that we can not add extra variables which also do not vary over time, such as country size for example, as this variable will be perfectly co-linear with the fixed effect.

(2) In some cases it may involve a very large number of dummy constants as some panels may have many thousand individual members, for example large survey panels. In this case the fixed effect model would use up *N* degrees of freedom. This is not in itself a problem as there will always be many more data points than *N*. However computationally it may be impossible to actually calculate many thousand different constants. In this case many researchers would transform the model by differencing all the variables or be taking deviations from the mean for each variable, which has the effect of removing the dummy/constants and avoids the problem of estimating so many parameters. However differencing the model, in particular may be undesirable as it may distort the parameter values and can certainly remove any long run effects.

It is also possible to extend the fixed effect model by including a set of time dummies as well. This is known as the two way fixed effect model and it has the further advantage of capturing any effects which vary over time but are common across the whole panel. For example if we were considering firms in the UK they might all be affected by a common exchange rate and the time dummies would capture this.

The fixed effect model is a very useful basic model to start from; however, traditionally, panel data estimation has been mainly applied to datasets where *N* is very large and in this case a simplifying assumption is sometimes made which gives rise to the random effects model.

The random effects method

An alternative method of estimating a model is the random effects model. The difference between the fixed effects and the random effects method is that the latter handles the constants for each section not as fixed, but as random parameters.

Hence the variability of the constant for each section comes from the fact that:

$$a_i = a + v_i \tag{18.9}$$

where v_i is a zero mean standard random variable.

The random effects model therefore takes the following form:

$$Y_{it} = (a + v_i) + \beta_1 X_{1it} + \beta_2 X_{2it} + \cdots + \beta_k X_{kit} + u_{it} \tag{18.10}$$

$$Y_{it} = a + \beta_1 X_{1it} + \beta_2 X_{2it} + \cdots + \beta_k X_{kit} + (v_i + u_{it}) \tag{18.11}$$

One obvious disadvantage of the random effects approach is that we need to make specific assumptions about the distribution of the random component. Also, if the unobserved group-specific effects are correlated with the explanatory variables, then the estimates will be biased and inconsistent. However, the random effects model has the following advantages:

1 It has fewer parameters to estimate compared to the fixed effects method.
2 It allows for additional explanatory variables that have equal value for all observations within a group (i.e. it allows us to use dummies).

Again in order to use random effects we have to be very careful to check whether there is any meaning to using them for our model compared to the fixed effects model. Comparing the two methods, one might expect that the use of the random effects estimator is superior compared to the fixed effects estimator, because the former is the GLS estimator and the latter is actually a limited case of the random effects model, as it corresponds to cases where the variation in individual effects is relatively large. But on the other hand the random effects model is built under the assumption that the fixed effects are uncorrelated with the explanatory variables, an assumption that in practice creates strict limitations in panel data treatment.

In general, the difference between the two possible ways of testing panel data models is this: the fixed effects model assumes that each country differs in its intercept term, whereas the random effects model assumes that each country differs in its error term. Usually, when the panel is balanced (i.e. contains all existing cross-sectional data), one might expect that the fixed effects model will work best. In other cases, where the sample contains limited observations of the existing cross-sectional units, the random effects model might be more appropriate.

The Hausman test

The Hausman test is formulated to assist in making a choice between the fixed effects and random effects approaches. Hausman (1978) adapted a test based on the idea that under the hypothesis of no correlation, both OLS and GLS are consistent but OLS is inefficient, while under the alternative OLS is consistent but GLS is not. More specifically, Hausman assumed that there are two estimators $\hat{\beta}_0$ and $\hat{\beta}_1$ of the parameter vector β and he added two hypothesis-testing procedures. Under H_0, both estimators are consistent but $\hat{\beta}_0$ is inefficient, and under H_1, $\hat{\beta}_0$ is consistent and efficient, but $\hat{\beta}_1$ is inconsistent.

For the panel data the appropriate choice between the fixed effects and the random effects methods investigates whether the regressors are correlated with the individual (unobserved in most cases) effect. The advantage of the use of the fixed effects estimator is that it is consistent even when the estimators are correlated with the individual effect. In other words, given a panel data model where fixed effects would be appropriate the Hausman test investigates whether random effects estimation could be almost as good. According to Ahn and Moon (2001), the Hausman statistic may be viewed as a distance measure between the fixed effects and the random effects estimators. Thus we actually test H_0, that random effects are consistent and efficient, versus H_1, that random effects are inconsistent (as the fixed effects will be always consistent). The Hausman test uses the following test statistic:

$$H = (\hat{\beta}^{FE} - \hat{\beta}^{RE})'[Var(\hat{\beta}^{FE}) - Var(\hat{\beta}^{RE})]^{-1}(\hat{\beta}^{FE} - \hat{\beta}^{RE}) \sim \chi^2(k) \qquad (18.12)$$

If the value of the statistic is large, then the difference between the estimates is significant, so we reject the null hypothesis that the random effects model is consistent and we use the fixed effects estimators. In contrast, a small value of the Hausman statistic implies that the random effects estimator is more appropriate.

Computer examples with panel data

Inserting panel data in EViews

One difficulty in working with panel data is that it is quite different from what we have seen so far using EViews. To use panel data requires specific data manipulation in order to insert the data in EViews in a way that will allow us to get results from the different panel methods of estimation we have seen above.

Consider the following case: assume we have a data set formed of three variables (Y, X and E), and that we have panel data for those three variables for eight different sections (i.e. $i = 1, 2, \ldots, 8$) and for 40 different time periods (i.e. $t = 1, 2, \ldots, 40$), for example yearly data from 1960 to 1999. We want to enter these data into EViews to estimate a panel regression of the form:

$$Y_{it} = a_i + \beta_1 X_{it} + \beta_2 E_{it} + u_{it} \qquad (18.13)$$

To do this we follow the following steps:

Step 1   *Create a workfile.* As a first step we need to create a new EViews workfile by going to **File/New/Workfile** and setting values for the start and end periods of our data set (in our case 1960 to 1999).

Step 2   *Create a pool object.* The next step is to create a pool object. To do this we go to **Object/New Object** and from the list of objects click on **Pool**, provide a name for our pool object in the top right-hand corner of the window **Name for the object** (let's say basic) and click <**OK**>. The pool object window will open with the first line reading:

Cross Section Identifiers: (Enter identifiers below this line)

In this window we enter names for our cross-section dimension. If, for example, we have different countries we can enter the names of the countries, specifying short names (up to three letters for each) to have an equal number of letters for the description of each. If we have different individuals, we could enter numbers instead of the names of the individuals and keep a log file in Excel to record numbers against names. Again in setting numbers as identifiers, an equal number of digits should be used for each section.

Step 3 *Enter the identifiers.* In our example we have eight different sections so we can enter the identifiers with either names or numbers as we choose. Because we do not have (in this specific example) any information about the nature of the cross-sectional dimension, we may simply enter numbers for identifiers as follows:

Cross Section Identifiers: (Enter identifiers below this line)
01
02
03
04
05
06
07
08

Step 4 *Generate a variable.* We can now proceed to generate variables that can be read in EViews as panel data variables. To do this click on the button **PoolGenr** in the Pool Object window. This opens the **generate series by equation** window, in which we specify our equation. Let's say that we want first to enter the Y variable; to do so we type:

    y_?=0

and click <**OK**>. This will create eight different variables in the Workfile window, namely the variables y_01, y_02, y_03,..., y_08. To explain this a bit more, it is the question mark symbol (?) that instructs EViews to substitute each of the cross-section identifiers at that point; and we have also used the underscore (_) symbol to make the names of the variables easy to see.

Step 5 *Copying and pasting data from Excel.* To do this we need to first explain how the data should look in Excel. If we open the eight variables (y_01, y_02, y_03,..., y_08) created from the previous step in a **group** (to do this select all eight variables and double click on them to go to **group**) we will have a matrix of 40 × 8 dimensions of zeros; 40 because of the number of years in our file and 8 because of the number of cross-sections. This matrix is viewed as what we call **'years down – sections across'**, so it looks like:

	section 1	section 2	section 3	$\cdots$	section 8
1960					
1961					
1962					
...					
...					
1999					

Therefore, it is very important that we have our data in the same format in Excel. If, for example, the downloaded data were in the form **'sections down – years across'**, we would have to transform them before entering them in EViews. (A simple way of doing this would be to select all the data, then copy the data (**Edit/Copy**) and finally paste the data into a different sheet using the **Paste Special** function (**Edit/Paste Special**) after clicking on the choice **transpose**, in order to reformat the data as we require.)

When we have the data in Excel as we want them (i.e. **'years down – sections across'**), then we simply copy all the data (the values of the data only, not the years or the variables/sections names) and then paste the data into the EViews group window with the zero values. In order to edit the group window and paste the data we need to activate the window by pressing the **edit +/−** button, and then go on **Edit/Paste**. After that we press the **edit +/−** button once more to deactivate the window.

The same procedure should be followed for the rest of the variables (X and E). The file panel_test.xls contains the raw data in Excel and the file panel_test.wf1 the same data transferred in EViews.

As a second example, consider the data in the file panel_eu.xls, that contains data for the 15 EU countries (so $N = 15$) for the years 1960–99 unbalanced (so max $T = 40$) for three variables, GDP growth, gross fixed capital formation as % of GDP and FDI inflows as % of GDP. The reader should try as an exercise to transfer the data from Excel to EViews. (The result is in a file labelled panel_test.wf1.) We have used the following cross-section identifiers:

BEL   for Belgium
DEN   for Denmark
DEU   for Germany
ELL   for Greece
ESP   for Spain
FRA   for France
IRE   for Ireland
ITA   for Italy
LUX   for Luxembourg
NET   for Netherlands
OST   for Austria
POR   for Portugal
RFI   for Republic of Finland
SWE   for Sweden
UKA   for United Kingdom

Note that only the three letters should be written as names for the cross-section identifiers in the pool object. We have also used the following variable names GDPGR95_?, FDITOGDP_? and GFCFTOGDP_? (see file panel_eu.wf1).

Table 18.1   Common constant

Dependent Variable: Y_?
Method: Pooled Least Squares
Date: 04/03/04 Time: 22:22
Sample: 1960 1999
Included observations: 40
Number of cross-sections used: 8
Total panel (balanced) observations: 320

Variable	Coefficient	Std. Error	t-Statistic	Prob.
C	50.27199	2.040134	24.64151	0.0000
X_?	0.496646	0.018320	27.10964	0.0000
E_?	1.940393	0.153886	12.60930	0.0000
R-squared	0.739693	Mean dependent var		105.2594
Adjusted R-squared	0.738051	S.D. dependent var		5.254932
S.E. of regression	2.689525	Sum squared resid		2293.034
Log likelihood	−769.1500	F-statistic		450.3965
Durbin–Watson stat	1.061920	Prob(F-statistic)		0.000000

Table 18.2   Fixed effects

Dependent Variable: Y_?
Method: Pooled Least Squares
Date: 04/03/04 Time: 22:23
Sample: 1960 1999
Included observations: 40
Number of cross-sections used: 8
Total panel (balanced) observations: 320

Variable	Coefficient	Std. Error	t-Statistic	Prob.
X_?	0.473709	0.021889	21.64181	0.0000
E_?	1.845824	0.157163	11.74465	0.0000
Fixed Effects				
01–C	53.24391			
02–C	53.35922			
03–C	52.37416			
04–C	52.89543			
05–C	52.64917			
06–C	53.34308			
07–C	52.76667			
08–C	51.85719			
R-squared	0.746742	Mean dependent var		105.2594
Adjusted R-squared	0.739389	S.D. dependent var		5.254932
S.E. of regression	2.682644	Sum squared resid		2230.940
Log likelihood	−764.7575	F-statistic		914.0485
Durbin–Watson stat	1.030970	Prob(F-statistic)		0.000000

Estimating a panel data regression

After transferring the data into EViews, panel data estimation is done by the use of the **pool object**. Always double click on **pool object** (labelled as **basic**) and work from there. Let us assume that we have the panel_test file open and that we want to estimate the following model:

$$Y_{it} = a_i + \beta_1 X_{it} + \beta_2 E_{it} + u_{it} \qquad (18.14)$$

To do so from the **basic (pool object)** we should first click on the **Estimate** button. The **Pooled Estimation** window opens which asks us to provide names for the dependent variable and the regressors. For the model above we need to insert as **dependent variable** Y_? (the ? indicates that the computer will include the data for all cross-sections from 1 to 8) and as regressors in the field that says **common coefficients** we include X_? and E_?. We also have the option to change the sample (by typing different

Table 18.3 Random effects

Dependent Variable: Y_?
Method: GLS (Variance Components)
Date: 04/03/04 Time: 22:24
Sample: 1960 1999
Included observations: 40
Number of cross-sections used: 8
Total panel (balanced) observations: 320

Variable	Coefficient	Std. Error	t-Statistic	Prob.
C	47.30772	1.340279	35.29692	0.0000
X_?	0.523554	0.012030	43.52132	0.0000
E_?	2.220745	0.149031	14.90118	0.0000

Random Effects

01–C	0.258081
02–C	−2.415602
03–C	0.848119
04–C	−1.775884
05–C	1.190163
06–C	−1.573142
07–C	0.472518
08–C	2.995747

GLS Transformed Regression

R-squared	0.716534	Mean dependent var	105.2594
Adjusted R-squared	0.714746	S.D. dependent var	5.254932
S.E. of regression	2.806617	Sum squared resid	2497.041
Durbin–Watson stat	1.140686		

Unweighted Statistics including Random Effects

R-squared	0.594095	Mean dependent var	105.2594
Adjusted R-squared	0.591534	S.D. dependent var	5.254932
S.E. of regression	3.358497	Sum squared resid	3575.601
Durbin–Watson stat	0.796605		

starting and ending periods in the corresponding box), to include cross-section-specific coefficients for some of the explanatory variables (to induce heterogeneity – we will examine this later), and to choose a number of different estimation techniques including the common constant, fixed effects and random effects methods that we have examined before. By clicking next to common constant we get the results presented in Table 18.1.

The interpretation of the results is as standard. If we want to take the fixed effects estimator we should click on estimate again, leave the equation specification as it is and click on the button next to fixed effects instead of common constant. The results are given in Table 18.2. Similarly we can obtain results for random effects, and these are given in Table 18.3.

We leave it to the reader to estimate a model (using the data in the panel_eu.wf1 file) that examines the effects of gross fixed capital formation and FDI inflows to gdp growth for the 15 EU countries.

19 Dynamic Heterogeneous Panels

A dynamic model is characterized by the presence of a lagged dependent variable among the regressors. The basic model is:

$$Y_{i,t} = a_i + \beta_i' X_{i,t} + \gamma Y_{i,t-1} + u_{i,t} \qquad (19.1)$$

where γ is a scalar, and β and $X_{i,t}$ are each $k \times 1$. Dynamic models are very important, especially in economics, because many economic relationships are dynamic in nature and should be modelled as such. The time dimension of panel data (unlike cross-sectional studies) enables us to capture the dynamics of adjustment.

In this simple dynamic model the only heterogeneity comes from the individual intercepts a_i which are allowed to vary among different sections. However, sometimes in economics it is necessary to induce more heterogeneity in order to find specific coefficients for different groups for some cases. Later we will consider the mean group and pooled mean group estimators that allow for larger heterogeneity in panel data models.

The problem with the dynamic panels is that the traditional OLS estimators are biased and, therefore, different methods of estimation need to be introduced. These issues are examined analytically in the next sections of this chapter.

Bias in dynamic panels

Bias in the simple OLS estimator

The simple OLS estimator for simple static panels is consistent as n or $T \to \infty$ only when all explanatory variables are exogenous and are uncorrelated with the individual specific effects. However, due to the fact that the OLS estimator ignores the error-component structure of the model, it is not efficient. Also, things are quite different when the model includes a lagged dependent variable.

Consider the basic model presented in equation (19.1) which can be rewritten (omitting the $X_{i,t}$ regressors for simplicity) as:

$$Y_{i,t} = a_i + \gamma Y_{i,t-1} + u_{i,t} \qquad (19.2)$$

It is easy to show that the OLS estimator for this model will be seriously biased due to correlation of the lagged dependent variable with the individual specific effects (a_i) either random or fixed. Since $Y_{i,t}$ is a function of a_i, then $Y_{i,t-1}$ is a function of a_i as well. Therefore $Y_{i,t-1}$, which is a regressor in the model, is correlated with the error term and this obviously causes OLS estimators to be biased and inconsistent even if the error terms are not serially correlated. (The proof of this is quite difficult and requires lots of calculations using matrix algebra, beyond the scope of this text. Readers who would like a better insight into dynamic panels should read Baltagi (1995) chapter 8, or Hsiao (1986) chapter 6.)

Bias in the fixed effects model

The bias and inconsistency of the OLS estimator stems from correlation of the lagged dependent variable with the individual specific effects. It might therefore be thought that the within-transformation of the fixed effects model, given by:

$$Y_{i,t} - \bar{Y}_i = \gamma(Y_{i,t-1} - \bar{Y}_{i,t-1}) + (u_{i,t} - \bar{u}_i) \tag{19.3}$$

would eliminate the problem because now the individual effects (a_i) are cancelled out. However, the problem is not solved that easily.

Consider again the model in equation (19.1) which can be rewritten as:

$$Y_{i,t} = \mu_i + \gamma Y_{i,t-1} + u_{i,t} \tag{19.4}$$

where μ_i are now fixed effects. Let $\bar{Y}_i = 1/T \sum_{t=1}^{T} Y_{i,t}$; $\bar{Y}_{i,t-1} = 1/T \sum_{t=1}^{T-1} Y_{i,t-1}$ and $\bar{u}_i = 1/T \sum_{t=1}^{T} u_{i,t}$. It can be shown again that the fixed estimator will be biased for small 'fixed' T. The bias this time is caused by having to eliminate the unknown individual effects (constants) from each observation, which creates a bias $1/T$ between the explanatory variables in the 'within' transformed model and the residuals. Because $Y_{i,t}$ is correlated with $\bar{u}_i$ by construction (consider that $\bar{u}_i$ is an average containing $u_{i,t-1}$, which is obviously correlated with $Y_{i,t-1}$), $(Y_{i,t-1} - \bar{Y}_{i,t-1})$ will be correlated with $(u_{i,t} - \bar{u}_i)$ even if u_{it} are not serially correlated.

Bias in the random effects model

The problem with the generalized least-squares (GLS) method of estimation of the random effects model is similar to that of the least-squares dummy variables (LSDV) estimation of the fixed effects model. In order to apply GLS, we have to quasi-demean the data. This demeaning unavoidably causes the quasi-demeaned dependent variable to be correlated with the quasi-demeaned residuals, and therefore the GLS estimator will also be biased and inconsistent.

Solutions to the bias problem (due to the dynamic nature of the panel)

There are two proposed solutions to the bias problem presented above. One is to *introduce exogenous variables* in the model. If exogenous variables are added (to a first-order autoregressive process), the bias in the OLS estimator is reduced in magnitude but remains positive. The coefficients on the exogenous variables are biased towards zero. However, the LSDV estimator, for small T, remains biased even with added exogenous variables. A second way is to use the *instrumental variable methods* proposed by Anderson and Hsiao (1981 and 1982) and Arellano and Bond (1991). The instrumental variable methods are quite complicated and beyond the scope of this text, but we mention them here since they are widely used in panels with small T dimensions. These instrumental variable estimators are sometime referred to as GMM estimators.

Bias of heterogeneous slope parameters

All Panel data models make the basic assumption that at least some of the parameters are the same across the panel; this is sometimes refered to as the pooling assumption. Serious complications can arise if this assumption is not true and we can again get bias arising in both static and dynamic panels under certain circumstances. When the pooling assumation does not hold we refer to a panel as a heterogeneous panel, this simply means that some of the parameters actually vary across the panel. If we impose a constant parameter assumption incorrectly then serious problems may arise. Consider the following heterogeneous static model:

$$Y_{i,t} = \mu_i + \beta_i' X_i + u_{i,t} \tag{19.5}$$

where heterogeneity is introduced, for example, because we consider as cross-sections a large number of countries that are in differing stages of economic development, or have different institutions, customs etc. For simplicity assume that we have only one explanatory variable, X_{it}, and also suppose that the now heterogeneous β_i coefficients are:

$$\beta_i = \beta + v_i \tag{19.6}$$

In this case, Pesaran and Smith (1995) prove that both the Fixed Effects (FE) and the Random Effects (RE) estimators may be inconsistent.

Consider now the dynamic autoregressive distributed lag (ARDL) model:

$$Y_{i,t} = a_i + \gamma_i Y_{i,t-1} + \beta_i X_{it} + e_{i,t} \tag{19.7}$$

where all coefficients are allowed to vary across cross-sectional units. If we want to consider long-run solutions we have that:

$$\theta_i = \frac{\beta_i}{1 - \gamma_i} \tag{19.8}$$

is the long-run coefficient of X_{it} for the *i*th cross-sectional unit. Using this we can rewrite equation (19.7) as:

$$\Delta Y_{i,t} = a_i - (1 - \gamma_i)(Y_{i,t-1} - \theta_i X_{it}) + e_{i,t} \tag{19.9}$$

or substituting $(1 - \gamma_i)$ with ϕ_i:

$$\Delta Y_{i,t} = a_i - \phi_i(Y_{i,t-1} - \theta_i X_{it}) + e_{i,t} \tag{19.10}$$

Let's consider now a random coefficients model, which will mean that:

$$\phi_i = \phi + v_i \tag{19.11}$$

$$\theta_i = \theta + w_i \tag{19.12}$$

where v_i and w_i are two iid error terms. From this we have that the original coefficients in (19.7) are:

$$\beta_i = \theta_i \phi_i = \theta\phi + \phi w_i + \theta v_i + w_i v_i \qquad (19.13)$$

Having that $\gamma = 1 - \phi$, and that $\beta = \theta\phi$, and substituting these two in (19.7) we get:

$$Y_{i,t} = a_i + \gamma_i Y_{i,t-1} + \beta_i X_{i,t} + v_{i,t} \qquad (19.14)$$

$$v_{i,t} = e_{i,t} - v_i Y_{i,t-1} + (\phi w_i + \theta v_i + w_i v_i) X_{i,t} \qquad (19.15)$$

From this analysis, it is clear that $v_{i,t}$ and $Y_{i,t-1}$ are correlated and therefore both the FE and the RE estimators are now inconsistent. This is an expected result given that we know that the FE and RE estimators are inconsistent for small T and infinite N. The big problem, here, is that both estimators will be inconsistent even for $T \to \infty$ and $N \to \infty$.

Solutions to heterogeneity bias: alternative methods of estimation

Pesaran, Shin and Smith (1999) suggest two different estimators in order to resolve the bias due to heterogeneous slopes in dynamic panels. These are the mean group (MG) estimator and the pooled mean group (PMG) estimator. Both methods are presented briefly below.

The mean group estimator

The MG estimator derives the long-run parameters for the panel from an average of the long-run parameters from ARDL models for individual countries. For example, if the ARDL is the following

$$Y_{i,t} = a_i + \gamma_i Y_{i,t-1} + \beta_i X_{it} + e_{i,t} \qquad (19.16)$$

for country i, where $i = 1, 2, \ldots, N$, then the long-run parameter θ_i for country i is:

$$\theta_i = \frac{\beta_i}{1 - \gamma_i} \qquad (19.17)$$

and the MG estimators for the whole panel will be given by:

$$\hat{\theta} = \frac{1}{N} \sum_{i=1}^{N} \theta_i \qquad (19.18)$$

$$\hat{a} = \frac{1}{N} \sum_{i=1}^{N} a_i \qquad (19.19)$$

It can be shown that MG estimation with sufficiently high lag orders yields super-consistent estimators of the long-run parameters even when the regressors are $I(1)$ (see Pesaran, Shin and Smith, 1999). The MG estimators are consistent and have asymptotic normal distributions for N and T sufficiently large. However, when T is small, the MG estimator of the dynamic panel data model is biased and can lead to misleading results, and therefore should be used cautiously.

The pooled mean group (PMG) estimator

Pesaran and Smith (1995) show that, unlike in static models, pooled dynamic heterogeneous models generate estimates that are inconsistent even in large samples. (The problem cannot be solved by extending the sample, as it flows from heterogeneity: extending the dimension of the cross-section increases the problem. Baltagi and Griffin (1997) argue that the efficiency gains of pooling the data outweigh the losses from the bias induced by heterogeneity. They support this argument in two ways. First, they informally assess the plausibility of the estimates they obtain for a model of gasoline demand using different methods. This is hard to evaluate as it relies upon a judgement about what is 'plausible'. Monte Carlo simulations would make the comparison clearer. Second, they compare forecast performance. However, this is a weak test to apply to the averaging technique, which is designed only to estimate long-run parameters and not the short-run dynamics. Baltagi and Griffin do not consider the next method to be discussed, (the PMG.) In the type of data set we are considering T is sufficiently large to allow individual country estimation. Nevertheless, we may still be able to exploit the cross-section dimension of the data to some extent. Pesaran and Smith (1995) observe that while it is implausible that the dynamic specification is common to all countries, it is at least conceivable that the long-run parameters of the model may be common. They propose estimation by either averaging the individual country estimates, or by pooling the long-run parameters, if the data allows, and estimating the model as a system. Pesaran, Shin and Smith (1999) (henceforth PSS) refer to this as the pooled mean group estimator, or PMG. It combines the efficiency of pooled estimation while avoiding the inconsistency problem flowing from pooling heterogeneous dynamic relationships.

The PMG method of estimation occupies an intermediate position between the MG method, in which both the slopes and the intercepts are allowed to differ across countries, and the classical fixed effects method in which the slopes are fixed and the intercepts are allowed to vary. In PMG estimation, only the long-run coefficients are constrained to be the same across countries, while the short-run coefficients are allowed to vary.

Setting this out more precisely, the unrestricted specification for the ARDL system of equations for $t = 1, 2, \ldots, T$ time periods and $i = 1, 2, \ldots, N$ countries for the dependent variable Y is:

$$Y_{it} = \sum_{j=1}^{p} \lambda_{ij} Y_{i,t-j} + \sum_{j=1}^{q} \delta'_{ij} X_{i,t-j} + \mu_i + \varepsilon_{it} \tag{19.20}$$

where $X_{i,t-j}$ is the $(k \times 1)$ vector of explanatory variables for group i and μ_i represents the fixed effects. In principle the panel can be unbalanced and p and q may vary across countries. This model can be reparametrized as a VECM system:

$$\Delta Y_{it} = \theta_i(Y_{i,t-1} - \beta_i' X_{i,t-1}) + \sum_{j=1}^{p-1} \gamma_{ij} \Delta Y_{i,t-j}$$

$$+ \sum_{j=1}^{q-1} \gamma_{ij}' \Delta X_{i,t-j} + \mu_i + \varepsilon_{it} \qquad (19.21)$$

where the β_i are the long-run parameters and θ_i are the equilibrium (or error)-correction parameters. The pooled mean group restriction is that the elements of β are common across countries:

$$\Delta y_{it} = \theta_i(y_{i,t-1} - \beta' x_{i,t-1}) + \sum_{j=1}^{p-1} \gamma_{ij} \Delta y_{i,t-j}$$

$$+ \sum_{j=1}^{q-1} \gamma_{ij}' \Delta x_{i,t-j} + \mu_i + \varepsilon_{i,t} \qquad (19.22)$$

Estimation could proceed by OLS, imposing and testing the cross-country restrictions on β. However, this would be inefficient as it ignores the contemporaneous residual covariance. A natural estimator is Zellner's SUR method, which is a form of feasible GLS. However, SUR estimation is only possible if N is smaller than T. Thus PSS suggest a maximum likelihood estimator. All the dynamics and the ECM terms are free to vary. Again it is proved by PSS that under some regularity assumptions, the parameter estimates of this model are consistent and asymptotically normal for both stationary and non-stationary I(1) regressors. Both MG and PMG estimations require selecting the appropriate lag length for the individual country equations. This selection was made using the Schwarz Bayesian criterion.

There are also issues of inference. PSS argue that in panels, omitted group-specific factors or measurement errors are likely to severely bias the country estimates. It is a commonplace in empirical panels to report a failure of the 'poolability' tests based on the group parameter restrictions. (For example, Baltagi and Griffin (1997, p. 308) state that although the poolability test is massively failed ($F(102,396) = 10.99$; critical value about 1.3), 'like most researchers we proceed to estimate pooled models'.) So PSS propose a Hausman test. This is based on the result that an estimate of the long-run parameters in the model can be derived from the average (mean group) of the country regressions. This is consistent even under heterogeneity. However, if the parameters are in fact homogeneous, the PMG estimates are more efficient. Thus we can form the test statistic:

$$H = \hat{q}'[var(\hat{q})]^{-1}\hat{q} \sim \chi_k^2$$

where $\hat{q}$ is a $(k \times 1)$ vector of the difference between the mean group and PMG estimates and $var(\hat{q})$ is the corresponding covariance matrix. Under the null that the two estimators are consistent but one is efficient, $var(\hat{q})$ is easily calculated as the difference between the covariance matrices for the two underlying parameter vectors. If the poolability assumption is invalid, then the PMG estimates are no longer consistent and we fail the test.

Application: the effects of uncertainty in economic growth and investments

Asteriou and Price (2000) examine the interactions between uncertainty, investment and economic growth, using panel data for a sample of 59 industrial and developing countries between 1966 and 1992 to estimate the reduced form equation:

$$\Delta \hat{y}_{i,t} = a_{0,i} + a_{1,i} h_{i,t} + \alpha_i \Delta \hat{k}_{i,t} + \epsilon_{i,t} \tag{19.23}$$

in order to explore the possible effects of uncertainty on economic growth and investments. The data used in their analysis are annual observations for GDP per capita (worker) (y_{it}) and capital per capita (k_{it}) taken from the Penn World Tables. Prior to estimation of the main model, they estimate GARCH(1,1) models for GDP per capita growth in order to obtain the variance series, used as uncertainty proxies ($h_{i,t}$) in the subsequent analysis.

Evidence from traditional panel data estimation

Asteriou and Price begin by estimating their main model using traditional panel data techniques: i.e. fixed effects and random effects. Acknowledging that these methods of estimation are inappropriate, they report them partly to illustrate how misleading they may be. The results are presented in Table 19.1, which reports estimates of equation (19.23) for three alternative cases: first, assuming that the constant in the model is common and homogeneous for all countries, which is a rather restrictive assumption; second, assuming fixed effects; and third, assuming the existence of random effects (the country-specific constants have been omitted from Table 19.1). In all cases (see columns (a), (c) and (d) of Table 19.1), the reported coefficients are similar and significant. Where capital growth is included, the uncertainty proxy enters the equation negatively, so that higher levels of uncertainty are associated with lower levels of growth. Capital growth has the expected positive sign. However, when the growth rate of capital per capita term is excluded from the equation, the uncertainty proxy coefficients obtained are positive and highly significant (see columns (b), (d) and (f) of Table 19.1). This implies investment is increasing in uncertainty. But regressions of the growth rate of capital on uncertainty (not reported) reveal that uncertainty has a significant negative impact. These results are therefore hard to interpret.

Mean group and pooled mean group estimates

Next, Asteriou and Price (2000) estimate and report results of the MG and PMG methodology. Table 19.2 shows the effects of uncertainty on GDP per capita growth in three cases: pooling only the effect of uncertainty; pooling only capital; and pooling

Table 19.1 Results from traditional panel data estimation

Variable	Common constant		Fixed effects		Random effects	
	(a)	(b)	(c)	(d)	(e)	(f)
constant	0.01	0.01			0.01	0.02
	(12.6)	(5.13)			(8.5)	(9.7)
$h_{i,t}$	−0.10	0.63	−0.06	0.92	−0.08	0.48
	(−5.7)	(13.5)	(−2.6)	(13.5)	(−4.1)	(14.0)
$\Delta \hat{k}_{i,t}$	0.12		0.10		0.11	
	(7.2)		(6.4)		(6.7)	
R^2	0.05	0.08	0.14	0.11	0.13	0.05

Note: *t* statistics in parentheses in this and subsequent tables.

Table 19.2 MG and PMG estimates: dep. var. output growth

Variable	PMG estimates		MG estimates		h-test
	coef.	t-ratio	coef.	t-ratio	
A. common parameter on h					
Common long-run coefficients					
h	−0.061	−1.891	−26.618	−1.967	3.85[0.05]
Unrestricted long-run coefficients					
Δk	0.086	1.323	−0.214	−0.487	—
Error-correction coefficients					
ϕ	−0.952	−32.988	−0.926	−22.300	—
B. common parameter on Δk					
Common long-run coefficients					
Δk	0.061	3.324	−0.214	−0.487	1.19[0.27]
Unrestricted long-run coefficients					
h	−10.325	−1.762	−26.618	−1.967	—
Error-correction coefficients					
ϕ	−0.929	−25.798	−0.926	−22.300	—
C. common parameter on Δk **and** h					
Common long-run coefficients					
Δk	0.160	7.949	−0.214	−0.487	2.21[0.14]
h	−0.027	−1.019	−26.618	−1.967	3.86[0.05]
Joint Hausman test: 3.89[0.14]					
Error-correction coefficients					
ϕ	−0.945	−35.920	−0.926	−22.300	—

Table 19.3 MG and PMG estimates: dep. var. capital growth

Variable	PMG estimates		MG estimates		h-test
	coef.	t-ratio	coef.	t-ratio	
h	−5.956	−4.310	−316.0	−1.003	0.97[0.33]
Error-correction coefficients					
ϕ	−0.345	−5.972	−0.414	−7.409	—

both uncertainty and capital. The results show that the Hausman test rejects pooling of the long-run variance term, but accepts pooling of the capital stock effect. The joint test in column (c) accepts, but the individual test rejects. Thus the key results are in column (b). (The inefficient MG results are given for comparison; the Δk term is incorrectly signed but insignificant.) The PMG coefficient on Δk is on the small side but correctly signed and significant. (As usual in growth studies, one has a potential difficulty interpreting these results, as the equation is specified in first differences. These are marginal effects we are observing.) The impact of uncertainty is apparently large, but the variance terms are small. The (average) error-correction coefficients reported show adjustment is rapid, 93% occurring within one year. Compared to the traditional estimates, the variance effect is larger by two orders of magnitude.

Table 19.2 shows the effect of uncertainty over and above that working through investment, while Table 19.3 reports the direct impact on investment. The PMG specification is easily accepted by the Hausman test. As discussed above, the impact of uncertainty is ambiguous, but we expect a negative coefficient; this is the case. Thus the conclusion from this application is that certainly MG and PMG estimators are appropriate for a dynamic heterogeneous panel of this nature, while the results from the estimation suggest that uncertainty (as proxied by the variance series of GARCH(1,1) models of the GDP per capita) negatively affects both growth rates and investments.

20 Non-Stationary Panels

Panel data studies, until very recently, have ignored the crucial stationarity (ADF and Phillips–Perron) and cointegration (Engle–Granger and Johansen) tests. However, with the growing involvement of macroeconomic applications in the panel data tradition, where a large sample of countries constitute the cross-sectional dimension providing data over lengthy time series, the issues of stationarity and cointegration have emerged in panel data as well. This was mainly due to the fact that macro panels had both large N and T compared to micro panels with large N but small T. Consider, for example, the Penn World Tables data (available from the NBER at http://www.nber.org) where data are available for a large set of countries and at least some of the variables (GDP for example) are expected to have unit roots. This has brought a whole new set of problems in panel data analysis that were previously ignored.

Although the relative literature on time-series studies successfully answers stationarity issues, the adoption and adjustment of similar tests on panel data is yet in progress, mainly due to the complexity of considering relatively large T and N samples in the later studies. We can summarize the major differences between time-series and panel unit-root tests as follows:

1 Panel data allows us to test the various approaches with different degrees of heterogeneity between individuals.

2 In the panel data analysis, so far, one cannot be sure as to the validity of rejecting a unit root.

3 The power of panel unit-root tests increases with an increase in N. This power increase is much more robust than in the size of the one observed in the standard low-power DF and ADF tests applied for small samples.

4 The additional cross-sectional components incorporated in panel data models provide better properties of panel unit-root tests, compared with the low-power standard ADF for time-series samples.

Panel unit-root tests

Both DF and ADF unit-root tests are extended to panel data estimations, to consider cases that possibly exhibit the presence of unit roots. Most of the panel unit-root tests are based on an extension of the ADF test by incorporating it as a component in regression equations. However, when dealing with panel data, the estimation procedure is more complex than that used in time series. The crucial factor in panel data estimation appears to be the degree of heterogeneity. In particular it is important to realize that all the individuals in a panel may not have the same property, that is to say they may not all be stationary or non-stationary (or cointegrated or not cointegrated). So if we carry out a panel unit root test where some of the panel have a unit root and some do not the situation becomes quite complex.

A wide variety of procedures have been developed with an emphasis on the attempt to combine information from the time series dimension with that obtained from the cross-sectional dimension, hoping that in taking into account the cross-sectional dimension the inference about the existence of unit roots will be more precise and straightforward.

However, a variety of issues arise from this: one is that some of the tests proposed require balanced panels (not missing any data for either i or t), whereas others allow for unbalanced panel setting. A second issue has to do with the formulation of the null hypothesis; one may form the null as a generalization of the standard DF test (i.e. that all series in the panel are assumed to be non-stationary) and reject the null if some of the series in the panel appear to be stationary, while on the other hand one can formulate the null hypothesis in exactly the opposite way, presuming that all the series in the panel are stationary processes, and rejecting it when there is sufficient evidence of non-stationarity. In both cases, the consideration of a set of time series leads to a 'box-score' concept, wherein one makes an inference on the set of the series depending on the predominating evidence.

Another important theoretical consideration in the development of the panel unit-roots literature has to do with the asymptotic behaviour of a panel's N and T dimensions. Various assumptions can be made regarding the rates at which these parameters tend to infinity. One may fix, for example, N and let T go to infinity and after that let N tend to infinity. Alternatively, one may allow the two indices to tend to infinity at a controlled rate, i.e. as $T = T(N)$, while a third possibility is to allow both N and T to tend to infinity simultaneously (see Phillips and Moon, 2000). All these are quite complicated issues and beyond the scope of this text. In the next section our aim is to present as simply as possible the major tests for unit roots and cointegration in panels and provide guidelines on how to apply these tests in applied econometric work.

The Levin and Lin (LL) test

One of the first panel unit-root tests was that developed by Levin and Lin (1992). (The test was originally presented in a working paper by Levin and Lin in 1992. Their work was finally published in 2002 with Chu as co-author (see Levin, Lin and Chu, 2002) but the test is still abbreviated as LL by the initials of the first two authors.) Levin and Lin adopted a test that can actually be seen as an extension of the DF test. Their model takes the following form:

$$\Delta Y_{i,t} = a_i + \rho Y_{i,t-1} + \sum_{k=1}^{n} \phi_k \Delta Y_{i,t-k} + \delta_i t + \theta_t + u_{it} \qquad (20.1)$$

This model allows for two-way fixed effects, one coming from the a_i and the second from the θ_t. So we have both unit-specific fixed effects and unit-specific time trends. The unit-specific fixed effects are a very important component because they allow for heterogeneity since the coefficient of the lagged Y_i is restricted to be homogeneous across all units of the panel.

The null hypothesis of this test is that:

$$H_0: \quad \rho = 0$$
$$H_0: \quad \rho < 0$$

Like most of the unit root tests in the literature, the LL test also assumes that the individual processes are cross-sectionally independent. Under this assumption, the test derives conditions for which the pooled OLS estimator of ρ will follow a standard normal distribution under the null hypothesis.

Thus, the LL test may be viewed as a pooled DF or ADF test, potentially with different lag lengths across the different sections in the panel.

The Im, Pesaran and Shin (IPS) test

The major drawback of the LL test is that it restricts ρ to be homogeneous across all i. Im, Pesaran and Shin (1997) extended the LL test allowing heterogeneity on the coefficient of the $Y_{i,t-1}$ variable and proposing as a basic testing procedure one based on the average of the individual unit-root test statistics.

The IPS test provides separate estimations for each i section, allowing different specifications of the parametric values, the residual variance and the lag lengths. Their model is given by:

$$\Delta Y_{i,t} = a_i + \rho_i Y_{i,t-1} + \sum_{k=1}^{n} \phi_k \Delta Y_{i,t-k} + \delta_i t + u_{it} \tag{20.2}$$

while now the null and the alternative hypotheses are formulated as:

$$H_0: \quad \rho_i = 0 \text{ for all } i$$

$$H_0: \quad \rho < 0 \text{ for at least one } i$$

Thus, the null of this test is that all series are non-stationary processes under the alternative that a fraction of the series in the panel are assumed to be stationary. This is in sharp contrast with the LL test, which presumes that all series are stationary under the alternative hypothesis.

Im, Pesaran and Shin (1997) formulated their model under the restrictive assumption that T should be the same for all cross-sections, requiring a balanced panel to compute the $\bar{t}$ test statistic. Their $\bar{t}$ statistic is nothing else than the average of the individual ADF t-statistics for testing that $\rho_i = 0$ for all i (denoted by t_{ρ_i}):

$$\bar{t} = \frac{1}{N} \sum_{i=1}^{N} t_{\rho_i} \tag{20.3}$$

Im, Pesaran and Shin (1997) also showed that under specific assumptions t_{ρ_i} converges to a statistic denoted as t_{iT} which they assume that is iid and that also has finite mean and variance. They then computed values for the mean ($E[t_{iT}|\rho_i = 1]$) and for the variance ($Var[t_{iT}|\rho_i = 1]$) of the t_{iT} statistic for different values of N and lags included in the augmentation term of equation (20.1). Based on those values, they then constructed the IPS statistic for testing for unit roots in panels given by:

$$t_{IPS} = \frac{\sqrt{N} \left(\bar{t} - 1/N \sum_{i=1}^{N} E[t_{iT}|\rho_i = 0] \right)}{\sqrt{Var[t_{iT}|\rho_i = 0]}} \tag{20.4}$$

which they have proved follows the standard normal distribution as $T \to \infty$ followed by $N \to \infty$ sequentially. The values of $E[t_{iT}|\rho_i = 0]$ and $Var[t_{iT}|\rho_i = 0]$ are given in their paper. Finally, they also suggested a group mean Lagrange multiplier test for testing for panel unit roots. Performing Monte Carlo simulations they proved that both their LM and t statistics have better finite sample properties that the LL test.

The Maddala and Wu (MW) test

Maddala and Wu (1999) attempted to improve to some degree the drawbacks of all previous tests by proposing a model that could also be estimated with unbalanced panels. Basically, Maddala and Wu are in line with the assumption that a heterogeneous alternative is preferable, but they disagree with the use of the average ADF statistics by arguing that it is not the most effective way of evaluating stationarity. Assuming that there are N unit-root tests, the MW test takes the following form:

$$\Pi = -2 \sum_{i=1}^{N} \ln \pi_i \qquad (20.5)$$

where π_i is the probability limit values from regular DF (or ADF) unit-root tests for each cross-section i. Because $-2 \ln \pi_i$ has a χ^2 distribution with 2 degrees of freedom, the Π statistic will follow a χ^2 distribution with $2N$ degrees of freedom as $T_i \to \infty$ for finite N. In order to consider the dependence between cross-sections, Maddala and Wu propose obtaining the π_i-values by using bootstrap procedures by arguing that correlations between groups can induce significant size distortions for the tests. (The bootstrapping method of estimation is quite complicated and therefore not presented in this text. For this reason, and only for illustrative purposes in the examples given in the next section for the MW test, we use π values that are given by the standard OLS method of the DF (or ADF) tests.)

Computer examples of panel unit-root tests

Consider the data in the panel_unit_root.wf1 file for 14 EU countries (Luxembourg is excluded due to limited data availability) and for the years 1970–99. We have two variables, namely GDP per capita (GDPPC) and FDI inflows. First we want to calculate the $\bar{t}$ statistic from the IPS (1997) paper. In order to do that we estimated 14 different regression equations of the standard ADF unit-root test using first only a constant and then a constant and a trend in the deterministic components. From those tests we extracted the ADF test statistics for each section which we report in Table 20.1. The $\bar{t}$ statistic is simply the average from the individual ADF statistics so we can put the data in Excel and calculate the average of the $N = 14$ different ADF statistics. The $\bar{t}$ statistic is also reported in Table 20.1. Finally we calculated the t_{IPS} statistic given by equation (20.4). The commands for these calculations in Excel are quite easy and are indicated for the first two cases in Table 20.1 (where $E[t_{iT}|\rho_i = 0] = -1.968$ and $Var[t_{iT}|\rho_i = 0] = 0.913$ are taken by the IPS paper for $N = 25$ and number of lags equal to 4. We have used the same number of lags (i.e. 4) for all ADF models for simplicity. If the lag length is different for each case the formula is slightly more complicated because the mean of the $E[t_{iT}|\rho_i = 0] = -1.968$ and the $Var[t_{iT}|\rho_i = 0] = 0.913$ need

Table 20.1   IPS panel unit-root tests

	Intercept		Intercept and trend	
	FDIINFL	GDPPC	FDIINFL	GDPPC
Belgium	2.141	0.963	1.304	−1.797
Denmark	5.873	1.872	3.381	−1.981
Germany	2.852	0.603	2.561	−2.900
Greece	−2.008	2.466	−2.768	−0.156
Spain	−1.099	1.169	−2.958	−1.917
France	1.991	−0.189	0.558	−4.038
Ireland	2.718	2.726	2.465	1.357
Italy	−0.478	0.620	−2.392	−2.211
Netherlands	2.104	1.804	1.271	−0.990
Austria	−0.140	1.061	−0.577	−2.886
Portugal	−1.257	1.810	−2.250	−0.443
Finland	1.448	−0.008	0.809	−2.303
Sweden	3.921	−0.013	4.900	−2.361
United Kingdom	1.010	2.088	−0.996	−1.420
t-bar	1.362*	1.212	0.379	−1.718
IPS-stat	10.172**	9.612	9.191	0.980
ADF critical	−2.985	−2.959	−3.603	−3.561
IPS critical 5%	−1.960	−1.960	−1.960	−1.960

Notes: * = AVERAGE(B4:B17); ** = (SQRT(14)*(B19 − (−1.968)))/(SQRT(0.913)).

Table 20.2   Maddala and unit-root tests

	Intercept				Intercept and Trend			
	FDIINFL		GDPPC		FDIINFL		GDPPC	
	pi	−2ln(pi)	pi	−2ln(pi)	pi	−2ln(pi)	pi	−2ln(pi)
Belgium	0.045	2.685*	0.345	0.925	0.209	1.361	0.085	2.142
Denmark	0.000	9.858	0.073	2.275	0.003	4.955	0.059	2.457
Germany	0.010	3.984	0.552	0.516	0.020	3.413	0.008	4.209
Greece	0.061	2.433	0.021	3.360	0.014	3.725	0.877	0.114
Spain	0.286	1.089	0.253	1.193	0.008	4.149	0.067	2.346
France	0.061	2.428	0.852	0.140	0.583	0.468	0.000	6.639
Ireland	0.014	3.731	0.012	3.876	0.024	3.241	0.187	1.455
Italy	0.638	0.390	0.541	0.533	0.028	3.110	0.037	2.869
Netherlands	0.049	2.621	0.083	2.159	0.220	1.315	0.332	0.958
Austria	0.890	0.101	0.299	1.049	0.571	0.487	0.008	4.180
Portugal	0.226	1.293	0.082	2.169	0.039	2.821	0.662	0.359
Finland	0.164	1.570	0.994	0.005	0.429	0.735	0.030	3.038
Sweden	0.001	6.074	0.990	0.009	0.000	7.875	0.027	3.148
United Kingdom	0.325	0.976	0.047	2.653	0.332	0.957	0.169	1.547
MW stat		39.233**		20.862		38.611		35.461
MW critical	41.330							

Notes: * = − 2*log(C5); ** = Sum(C5:C19).

to be used instead. We leave this as an exercise for the reader.). From the results we see that, first, from the simple ADF test for each section we have unit roots in all cases apart from the rare exception of France for the GDPPC with trend and intercept which appears to be trend-stationary. However, from the t_{IPS} we conclude that the whole panel is stationary because the statistical values are clearly bigger than the critical value (distributed under the normal distribution).

For the Maddala and Wu test, the results are reported in Table 20.2. Here the first column reports statistics regarding the p values (π) for each of the 14 cross-sections. Then in the next column we calculate the value $-2\ln\pi_i$ for each of the cross-sections and at the end we take the sum of these values in order to construct the MW statistic given by equation (20.5). The basic commands in Excel are reported belowf Table 20.2.

In general, panel unit-root tests are quite tedious and complicated, so various routines have been developed in order to achieve easy and effective calculations of these statistics. Unfortunately these algorithms are not performed in tests using user-friendly econometric packages like EViews and Microft, and they are not easy to find either. Panel unit-root tests are a very new topic in econometrics and developments in this area need to be followed at higher levels of research which are beyond the scope of this text. To our knowledge there is no econometrics textbook yet (even from textbooks that examine panel data only) that discusses these issues in a simplified context.

Panel cointegration tests

Introduction

The motivation towards testing for cointegration is primarily linked with the provision of investigating the problem of spurious regressions, which exists only in the presence of non-stationarity. The cointegration test among two variables is a formal way of investigating between:

1 a simple spurious regression where both X_{it} and Y_{it} are integrated of the same order and the residuals of regressing Y_{it} to X_{it} (i.e. the u_{it} sequence of this panel data model) contains a stochastic trend; or

2 the special case in which, again, both X_{it} and Y_{it} are integrated of the same order, but this time the u_{it} sequence is stationary.

Normally in the first case we apply first differences to reestimate the regression equation, while in the second case we conclude that the variables X_{it} and Y_{it} are cointegrated. Thus, in order to test for cointegration it is important to ensure that the regression variables are *a priori* integrated of the same order.

There are different possible tests for cointegration in panels, and the best-known cointegration tests are based on the Engle and Granger cointegration relationship. In the time series framework the remarkable outcome of the Engle–Granger (1987) procedure is that if a set of variables are cointegrated, then there always exists an error-correcting formulation of the dynamic model, and vice versa. Their analysis consists of a standard ADF test on the residuals u_t under the null H_0: the variables are not cointegrated, versus the alternative H_a: the variables are cointegrated. If we observe that the ADF statistic is less than the appropriate critical value, we reject the null that there are no cointegrating relationships between the variables and we continue with the estimation of the ECM. The Engle–Granger procedure can also be used for the estimation of either heterogeneous or homogeneous panels, under the hypothesis of a single cointegrating vector, as we will show below.

The Kao test

Kao (1999) presented DF and ADF-type tests for cointegration in panel data. Consider the model:

$$Y_{it} = a_i + \beta X_{it} + u_{it} \tag{20.6}$$

According to Kao, the residual-based cointegration test can be applied to equation:

$$u_{it} = e u_{it-1} + v_{it} \tag{20.7}$$

where $\hat{u}_{it}$ is the estimated residuals from equation (20.6) above. The OLS estimate of ρ is given by:

$$\hat{\rho} = \frac{\sum_{i=1}^{N} \sum_{t=2}^{T} u_{it} u_{it-1}}{\sum_{i=1}^{N} \sum_{t=2}^{T} u_{it}^2} \tag{20.8}$$

and its corresponding t statistic is given by:

$$t_\rho = \frac{(\hat{\rho} - 1)\sqrt{\sum_{i=1}^{N} \sum_{t=2}^{T} u_{it}^2}}{1/(NT) \sum_{i=1}^{N} \sum_{t=2}^{T} (u_{it} - \hat{\rho} u_{it-1})^2} \tag{20.9}$$

Kao proposed four different DF-type tests that are given below:

$$DF_\rho = \frac{\sqrt{N}T(\hat{\rho} - 1) + 3\sqrt{N}}{\sqrt{10.2}} \tag{20.10}$$

$$DF_t = \sqrt{1.25} t_\rho + \sqrt{1.875N} \tag{20.11}$$

$$DF_\rho^* = \frac{\sqrt{N}T(\hat{\rho} - 1) + 3\sqrt{N}\hat{\sigma}_v^2/\hat{\sigma}_{0v}^2}{\sqrt{3 + 36\hat{\sigma}_v^4/(5\hat{\sigma}_{0v}^4)}} \tag{20.12}$$

$$DF_t^* = \frac{t_\rho + \sqrt{6N}\hat{\sigma}_v/(2\hat{\sigma}_{0v})}{\sqrt{\hat{\sigma}_{0v}^2/(2\hat{\sigma}_v^2) + 3\hat{\sigma}_v^2/(10\hat{\sigma}_{0v}^2)}} \tag{20.13}$$

of which the first two (DF_ρ and DF_t) are for cases where the relationship between the regressors and the errors is strongly exogenous, and the last two (DF_ρ^* and DF_t^*) are for cases where the relationship between the regressors and the errors is endogenous.

Kao (1999) also proposes an ADF test, where one can run the following regression:

$$u_{i,t} = \rho u_{i,t-1} + \sum_{j=1}^{n} \phi_j \Delta u_{i,t-j} + v_{it} \tag{20.14}$$

The null hypothesis for this test as well as for the DF tests is that of no cointegration, and the ADF test statistic is calculated by:

$$ADF = \frac{t_{ADF} + \sqrt{6N}\hat{\sigma}_v/(2\hat{\sigma}_{0v})}{\sqrt{\hat{\sigma}_{0v}^2/(2\hat{\sigma}_v^2) + 3\hat{\sigma}_v^2/(10\hat{\sigma}_{0v}^2)}}$$ (20.15)

where t_{ADF} is the ADF statistic of regression (20.14). All five test statistics follow the standard normal distribution.

Kao's test imposes homogeneous cointegrating vectors and AR coefficients, but it does not allow for multiple exogenous variables in the cointegrating vector. Another drawback is that it does not address the issue of identifying the cointegrating vectors and the cases where more than one cointegrating vector exists.

The McCoskey and Kao test

McCoskey and Kao (1998) use a Lagrange multiplier test on the residuals. The major contribution of this approach is that it tests for the null of cointegration rather than the null of no cointegration. The model is:

$$Y_{it} = a_i + \beta_i X_{it} + u_{it}$$ (20.16)

where

$$u_{it} = \theta \sum_{j=1}^{t} e_{ij} + e_{it}$$ (20.17)

Thus, the test is analogous to the locally best unbiased invariant for a moving average unit root and is also free of nuisance parameters. The null hypothesis is then H_0: $\theta = 0$, implying that there is cointegration in the panel, since for $\theta = 0$, $e_{it} = u_{it}$. The alternative H_a: $\theta \neq 0$, is the lack of cointegration. The test statistic is obtained by using the following equation:

$$LM = \frac{1/N \sum_{i=1}^{N} 1/T^2 \sum_{t=2}^{T} S_{it}^2}{s^*}$$ (20.18)

where S_{it} is the partial sum process defined as $S_{it}^2 = \sum_{j=1}^{t} u_{ij}$ and s^* is defined as $s^* = 1/NT \sum_{i=1}^{N} \sum_{t=2}^{T} u_{it}^2$.

Estimation of the residuals can be applied by using OLS estimators and, more specifically, through the use of either FMOLS (fully modified OLS) or the DOLS (dynamic OLS) estimator.

The Pedroni tests

Pedroni (1997, 1999 and 2000) proposed several tests for cointegration in panel data models that allow considerable heterogeneity. Pedroni's approach differs from that of McCoskey and Kao presented above in assuming trends for the cross-sections and in considering as the null hypothesis that of no cointegration. The good features of Pedroni's tests are the fact they allow for multiple regressors, for the cointegration vector to vary across different sections of the panel, and also for heterogeneity in the errors across cross-sectional units.

The panel regression model that Pedroni proposes has the following form:

$$Y_{i,t} = a_i + \delta_t + \sum_{m=1}^{M} \beta_{mi} X_{mi,t} + u_{i,t} \tag{20.19}$$

Seven different cointegration statistics are proposed to capture the within and between effects in his panel, and his tests can be classified into two categories. The first category includes four tests based on pooling along the 'within' dimension (pooling the AR coefficients across different sections of the panel for the unit-root test on the residuals). These tests are quite similar to those discussed above, and involve calculating the average test statistics for cointegration in the time series framework across the different sections. The test statistics of these tests are given below:

1 the panel v statistic

$$T^2 N^{3/2} Z_{\hat{v}NT} = \frac{T^2 N^{3/2}}{\left(\sum_{i=1}^{N} \sum_{t=1}^{T} \hat{L}_{11i}^{-2} \hat{u}_{it}^2 \right)} \tag{20.20}$$

2 the panel ρ statistic

$$T\sqrt{N} Z_{\hat{\rho}NT} = \frac{T\sqrt{N} \left(\sum_{i=1}^{N} \sum_{t=1}^{T} \hat{L}_{11i}^{-2} \left(\hat{u}_{it-1}^2 \Delta \hat{u}_{it}^2 - \hat{\lambda}_i \right) \right)}{\left(\sum_{i=1}^{N} \sum_{t=1}^{T} \hat{L}_{11i}^{-2} \hat{u}_{it}^2 \right)} \tag{20.21}$$

3 the panel t statistic (non-parametric)

$$Z_{tNT} = \sqrt{ \tilde{\sigma}_{NT}^2 \sum_{i=1}^{N} \sum_{t=1}^{T} \hat{L}_{11i}^{-2} \hat{u}_{it-1}^2 } \left(\sum_{i=1}^{N} \sum_{t=1}^{T} \hat{L}_{11i}^{-2} \left(\hat{u}_{it-1}^2 \Delta \hat{u}_{it}^2 - \hat{\lambda}_i \right) \right) \tag{20.22}$$

4 the panel t statistic (parametric)

$$Z_{tNT} = \sqrt{ \tilde{\sigma}_{NT}^{*2} \sum_{i=1}^{N} \sum_{t=1}^{T} \hat{L}_{11i}^{-2} \hat{u}_{it-1}^{*2} } \left(\sum_{i=1}^{N} \sum_{t=1}^{T} \hat{L}_{11i}^{-2} \left(\hat{u}_{it-1}^{*2} \Delta \hat{u}_{it}^{*2} - \hat{\lambda}_i \right) \right) \tag{20.23}$$

The second category includes three tests based on pooling the 'between' dimension (averaging the AR coefficients for each member of the panel for the unit-root test on the residuals). So, for these tests the averaging is done in pieces and therefore the limiting distributions are based on piecewise numerator and denominator terms.

These test statistics are given below:

5 the group ρ statistic (parametric)

$$T\sqrt{N}\tilde{Z}_{\tilde{\rho}NT} = T\sqrt{N}\frac{\sum_{t=1}^{T}\left(\hat{u}_{it-1}^2\Delta\hat{u}_{it}^2 - \hat{\lambda}_i\right)}{\sum_{i=1}^{N}\left(\sum_{t=1}^{T}\hat{u}_{it-1}^2\right)} \tag{20.24}$$

6 the group t statistic (non-parametric)

$$\sqrt{N}\tilde{Z}_{tNT-1} = \sqrt{N}\sum_{i=1}^{N}\left(\sqrt{\tilde{\sigma}_i^2\sum_{t=1}^{T}\hat{u}_{it-1}^2}\right)\sum_{t=1}^{T}\left(\hat{u}_{it-1}^2\Delta\hat{u}_{it}^2 - \hat{\lambda}_i\right) \tag{20.25}$$

7 the group t statistic (parametric)

$$\sqrt{N}\tilde{Z}_{tNT-1}^* = \sqrt{N}\sum_{i=1}^{N}\left(\sqrt{\tilde{s}_i^{*2}\sum_{t=1}^{T}\hat{u}_{it-1}^{*2}}\right)\sum_{t=1}^{T}\left(\hat{u}_{it-1}^{*2}\Delta\hat{u}_{it}^{*2}\right) \tag{20.26}$$

A major drawback of the above procedure is the restrictive *a priori* assumption of a unique cointegrating vector.

The Larsson *et al.* test

Larsson *et al.* (2001), contrary to all the above tests, based their test on Johansen's (1988) maximum likelihood estimator, avoiding using unit-root tests on the residuals and contemporaneously relaxing the assumption of a unique cointegrating vector (thus this model allows us to test for more multiply-cointegrating vectors). The model that they proposed starts from the assumption that the data generating process for each of the cross-sections can be represented by an ECM specification. So, we have the following model:

$$\Delta Y_{i,t} = \Pi_i Y_{i,t-1} + \sum_{k=1}^{n}\Gamma_{ik}\Delta Y_{i,t-k} + u_{i,t} \tag{20.27}$$

Larsson *et al.* propose the estimation of the above model separately for each cross-section using maximum likelihood methods for the calculation of the trace statistic for each cross-sectional unit LR_{iT}. Then, the panel rank trace statistic, LR_{NT}, can be obtained as the average of the N cross-sectional trace statistics. The null and alternative hypotheses for this test are:

$$H_0: \quad rank(\Pi_i) = r_i \leq r \quad \text{for all } i = 1,\dots,N \tag{20.28}$$

$$H_a: \quad rank(\Pi_i) = p \quad \text{for all } i = 1,\dots,N \tag{20.29}$$

where p is the number of variables that we use in order to test for possible cointegration among them.

The standardized panel cointegration rank trace test-statistic (denoted by Y_{LR}) is then given by:

$$Y_{LR} = \frac{\sqrt{N}(LR_{NT} - E[Z_k])}{\sqrt{Var(Z_k)}} \tag{20.30}$$

where LR_{NT} is the average of the trace statistic for each cross-sectional unit, and $E[Z_k]$ and $Var[Z_k]$ are the mean and variance of the asymptotic trace statistic reported in Larsson *et al.* (2001).

Computer examples of panel cointegration tests

In order to perform the panel cointegration tests in EViews the algorithm provided freely by Pedroni (downloadable from http://fmwww.bc.edu/repec/bocode/m/multi-pc2d-pedroni.prg) was used in the panel_unit_root.wf1 data set. Unfortunately again, as with the panel unit-root tests, these algorithms cannot be used in conventional programs like EViews. The results for the seven Pedroni test statistics are reported in Table 20.3.

The mean and variance used for calculating the Pedroni statistics were obtained from Pedroni (1999, table 2); the number of lag truncations was set to four. The Pedroni tests are all one-sided. All statistics, with the exception of the v statistic, have a critical value of -1.64, which means that if the statistical value is bigger than -1.64 then this implies rejection of the null of no cointegration. From our results we can see that in all cases we have strong evidence for existence of cointegration among the FDIINFL and the GDPPC variables. The v statistic has a critical value of 1.64; so if v statistic > 1.64 then we can reject the null of no cointegration. In our case we again reject the null and conclude in favour of cointegration. Finally, the McCoskey and Kao LM test is again one-sided with a critical value of 1.64 (thus LM-statistic > 1.64 implies rejection of the null hypothesis of cointegration). The mean and variance used for calculating the McCoskey and Kao statistic were taken from McCoskey and Kao (1998) table 2.

We continue by applying the Larsson *et al.* (2001) test. In order to do so we check for cointegration using the Johansen approach for the three variables in the file (FDITOGDP, GDPGR95 and GFCFTOGDP) for each of the 13 EU countries (Luxembourg and Netherlands are excluded due to insufficient data). From this test we take the trace statistics and report them in Excel as in Table 20.4.

Table 20.3   Panel cointegration tests

panel v statistic	8.25
panel ρ statistic	−5.11
panel t statistic (non-parametric)	−5.02
panel t statistic (parametric)	−5.01
group ρ statistic	−4.71
group t statistic (non-parametric)	−6.25
group t statistic (parametric)	−6.33
McCoskey and Kao *LM* statistic	−4.32

Notes: Nsecs = 14, Tperiods = 30, no. regressors = 1.

Table 20.4 Larsson *et al.* (2001) panel cointegration test results

	$r = 0$	$r = 1$	$r = 2$
Belgium	30.874*	8.829	2.007
Denmark	28.272	11.352	0.256
Germany	43.978*	10.007	0.351
Greece	32.213*	12.482	2.943
Spain	39.212*	16.135*	3.225
France	28.347	12.154	2.041
Ireland	33.003*	8.207	0.346
Italy	33.614*	14.078	0.385
Austria	33.238*	14.364	0.439
Portugal	44.678*	21.654*	4.212
Finland	36.948*	8.745	1.148
Sweden	46.346*	19.704*	3.234
United Kingdom	28.427	9.781	3.634
5% critical	29.68	15.41	3.76
LR_{NT}	35.319[a]	12.884	1.863
Y_{LR}-test	14.764[b]	7.552	1.760
$E(Z_k)$	14.955	6.086	1.137
$Var(Z_k)$	24.733	10.535	2.212
N	13	13	13

Notes: The values for $E(Z_k)$ and $Var(Z_k)$ were obtained from Larsson *et al.* (2001)
a = AVERAGE(B3:B15); b = (SQRT(B24)*(B19-B22)/(SQRT(B23))).

The command for the cointegration test in EViews is:

```
coint gdpgr95_bel fditogdp_bel gfcftogdp_bel
```

for the case of Belgium (which is why we use the cross-section identifier **bel**), and changing the cross-section identifier for every other group. The model we have chosen for this test is the one that includes a linear deterministic trend in the data and intercept in both CE and VAR. The lag length, for simplicity, was chosen in all cases to be equal to 1. After obtaining the statistics it is very easy to do the calculations (simply taking the average of all the trace statistics for each section) in order to compute LR_{NT}, and then using the $E[Z_k]$ and $Var[Z_k]$ obtained from Larsson *et al.* (2001) to calculate:

$$Y_{LR} = \frac{\sqrt{N}(LR_{NT} - E[Z_k])}{\sqrt{Var(Z_k)}} \qquad (20.31)$$

The commands for the calculations in Excel are given in Table 20.4. From the results for the individual cointegration tests we see that we can reject the null of no cointegration and accept that there is one cointegrating vector for all the cases apart from three (Denmark, France and UK suggest no cointegration among their variables) and also reject the null of only one cointegrating vector in favour of two cointegrating vectors for three out of the 13 cases (Spain, Portugal and Sweden). However, the Y_{LR} statistic suggest that in the panel we have two cointegrating vectors based on the fact that the statistical values are bigger than the 1.96 critical value of the normal distribution.

21 Practicalities in Using EViews and Microfit

About Microfit

Creating a file and importing data

To input data directly from the keyboard is the most basic method of entering data. First make sure that you know:

- the frequency of the data (whether the data are undated, or are annual, half-yearly, quarterly or monthly);
- the number of variables in the dataset; and
- sample period of observations.

To input a new data set, click on the [File] menu and then choose [new. . .]. A window will open with different options for data frequency, start and end dates and number of variables. Under frequencies there are the following options:

[Undated] This option is relevant for entering cross-sectional observations and Microfit assumes that the observations are unordered, and asks how many observations you have. If we have data containing variables such as employment, output, and investment on a number of firms, then each firm represents an observation and the number of observations will be equal to the number of firms in your dataset. If we have time-series covering the period from 1990 to 2000 inclusive and wish to enter them as undated, the number of observations in the data will equal 11.

[Annually, Half-yearly, Quarterly and Monthly] All these choices are for time series data. The program supplies the dates and you do not need to type them in. However, you will be asked to specify the dates for the start and end of your data by typing them in the corresponding cells. The next step is to type in and specify the number of variables you wish to have in your file.

Entering variable names

The variables window contains the default variable names X1, X2, X3, etc. You can enter your own choice of variables and/or add a description if you wish. When you are entering the desired names keep in mind the following:

- A valid variable can be at most 9 characters long and must begin with a letter not a symbol.
- MFit is not case sensitive. Lower- and upper case letters are treated as equivalent.
- The underscore (_) character is allowed.
- Variable descriptions can be up to 80 characters long.

- You can return to the variables window to edit your data by clicking the variables button.
- When you have finished entering your observations, click CLOSE.

Copying/pasting data

Pasting data in Microfit

To paste data from the clipboard into the Data Editor, choose Paste Data from the Edit menu. Then choose the frequency of your data by clicking the appropriate button. When you have finished entering your information, press OK. You will be asked to specify whether the variable names (up to 9 characters) and/or variable description (up to 80 characters) is included in the copied area of your data set. This relates to the format in which your copied data appear on the clipboard.

Copying data from MFit to the clipboard

Move to the Data Editor and choose Copy from the Edit menu. A dialog appears giving you various choices about how much of the data you want to copy and in what format. The complete data set is selected by default. If you want to copy less that the full set, specify the first and the last variable and/or observation on the appropriate field. By default, variable names are copied to the first row of the clipboard and variable descriptions are copied to the second row. If you want to disable either of these options, remove the tick as appropriate.

Saving data

To save your current data file, select [Save as…] from the File menu or click the 'Save' button. Then select the type of file in which you want to save your data from the drop-down list. If you are working with a file you have already saved previously, you save it again by choosing [Save] from the File menu.

Description of MFit tools

The rectangular buttons across the top of the Command Editor are used to access other parts of the application.

[PROCESS]: when the data has been successfully inserted, the program opens the Command Editor. This is MFit's gateway to data transformations and preliminary data analyses.

[VARIABLES]: to view your variables and edit their names and/or descriptions.

[DATA]: to view your data.

[SINGLE]: to access the Single Equation Estimation window.

[MULTI]: to access the System Estimation window.

Creating a constant term

To create a constant term, click on the CONSTANT button in the process menu or choose Constant (intercept) from the EDIT. Constant is a variable with all its all elements equal to unity and asks you to supply a name (C, CON, INT and ALPHA are the most common choices).

Basic commands in MFit

The Command Editor is where you can type one or more formula(e) or command(s). The different formulae need to be separated by semicolons (;). Standard arithmetic operators such as +, −, /, ∗ can also be used as well as a wide range of built-in functions. For example, to create a new variable (e.g. LOGX) which is the logarithm of an existing variable (e.g. X) you need to type in the Command Editor [PROCESS]:

$$LOGX = LOG(X) \tag{21.1}$$

and then click on [GO]. This operation places the natural logarithm of X in *LOGX*. Click on the [VARIABLES] and [DATA] buttons underneath the FILE to view the new variable. In this context, you can also create the first differences (returns) of the series. To create a new variable (e.g. D1X) which is the first differences of the series of an existing variable (e.g. X), type:

D1X = X − X (−1) if the variable is daily, yearly or undated

D1X = X − X (−4) if the variable is quarterly

D1X = X − X (−12) if the variable is monthly

in the Command Editor [PROCESS] and then click on GO.

About EViews

We need to familiarize ourselves with the following main areas in the EViews window:

The title bar

The title bar, labelled EViews, is at the very top of the main window. When EViews is the active program in Windows, as is usual in windows the title bar colour is enhanced; when another program is active, the title bar will be lighter. EViews may be activated by clicking anywhere in the EViews window or by using Alt+Tab to cycle between applications until the EViews window is active.

The main menu

Just below the title bar is the main menu. If we move the cursor to an entry in the main menu and left-click on it, a drop-down menu will appear. Clicking on an entry in the drop-down menu selects the highlighted item. Some of the items in the drop-down may be black, others grey; grey items are not available, to be executed.

The command window

Below the menu bar is an area called the command window, in which EViews commands may be typed. The command is executed as soon as you hit ENTER. The vertical bar in the command window is called the insertion point, and shows where the letters that you type on the keyboard will be placed. As with standard word processors, if we type something in the command area, we can move the insertion point by pointing to and clicking on a new location. If the insertion point is not visible, it probably means that the command window is not active; simply click anywhere in the command window to activate it.

We can move the insertion point to previously executed commands, edit the existing command, and then press ENTER to execute the edited version of the command. The command window supports Windows cut-and-paste so that we can easily move text between the command window, other EViews text windows, and other Windows programs. The contents of the command area may also be saved directly into a text file for later use (make certain that the command window is active by clicking anywhere in the window, and then select File/Save As from the main menu).

If we enter more commands than will fit in the command window, EViews turns the window into a standard scrollable window. Simply use the scroll bar or up and down arrows on the right-hand side of the window to see various parts of the list of previously executed commands.

You may find that the default size of the command window is too large or small for your needs. It can be resized by placing the cursor at the bottom of the command window, holding down the mouse button and dragging the window up or down. Release the mouse button when the command window is the desired size.

The status line

At the very bottom of the window is a status line which is divided into several sections. The left section will sometimes contain status messages sent to you by EViews. These messages can be cleared manually by clicking on the box at the far left of the status line. The next section shows the default directory that EViews uses to look for data and programs. The last two sections display the names of the default database and workfile.

The work area

The area in the middle of the window is the work area where EViews displays the various object windows that it creates. Think of these windows as similar to the sheets of paper you might place on your desk as you work. The windows will overlap each other with the foremost window being in focus or active. Only the active window has a darkened titlebar. When a window is partly covered, you can bring it to the top by clicking on its titlebar or on a visible portion of the window. You can also cycle through the displayed windows by pressing the F6 or CTRL+TAB keys. Alternatively, you may directly select a window by clicking on the window menu item, and selecting the desired name. You can move a window by clicking on its title bar and dragging the window to a new location, or change the size of a window by clicking at the lower-right corner and dragging the corner to a new location.

Creating a workfile and importing data

To create a workfile to hold your data, select **File/New/Workfile**, which opens a dialogue box to provide information about the data. Here we specify the desired frequency of the data set, for example daily, 5 days a week, and the start and end dates for example 01:01:85 and 12:31:99 (note the order of month, then day, then year).

After filling out the dialogue, click on **OK**. EViews will create an untitled workfile, and display the workfile window. For now, notice that the workfile window displays two pairs of dates: one for the range of dates contained in the workfile, and the second for the current workfile sample. Note also that the workfile contains the coefficient vector **C** and the series **RESID**. All EViews workfiles will contain these two objects.

Copying and pasting data

Copying data

The next step is to copy and paste the data. Note that while the following discussion involves an example using an Excel spreadsheet, these basic principles apply for any other Windows applications. The first step is to highlight the cells to be imported into EViews. Note that if we include in our selection column headings, these will be used as EViews variable names, so we don't leave empty cells after the variable name but start with the data. Since EViews understands dated data, and we are going to create a daily workfile, we do not need to copy the date column. Instead, click on the column label B and drag to the column label desired. The selected columns of the spreadsheet will be highlighted. Select **Edit/Copy** to copy the highlighted data to the clipboard.

Pasting into new series

Select **Quick/Empty Group (Edit Series)**. Note that the spreadsheet opens in edit mode so there is no need to click the **Edit +/−** button. If we are pasting in the series names, we click on the up arrow in the scroll bar to make room for the series names. Place the cursor in the upper-left cell, just to the right of the second observation label. Then select **Edit/Paste** from the main menu (not **Edit +/−** in the toolbar). The group spreadsheet will now contain the data from the clipboard.

You may now close the group window and delete the untitled group without losing the two series. Note that when importing data from the clipboard, EViews follows the Windows standard of tab-delimited free-format data with one observation per line. Since different applications use different whitespace and delimiter characters, attempting to cut-and-paste from non-standard applications may produce unanticipated results.

Pasting into existing series

We can import data from the clipboard into an existing EViews series or group spreadsheet by using Edit/Paste in the same fashion. There are only a few additional issues to consider:

1 To paste several series, first open a group window containing the existing series. The easiest way to do this is to click on Show, and then type the series names in the order they appear on the clipboard. Alternatively, we can create an untitled group by selecting the first series, click/select each subsequent series (in order), and then double-click to open.

2 Next, make certain that the group window is in edit mode. If not, press the Edit $+/-$ button to toggle between edit mode and protected mode. Place the cursor in the target cell, and select Edit/Paste.

3 Finally, click on **Edit** $+/-$ to return to protected mode.

Verifying the data

First we verify that the data have been read correctly. Here we create a group object that allows us to examine all our series. Click on the name of the first variable in the workfile window, and then press Ctrl and click on all the rest of them (do not include resid and c). All of the new series should be highlighted. Now place the cursor anywhere in the highlighted area and double-click the left mouse button. EViews will open a popup menu providing several options. Choose Open Group. EViews will create an untitled group object containing all four of the series. The default window for the group shows a spreadsheet view of the series, which we can compare with the top of the Excel worksheet to insure that the first part of the data have been read correctly. We can use the scroll bars and scroll arrows on the right side of the window to verify the remainder of the data.

Once satisfied that the data are correct, save the workfile by clicking **Save** in the workfile window. A save dialog will open, prompting for a workfile name and location; enter a name and click **OK**. EViews will save the workfile in the specified directory with the name specified. A saved workfile can be opened later by selecting **File/Open/Workfile** from the main menu.

Examining the data

We can use basic EViews tools to examine the data in a variety of ways. For example, if we select View/Multiple Graphs/Line from the group object toolbar, EViews displays line graphs of each of the series. We can select View/Descriptive Stats/Individual Samples to compute descriptive statistics for each of the series. Click on View/Correlations, for example, to display the correlation matrix of the selected (grouped) series.

We can also examine characteristics of the individual series. Since the regression analysis below will be expressed in either logarithms or growth rates (first differences in logarithms; or returns), we can construct variables with the genr command (for generate).

Commands, operators and functions

The GENR command

The genr command generates new series according to an equation specified by the user, in either of two ways. The first is to press genr from the workfile area. A new window pops up, which asks us to enter the equation required. We need to define a new name and then enter the equation next to the name (followed by the = sign). For example, if we want to take the logarithm of series X01 we can write:

$$LX01 = LOG(X01) \tag{21.2}$$

Which will generate a new series named $LX01$ which will be the logarithm of $X01$ (note that you can choose whichever name you like before the = sign).

Another way is to use the command line where you can simply write:

$$genr\ lx01 = log(x01) \tag{21.3}$$

and get the same result as before. This way is sometimes very convenient because you might have to take logs of tenths of series that we named them like x?? (? denotes number from 1 to 9). We can then return to the command line and change only the numbers in each case.

Obviously taking logarithms is one of the many things we can use for generating new series. The following tables show the basic operators, mathematical functions and time series functions that can be used with the genr command.

Operators

All of the operators described in Table 21.1 may be used in expressions involving series and scalar values. When applied to a series expression, the operation is performed for each observation in the current sample. The precedence of evaluation is listed below. Note that you can enforce order-of-evaluation using appropriate parentheses.

Mathematical functions

The functions listed in Table 21.2 are designed to perform basic mathematical operations. When applied to a series, they return a value for every observation in the current sample. When applied to a matrix object, they return a value for every element of the matrix object. The functions will return NA (not applicable) values for observations where the input values are NAs, and for observations where the input

Table 21.1 Operators

Expression	Operator	Description
+	Add $x + y$	Adds the contents of x and y
−	Subtract $x - y$	Subtracts the contents of y from x
*	Multiply $x*y$	Multiplies the contents of x by y
/	Divide x/y	Divides the contents of x by y
^	Raise to the power $x^\wedge y$	Raises x to the power of y

Table 21.2   Mathematical function

Function	Name	Examples/description
@abs(x); abs(x)	Absolute value	@abs(-3) = 3; abs(2) = 2
@ceiling(x)	Smallest integer	@ceiling(2.34) = 3; @ceiling(4)=4
@exp(x); exp(x)	Exponential, e^x	@exp(1) = 2.71813
@fact(x)	Factorial, $x!$	@fact(3) = 6; @fact(0) = 1
@floor(x)	Largest integer	@floor(1.23) = 1; @floor(3) = 3
@inv(x)	Reciprocal, $1/x$	@inv(2) = 0.5
@log(x)	Natural logarithm ln(x)	@log(2) = 0.693; log(2.71813)=1
@sqrt(x)	Square root	@sqrt(9) = 3; sqr(4) = 2

Table 21.3   Time series functions

Function	Name and description
d(x)	First difference; $(1 - L)X = X - X(-1)$
d(x, n)	nth order difference; $(1 - L)^n X$
d(x, n, s)	nth order difference with a seasonal difference at s; $(1 - L)^n(1 - L^s)X$
dlog(x)	First difference of the logarithm
dlog(x, n)	nth order difference of the logarithm
dlog(x, n, s)	nth order difference of the logarithm with a seasonal difference at s
@movav(x, n)	n-period backward moving average; @movav(x,3) = $(X + X(-1) + X(-2))/3$
@movsum(x, n)	n-period backward moving sum; @movsum(x,3) = $X + X(-1) + X(-2)$
@pch(x)	One-period percentage change (in decimal)
@pcha(x)	One-period percentage change annualized (in decimal)
@pchy(x)	One-year percentage change (in decimal)
@seas(n)	Seasonal dummy: returns 1 when the quarter or month equals n and 0 otherwise

values are not valid. For example, the square-root function *@sqrt*, will return NA values for all observations that are less than zero. Note that the logarithmic functions are base-e (natural logarithms). To convert the natural logarithm into log10, you should use the relationship: $log_{10}(x) = log_e(x)/log_e 10$.

Time series functions

The functions in Table 21.3 facilitate working with time series data. Note that NAs will be returned for observations for which lagged values are not available. For example, d(x) returns a missing value for the first observation in the workfile, since the lagged value is not available.

Bibliography

Ahn S.C. and H.R. Moon (2001) 'Large-N and Large-T Properties of Panel Data Estimators and the Hausman Test, August 2001', USC CLEO Research Paper No. C01–20.

Akaike, H. (1970) 'Statistical Predictor Identification', *Annals of the Institute of Statistical Mathematics*, 22, pp. 203–17.

Akaike, H. (1974) 'A New Look at Statistical Model Identification', *IEEE Transactions on Automatic Control*, 19, pp. 716–23.

Almon, S. (1965) 'The Distributed Lag Between Capital Appropriations and Expenditures', *Econometrica*, 30, pp. 178–96.

Anderson, T.W. and C. Hsiao (1981) 'Estimation of Dynamic Models with Error Components', *Journal of the American Statistical Association*, 76, pp. 598–606.

Anderson, T.W. and C. Hsiao (1982) 'Formulation and Estimation of Dynamic Models Using Panel Data', *Journal of Econometrics*, 18, pp. 47–82.

Arellano, M. and S. Bond (1991) 'Some Tests of Specification for Panel Data: Monte Carlo Evidence and an Application to Employment Equations', *Review of Economic Studies*, 58, pp. 277–320.

Asteriou, D. and G. Kavetsos (2003) 'Testing for the Existence of the January Effect in Transition Economies', City University Working Paper no. 107.

Asteriou, D. and S. Price (2000a) 'Financial Development and Economic Growth: Time Series Evidence for the Case of UK', *Ekonomia*, 4(2), pp. 122–41.

Asteriou, D. and S. Price (2000b) 'Uncertainty, Investment and Economic Growth: Evidence from a Dynamic Panel', City University Working Paper no. 88.

Asteriou, D. and S. Price (2001) 'Political Uncertainty and Economic Growth: UK Time Series Evidence', *Scottish Journal of Political Economy*, 48(4), pp. 383–9.

Baltagi, B.H. (1995) *Econometric Analysis of Panel Data*. New York, NY: John Wiley and Sons.

Baltagi, B.H. and J.M. Griffin (1997) 'Pooled Estimators vs their Heterogeneous Counterparts in the Context of Dynamic Demand for Gasoline', *Journal of Econometrics*, 77, pp. 303–27.

Bencivenga, V., B. Smith and R. Starr (1996) 'Equity Markets, Transactions Costs, and Capital Accumulation: An Illustration', *The World Bank Economic Review*, 10(2), pp. 241–65.

Banerjee, A., J.J. Dolado, J.W. Galbraith and D.F. Hendry (1993) *Cointegration, Error-Correction and the Econometric Analysis of Non-Stationary Data*. Oxford: Oxford University Press.

Berra, A.K. and M.L. Higgins (1993) 'ARCH Models: Properties, Estimation, and Testing', *Journal of Economic Surveys*, 7, pp. 305–62.

Bollerslev, T. (1986) 'Generalised Autoregressive Conditional Heteroskedasticity', *Journal of Econometrics*, 31, pp. 307–27.

Bollerslev, T., R.F. Engle and D.B. Nelson (1994), 'ARCH Models', in R.F. Engle and D. McFadden (eds.), *Handbook of Econometrics*, Volume IV, 2959–3038. Amsterdam: North-Holland.

Box, G.E.P. and D.R. Cox (1964) 'An Analysis of Transformations', *Journal of the Royal Statistical Sociey*, Series B.

Box, G.E.P. and G.M. Jenkins (1976) *Time Series Analysis: Forecasting and Control*, revised edition. San Francisco Holden-Day.

Breusch, T. (1978) 'Testing for Autocorrelation in Dynamic Linear Models', *Australian Economic Papers*, 17, pp. 334–55.

Breusch, T. and A. Pagan (1979) 'A Simple Test for Heteroskedasticity and Random Coefficient Variation', *Econometrica*, 47, pp. 1278–94.

Cagan, P. (1956) 'The Monetary Dynamics of Hyper Inflations', in M. Friedman (eds), *Studies in the Quantity Theory of Money*. Chicago: University of Chicago Press.

Campbell, H.Y, A.W. Lo and A.C. MacKinley (1997) *The Econometrics of Financial Markets*. Princeton, NJ: Princeton University Press.

Chow, G. (1960) 'Tests of Equality between Sets of Coefficients in Two Linear Regressions', *Econometrica*, 28, pp. 591–605.

Cochrane, D. and G. Orcutt (1949) 'Application of Least Squares Regression to Relationships Containing Autocorrelated Error Terms', *Journal of the American Statistical Association*, 44, pp. 32–61.

Craven, P. and G. Wahba (1979) 'Smoothing Noisy Data with Spline Functions', *Numerische Mathematik*, 31, pp. 377–403.

Cuthbertson, K., S.G. Hall and M.P. Taylor (1992) *Applied econometric techniques*. New York: Simon and Schuster.

Davidson, R. and J.G. MacKinnon (1993) *Estimation and Inference in Econometrics*, Oxford University Press.

Demetriades, P.O. and K.A. Hussein (1996) 'Does Financial Development Cause Economic Growth? Time-Series Evidence from 16 Countries', *Journal of Development Economics*, 51, pp. 387–411.

Dickey, D.A. and W.A. Fuller (1979) 'Distribution of the Estimators for Autoregressive Time Series with a Unit Root', *Journal of the American Statistical Association*, 74, pp. 427–31.

Dickey, D.A. and Fuller W.A. (1981) 'Likelihood Ratio Statistics for Autoregressive Time Series with a Unit Root', *Econometrica*, 49, pp. 1057–72.

Doldado, J., T. Jenkinson and S. Sosvilla-Rivero (1990) 'Cointegration and Unit Roots', *Journal of Economic Surveys*, 4, pp. 249–73.

Durbin, J. (1970) 'Testing for Serial Correlation in Least Squares Regression – When Some of the Variables are Lagged Dependent Variables', *Econometrica*, 38, pp. 410–21.

Durbin, J. and G. Watson (1950) 'Testing for Serial Correlation in Least Squares Regression I', *Biometrica*, 37, pp. 409–28.

Enders, W. (1995) *Applied Econometric Time Series*. New York: John Wiley.

Engle, R.F. (1982) 'Autoregressive Conditional Heteroskedasticity with Estimates of the Variance of U.K. Inflation', *Econometrica*, 50, pp. 987–1008.

Engle, R.F. (1995) *ARCH Selected Readings (Advanced Texts in Econometrics)*. Oxford: Oxford University Press.

Engle, R.F. and C.W.J. Granger (1987) 'Co-integration and Error Correction: Representation, Estimation, and Testing', *Econometrica*, 55, pp. 251–76.

Engle, R.F., D.M. Lilien and R.P. Robins (1987) 'Estimating Time Varying Risk Premia in the Term Structure: The ARCH-M Model', *Econometrica*, 55, pp. 391–407.

Engle, R.F. and B. Yoo (1987) 'Forecasting and Testing in Cointegrated Systemts', *Journal of Econometrics*, 35, pp. 143–59.

Fuller, W.A. (1976) *Introduction to Statistical Time Series*. New York: John Wiley.

Gilbert, C.L. (1986) 'Professor Hendry's Econometric Methodology', *Oxford Bulletin of Economics and Statistics*, 84, pp. 283–307.

Glesjer, H. (1961) 'A New Test for Multiplicative Heteroskedasticity', *Journal of the American Statistical Association*, 60, pp. 539–47.

Glosten, L., R. Jogannathan and D. Ruknle (1993) 'Relations between the Expected Nominal Stock Excess Return, the Volatility of the Nominal Excess Return and the Interest Rate', *Journal of Finance, December*, 48(5), pp. 1779–801.

Godfrey, L.G. (1978) 'Testing for Higher Order Serial Correlation in Regression Equations when the Regressions Contain Lagged Dependent Variables', *Econometrica*, 46, pp. 1303–10.

Goldfeld, S. and R. Quandt (1965) 'Some Tests for Homoscedasticity', *Journal of the American Statistical Association*, 60, pp. 539–47.

Goldsmith, R. (1969) *Financial Structure and Development*. New Haven: Yale University Press.

Granger, C.W.J. (1969) 'Investigating Causal Relations by Econometric Models and Cross Spectral Methods', *Econometrica*, 35, pp. 424–38.

Granger, C.W.J. (1981) 'Some Properties of Time Series Data and their Use in Econometric Model Specification', *Journal of Econometrics*, 16, pp. 121–30.

Granger, C.W.J. (1988) 'Some Recent Developments in the Concept of Causality', *Journal of Econometrics*, 39, pp. 199–211.

Granger, C.W.J. and P. Newbold (1974) 'Economic Forecasting: The Atheist's Viewpoint,' in G.A. Renton (ed.), *Modeling the Economy*. London: Heinemann.

Granger, C.W.J. and J. Lin (1995) 'Causality in the Long-run', *Econometric Theory*, 11, pp. 530–36.

Granger, C.W.J. and P. Newbold (1996) *Forecasting Economic Time Series*. New York: Academic Press.

Greenslade J.V., S.G. Hall and S.G.B. Henry (1999) 'On the Identification of Cointegrated Systems in Small Samples: Practical Procedures with an Application to UK Wages and Prices', *Computing in Economics and Finance* 1999, 643, Society for Computational Economics.

Gujarati, D. (1978) *Basic Econometrics*. New York: McGraw-Hill.

Gultekin, M.N. and N.B. Gultekin (1983) 'Stock Market Seasonality: International Evidence', *Journal of Financial Economics*, 12, pp. 469–81.

Gurley, J.G. and E.S. Shaw (1955) 'Financial Aspects of Economic Development', *American Economic Review*, 45, pp. 515–38.

Hall, S.G., D.K. Miles and M.P. Taylor (1990) 'A Multivariate Garch in Mean Estimation of the Capital Asset Pricing Model', in K.D. Patterson and S.G.B. Henry (eds), *Issues in Economic and Financial Modelling*. Chapman Hall.

Hannan, E.J. and B. Quin (1979) 'The Determination of the Order of an Autoregression', *Journal of the Royal Statistical Society*, Series B14, pp. 190–5.

Harris, R. (1997) *Using Cointegration Analysis in Econometric Modeling*. City: Prentice Hall.

Harvey, A. (1976) 'Estimating Regression Models with Multiplicative Heteroscedasticity', *Econometrica*, 44, pp. 461–5.

Hausman, J. (1978) 'Specification Tests in Econometrics', *Econometrica*, 46, pp. 1251–71.

Hendry, D.F., A.R. Pagan and J.D. Sargan (1984) 'Dynamic Specification', in Z. Griliches and M.D. Intriligator (eds) *Handbook of Econometrics*. Amsterdam: North Holland.

Hendry, D.F. and J.F. Richard (1983) 'The Econometric Analysis of Economic Time Series', *International Statistics Review*, 51, pp. 3–33.

Hildreth, C. and J. Lu (1960) 'Demand Relations with Autocorrelated Disturbances' Technical Bulletin no. 276, Michigan State University Agricultural Experiment Station.

Holmstrom, B. and J. Tirole (1993) 'Market Liquidity and Performance Monitoring', *Journal of Political Economy*, 101(4), pp. 678–709.

Hsiao, C. (1986) *Analysis of Panel Data, Econometric Society Monographs* No. 11. Cambridge, United Kingdom: Cambridge University Press.

Im, K.S., M.H. Pesaran and Y. Shin (1997) Testing for Unit Roots in Heterogeneous Panels, manuscript, Department of Applied Economics, University of Cambridge.

Jaffe, J.F. and R. Westerfield (1989), 'Is there a Monthly Effect in Stock Market Return?', *Journal of Banking and Finance*, 13, pp. 237–44.

Jarque, C.M. and A.K. Berra (1990) 'Efficient tests for Normality, Homoskedasticity and Serial Independence of Regression Residuals', *Economic Letters*, 6, pp. 255–9.

Johansen, S. (1988) 'Statistical Analysis of Cointegration Vectors', *Journal of Economics Dynamics and Control*, 12, pp. 231–54.

Johansen, S. (1991) 'Estimation and Hypothesis Testing of Cointegration Vectors in Gaussian Vector Autoregressive Models', *Econometrica*, 59, pp. 1551–80.

Johansen, S. (1992) 'Determination of Cointegration Rank in the Presence of a Linear Trend', *Oxford Bulletin of Economics and Statistics*, 54, pp. 383–97.

Johansen, S. (1995a) *Likelihood-based Inference in Cointegrated Vector Autoregressive Models*. Oxford: Oxford University Press.

Johansen, S. (1995b) A Statistical Analysis of I(2) Variables, *Econometric Theory*, 11, pp. 25–59.

Johansen, S. and K. Juselius (1990) 'The Maximum Likelihood Estimation and Inference on Cointegration – with Application to Demand for Money', *Oxford Bulletin of Economics and Statistics*, 52, pp. 169–210.

Kao, C. (1999) 'Spurious Regression and Residual-Based tests for Cointegration in Panel Data', *Journal of Econometrics*, 90, pp. 1–44.

King, R. and R. Levine (1993a) 'Finance and Growth: Schumpeter Might Be Right', *Quarterly Journal of Economics*, 108(3), pp. 717–38.

King, R. and R. Levine (1993b) 'Finance, Enterpreneurship and Growth Theory and Evidence', *Journal of Monetary Economics*, 32(3), pp. 513–42.

Klein, L.R. and J.N. Morgan (1951) 'Results on Aftermatical Statistical Treatment of Sample Survey Data', *Journal of American Statistical Association*, 47, pp. 399–407.

Kmenta, J. (1986) *Elements of Econometrics*. New York: Macmillan.

Koyck, L.M. (1954) *Distributed Lags and Investment Analysis*. New York: North-Holland.

Larsson, R., J. Lyhagen and M. Lothgren (2001) 'Likelihood Based Cointegration Tests in Heterogeneous Panels', *Econometrics Journal*, 4, pp. 109–42.

Levin, A. and C.F. Lin (1992) 'Unit Root Tests in Panel Data: Asymptotic and Finite Sample Properties', University College of San Diego Working Paper no. 92–3.

Levin, A., C.F. Lin and C.S. Chu (2002) 'Unit Root Tests in Panel Data: Asymptotic and Finite Sample Properties', *Journal of Econometrics*, 108, pp. 1–24.

Ljung, G. and G. Box (1979) 'On a Measure of Lack of Fit in Time Series Models', *Biometrika*, 66, pp. 265–70.

MacKinnon, J.G. (1991) 'Critical Values for Cointegration Tests', R.F. Engle and C.W.J. Granger (eds), in *Long-run Economic Relationships: Readings in Cointegration*. Oxford: Oxford University Press.

Maddala G.S. (2001) *Introduction to Econometrics*. London: Wiley and Sons.

Maddala, G.S and S. Wu (1999) 'A Comparative Study of Unit Root Tests with Panel Data and a New Simple Test', *Oxford Bulletin of Economics and Statistics*, special issue, 61, pp. 631–52.

Mahmoud, E. (1984) 'Accuracy in Forecasting: A Survey', *Journal of Forecasting*, 3, pp. 139–59.

McCoskey, S. and C. Kao (1998) 'A Residual-Based Test for the Null of Cointegration in Panel Data', *Econometric Reviews*, 17, pp. 57–84.

McCulloch, J. Huston (1985) 'On Heteroskedasticity', *Econometrica*, p. 483.

McNees, S. (1986) 'Forecasting Accuracy of Alternative Techniques: A comparison of US Macroeconomic Forecasts', *Journal of Business and Economic Statistics*, 4, pp. 5–15.

Mitchell, B. (1998), *International Historical Statistics: Europe, 1750–1993* (4th edn). Basingstoke: Palgrave MacMillan.

Mizon, G. and J. Richard (1986) 'The Encompassing Principle and its Application to Testing Nonnested Models', *Econometrica*, 54, pp. 657–78.

Nehru, V. and A. Dhareshwar (1993) 'A New Database on Physical Capital Stock: Sources, Methodology and Results', *Rivista de Analisis Economico*, 8(1), pp. 37–59.

Nelson, D.B. (1991) 'Conditional Heteroskedasticity in Asset Returns: A New Approach', *Econometrica*, 59, pp. 347–70.

Newey, W. and K. West (1987) 'A Simple Positive Semi-Definite, Heteroskedasticity and Autocorrelation Consistent Covariance Matrix', *Econometrica*, p. 51.

Okun, A. (1962) 'Potential GNP: Its Measurement and Significance', *Proceedings of the Business and Economics Statistics Section of the American Statistical Association*, pp. 98–104.

Osterwald-Lenum, M. (1992) 'A Note with Fractiles of the Asymptotic Distribution of the Likelihood Rank Statistics: Four Cases', *Oxford Bulletin of Economics and Statistics*, 54, pp. 461–72.

Park, R. (1966) 'Estimating with Heteroscedastic Error Terms', *Econometrica*, 34, p. 888.

Pedroni, P. (1997) 'Panel Cointegration: Asymptotic and Finite Sample Properties of Pooled Time Series with an Application to the PPP Hypothesis: New Results', Working Paper, Indiana University.

Pedroni, P. (1999) 'Critical Values for Cointegration Tests in Heterogeneous Panels with Multiple Regressors', *Oxford Bulletin of Economics and Statistics*, special issue, November, 61, pp. 653–70.

Pedroni, P. (2000) 'Fully Modified OLS for Heterogeneous Cointegrated Panel', *Advances in Econometrics*, 15, pp. 93–130.

Pesaran, M.H., Y. Shin and R. Smith (1999) 'Pooled Mean Group Estimation of Dynamic Heterogeneous Panels', *Journal of the American Statistical Association*, 94, pp. 621–34.

Pesaran, M.H. and R. Smith (1995) 'Estimation of Long-run Relationships from Dynamic Heterogeneous Panels', *Journal of Econometrics*, 68, pp. 79–113.

Phillips, P.C.B. (1986) 'Understanding Spurious Regression', *Journal of Econometrics*, 33, pp. 311–40.

Phillips, P.C.B. (1987) 'Time Series Regressions with a Unit Root', *Econometrica*, 55, pp. 165–93.

Phillips, P.C.B. and H.R. Moon (2000) 'Linear Regression Theory for Non-stationary Panel Data', *Econometrica*, 67, pp. 1057–111.

Phillips, P.C.B. and P. Perron (1988) 'Testing for a Unit Root in Time Series Regression', *Biometrika*, 75, pp. 335–46.

Phillips, P.C.B. and S. Ouliaris (1990) 'Asymptotic Properties of Residual Based Tests for Cointegration', *Econometrica*, 58, pp. 165–93.

Ramsey, J. B. (1969) 'Tests for Specification Error in Classical Least Squares Regression Analysis', *Journal of the Royal Statistical Society* , B31, pp. 250–71.

Rice, J. (1984) 'Bandwith Choice for Nonparametric Kernel Regression', *Annals of Statistics*, 12, pp. 1215–30.

Roubini, N. and X. Sala-i-Martin (1992) 'Financial Repression and Economic Growth', *Journal of Development Economics*, 39, pp. 5–30.

Runkle, D.E. (1987) 'Vector Autoregression and Reality', *Journal of Business and Economic Statistics*, 5, pp. 437–54.

Schwarz, G. (1978) 'Estimating the Dimension of a Model', *Annals of Statistics*, 6.

Shibata, R (1981) 'An Optimal Selection of Regression Variables', *Biometrica*, 68, pp. 45–54.

Sims, C.A. (1972) 'Money, Income and Causality', *American Economic Review*, 62, pp. 540–52.

Sims, C.A. (1980) 'Macroeconomics and Reality', *Econometrica*, 48, pp. 1–48.

Stock, J. and M. Watson (1988) 'Testing for Common Trends', *Journal of the American Statistical Association*, 83, pp. 1097–107.

Studenmund, A.H. (2001) *Using Econometrics: A Practical Guide*. Reading, Mass.: Addison-Wesley Longman Inc.

White, H. (1980) 'A Heteroscedasticity-Consistent Covariance Matrix Estimator and a Direct Test for Heteroscedasticity', *Econometrica*, 48, pp. 817–38.

Zakoian, J.-M. (1994) 'Threshold Heteroskedastic Models', *Journal of Economic Dynamics and Control*, 18, pp. 931–55.

Index